Global Middle East

GL●BAL SQU■RE

Edited by
Matthew Gutmann, Brown University
Jeffrey Lesser, Emory University

The Global Square series features edited volumes focused on how regions and countries interact with the rest of the contemporary world. Each volume analyzes the tensions, inequalities, challenges, and achievements inherent in global relationships. Drawing on work by journalists, artists, and academics from a range of disciplines—from the humanities to the sciences, from public health to literature—The Global Square showcases essays on the histories, cultures, and societies of countries and regions as they develop in conjunction with and contradiction to other geographic centers.

Each volume in The Global Square series aims to escape simplistic truisms about global villages and to provide examples and analysis of the magnitude, messiness, and complexity of connections. Anchoring each book in a particular region or country, contributors provoke readers to examine the global and local implications of economic and political transformations.

1. *Global Latin America: Into the Twenty-First Century,* edited by Matthew Gutmann and Jeffrey Lesser

2. *Global Africa: Into the Twenty-First Century,* edited by Dorothy L. Hodgson and Judith A. Byfield

3. *Global Middle East: Into the Twenty-First Century,* edited by Asef Bayat and Linda Herrera

Global Middle East

INTO THE TWENTY-FIRST CENTURY

Edited by
Asef Bayat and Linda Herrera

UNIVERSITY OF CALIFORNIA PRESS

University of California Press
Oakland, California

© 2021 by The Regents of the University of California

Cataloging-in-Publication Data is on file at the Library of Congress.

ISBN 978-0-520-29533-9 (cloth : alk. paper)
ISBN 978-0-520-29535-3 (pbk. : alk. paper)
ISBN 978-0-520-96812-7 (ebook)

30 29 28 27 26 25 24 23 22 21
10 9 8 7 6 5 4 3 2 1

CONTENTS

ILLUSTRATIONS

FIGURES

TABLE

PREFACE

As we write, the world is overwhelmed by the impact of the novel COVID-19 pandemic. It has resulted in massive disruptions to travel and movement of people and goods, locked-down cities, economic freefall, mass unemployment, and millions sick and nearly 650,000 dead. Seen from a lens with silver linings, the pandemic has resulted in cleaner air, less fossil-fuel consumption, more opportunities for wildlife to flourish, novel forms of global solidarity, to name just a few effects. The virus that first appeared in Wuhan, the capital of China's Hubei province, in December 2019, spread to and profoundly altered lives and environments in every region of the globe. Perhaps nothing better than this event illustrates how the world is interconnected, that an impactful event, idea, or object emerging in one corner of the planet may indelibly change lives in far-flung places.

This book is about the global interconnectedness seen from the prism of the Middle East, both "global-in" and "global-out." The volume shows how the region's economic, political, cultural, intellectual, and artistic formations have come about from a complex set of flows, innovations, effects, interactions, and exchanges. It covers topics that range from God to Rumi, food, film, fashion, and music, sports and science, to the flow of people, goods, and ideas. It discusses social and political movements from human rights, Salafism, and cosmopolitanism to radicalism and revolutions. The book is interdisciplinary by design, incorporating perspectives from history, anthropology, sociology, political science, philosophy, religious studies, literature, film studies, and philosophy. We have been adamant to produce short, clear, and jargon-free chapters with minimal notes accessible to lay readers and students, written by seasoned scholars with established expertise in their areas of inquiry.

A volume of this nature relies on the support, hard work, and collegiality of many people. We would like to thank the contributors who, as one reviewer noted, "strike gold" in their chapters. They approach their topics with a spirit of rigorous scholarship, artistry, and passion. The editors of the Global Square series at the University of California Press, Matthew Gutmann and Jefferey Lesser, have provided encouragement and direction from the start. At the University of Illinois at Urbana-Champaign, we are grateful to the Center for South Asian and Middle East Studies (CSAMES) for hosting a workshop for authors to present earlier versions of their chapters, the Department of Sociology, the College of Education, and the Center for Global Studies. Thanks to Heba Shama for her help with the photos. Gratitude goes to the Estate of Edward Said for permission to reprint Said's seminal essay "Reflections on Exile," to Verso Press for permission to reprint an excerpt from Timothy Mitchell's book *Carbon Democracy*, and to Seyla Benhabib for her interview.

To our many students, colleagues, and friends with whom we have had lively discussion about this book, thanks for providing such a fertile ground for sharing and exploring ideas.

Asef Bayat and Linda Herrera
Champaign, Illinois
August 2020

PART ONE

Introduction

ONE

Global Middle East

Asef Bayat and Linda Herrera

> Not Christian or Jew or Muslim, not Hindu, Buddhist, sufi, or
> zen. Not any religion or cultural system.
>   I am not from the East or the West, not out of the ocean or
> up from the ground, not natural or ethereal, not composed of
> elements at all.
>
> RUMI (1207–1273)

RARELY DO LOCALITIES, COUNTRIES, AND REGIONS develop over
centuries and millennia in isolation; rather, they develop in complex interaction with others. The societies of the Middle East and North Africa
(MENA), a region also referred to as North Africa and West Asia (NAWA),
are not an exception. Their economic, political, cultural, scientific, intellectual, and artistic formations have come about from a complex set of flows,
innovations, interactions, and exchanges with those outside and within the
region. Ever since the idea of "global" or "worldliness" has been part of people's consciousness, the region has been immensely influenced by various
global forces. It has also profoundly impacted developments in other parts
of the world, including what is generally called the "West."

Yet the Middle East has long been viewed from an "exceptionalist" lens
in much of the Western press, cinema, television, literature, and scholarship.
This exceptionalism depicts peoples and societies as being resilient to change,
entrapped by their own history, culture, and religion, and prone to tribalism
and nativism. In such a view, culture and religion rarely change, and contemporary conflicts are often attributed to stubborn religious and sectarian
rivalries dating back centuries, if not millennia. News media, for instance,
are replete with explanations of the Middle East as a region of continuous
war, sectarian bloodshed, the cradle of extremism, oppression of women, and
religious conflicts, as if these are the result of an innate, inward-looking,
and change-resistant culture. Only rarely do analysts take into consideration

how the role of geopolitics, multinational entanglements, arms sales (which are among the highest in the world), military interventions, climate change, technological advances, social media networks, high rates of internal and external migrations (the list goes on) influence, transform, and alter societies, from all directions.

For a short period during the Arab Uprisings of late 2010 through 2013, a break to the mainstream narrative occurred. Media from much of North America and Europe celebrated the protestors as global models of pro-democracy, nonviolent warriors from progressive youth movements.[1] However, the so-called Arab Spring soon turned into what countless analysts prosaically dubbed the "Arab Winter," and a return to the old paradigms of regional stagnation and sectarianism ensued. This resorting to stereotypes to understand the region while sidelining crucial developments in geopolitics, markets, technology, social policies, climate change, grassroots movements, and other dynamics is partially rooted in what Edward Said famously termed "Orientalism." This refers to a systematic body of knowledge production that constructs a totalizing image of the Middle East as an object of prejudice. It considers Muslim-majority populations as static, while neglecting differentiation and change brought about by exchanges among various societies and peoples in the region.

Today a powerful neo-Orientalist approach depicts the region as largely homogenous, closed, parochial, and resistant to change. Imagined in this fashion, the Middle East has little of value to offer to the world and is responsible for its own troubles. This binary of the (Middle) East versus the West has come to occupy a central place in the well-known "clash of civilizations" theory advanced by political scientist Samuel Huntington in 1993. Huntington viewed an essential opposition between the Western and Islamic civilizations. The idea of this clash has considerably shaped perceptions in the United States about Islam and the Muslim-majority Middle East, in the media and foreign policy circles as well as among different publics.[2] Even the very term the "Middle East" is a colonial construct coined in the 1850s by the British India Office, popularized in the late 1930s in the British outpost in Egypt (Egypt was the "middle" point between Britain and India, the "East"). The term traveled to the United States in 1946 with the establishment of the Middle East Institute in the nation's capital. The Middle East thus became a specific object of policy and research.

Few would deny that in past decades countries in the region have suffered from debilitating wars, stifling political repression, new forms of patriarchy, growing inequality, and more entrenched religious extremism and radicalism. But are these features rooted in local culture and an outgrowth of long-held traditions? Take, for instance, Islamic radicalism, jihadi terrorism, or the phenomenon of the so-called Islamic State (ISIS). If these were inherent landscapes of local cultures and traditions, why did they emerge largely after the 1970s and seldom appeared before that time? How do we explain the fact that only "very few radicals have a past of long-standing piety, and most of them are religiously illiterate," as Olivier Roy suggests (chapter 21) in this book?

The truth is that jihadi terrorism did not naturally arise from certain values intrinsic to local culture. Rather, it was imported and spread by thousands of youths from diverse national, class, and educational backgrounds who joined the Mujahedin in Afghanistan during the Cold War. The Mujahedin, with the support of the United States, worked to expel the Soviet invaders. At the time, al-Qaeda was under the leadership of Osama Bin Laden, the son of a construction magnate with close ties to the Saudi royal family, who advanced the cause of global terrorism in the name of Islam. He turned on his former US ally and is widely reputed to have masterminded the September 11, 2001, terrorist attacks. As Roy argues, violent radicalism of militant Islamists or jihadi terrorists has little in essence to do with the idea of "jihad" as understood in the legal Islamic tradition. As such, Roy writes, "Jihad was traditionally defined as a collective duty to defend a part of the Muslim territory under attack." No individual could call for jihad or bestow on himself the quality of being a "jihadi." Instead, militant Islamists deployed the language of jihad to *Islamize* an emerging radicalism that was embedded in youth nihilism and fascination with death—a narrative in which successive movements embodied in ISIS and other global jihadi groups found a perfect fit.

Another example can be found in the ongoing conflict between Palestinians and successive Israeli governments. Although some analysts try to shape the narrative by claiming Israel's "biblical right" to the land of Palestine, or reduce the conflict to "age-old" hostilities between Islam and Judaism, the conflict is in fact rooted in far more recent history, particularly since World War I. This history includes British support for the establishment of a "national home for the Jewish people" with the Balfour Declaration of 1917, European anti-Semitism that culminated in the horrors of the Holocaust, the development of strong strategic alliances between the United States and Israel, and the capitulation of certain authoritarian Arab states to the status quo. More recently, Evangelical Christians in the

United States have been pointing to end-time prophecies in their support of the modern state of Israel. As conflicts escalate in Israel and the Occupied Territories of the West Bank and Gaza Strip around Palestinian rights, security, and sovereignty, Evangelical Christians have been propounding Israel's "biblical right" to Palestine.[3]

According to a 2013 Pew Research Center poll, American Evangelicals are even stronger supporters of Israel than are American Jews. If jihadi radicals are in effect *Islamizing* terrorism by deploying the language of jihad, Zionist radicals are *Christianizing* the occupation of Palestinian lands by deploying a language of "biblical rights." Ilana Feldman's chapter in this book (chapter 22) offers a much needed context to understand the transnational connections and solidarity networks involved in this conflict, with a myriad of players and interests.

Each chapter in this edited volume is a testimony to the global interlinkages of the Middle East in the political, economic, cultural, intellectual, and artistic domains. The authors narrate how these domains have been shaped by interconnections to transnational forces, peoples, and geographies. But this globality has been complex, taking different expressions and involving different layers, scales, and directions. Sometimes it is expressed in how certain events or interests from outside *affect* a particular society; other times it is manifested in how persons, products, or cultural registers *circulate*, travel through national boundaries to be taken on and shared by others. Interlinkages are displayed in the way societies trade, give, take, and *exchange* cultural and material goods—a process that tends to advance those goods; in other instances, they are revealed in the way persons, ideas, or emotions express belonging to not one but many geographies, taking the *world as home*.

GEOPOLITICAL EFFECTS

Although we do not hold the Orientalist view of cultural exceptionalism, there does exist a kind of "geopolitical exceptionalism" in the region, forged by the trilogy of geography, oil, and Israel—elements that have historically heightened imperial dominance and intraregional rivalry. In the aftermath of World War I, Ottoman provinces were carved into zones of British and French influence in the infamous Sykes-Picot/Asia Minor Agreement of 1916. These artificial borders divided peoples and historic communities, splitting contiguous groups like the Kurds and Druze. In the postcolonial period of the 1950s through the 1970s, the forced creation of distinct nation-states planted the seeds of territorial claims and conflicts, instigating wars between neighboring countries.

Thirst for raw materials and control over trade routes brought the lives of the colonized people into global circuits of trade and transportation, production and profit. In the late nineteenth century, for instance, 80 percent to 90 percent of Egyptian exports, mainly cotton, went to British and European textile mills, not only because the American Civil War (1861–65) cut down the US cotton production in the world market, but especially because British colonists wanted Egypt to export its raw material rather than produce its own textiles. Today, even though it is theoretically free from colonial control, Egyptian cotton is entangled in a global network that connects a cotton grower in the Nile Delta to a seaport in Alexandria, a cotton exchange in Liverpool, a factory in Lancashire, a retailer in America, and courtrooms in various major capitals of the world.

To add salt to the wound, the highly desirable commodity of Egyptian cotton used to make sheets and shirts may not even originate in Egypt because, as Ahmed Shokr discusses (chapter 15), the label "Egyptian cotton" in legal and commercial parlance is not a national marker but a quality brand. Beyond the global circuits of politics, trade, and markets, the fortune of Egyptian cotton also depends on a critical and strategic natural resource—water. With 80 percent spent on agriculture, water remains vulnerable to climate change, energy crisis, local politics and management, as well as regional geopolitics. A number of countries in the MENA region— Iran, Iraq, Palestine, Sudan, and Syria to name but a few—already suffer from inadequate water and energy, and in some areas the situation is dire. As Jeannie Sowers relates (chapter 13), key human factors contributing to drought and other forms of environmental degradation include wars, civil strife, occupation, and mismanagement. Egypt shares the river Nile with Sudan, Ethiopia, and Uganda, and conflict between these countries can very quickly trigger crisis in the supply of water, energy, and agricultural products—elements that are so deeply interconnected.

The discovery of oil in the Arabian Peninsula transformed geopolitics and transnational trade, triggering massive transregional migration flows as well as economic and social developments. Since the 1970s, Iran and the Gulf Arab countries gained immense revenues from oil and in turn experienced remarkable economic growth, the rise of a middle class, infrastructural development, social changes, and quests for democracy.[4] At the same time, oil enabled autocratic and authoritarian governments to rule as "rentier states." They dispensed welfare to their citizens and attempted to appease and essentially buy off dissenting groups. More significantly, as oil became an energy source driving global economic growth, foreign powers and their corporations (initially from Britain, the United States, France, and the Netherlands, with Russia and China later gaining dominance in this lucrative market) established influence in the region and supported autocratic regimes in exchange for direct access to oil and economic and political favors.

As Timothy Mitchell shows (chapter 14), the largest oil-importing countries encouraged massive arms sales to recycle the money they would pay for importing oil. For instance, in 1953, after the popular prime minister of Iran, Mohamed Mossadegh, nationalized Iranian oil, the United States and Britain organized a coup to topple his secular democratic government in favor of the pro-US monarch Shah Mohammad Reza Pahlavi, who became the biggest buyer of US arms in the region. The Shah was later overthrown by the Iranian Revolution of 1979. The support of repressive rulers of oil-rich countries is an old story and continues to present times. In 2019, for example, even after the US Senate passed a resolution in March to end US support for the Saudi-led coalition in Yemen (only to be vetoed by President Donald Trump in April of the same year), after the Central Intelligence Agency (CIA) concluded in a November 2018 report that the Crown Prince of Saudi Arabia, Mohammed Ben Salman (MBS), had ordered the killing and dismemberment of Saudi journalist and US resident Jamal Khashoggi, and despite numerous reports of staggering repression of dissent and violation of human rights of women, young activists, artists, and other members of the royal family, Trump continued to wholeheartedly support and defend MBS and continue unabated with trade and arms deals to the country.

In other words, the absence of democratic rule in the region is not simply an outcome of religion or age-old traditions or cultural practices. After all, the Arab uprisings meant to bring more accountable and democratic governance in the Arab world. Rather, this absence is largely linked to the region's political economy and powerful enablers of repression and autocracy. People in the region have responded to these challenges partly by deploying the language of "human rights" adopted from United Nations (UN) charters, conventions, and international NGOs. The 1948 United Nations Declaration of Human Rights (UDHR), a document born out of the devastation of World War II, was an attempt to lay out a set of international principles for the protection of all peoples. Prominent rights advocates from the region, including Charles Malik (Lebanese) and Bedia Afnan (Iraqi), were influential members of the UN Human Rights Commission. Yet as Lori Allen illustrates (chapter 23), "human rights" have been torn between the imperial desire to use them as a tool of geopolitical dominance (e.g., invading foreign countries in the name of "bringing democracy," "enforcing human rights," and "protecting women and children") and the indigenous urge to invoke rights as an empowering language for social struggle. Although the process of imperializing human rights has rendered some people in the region to suspect the concept, others have sought to "define the meaning and substance of rights in ways that make sense to them, and in which they try to defend them on their own terms." In sum, geopolitics, while a critical force in the region, is not destiny. People and movements transcend regional particularities to act as players in refiguring the global order.

CIRCULATING BELIEFS, ARTS, AND FOODS

If global forces and processes—such as colonialism, oil markets, or arms sales—have deeply influenced the politics and economies of individual countries in the Middle East, ideas and cultural products from the region have equally shaped the social and cultural landscapes outside the region. The remarkable global circulation of belief systems, technologies, music, and foods that originated in the Middle East profoundly transformed the course of human history. The very idea of monotheism as a state religion likely originated in ancient Egypt during the reign of Pharaoh Akhenaten (1353–1336 BCE). The idea of a single universal deity has been the cornerstone of the three main Abrahamic religions—Judaism, Christianity, and Islam—all of which were born in what we now refer to as the Middle East. It is remarkable to note that in the twenty-first century, more than half the world's population adheres to an Abrahamic religion, a topic pondered by Ebrahim Moosa (chapter 2). Moosa shows how the idea of prophecy in these monotheistic religions underlined the impulse to create a worldly political order in which God occupied a central place, beginning with the notion of "heavenly king" and continuing with today's religious fundamentalisms. The monotheistic God has had enormous global staying power and remains as strong a phenomenon as ever despite relentless challenges from science and secular sensibilities.

As notions of prophecy and worship traveled with merchant ships, pilgrim caravans, and migrants, so too did food and recipes. Today we take for granted certain food or drinks but have little knowledge of their origins. Sami Zubaida (chapter 9) lays out the historical circulation and art of food. As empires spread, so too did their quest for culinary distinction. During the Muslim expansions, food items brought mostly from India and China—such as rice, hard wheat, sugarcane, citrus fruit, spinach, and aubergine—traveled to Europe, the Iberian Peninsula, and Sicily. Today, European names for "rice" come from the Arabic *arruz*, "sugar" from *sukkar*, "aubergine" from Arabic and Persian *badinjan*, "alcohol" from the Arabic *al-kuhl* (antimony eyeliner), "lime" or "lemon" from *limu*, and "orange" from *narinji*. The diffusion of small dishes or appetizers known collectively as "mezze" (originally a Persian word) into global diets has transformed the traditional European meal pattern from full course meal into largely shared "small plates." Nowadays, in what Zubaida calls a global "foodie milieu" in the Western foodscape, such Middle Eastern foods as kebab, hummus, falafel, baklava, or mezze have entered common food vocabularies.

Like food, music holds an extraordinary capacity to spread and merge cultures. With an intangible nature, semantic ambiguity, and no impassible social boundaries, music remains a most "globalizable expressive substance," as Michael Frishkopf recounts (chapter 11). Musical instruments and sounds of the region traversed Europe, the United States, and Latin America through such channels as West African Islam, the slave trade, colonial encounters, and immigration. Even though certain genres from traditional music and dance became tropes in fanciful Orientalist stereotypes (like a sonic background to belly dancing mixed with exotic femininity), musical repertoires and movements from the Middle East circulated widely. They have been adapted and incorporated into local musical genres, from hip-hop to Hollywood soundtracks. Without a doubt, the "impact of the Middle East over nearly eight centuries" in music, poetry, dance, sounds has been enduring.

Hollywood and Bollywood may dominate global commercial cinema, but Middle East cinema has carved an important niche. Egyptian films and especially television serials have enjoyed large audiences throughout the Arab world, as have Turkish shows popular among Arabs and West Africans. The avant-guard and highly acclaimed Iranian cinema has gained worldwide audiences. While US and UK film cultures have informed broad frames of cinema in the Middle East, "resistant cinema" from the socialist USSR inspired parallels in places as far-flung as Algeria, Angola, Latin America, Palestine, South Africa, and Vietnam. Kamran Rastegar (chapter 10) takes three examples—from Egypt (Yousef Shahin), Iran (Mohsen Kiarostami), and Lebanon (Nadine Labaki)—to trace changes and influences in Middle Eastern cinema. He grapples with questions of art and power and asks, "Can global be reimagined as a more revolutionary possibility, a world of new connections and opportunities that surpass the limits of nationalism and regionalism?" Cinema exemplifies a globality of multidirectional flows that strives to modify the prevailing pattern of center-periphery flows.

EXCHANGE AND TRANSMUTATIONS

From the period of modern colonialism the diffusion of knowledge often appeared to be a one-way street, typically flowing from the rich to the poor nations or from the center to periphery. Things looked different before. During the Umayyad (661–750) and Abbasid dynasties (750–1258), with seats of power in Damascus and Baghdad respectively, new knowledge and staggering scientific discoveries occurred within a multilingual and "transregional scientific culture" that "continued through the nineteenth-century encounter with modern science," as Robert Morrison points out (chapter 3). Since the history of science begins before the advent of modernity, scholars never use the term "Middle Eastern science"; rather, they speak of "science in Islamic (or Islamicate) societies." Morrison cautions that because "Islam was the religion of the powerful in these societies, Islamic science is a concise shorthand so long as one understands that the relationship between the sciences and Islam was nuanced, variable, and historically contingent."

The term "Arabic science" is often used in replace of "Islamic science" since Arabic was the lingua franca of science, so to speak. But even this term lacks accuracy, Morrison explains, "as more and more scientific literature in Islamic languages other than Arabic comes to light." Thus medicine, philosophy, and mysticism conversed and converged with various linguistic, regional, and ethnic communities of learning and worship. The translation movement (from Greek to Arabic and Arabic to other languages) was for centuries a key factor in advances in science, medicine, alchemy, navigation, and astronomy, among other fields. The life of the itinerant astronomer and physician Abdel

Rhaman al-Sufi (d. 986) represents the richness of encounters and cultures of learning. This onetime personal physician of the Abbasid caliph traveled to India to study medicine, as Indians journeyed to Baghdad to learn astronomy. In the thirteenth century the famous Maraghah Observatory, located in modern-day Northwest Iran, hosted scholars from Islamic societies from as far as China. Khawrazmi's algebra (from the Arabic *al-jabr*, the reunion of broken parts) drew on some Indian, Hebrew, and Greek contributions to build a discipline that later traveled to the Latin world to undergo further advancement during the Renaissance. As much as they are elevated in world histories of science, Morrison writes, the "scientific cultures of Islamic societies and Renaissance Europe owe much to other parts of the world."

Whether it is effect, exchange, or simply circulation, globalizing cultural registers often get modified, transfigured, indigenized, and take new meanings. Thus, as culinary cultures traveled in and out of the societies of the Middle East, both their vocabularies and their textures changed. If the celebrated dish ceviche is a derivative from the old Persian *sikbaj*, it was substantially modified and found life of its own in Peru and the Latin world. Many cultural registers may lose their original identities when they travel and are indigenized. Just as this has been the case with food, science, and music, so too with cultural artifacts. One such intriguing artifact, which has assumed cultural-political features, is the Palestinian kufiya. As Ted Swedenburg traces (chapter 12), this form of headwear originated with peasant-guerrillas fighting the British occupation. In the late 1960s and early 1970s, the kufiya became the key symbol of resistance of the Palestinian peoples against the Israeli occupation. It was soon taken up by people around the world to exhibit solidarity with Palestinians. But the kufiya, once imbued with specific symbolic meaning, has taken different turns, sometimes hardly related to its original purpose. The kufiya entered the world of youth chic and high street/shopping mall fashion. The trendy chain Urban Outfitters offered it for sale in various playful colors and marketed it as an "antiwar" scarf, and Israeli designers appropriated it as a fashion rather than political object. The kufiya has also served as a general sign of resistance worn by protesters in political causes ranging from a right-wing militias in the United States to protesters of the Saudi–United Arab Emirates (UAE)–led war against Yemen. But, as Swedenburg concludes, "in whatever context and whatever form, as it continues its transnational migrations and transfigurations, the kufiya in some manner or the other usually refers back to Palestine, and its struggles."

The story of the kufiya is at once a story of travel and origin, of going off in the world yet knowing its home. What can we say about a form of globality where the home is the world—the kind of world that one might capture in John Lennon's lasting "Imagine" lyrics inspired by Yoko Ono? Here is a perception of home, world, and belonging that is not anchored to a specific place or even region but carries within it a multiplicity of cultures, echoes of a common humanity. The life, cultural habitat, and intellectual sensibilities of the thirteenth-century poet Jalal al-Din Rumi embodies such a vision of world as home—a vision that the Persian word *jahan-vatani* perfectly captures.

Rumi's life and poetry represent the quintessential timeless figure who traversed multiple lands, life worlds, and cultures. Born in Vakhsh in present-day Afghanistan, Rumi lived in Iran, Syria, and then Turkey, and died in the multilingual and multireligious city of Konya in 1273. Most of his poetry is in Persian, but he also left verses in Arabic and Turkish. As highlighted by Fatemeh Keshavarz (chapter 4), "his goal was simple—to speak through a language that transcended barriers such as class, ethnicity, culture, and religion, that would reach Hindus, Muslims, Christians, Jews, and atheists alike." Rumi lived a cosmopolitan life and reflected on its merits in his poetry. No wonder such a timeless and "cultureful" poetry would find appeal almost everywhere and across the centuries. Literary creations traveled and connected cultures in societies where knowledge of different languages was central to this historic literary circulation.

In contemporary times, characterized by unprecedented levels of human flows, we witness a different kind of worlding experienced by the exiled, banished from home, out of place with an endless melancholy and longing for the homeland. Exiles, refugees, and displaced people wander between the world and home. The condition of uprootedness and striving for a sense of home has been common to Jews who have fled inquisitions, pogroms, and the Holocaust; Palestinians expelled from their lands by wars and policies of the Israeli state; Armenians who fled genocides; and now millions of Iraqis, Syrians, and Yemenis escaping the calamities of war. Around the globe, these peoples strive to rebuild a "home" through their language, networks, food, music, and memory. "The exile's new world, logically enough, is unnatural and its unreality resembles fiction," writes Edward Said in his seminal essay, "Reflections on Exile."[5] Yet precisely because of this "fictional" character, the experience of exile can lend itself to immense intellectual empowerment and resilience—think of Karl Marx, Hannah Arendt, or Said himself. His essay is a reflection on his own exiled and global life. Displaced from his home in Jerusalem, now occupied by the International Christian Embassy, a right-wing Christian fundamentalist organization, Said lived and studied in Palestine then Egypt, Lebanon, and the United States, where he rose to fame as an exemplary intellectual of the late twentieth century. He identified emotionally and intellectually with at once his lost home and the world—the United States, Europe, Latin America, Africa, and South Asia.

The kind of life experienced by Rumi, Marx, or Said is often described in terms of "cosmopolitanism," which refers to both social conditions and an ethical project. In one sense, it signifies certain social processes, such as migration and exile, that compel people of diverse communal, national, or racial affiliations to associate, work, and live together—for good and for bad. These processes may potentially lead to diminishing cultural homogeneity in favor of diversity, variety, and plurality of cultures, religions, and lifestyles. Cosmopolitanism also has ethical and normative dimensions; it is a project, something to be cherished. In this sense, cosmopolitanism is deployed to challenge the language of separation and antagonism, to confront cultural superiority and ethnocentrism. It further stands opposed to communalism and narrow identitarian politics, where the inward-looking and closed-knit ethnic or religious collectives espouse narrow, exclusive, and selfish interests. Cosmopolitanism of this sort overrides the "multiculturalist" paradigm. Because although multiculturalism calls for equal coexistence of different cultures within a national society, it is still preoccupied with cultural boundaries—an outlook that departs from cosmopolitan life-world where intense interaction, mixing, and sharing tend to blur communal boundaries, generating hybrid and "impure" cultural practices.[6]

The social environment, fascinating life trajectory, and influential body of work of the philosopher Seyla Benhabib represent an aspect of such cosmopolitanism. In an interview with Benhabib (chapter 24), Linda Herrera seeks to "tease out connections between biography, political philosophy linked to cosmopolitanism, and global Middle East." Benhabib recounts her memory of the "incredibly cosmopolitan" Istanbul where her Sephardi Jewish family lived next to Greeks, Italians, Kurds, and Turks in the 1970s. She traces her own political awakenings, life trajectories, and studies that enabled her to make contributions in the areas of German philosophy, feminism, and the rights of stateless people and migrants. Benhabib's ideas in political philosophy resonate with the plight of migrants and refugees throughout the world, including those from across the region.

Sadly, that type of cosmopolitanism that Istanbul enjoyed began to fade following the Arab-Israeli War and the rise of religious politics in Turkey since the 1980s. However, a new kind of cultural diversity has emerged in the Persian Gulf with the heavy presence of foreign residents and migrant laborers. As a result, places like Dubai have come to represent a "cosmopolitan" city-state in the Persian Gulf in that it juxtaposes individuals and families of diverse national, cultural, and racial belongings, who live and work next to one another within a small geographical space. But can we call this cosmopolitanism? Indeed, what Dubai represents is not unique in the region. As Ahmed Kanna demonstrates (chapter 18), the massive presence of foreign workers in Bahrain, Kuwait, Oman, Qatar, Saudi Arabia, and the United Arab Emirates has virtually turned the area into a non-Arab region where 90 percent of the population in UAE and Qatar—and 50 percent in the region as a whole—are currently immigrants. Indeed, migration has essentially altered the meaning of "nation" in this part of the region and the world.

The great ports of the Persian Gulf have historically drawn people from a mix of Arab, Persian/Iranian, African, and South Asian cultures. Ports are in essence worldly spaces, as Laleh Khalili reveals (chapter 16), "not only because of goods transiting through their harbors, but because of the flows of merchants and mariners, capitalists and colonizers, soldiers, sailors and spies, and adventurers and dreamers." Indeed, the great Arab ports on the Mediterranean, the Red Sea, and the Gulfs (Arabian/Persian, Aden, and Oman) played such a role in their very long "histories that predate the birth of Christianity and Islam." They created the conditions for cosmopolitan environments of sorts in what seemed to be remote and disconnected locations. The port cities around the harbors teemed with "languages, sounds, flavors, and smells from all around the Indian Ocean and even further afield." Today the port of Jabal Ali in Dubai embodies a global space par excellence. It is operated by a mix of western Europeans, Lebanese, Syrians, Indians, Punjabi, Filipinos, Pashtun, Nepalese, and South Asians whose assembly reflects Dubai itself, a "cosmopolitan" if highly unequal global city.

The question to ask is how many elite professional expatriates residing in places like Dubai or Doha share cultural life with the poor, stateless, and deprived migrants of the host society? In truth, the objective possibility to experience mixing, mingling, and sharing is not the same as the genuine desire to do so. At closer examination, cosmopolitan Dubai turns out to be no more than a city-state of relatively gated communities marked by sharp communal and spatial boundaries, with labor camps (of South Asian migrants) and the segregated milieu of parochial jet-setters, or the cosmopolitan ghettoes of the Western elite expatriates who remain bounded within the physical safety and cultural purity of their own reclusive collectives. Ahmed Kanna shows how the extraordinary labor migration to the Gulf has substantially altered the economic and cultural landscapes of these societies. These states have reinforced colonial patterns of segmented labor where the highest paid managerial jobs go to Western elites, while the menial, back-breaking, and domestic labor is assigned largely to South and East Asian men and women. They endure severe exploitation, often long hours, and low pay. Construction workers in Dubai earn as little as fifty to eighty cents per hour in ten-hour-six-day-week routines, trapped mainly in temporary contracts and a system of work sponsorship known as *kafala*. Laborers live in residential compounds that further entangle them in already hyperexploitative relations of debt, in conditions of particularly "exploitative forms of bonded labor." Rather than being regionally specific, this pattern of exploitation is organically linked to the structure of global capital and its logic of profit-making.

If seaports have long been key loci of travel and exchange of people and goods in the region, airports have dramatically increased the volume of travelers, tourists, and pilgrims since World War II. Waleed Hazbun (chapter 17) recounts how from colonial times, the Middle East became a destination for millions of people to visit ancient monuments, religious sites, and the expanding tourist resorts. Beirut famously became the "Paris of the Middle East" in the 1960s before the civil war and the Arab-Israeli conflict ended its fortunes. But Holy Land tourism and the Muslim Pilgrimage, the Hajj, to Saudi Arabia has continued to attract two million Muslim visitors from around the world every year. Tourism does not necessarily bring about more exchange and human connection, particularly if it remains an "enclave" industry concentrated in pockets across the region. Tourism can also perpetuate global hierarchies and zones of exclusion.

COUNTERCURRENTS

"Cultural imperialism"—a term that conveys how flows of knowledge and paradigms for understanding the world tend to move from the rich countries of the Global North (the "center") to the poorer nations of the Global South (the "periphery")—is often a reality but not a given. Good ideas and cultural traits that resonate with global humanity can stir countercurrents capable of breaking barriers and shifting the direction of history. The spectacular Arab uprisings that began in Tunisia in December 2010 and quickly spread to Egypt and several other Arab countries inspired and informed the imagination of millions of people around the globe who were fighting for social justice. Asef Bayat (chapter 20) discusses how Tahrir Square in Egypt became a global emblem, a model for the global Occupy Movements that emerged in eighty countries and five hundred cities around the world, including Athens, Madrid, New York, and Tel Aviv.

How did the Tahrir repertoire exude such a remarkable global reception, especially when the idea came from a region, the Arab Middle East, that was deemed in the Western media as a cultural backwater? Tahrir represented an extraordinary mix of a political space ("liberated square") and political practice (noninstitutional, mass-based, and horizontal movement) that many around the world found appealing to address their own predicaments. As a model, it stirred millions of activists in the streets of the "Center" to exchange ideas with Egyptian activists and create their own Tahrir squares— to resist the staggering inequality of wealth, precarious life, and governmental politics that had become subservient to corporate and elite interests.

Egypt had championed a different global movement some five decades earlier. It was not a fight against autocracy and neoliberalism but a nationalist movement to undercut imperialist domination. The Egyptian leader Gamal Abdel Nasser, who was instrumental in leading a coup against the monarchy and British rule in Egypt, spearheaded a worldwide Non-Aligned Movement along with Jawaharlal Nehru of India, Josip Tito of Yugoslavia, Kwame Nkrumah of Ghana, and Fidel Castro of Cuba. Their aim was to unite the postcolonial nations against the dominance of both the capitalist West and the Soviet bloc. As Khaled Fahmy elaborates (chapter 8), while Nasser's autocratic military rule decisively reshaped Egypt's politics away from liberalism, his anti-imperialist and pro-Palestinian posture made him a hero of the Third World masses. His nationalization of the Suez Canal in 1956 triggered Israel, Britain, and France to form an alliance and invade Egypt, but it also inspired anti-imperialist sentiments in Latin America, notably in Panama, where its nationalist leader Omar Torrijos reclaimed control of the Panama Canal from the United States in 1977. Broadly, a form of Latin American Nasserism had emerged far away from Egypt, marked by populism, radical independence, national development, and social progress.[7]

These South-South relations between Egypt and Latin America were partially aided by a long-standing Arab diaspora largely from the Levant. As John Tofik Karam observes (chapter 19), this group who were labeled as *turcos* (people of Ottoman lands) warmly embraced the ideas of their fellow Arab leader, Nasser. Arab migration had begun in the late nineteenth and early twentieth centuries and has continued ever since. This vocal and visible diaspora consists of generations of communities that have distinguished themselves in business, the arts, and politics—from both right and leftist orientations. Today in Mexico the business magnet Carlos Slim Helu, one of the richest men in the world, came from a Lebanese family. His right-wing politics mirrored the infamous Carlos Menem, from Syria, who ruled Argentina between 1989 and 1999. But back in the 1960s and 1970s, ideologies like Nasserism and leftist politics enjoyed the support of the Arab diaspora. That era has certainly passed; and today perhaps few people may even be able to tell who Nasser is, except perhaps in Venezuela, where many consider Hugo Chavez as the "Soldier of Nasser."[8]

Today, people are much more likely to know the great Egyptian soccer star, Mo Salah. Like Nasser, Mohammed "Mo" Salah also comes from humble beginnings and, like Nasser, he represents Arabs and Muslims in the world. Salah is arguably more known and famous than Nasser was in his time. Of course, Salah is one of the best soccer players in a game that boasts some four billion fans worldwide, more than any other sport. But there are many celebrated soccer players, like the Algerian-French Zinedine Zeidan, who are not as global and cherished as Salah. In a sense, as Amro Ali recounts(chapter 7), Salah compensates for the absence of an Arab leader of the stature of Nasser. Salah "is a redemption of something lost, a substitute in an era devoid of real Muslim leaders." But for the rest of the world, particularly Europe, "he is the disrupter of the secular realm and obstacle to bigotry who can jam the wires of Islamophobia." Chants by English fans describe Salah as a "gift from Allah."

In a sense, Ali writes, "Salah encodes the somebodiness that restores a sense of dignity to the Egyptian at home, and to Arabs and Muslims abroad, while delivering a reckoning for which the West has to deal." What Salah brings to the world is not simply the stunning athletic beauty he displays in the soccer pitch but, despite the occasional falls from grace, an extraordinary humanity, decency, empathy, and integrity that is missing in today's world of sports. He even exhibits a deep empathy for teams that lose by his wins. In short, Salah's globality lies in displaying the kind of moral code, beauty, charity, and humility that transcend culture, religion, and national boundaries.

CONCLUSION

Why should we get surprised about the globality of the Middle East, if not for the all-too-common and widespread assumptions about the innate parochiality and nativism of the region frozen in time? Indeed, a large part of this discourse about globality or parochialism of the Middle East has concerned the modern era, the era of nation-states, when the territorial borders came to shape national and cultural hierarchies. Otherwise, as Hamid Dabashi highlights (chapter 5), before the very designation of the term "the Middle East" by European colonists, the region was integral in at least "three global Muslim empires that ruled half of the civilized world: the Mughals, the Safavids/Qajars, and the Ottomans." The region we currently call the Middle East was historically the loci of widespread trade, travel, exchange of goods, people, capital, and cultural products that together lend themselves to the integration of cultures.

Perhaps notions of diffusion, of give-and-take, are too simple to capture the complexities and myriad ways cultural landscapes have been interconnected. Consider how much, as Dabashi shows, Persian philosophy, poetry, prophets, and figurative symbols found their ways into the works of thinkers like the ancient Greek philosopher Xenophon, into the Hebrew Bible, in Montesquieu's *Persian Letters*, Nietzsche's *Thus Spoke Zarathustra*, or Mozart's *Magic Flute*. These display not simply the influence of Persian culture on the European literary consciousness—the opposite of which would be that infamous Westernization of the rest. Rather, they point to the operation of what Dabashi calls a "transnational public sphere," a sphere of the circulation of cultural registers that is embraced by nations without borders but emasculated by the states with walls. The challenge is to retrieve such interconnected cultural worlds that Europe repressed by universalizing itself and provincializing the others.

Looking from this lens, the notion that certain knowledge "belongs" to a certain culture, society, or country may seem too simplistic or even irrelevant. Although it is undeniable that local cultures influence the mode, direction, or even the value of knowledge production, the narratives of astronomy, algebra, or Rumi, of food, fashion, and music described in this book, show that knowledge, ideas, or artifacts are often the outcome of accumulated layers of old, new, and ongoing additions, modification, and transfigurations, coming from sources and places beyond where they originated. In the age of the nation-state and the current outflow of offensive nationalism and nativism, nations may take pride in this or that discovery, idea, or famous personality.

But in truth there is no totally pure people, thought, or culture with a fixed geography. In the large span of time and space, humans have moved around, gained new experiences, and their ideas have circulated over time and in the expanse of this planet. From this standpoint the homeland is our shared world to which all of us—peoples, knowledges, and ways of living—belong. The claims about which notable figure or ideas belongs to which place and time are often associated with desire for power, superiority, or otherwise resisting power and building hegemony. In the current global order marked by hierarchy and dominance, peripheral nations or liberation movements may deploy cultural symbols to gain recognition. But recognition is one thing, ownership is another. Otherwise what is the relevance of the question of where Rumi belongs—to Persia, Afghanistan, the Arab world, or Turkey? Why should it matter? For in truth, he belongs to all of these lands, his space was borderless, his speech multiple, and his poetry universal. In this sense, he belonged to our world, to everyone, and perhaps to all times.

NOTES

1. This point has been elaborated in Linda Herrera, *Revolution in the Age of Social Media: The Egyptian Popular Insurrection and the Internet* (New York: Verso, 2014).

2. Fortunately, advances in both global studies and Middle East studies have been changing the conversation and opening avenues of inquiry and understanding. A growing critical mass of outstanding and pioneering scholars, artists, activists, and social media influencers—a selection of whom have authored chapters in this edited volume—have been providing rigorous and more integrated readings of history, politics, economy, and society. These perspectives are needed more than ever to make sense of and find solutions to the state of global change and challenges.

3. Michael Lipka, "More White Evangelicals Than American Jews Say God Gave Israel to the Jewish People," Pew Research Center, October 3, 2013, http://pewrsr.ch/15MZZA2 (accessed June 1, 2019).

4. Tim Mitchel, *Carbon Democracy: Political Power in the Age of Oil* (London: Verso Books, 2011).

5. Edward Said, "Reflections on Exile," *Granta* 13 (1984): 159–172.

6. This discussion draws on Asef Bayat, "Everyday Cosmopolitanism," *ISIM Review* 22 (Autumn 2008), https://openaccess.leidenuniv.nl/bitstream/handle/1887/17246/ISIM_22_Everyday_Cosmopolitanism.pdf?sequence=1.

7. Yasmin Helal, "The Phantom of Nasserism in Latin America," Jadaliyya.com, April 9, 2019, http://jadaliyya.com/Details/38541?fbclid=IwAR3Pwl6gEp8Eh7.

8. Helal, "Phantom of Nasserism."

PART TWO

Nations without Borders

TWO

God

Ebrahim Moosa

ALMOST HALF OF THE POPULATION of the modern world adopted some version of the idea of God that originated in the global Middle East. Stirrings of a God who first became known to people in the Middle East and then to regions beyond roughly dates back to the fifth century BCE. This period coincided with the advent of the patriarch Abraham and the rise and flourishing of Judaism, Christianity, and Islam—the main contenders for the moniker of monotheism rooted in the Middle East. Other traditions among Babylonian and Persian religions also bear traces of monotheism; however, they have not survived the growth and competition from the three subsequent monotheistic faiths.

By today's nomenclature we call Judaism, Christianity, and Islam "world religions" for a simple reason: each are distributed across many cultures, language groups, and ethnicities in an unparalleled manner. Although each tradition might have originated in the Middle East region, these religions made their biggest impact beyond their geographical boundaries and grew in places that look very different from their original habitats. Christianity and Islam today have more adherents outside the Middle East than the total population of each faith within the region. And until the twentieth century, Judaism was distributed among different linguistic communities in the Middle East and in Europe. Since the formation of the state of Israel in 1948, Judaism has had a concentrated presence in Israel, with significant minorities of Jews in Europe and North America.

Many people think of God as an unseen and hidden figure who is an all-powerful and all-knowing entity. This God is relatable with the authority of the divine often being projected as that of the king of the world or the lord of the universe who created all living beings, animals, vegetation, and all inanimate substances. When we talk about a deity with these features, we are certainly talking about the idea of a God with a heredity that is distinct to the broader Middle East. Needless to say, the very idea of God has evolved over a long time. From the outer and adjacent regions of Asia, from the locations to the west of the Middle East, known as West Asia, and abutting Europe, there are unmistakable influences that seeped into the conceptions of the deity that originated in what is today called the Middle East. The Romans who ruled parts of North Africa and the Middle East recognized very early on that there were key differences between Roman deities and the one cherished by the Jews and the Persians. Zoroastrianism was followed in the area of what is today modern Iran. Followers of this faith who survived in India are known as the Parsees. Greek philosophy gradually inscribed itself on descriptions of God found in Judaism, Christianity, and Islam. All three religions developed elaborate creeds, spawned beliefs about the world, and offered descriptions as to how their deity acts in the world and relates to followers. "Theology" is the name for a language of rational accounts of how God works in the world and engages people and the world.

JUDAISM

Among the oldest of the three monotheistic faiths, Judaism holds the idea of God as Yahweh. Biblical Israel is the old name for the northern region of modern Israel. Nearby in the Levant area is a country named Canaan, which was sometimes independent and at other times a tributary of ancient Egypt. Judaism's God is primarily derived from the preexisting polytheistic religion and divinities of Israel. Israelite religion identifies God as Yahweh, as the proper name of God. Yahweh was originally the lord above all other deities. There are striking similarities and some differences between Israelite and Canaanite deities.

Yahweh was transformed through theological processing as the sole high god from the debris of polytheistic deities. God was also called El or Elohim, also meaning God, but the term is derived from the word meaning a plurality of deities. Yahweh is a high God who is served by other deities. Yahweh is the beneficent patriarch, judge, and warrior who watches over the people of Israel and is exclusively the God of the Israelites, just like other communities, tribes, and ethnicities have their own gods. Because Yahweh delivered spectacular feats for his people, such as delivering them from bondage and slavery,

FIGURE 2.1 "Yahweh" in Hebrew script.

he demands exclusive loyalty and adherence. Yahweh serves to cement God and the people of Israel by prescribing a strict culture that separates the followers of Yahweh from the followers of other deities.

In earlier incarnations of Israelite religion, Yahweh and his people could at least acknowledge the existence of other gods in a system called henotheism (belief in one god), without denying the existence of subsidiary gods. Over time a more thoroughgoing monotheism took root from the eighth to the sixth centuries BCE. It allowed for the souls of the human dead and the statues of the human dead to be summoned by sorcerers and supernatural forces. These entities were also referred to as gods or shades of the dead, even though Deuteronomy 18:11 ("or casts spells, or who is a medium or spiritist or who consults the dead") prohibited the worship of such gods. So while Yahweh was in heaven, other gods with some autonomy dwelled in the earthly regions below.

In Israelite religion the king functioned as a quasi-divine intermediary between God and humans. For that reason the king is also sometimes referred to as the "son" of God, or the first born of God. In that role the king is God's representative or intermediary on earth managing the harmony and peace of the human and cosmic orders. From 536 through 70 BCE, in the absence of a reigning king, the very idea of a divine king stimulated the expectation of a royal messiah who would be equipped by the divinity to permanently defeat chaos. This sets the conceptual grounds for what happens later with the rise of Christianity, where Jesus is crowned messiah and the "king" of the Jews.

CHRISTIANITY

The idea of God in Christianity cannot be detached from what preceded it, especially as documented in the Hebrew Bible (Old Testament). If Israel's God is that of a people and a family, then the Christian God departs from that framework. The idea of the Lord of the nation of Israel morphs to become the Lord of all creation: beyond time, place, and history. Over time, this idea of the divine is further evolved and refined as Christendom's early communities spread into the Greek-speaking world.

One major development was a change in the way God was described: first God was described in anthropomorphic (exhibiting humanlike) ways, as a continuation of the thread of Israelite religion. God was featured as having humanlike qualities as a deity who can speak as well as see and hear all things. Biblical passages show how God is jealous or regrets creating humans, revealing a God who acts like a disappointed parent who chastises a disobedient child. The description of God in humanlike qualities meant that God was accessible to human beings, but there was also an acute awareness that God was beyond human imagination and character. At the same time, the deity was beyond anything humans could imagine, hence the prohibition on images and material representations of God. Humans could have access to a personal and living God and those loyal to God able to experience the gentleness and compassion of the divine, while the wrath and destruction of God are reserved for the disobedient and the enemies of God.

Christianity in contact with Greek culture and practices developed two kinds of vocabularies to describe the divine. One was a more abstract description of God as a Supreme Being, a First Cause who was the ruler of the world. God was described as eternal, intelligent, omnipotent, omniscient, the source of all good and to whom humans owed obeisance. The second vocabulary was to develop the divine as consisting of three divine persons but in one divine nature—Father, Son, and Holy Spirit. This is Christianity's signature doctrine, setting itself apart from both Judaism before it and Islam after it. Insistent on its monotheism, the idea of a triune god sharing in one divine person has challenged adherents in different ways and generated some minor schisms over time around the idea of an unitarian or monotheistic God. However, in most denominations of Christianity, the trinity is a critical feature of the divinity.

ISLAM

Theocentrism, the claim that God is at the center of all natural and supernatural reality, was Islam's signature expression of the doctrine of monotheism (*tawḥīd*). Professing the oneness of God means one must insist that the authority and sovereignty of Allāh, who was previously the high god of the polytheistic Arabs of the Arabian Peninsula, cannot be compromised with anyone. The Qur'ān, the revelation vouchsafed to Muhammad as the

FIGURE 2.2 "Allah" in Arabic script.

Prophet of God, and the sayings of Muhammad are replete with antipolytheistic themes. Allāh can have no partners, intermediaries, assistants, offspring, or be seen to associate with natural or supernatural forces.

Muslim theology infuses Greek philosophy to make its case for the character of the divine. God is described with the terms "independent," "necessary," "absolute," and "transcending"; God is compassionate and forgives. When they break moral norms, humans engage in sin and thus offend the majesty of God. When humans repent, Islam accepts their contrition. But offenses against one's fellows can only be sought from humans. Therefore a human being can only be morally raised and attain salvation once one reconciles with fellow humans. Like Judaism and Christianity that preceded it, Islam admits humanlike qualities in God, with the proviso that the qualities in each, God and humans, are utterly different.

COVENANT

Judaism, Christianity, and Islam see themselves in a covenantal or contractual relationship with God. However, in each tradition the covenantal elements differ and hence each works differently. Key to the covenant is the figure of Abraham (Abram in the Jewish tradition, Ibrahim in the Arabic tradition). God promises Abraham land and posterity. Abraham is blessed with two sons: the elder son Ishmael/Isma'il from his slave, Hagar, through whom the promise to the Arabic-speaking prophet, Muhammad, runs. The younger son is Isaac/Ishāq from Abraham's long sterile wife, Sarah, in whose line the patriarch Jacob, the father of Israel, rises. God then tests Abraham to sacrifice his son as an act of obedience. In the Jewish and Christian tradition the house of Isaac and his son Jacob, also known as Israel, as well as his offspring, are blessed with God's activity and presence in their lives.

For Christians this story takes an elaborate twist, especially in the hands of Saint Paul, who stresses that a promise can take two forms: one is a promise "according to the flesh" (meaning through blood lines and genetics as the Jews believed); the other is a promise "according to the spirit" (by way of faith and belief). The latter mode of promise by faith for Christians materializes in faith and belief in the messiah Jesus. For Muslims this promise to Abraham finds expression in Ishmael, who is viewed as the father of the Arabs and whose seed culminates in the prophecy of Muhammad, the son of Abdullah. The Qur'ān frequently refers to Abraham as the progenitor of the model monotheist whose profession of faith is most wholesomely expressed in Islam. Muslims also adhere to a spiritual covenant of obedience made to God in pre-eternity, when all souls were asked whether they accept God as Lord, and to which they replied, "Yes we do."

Judaism and Islam signal the covenant through adherence to certain practices and rules known as the *halakha* and the sharī'a respectively as a manifest form of obedience. In the Christian narrative, Abraham, Isaac, and Sarah are the true spiritual forebears of Jews as well as Gentiles. But unlike the importance of the law in Judaism and Islam, it is the belief in the messiah that serves as the focal point of salvation in Christianity.

MADE IN THE IMAGE OF GOD

All three traditions firmly hold that humans have been created in the image of God. Each see this claim slightly differently, but it nevertheless plays a critical role in moral theology and especially in doctrines centered on human personhood for the purpose of ethics. The image of God signifies a special relationship with God. If God is the king then this imagery serves to democratize the divine aura with a special status. Humans are lesser than gods but higher than animals. For this reason, humans are regarded as reaching the pinnacle of divine creation and therefore can boast a spiritual, moral, and intellectual dimension that surpasses other creation.

Early Yahwistic religion saw the human being as a laborer in the garden of Eden in order to protect the garden. This narrative resonated with older Mesopotamian creation myths where humans became like gods with knowledge of good and evil. The preeminent Muslim theologian Abu Hamid al-Ghazali (d. 1111) explained that the word "image" (as in being created in the image of God) cannot be taken literally since God is ineffable. Meanings are arranged in forms, he explained, and therefore it is best to think of humans cultivating an intimate and personal relationship with God. Creation in the image of God becomes the lodestone for ethics, morality, and personhood in modern expressions of these three Middle Eastern religious traditions. The abolition of slavery, campaigns in support of the rights of women and ethnic minorities, human rights, and ecological debates draw on this morality tale. They tie human action directly to theistic sources with strong divine resonances in morals and ethics. One advantage this moral scheme provides is that it offers a unique ethical effect: obedience to a moral command means that one is directly communing with a personal God. This enhances both the divine command and the feeling of fulfillment of one's human dignity, a concept that is uniquely tied to God's essence.

REVELATION AND PROPHECY

Although multiple religions outside the greater Middle East have a concept of "revelation," what is distinctive about religion in this region is that it combines revelation with prophecy. Revelation is a divine communication to a human being in a wide variety of forms from direct inspiration to dreams and forms of personal intuition and oracles. Each tradition develops an elaborate theology around revelation, sanctioning certain forms of divine communication to be legitimate and disapproving of other means, such as magic and sorcery. Christianity gave the idea of revelation a special character. Christian revelation is framed as God's self-revelation to humanity in the form of the divine incarnation in Christ. It is a disclosure of the truth of God that Christianity facilitates with direct access to the divine person.

Judaism and Islam also allow for access to God but in more ineffable ways. Hence the German Christian theologian Dietrich Bonhoeffer and others can boldly claim that Christianity alone possessed a revelation, especially when the divine is self-revealed in Jesus Christ. That self-revelation for Christians is divine love for humanity. In Islam, revelation in the strict sense is only vouchsafed to specific figures known as prophets (*nabī* pl. *anbiyā*) and those select figures who are given a normative order or law who are called messengers (*rasūl* pl. *rusul*) and are ranked higher than prophets. The Qur'ān as revelation is viewed as God's speech carrying knowledge of divine truths directed firstly at the messenger. Islam's concept of God is not one who self-discloses, but rather God gives humans access to divine knowledge. God mediates knowledge first to prophets via angels and then this knowledge is shared with communities. According to Islamic teachings, Muhammad is God's last prophet and messenger. Mystical illumination and intuitions received by saintly figures and mystics cannot serve as a normative teaching and authority for a community but are viewed as supplementary to the prophetic revelations. Hence mainstream Muslim theology's contestation with Bahaullah (1817–1892), the founder of Bahaism, a faith that initially grew in Persia, which has faced persecution since its inception in 1863.

In Judaism the pivotal revelatory moment is the gift of the Torah granted to Moses at Mount Sinai. Most Jews believe that revelation comes to an end around the fifth century BCE, during the second temple period. However, the interpretation of the revealed texts found in the Bible by the sages of the community took the place of revelation. Therefore the act of interpreting sacred texts could itself be viewed as a sort of secondary revelation. Here there is some overlap with Islam, where the revealed text of the Qur'ān and Muhammad's collected teachings are interpreted by the inspired leaders (imams) who descended from his family or the efforts of the founding jurist-theologians in early Islam. Their interpretations are treated reverentially, but aspects of their teachings are the subject of vehement contestation in modern Islam. Some Jews believe revelation to be continuous in the sense of secondary revelation by way of the ongoing interpretative process.

Revelation in Christianity is also continuous. The proclamation or preaching (kerygma) of the death of Christ for the salvation of humankind is the ongoing revelation of God in Christianity and an expression of the divine self-revelation. Judaism, Christianity, and Islam cemented the idea of revelation and prophecy as a manifestation of God's teachings to the world. These teachings take form of the community of Jews, the church in Christendom, and the ecumenical community (*umma/milla*) of Muslims over time.

GOD AND GLOBAL ORDER

A key feature of prophecy is that it made possible the ability for humans to imagine a future. Prophetic charisma gave birth to the concept of history. In Greek culture history was knowledge, narration, and inquiry. But the prophets turned out to be seers, and their labors contributed to a concept of a future time and history. Often the future was an afterworldly future, but until such End Times arrived, all three religions taught humanity could live on earth according to a set of norms and values that were inspired by God and in a state of peace as a preview of Eden. This impulse contributed to creating a worldly political order attributed to God or derived from the teachings of God's prophets in one way or another. From the early kingdoms of

Judaism, to the multiple empires of Christendom and Islamdom, the idea of God and the desire to govern the world in terms of God's will were taken very seriously by all three faith traditions. In fact, the two elements—obedience to God (religion) and obedience or compliance to a political order (politics)—were seen as almost identical during the age of empires. God as the heavenly king either authorized and sanctioned the earthly monarchs to rule in the name of the divine or the monarchs had to perform as representatives of the divine on earth. A political theology of empire was the currency of governance for a long time.

Of course, the idea of twinning obedience to God and monarchs was contested in various ways during the age of empire and hence a vast literature abounds to attest to the challenges and differentiation in the past. But the contest was always about what constitutes the best ethical life, in both public and private realms. With the advent of European modernity, roughly from the fourteenth century on, from the rediscovery of classical philosophy, a return to art and literature in the Renaissance period, through the Reformation and the split in Christendom's church and the Enlightenment, the connections between obedience to God (religion) as well as to earthly rulers as representatives of God were questioned. Such ties were later abandoned with the rise of secular politics. From now on, at least in Christian domains, politics will not be justified by divine fiat but by human reason and the authority of the people. Obedience to God or religion was not abandoned inasmuch as it no longer served as a justification as to who should rule and on what normative grounds they should rule. God's place and God's rule, observers noted, was restricted to the personal and private realms.

Secular empires followed by secular nation-states emerged following a model of where the justification of politics was separated from adherence to religion. However, the place of God in nation-state political models of governance is highly contested. In political systems around the world God had made a comeback in one way or another—from the Islamic Revolution in Iran in 1979, to political Islam in Pakistan and Sudan, to the twenty-first-century post-Islamist social upheavals in the Middle East, North Africa, and Indonesia. Resurgent modes of political and cultural Christianity are evident in political trends in North America, Europe, and Latin America. Resurgent Judaism, Hinduism, and Buddhism are highly visible and volatile in political contestations in such places as Israel, India, Myanmar, and Sri Lanka, respectively. Global trends have defied twentieth-century predictions about the end of religion and an end to the role of God in politics and society. Humanity might be on the cusp of another new moment where God, the environment, and human sociality might begin to offer new possibilities for both theology and politics.

At the same time, the scientific revolutions of the past two hundred years have radically altered our ideas of the cosmos and the place of the world in it. Where the early cosmologies placed the earth at the center of the universe, the modern scientific cosmology locates the earth as a speck in a process of evolution across billions of years in the formation of the known cosmos. This new cosmology challenges the inherited creation stories and the concept of God that a creator God spawned. German philosopher Friedrich Nietzsche fully realized that all our concepts and ideas of the universe and morality will be impacted by our new discoveries, including the idea and concept of God we had inherited from the past. Nietzsche impudently, and in the eyes of many blasphemously, asked the question on the lips of his prophetic figure Zarathustra: "Could it be possible! This old saint has not yet heard in his forest that God is dead!"

Albert Einstein, the renowned physicist, also challenged the idea of a personal God. In other words the very idea of God in a cosmos marked by contingency is now under question. While a multitude of theologies have already begun to reconceptualize humans and existence in this new cosmology, the debates are earnest, furious, and divisive. Many of the faithful hold onto the idea of God birthed in the greater Middle East while they continue to exist and inhabit a world fashioned and produced by the new deities of science and evolution—the ideas of Galileo, Newton, Darwin, and Einstein who tell a somewhat different story about creation and existence from what the prophets of Judaism, Christianity, and Islam taught. Yet it also seems that the God of the Abrahamic religions is resilient and capacious enough to allow for laypersons and theologians to experience the divinity in light of their changing experiences over time.

FURTHER READING

Gregg, Robert C. *Shared Stories, Rival Tellings: Early Encounters of Jews, Christians, and Muslims*. New York: Oxford University Press, 2015.

Hendel, Ronald S. "Israelite Religion." In *Encyclopedia of Religion*, edited by Lindsay Jones, vol. 7, 4742–50. Detroit, MI: Macmillan Reference USA, 2005.

Hoonhout, M. A., J. R. Gillis, and R. J. Buschmiller. "God." In *New Catholic Encyclopedia*, vol. 6, 270–90. Detroit, MI: Gale, 2003.

THREE

Algebra, Alchemy, Astronomy

Robert Morrison

THE ARABIC ETYMOLOGIES of common terms such as algebra (Arabic *al-jabr wa-l-muqābala*), alchemy (Arabic *al-kīmiyā'*), and algorithm (from the name al-Khwārazmī, d. 847 CE) hint at how an examination of the global Middle East would be incomplete without reference to science. However, because the history of science in the region, what is called today the Middle East, begins before the advent of modernity, the terminology for this chapter is different in two ways. First, scholars never speak of the history of Middle Eastern science but rather the history of science in Islamic (or Islamicate) societies. As Islam was the religion of the powerful in these societies, "Islamic science" is a concise shorthand so long as one understands that the relationship between the sciences and Islam was nuanced, variable, and historically contingent. In a nod to non-Muslims' participation in this scientific enterprise and to an important language of composition, the science has been called "Arabic science." But as more and more scientific literature in Islamic languages other than Arabic comes to light, "Arabic science" becomes a less accurate term. Second, because the historical actors did not conceive of the term "global," this chapter uses the term "transregional."

A perusal of even outdated secondary sources would communicate that Islamic societies, starting around 800 (all dates in this chapter are CE), built on the heritage of classical antiquity until the twelfth century at which time the Latin West (medieval Europe) translated Arabic sources into Latin, as the West embarked, at first fitfully, on the path to modern Western science. Even these contacts between classical antiquity and Islamic societies and, subsequently, Islamic societies and the Latin West, indicate a transregional scientific culture. During this period of translation that began in the eighth century and continued through the eleventh, much of the scientific heritage of ancient Greece, along with some scientific texts in Persian and Sanskrit, were appropriated into Arabic. Translation into Arabic never meant the end of intellectual life in the societies from whence the manuscripts came. Intellectual life in the Byzantine Empire continued and was nourished by translation, and scholars from Islamic societies continued to be interested in India. Older secondary sources portray a twelfth-century ascendance of Islamic orthodoxy that purportedly harmed science, coincident with what those older sources saw as Europe's stirrings from the Dark Ages in the twelfth century. In fact, transregional and transcultural scientific activity in Islamic societies continued through the nineteenth-century encounter with modern science.

This chapter focuses on algebra, alchemy, and astronomy—fields that represent, in different measures, the exact and natural sciences. The historical actors recognized these and other sciences' transregional character by classifying them as fields with truth claims that did not depend on revelation. Regarding Islamic astronomy, there is a plethora of primary sources and modern scholarship, whereas algebra and alchemy, though less studied subfields of Islamic science, are likely to be just as transregional. The historical actors acknowledged that these sciences were connected to other cultures, whether earlier or contemporaneous, and valued the geographic breadth of potential sources of knowledge in Islamic societies. The Prophet Muḥammad (ca. 570–632) was reported to have said that one should seek knowledge even in China. This saying reflects intellectual horizons that extended beyond the lands of Islam.

ASTRONOMY

Astronomy is the scientific discipline in which scholars from Islamic societies left the highest output and where evidence for transregional exchange throughout the centuries is in plain sight. The names of many stars and constellations in contemporary European languages originate in the ninth-century Arabic translations of Ptolemy's second-century *Almagest*. The *Almagest*, two books of which were a catalogue of stars and constellations, was the most influential astronomy text in Greek. Although it might not be surprising that a tenth-century lavishly illustrated Arabic text titled *Book of the Constellations* by 'Abd al-Raḥmān al-Ṣūfī (d. 986) informed thirteenth-century Latin and Spanish texts, it is remarkable that, even five centuries later, Vincenzo Coronelli's (d. 1718) celestial globe still featured Ṣūfī's terminology in Arabic script.[1] The enduring transregional career of Ṣūfī's text makes more sense after a closer look at the first translations of astronomy texts into Arabic.

The history of Islamic astronomy was, from its outset, multicultural. When the Islamic Empire went through a rapid expansion in the seventh century into the Fertile Crescent, Mesopotamia, and North Africa, the conquering Muslim armies left the former Byzantine and Sassanian functionaries in place. They were the first to apply mathematics and astronomy to the administrative needs of the Umayyad Caliphate, the first dynasty of successors to the Prophet Muḥammad. The earliest discrete scientific texts reported to be translated in Islamic societies during the 730s and 740s were handbooks of astronomy with tables (*azyāj*, sing. *zīj*). These handbooks with tables were important for calendar calculations, astrological forecasts, and timekeeping, among other applications, and illustrate the practice of astronomy. The first *azyāj* to be translated came from Pahlavi (pre-Islamic Persian) and Sanskrit originals. The mid-eighth-century translation of Pahlavi astrological texts, such as the *Book of Nativities* (Kitāb al-Mawālīd), reflected the coupling of astronomy with its astrological applications.

The rise of the Abbasid Caliphate (750–1258), the second dynasty of successors to the Prophet Muḥammad, went along with a marked increase in the volume and intensity of translation. A famous embassy from India to the court of al-Manṣūr (d. 775) brought texts that eventually became a foundation of the *Zīj al-Sindhind* (The Sindhind Astronomical Handbook with Tables). Manṣūr, in turn, used astrology publicly to find the best time for the construction of Baghdad, the new Abbasid capital. Historian Kevin van Bladel has recently argued that the Abbasids' interest in Indian astronomy (and Sanskrit texts more broadly) was driven by a desire to compete with the Tang Court in China, a significant consumer of Sanskrit culture. The Abbasid caliph Hārūn al-Rashīd's (d. 809) personal physician went to India to study medicine. In turn, Indian scholars came to Baghdad to study medicine and astrology.

Scholars have long held that theoretical Islamic astronomy after 900 depended mostly on the heritage of Greek (and not Pahlavi and Sanskrit) texts. They point to the contents of *al-Zīj al-Ṣābi'* (The Sabaean astronomical handbook with tables) of al-Battānī (d. 923) as evidence to support this claim. The Latin translations of al-Battānī's *zīj*, by Robert of Chester and Plato of Tivoli in the thirteenth century, in addition to Latin translations of

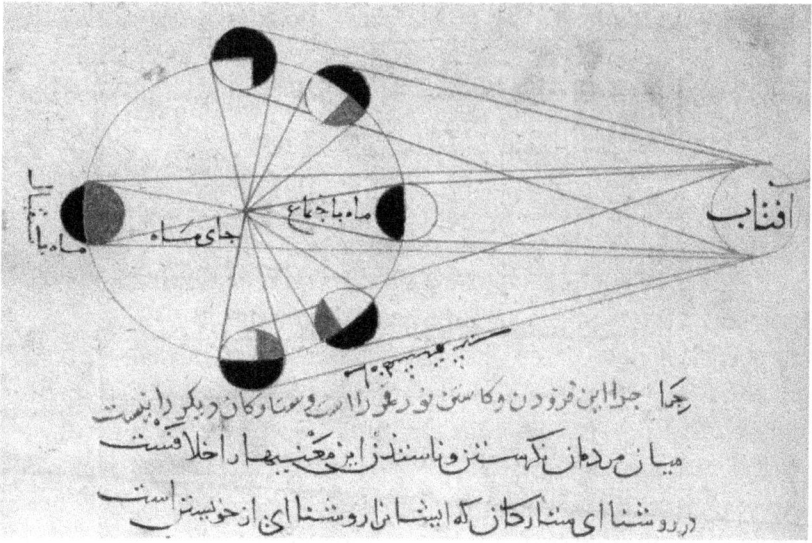

FIGURE 3.1 Al-Bīrūnī, "Illustration of different phases of the moon from manuscript of the *Kitab al-Tafhim* by Al-Biruni (973–1048)." Wikimedia Commons, https://en.wikipedia.org/wiki/File:Lunar_eclipse_al-Biruni.jpg.

the Arabic versions of Ptolemy's *Almagest*, introduced Ptolemaic astronomy to the Latin West. However, although the Greek influence on Islamic astronomy was indeed great, the intellectual life of India continued to matter. The most talented astronomer ever in the history of Islamic societies, al-Bīrūnī (d. 1048), paid a great deal of attention to astronomy from India. Al-Bīrūnī learned the relevant languages, devoted a significant portion of his *India* (Taḥqīq mā li-l-Hind) to astronomy, and made noteworthy contributions to the sudy of Indian chronology and astrology.

In fact, al-Bīrūnī cited Indian scholars to back up his own contention that earth may well be revolving daily about its own axis. All other astronomers writing in Arabic believed that earth did not revolve about its own axis. Al-Bīrūnī's study of Indian science was in the context of broader interests; India contained a clear-eyed explanation of religion in India. The Indian intellectual tradition that informed earlier translations into Arabic remained, after the rise of Islam, more vibrant and more attractive to al-Bīrūnī than the intellectual life of the Byzantine Empire. The Greek texts that were most influential for the science of Islamic societies came from the classical and Hellenistic periods, not from Byzantine scholars contemporaneous with the flourishing of intellectual life in Islamic societies.

The most famous institution in the history of Islamic astronomy, and a major locus for transregional exchanges, particularly with Chinese scholars, was the observatory founded by the (Mongol) Ilkhanid sultan Hülegü at Marāghah in 1259, in Northwest Iran. The Marāghah Observatory attracted scholars from other Islamic societies and other parts of the world. One such scholar who worked under Naṣīr al-Dīn al-Ṭūsī (d. 1274), the director of the observatory, was a Chinese scholar named Fu Mengchi (Fu Meng-zhi), who came from the Mongol Yuan dynasty in China. Information about Chinese astronomy penetrated works of the best-known astronomers at Marāghah. Although Ṭūsī's *Zīj-i Īlkhānī* (The Ilkhanid Astronomical Handbook with Tables) was not based on observations from Marāghah, it contained information about Chinese calendars, meaning that these scholars from China caught the attention of the observatory's director. The historian Yoichi Isahaya has argued that despite the presence of Chinese technical terms in *Zīj-i Īlkhānī*, there is no evidence that Ṭūsī translated a Chinese text.[2]

Rather, a Chinese astronomer at Marāghah was the presumed source of the information. Likewise, Muḥyī' al-Dīn al-Maghribī's (d. 1283) *zīj* incorporated both observations from Marāghah and information about Chinese calendars. Moving in the other direction, a Muslim scholar named Jamāl al-Dīn went to China in the mid-thirteenth century, built seven astronomical instruments, and was installed by Khubilai (d. 1294) as the superintendent of the newly established Institute of Muslim Astronomy. The 1383 *Huihui li* (Islamic Astronomical Calendrical System) was a translation of a Persian *zīj* that does not survive in the original. Connections between the Mongol dynasties that succeeded Genghis Khan facilitated these transregional connections.

After a couple of decades, the center of Ilkhanid intellectual life moved from Marāghah to nearby Tabriz. Gregory Chioniades (d. ca. 1320), a Byzantine Christian physician and scholar born in Constantinople and who spent much of his career in Trebizond, came to the Ilkhanid court in Tabriz in 1295–96. While in Tabriz, Chioniades was instructed by Shams al-Dīn al-Bukhārī (a.k.a. Wābkanawī, late thirteenth century), who was connected to astronomers from Marāghah. Among the works that Chioniades eventually translated into Greek are Bukhārī's text on the astrolabe and some *azyāj*, one of which may draw on Ṭūsī's *Zīj-i Īlkhānī*. Most important, Chioniades composed in Greek an introductory text to astronomy titled *The Schemata of the Stars* that contained many of the innovative theories associated with the astronomers affiliated with the Marāghah Observatory.[3] As Christian scholars during the European Renaissance could read Greek, and because one manuscript of the *Schemata* ended up in the Vatican, historians recognize Chioniades as a crucial intermediary for the passage of Islamic theoretical astronomy to Europe.

Since the Renaissance is seen as the origin of the modern West, there is much at stake in the question of connections between European Renaissance astronomy and Islamic astronomy. For several decades, historians have found numerous, precise parallels between Islamic astronomy and European Renaissance astronomy, most notably that of Copernicus. While there is no Islamic precursor for a sun-centered arrangement of the planets, all the other details of Copernicus's astronomy exist in Islamic texts. These parallels are all the more tantalizing because Copernicus clearly accessed and sometimes cited earlier texts connected to Islamic societies such as the *Alfonsine Tables* (produced by the order of King Alfonso X of Toledo by a team that included Jewish and Arab astronomers), as well as al-Biṭrūjī's *On the Principles of Astronomy* (Kitāb al-Hay'a), an Iberian astronomy text from around 1200 that was translated into Latin by Michael Scot (d. ca. 1235) in 1217 and which enjoyed greater readership in Latin than it did in Arabic. Although Copernicus did not cite scholars from Islamic societies who lived closer to his own time, he also did not mention nearly contemporary European astronomers whose work was undeniably foundational for his own. Chioniades's position as an intermediary could explain these numerous, uncited technical parallels with Islamic astronomy.

Chioniades's career was not the only connection between the European Renaissance and Islamic astronomy. After the Ottoman conquest of Constantinople in 1453, the Ottoman court in Istanbul became an intellectual center. Moses Galeano (d. after 1542), a rabbi and physician who was present at the Ottoman court and who wrote in Arabic and Turkish as Mūsā Jālīnūs, brought the planetary theories of Ibn al-Shāṭir (d. 1375) to the Vèneto, Venice and its environs, including the famous University of Padua where Copernicus studied, around 1500. Ibn al-Shāṭir was a Damascene scholar whose theoretical models built on the work of Marāghah astronomers such as Ṭūsī. Copernicus's first sun-centered models were geometric transformations of Ibn al-Shāṭir's earth-centered models; some of Copernicus's later sun-centered models included geometric transformations of other Marāghah models.

Galeano/Jālīnūs was a fascinating intermediary because he also exchanged astronomy less directly relevant to Copernicus's work. Galeano/Jālīnūs brought with him to the Vèneto a knowledge of the theories of Joseph Ibn

Naḥmias's (fl. 1400) *The Light of the World*; Ibn Naḥmias's theories were improvements on Biṭrūjī's *On the Principles of Astronomy*, a text widely diffused in Latin and Hebrew. Ibn Naḥmias wrote originally in Judeo-Arabic, a dialect of Arabic written in Hebrew characters, but Christian scholars in Padua most likely accessed *The Light of the World* through the Hebrew version, which included theories not found in the Judeo-Arabic original. This episode of transregional exchange was bidirectional. Galeano/Jālīnūs wrote an Ottoman Turkish text on pharmacology that cited Latin texts not available in any Islamic language. He also produced an Arabic version of the *Almanach Perpetuum*, a Latin astronomy text based originally on the Hebrew work of Abraham Zacut (d. 1507). Zacut himself fled the Inquisition in Portugal, settling finally in the Ottoman Empire, where he died.

The exchange of astronomy between Islamic societies and Europe did not end with the era of Galeano/Jālīnūs. Historian of Arabic and Islamic science George Saliba has studied the French scholar of Arabic Guillaume Postel (1510–1581) who, like Chioniades, traveled to Istanbul and procured, among other things, a manuscript of Ṭūsī's *al-Tadhkira fī 'ilm al-hay'a* (Memoir on astronomy) that now resides in the Vatican Library.[4] The *Tadhkira* contained some of the earliest theoretical innovations from Marāghah, innovations that reappeared in Chioniades's *Schemata*, Ibn al-Shāṭir and Copernicus's texts, and Ibn Naḥmias's *The Light of the World*. Postel's manuscript of the *Tadhkira* was accurately annotated in Latin, an acknowledgment of Arabic materials' ongoing value. John Greaves, a seventeenth-century English scholar, culled observations from Arabic and Persian texts such as the *zījes* of Ulugh Beg and Ṭūsī in order to "advance the contemporary study of astronomy and geography" in England. When Greaves traveled in the Ottoman Empire, he brought a copy of Tycho Brahe's *Astronomiae Instauratae Progymnasmata*, which was known to the Ottomans.[5] Thus, Coronelli's seventeenth-century celestial globe with Arabic labels, mentioned earlier, had a context. In the nineteenth century, Ottoman scholars from a religious milieu described the Copernican system and certain early modern European advances. Such knowledge had already penetrated other sectors of Ottoman intellectual life in earlier centuries through the work of Ibrahim Hakkı Erzurumi (d. 1780) and Ibrahim Müteferrika (d. 1745).

The scholarly exchange with India that fueled earlier translations and informed Bīrūnī endured. The Rajput Jai Singh (d. 1743) built several observatories in India with instruments inspired by those at Ulugh Beg's fifteenth-century observatory at Samarqand. He also produced the *Zīj*

Muḥammad Shāhī, which was based on Ulugh Beg's tables and on the *Tabulae Astronomicae* of Philippe de La Hire (d. 1718), both of which were clearly in Jai Singh's possession. Another example of what Saliba has called a "perfect circle" of scholarly exchange, hearkening back to earlier translations from Sanskrit, is the Sanskrit translation, produced with assistance from a Persian scholar, of al-Birjandī's (d. 1525) commentary on the chapter of Ṭūsī's *Tadhkira* with Ṭūsī's non-Ptolemaic theories.

ALGEBRA

Astronomy was the field in which scholars of Islamic societies were most productive, hence the quantity of transregional scholarly exchange. But transregional scholarly exchange occurred on a level proportional to scholars' output in other significant scientific fields. Algebra (*al-jabr wa-l-muqābala*), literally "restoring and equating," was the science of transforming and solving equations involving unknowns. Islamic algebra combined earlier work on arithmetic equations involving unknowns with geometry's ability to provide general solutions that would eliminate the need to plug in numbers as earlier Indian mathematicians had done. Algebra, given its etymology in Arabic, is frequently mentioned as a contribution of Islamic societies to the history of science, but algebra had significant, diverse foundations in earlier cultures. Writers on algebra in Islamic societies had different relationships with their predecessors in earlier cultures, revealing the complexity of transregional conversations. Muḥammad b. Mūsā al-Khwārazmī (d. c. 847), the author of the first book of algebra in an Islamic society, *al-Mukhtaṣar fī ḥisāb al-jabr wa-l-muqābala* (The Condensed Book on the Calculation of Algebra), was clearly interested in Indian mathematics as he also composed *The Book of Addition and Subtraction According to Hindu Calculation*.

Other material from India relevant to algebra entered the Abbasid Caliphate as part of the rise of Islamic astronomy. Indian scholars such as Aryabhata (d. 550) and Brahmagupta (d. 668) were interested in equations with multiple unknowns and solutions. These mathematical methods were contained in a text titled the *Brahmasphuta-Siddhanta* that was among those brought to Baghdad by the aforementioned embassy from India during the reign of the Abbasid caliph al-Manṣūr (d. 775) and which became a source of the astronomical handbook with tables titled *Zīj al-Sindhind*. Not only is algebra evidence of the relevance of Indian intellectual life for Islamic societies even when the discrete texts themselves were not translated, expositions of Indian mathematics continued to be produced through the middle of the eleventh century, long after the peak of translations into Arabic.

Although Khwārazmī did not name his sources, making the question of transregional exchange more complicated, historian of science Solomon Gandz has argued that, besides Indian sources, Khwārazmī's algebra drew also on the Hebrew text titled *Mishnat ha-Middot*. Babylonian mathematics has been identified as another source of Khwārazmī's algebra. Khwārazmī is known as a figure who looked to non-Hellenistic sources, but Hellenistic sources could have been the intermediary for Babylonian mathematics. Both the Babylonians and the ancient Greeks studied mathematical problems for which the solution was an unknown quantity. Both worded the problems in terms of geometrical quantities. In any case, Khwārazmī created a new discipline out of a variety of earlier fields and this discipline was the product of an Islamic context. For example, Khwārizmī's algebra treated problems of calculating inheritances. In this respect, Islamic algebra can be seen as an integration of distinctly Islamic practical and abstract approaches to mathematics and as a product of some of the social forces that had earlier led to a plethora of translations of scientific texts. Khwārazmī's work was important outside of Islamic societies. Both Gerard of Cremona and Robert of Chester produced Latin translations of the Arabic original of Khwārazmī's algebra. Khwārazmī's *zīj*, also called *Zīj al-Sindhind* but different from the first one from the eighth century, survives only in the Latin translation by Adelard of Bath.

Subsequently Abū Kāmil (d. 930) systematized Khwārazmī's numerous examples in his own *Algebra*, a commentary on Khwārazmī's work. Scholarship has found Abū Kāmil's algebra to be more dependent on Greek mathematical methods, such as Heron's, than Khwārazmī's. These Greek methods, in turn, had incorporated Babylonian mathematics. The differences between Abū Kāmil and Khwārazmī's algebras mean that these algebras preserve different strands in a broader conversation incorporating Islamic mathematics' transregional sources. Abū Kāmil's work, via a Latin translation, turned out to be very important for Leonardo Fibonacci's algebra; Abū Kāmil's text was also translated into Hebrew and probably Spanish.[6]

There is evidence of regional scientific traditions even in the medieval Islamic world. The contributions of figures from North Africa to algebra such as al-Samaw'al b. Yaḥyā al-Maghribī (d. ca. 1175), in laws of exponents and divisions of polynomials, and Ibn al-Bannā' (d. 1321), in new ways to approximate square roots, to algebra are notable. Historian of mathematics Mahdi Abdeljaouad has contended that algebraic symbols originated in North Africa when scholars migrated from Andalusia after the rise of the Almohads in the twelfth century. The Arabic letter *shin* (ش) stood for *shay'* (thing, x in modern notation) and the letter *mīm* (م) stood for *māl* (wealth, x^2 in modern notation). Changes in notation are noteworthy. Scholars such as Sabbetai Unguru (on the Greeks) and Eleanor Robson (on the Babylonians) have argued convincingly that moderns have inaccurately seen aspects of ancient mathematics as algebraic because of historians' tendency to present this ancient mathematics in modern notation.[7] The Greeks' more thoroughly geometrical analysis afforded a more rigorous treatment of irrational numbers—for example, the diagonal of the square with sides of one—than would be possible with modern notation. Different algebras in different Islamic societies mirrored the variety of Islamic algebra's pre-Islamic sources.

ALCHEMY

The Arabic etymology of the English word "alchemy" (Arabic: *al-kīmiyā'*), the science of transforming metals, is clear and succinctly communicates the transregional dimension of alchemy, which the historical actors themselves recognize. Literary dialogues that depict the passage of alchemical knowledge, which originated in ancient Egypt, from one culture to another, are a genre of alchemical literature. Although the historical accuracy of the Umayyad prince Khālid b. Yazīd's (d. 704 or 709) interest in alchemy has been debated by specialists, the alchemical literature itself frequently portrays him as the earliest Arab alchemist. One of these dialogues, *Masā'il Khālid li-Maryānus al-rāhib* (The Questions of Khalid to the Monk Maryānus), portrays an encounter between Khālid and a Byzantine monk named Maryānus. The narration communicates that Khālid knew about alchemy before this encounter. Not only did the dialogue discuss scholarly exchange, but the dialogue itself was "the very first text on alchemy to be known in the Latin West, probably in 1144."[8] Another dialogue, the *Kitāb Mihrārīs*, has Khālid being instructed by an Indian sage named Mihrārīs. According to that text, Khālid again knew much about alchemy before engaging Mihrārīs. The dialogues illustrate that Islamic alchemy preserved and extended the alchemical heritage of earlier cultures.

The text *Sirr al-asrār* (Secret secretorum) bridged regions, different types of alchemy, and the genre of literature that provided advice for political elites known as "mirror for princes." The connection between rulers and alchemy is represented in Islamic societies by how the Umayyad prince Khālid b. Yazīd is thought of as the first Islamic alchemist. This pseudo-Aristotelian text was translated into Arabic by Yaḥyā b. al-Biṭrīq (fl. 815) and subsequently into Latin and European vernaculars. Alchemy made transregional connections and exchanges in other sciences. The famous astronomer born in Madrid Maslama b. Aḥmad al-Majrīṭī (d. 1007) translated two well-known occult works into Latin at the Court of Alphonso X, the locus of the production for the *Alphonsine Tables*. One was on alchemy, *Rutbat al-ḥakīm* (The Station of the Wise), and the other was *Ghāyat al-ḥakīm* (The Goal of the Wise, known in Latin as the *Picatrix*), a compendium of astrology and magic. In astronomy, the Latin version of Khwārazmī's *Zīj al-Sindhind* incorporated Majrīṭī's revisions.

As was the case with Khwārizmī's *zīj*, the voyage of an alchemical text frequently affected its contents. An important Arabic alchemy text, the *Liber de Aluminibus et Salibus* (Arabic *al-Qawl fī al-milḥ*), had contents that varied from version to version; the Hebrew version of the text included many words transliterated from Italian, which could not have been in the Arabic original.[9] The manuscripts of the Latin translation outnumber those of the Arabic original, suggesting that the Latin version was more influential. Questions of the relationship between authorship and contents multiply in the case of Jābir b. Ḥayyān (eighth and ninth century), the best-known alchemist of the Islamic world. Many scholars believe he did not write all the texts attributed to him. Key themes of the Jābirian corpus include theories of balance and the elixir, which effected the transmutation of substances and the restoration of health. Latin alchemy texts attributed to Geber (Latin for Jābir) may not be translations from the Arabic; instead, the attribution may simply evoke the authority of the Jābirian corpus.

Abū Bakr al-Rāzī (d. 925 or 935) was an influential philosopher, physician, and alchemist. The intersection of his alchemy with philosophy led to questions of whether everything could be explained by the four elements as well-known philosophers such as Ibn Sīnā theorized. Rāzī's career is excellent evidence for how alchemy can be understood as part of the history of chemistry. Rāzī worked with a wide variety of substances, including some salts that came from India and Persia, mentioned in *Sirr al-asrār*.[10] Some of these substances could not be classified or understood as compounds of the four elements, a finding that led Rāzī to question mainstream theories of philosophy rather than his own empirical data.

Alchemy had its detractors in Islamic societies. Bīrūnī remarked in a chapter in India titled "On Hindu Sciences which Prey on the Ignorance of People" that the Indians had a "science similar to alchemy which is quite peculiar to them."[11] The science, Rasāyana—connected to the word for gold—was medical in that it purported, in Bīrūnī's words, to "restore the health of those who were ill beyond hope, and give back youth to fading old age, so that people become again what they were in the age near puberty." Bīrūnī presented an anecdote of a man from Ujayn named Vyāḍi who, to Bīrūnī, foolishly devoted his life to this science. Because the style of Indian alchemy texts was not always straightforward, a characteristic shared by Islamic alchemy texts, Vyāḍi mistook the word for human blood and oil to mean red myrobalan. The medicine did not work as advertised, but the king's saliva, so the story went, turned to gold and Vyāḍi and his wife gained the ability to fly. Even if the story was spurious, it reflected Bīrūnī's perception of the acceptance of alchemy in India and the Indians' blameworthy pursuit of gold. Bīrūnī hoped that alchemy would disappear. Bīrūnī's appropriation of Indian material for his critique of alchemy may have affected the precision of his argument because it transpired later that Rasa did not mean gold but mercury, cinnabar, and other substances.[12]

As the centuries progressed, alchemy's development in Europe came to Islamic societies. The Swiss Renaissance physician and alchemist Paracelsus (d. 1541) used alchemy as the foundation for a new, innovative chemical medicine. Paracelsan medicine entered the Ottoman Empire as the new medicine (*ṭibb-i cedid*).[13] The Ottoman physician Ḥasan Effendi (fl. 1720) produced a Turkish translation of an Arabic text on chemical medicine, depending on the work of Oswald Croll (d. 1609) and Daniel Sennert (d. 1637). Ottoman scholars attributed this medical knowledge to Paracelsus. Interestingly, European collectors prized Ibn Sallūm's (d. 1669) initial Arabic translation of Paracelsus's work. Ibn Sallūm was the most important alchemist at the court of the Ottoman Sultan Meḥmed IV. At the Ottoman court the new medicine came to replace the earlier practices of Islamic medicine that were based on an understanding of the humoral system. By the late eighteenth century, the new medicine had made scientific experimentation, and not philosophy, the dominant foundation of Ottoman medicine.

CONCLUSION

Modern historians of science pay a great deal of attention to particular cultural and historical contexts, and for good reason. The assertion that modern science is global faces little resistance and the preceding case studies of alchemy, algebra, and astronomy show that transregional and transcultural exchange was an important part of the scientific culture of premodern Islamic societies. Although these fields were in large part products of Islamic societies, the extensive evidence for translation and scholarly exchange shows that there was certainly a transregional and transcultural conversation.

The historian of science Jamil Ragep has remarked that the tendency of historians of science to understand science as the product of a given culture, a tendency Ragep calls "relativizing," has led historians of European science to overlook scholarly exchange as a factor in, say, Copernicus's astronomy. Islamic astronomy also benefited from exchange, in earlier centuries, with other living cultures—India and China. The question of Islamic algebra's connections to earlier cultures turned out to be one of exchange rather than of a unidirectional travel of a specific text. And alchemy presented an example of a meaningful exchange between Europe and the Ottoman Empire long after earlier historiography had presumed such contacts to have ceased. The scientific cultures of Islamic societies and Renaissance Europe owe much to other parts of the world.

NOTES

1. For an image of Coronelli's globe, see "Coronelli celestial globe," https://nla. gov.au/nla.obj-234355473/view (accessed July 9, 2020).

2. Mitsuaki Endo and Yoichi Isahaya, "Yuan Phonology as Reflected in Persian Transcription in the *Zīj-i Īlkhānī*," *Keizai Kenkuy* 経済研究 8 (2016): 1–38, at 1–2; and Isahaya, "*The Tārīkh-i Qitā* in the *Zīj-i Īlkhānī*—The Chinese Calendar in Persian," *Sciamus* 14 (2013): 149–258, at 202.

3. E. A. Paschos and P. Sotiroudis, *The Schemata of the Stars: Byzantine Astronomy from A.D. 1300* (Singapore: World Scientific, 1998).

4. George Saliba, "Arabic Science in Sixteenth-Century Europe: Guillaume Postel (1510–1581) and Arabic Astronomy," *Suhayl* 7 (2007): 115–64.

5. G. J. Toomer, *Eastern Wisedome and Learning* (Oxford, UK: Clarendon Press, 1996), 140 and 175.

6. Martin Levey, *The Algebra of Abū Kāmil: Kitāb al-jabr wa'l-muqābala in a Commentary by Mordecai Finzi* (Madison: University of Wisconsin Press, 1966), 6 and 217–20.

7. Sabbetai Unguru, "Rewriting the History of Greek Mathematics," *Archive for History of Exact Sciences* (1975): 67–114, at 69.

8. See Regula Forster, "The Transmission of Secret Knowledge," *al-Qanṭara* 27 (2016): 399–422.

9. Gabriele Ferrario, "Origins and Transmission of the Liber de aluminibus et salibus." *Chymists and Chymistry. Studies in the History of Alchemy and Early Modern Chymistry*, edited by L. Principe (Sagamore Beach, MA, 2007), 137–48, at 148 (Arabic MSS) and 144 (Hebrew version).

10. Julius Ruska, "Die Alchemie ar-Rāzī's," *Der Islam* 22 (1935): 281–319, at 306. See also L. E. Goodman, "al-Rāzī," in *Encyclopaedia of Islam*, 2nd edition, edited by P. Bearman, Th. Bianquis, C. E. Bosworth, E. van Donzel, and W. P. Heinrichs, http://dx.doi.org.ezproxy.bowdoin.edu/10.1163/1573-3912_islam_SIM_6267 (accessed November 3, 2017).

11. All quotes in this paragraph are from Bīrūnī, *Alberuni's India,* edited and translated by Sachau, vol. 1, 188–90.

12. J. Filliozat, "Al-Biruni and Indian Alchemy," in *Studies in the History of Science in India* (New Delhi: Editorial Enterprises, 1982), 338–43, at 340.

13. B. Harun Küçük, "New Medicine and the Ḥikmet-i Ṭabīʿiyye Problematic in Eighteenth Century Istanbul," in *Texts in Transit*, edited by Y. Tzvi Langermann and Robert G. Morrison, 222–42 (University Park: Pennsylvania State University Press, 2016).

FURTHER READING

Berggren, J. L. *Episodes in the Mathematics of Medieval Islam.* 1986; reprint, New York: Springer Verlag, 2016.

Bīrūnī, Muḥammad b. Aḥmad. *Alberuni's India: An Account of the Religion, Philosophy, Literature, Geography, Chronology, Astronomy, Customs, Laws and Astrology of India about AD 1030.* Edited, translated, and with notes and indexes by Edward C. Sachau. New Delhi: Oriental Reprint, 1983.

Forster, Regula. "The Transmission of Secret Knowledge." *al-Qanṭara* 27 (2016): 399–422.

Mavroudi, Maria. "Translations from Greek into Arabic and Latin during the Middle Ages: Searching for the Classical Tradition." *Speculum* 90, no. 1 (2015): 28–59.

Morrison, Robert. "A Scholarly Intermediary between the Ottoman Empire and Renaissance Europe." *Isis* 105 (2014): 32–57.

Robson, Eleanor. *Mesopotamian Mathematics 2100–1600 BC: Technical Constants in Bureaucracy and Education.* New York: Oxford University Press, 1999.

van Bladel, Kevin. *The Arabic Hermes: From Pagan Sage to Prophet of Science.* New York: Oxford University Press, 2009.

FOUR

Rumi, the Bridge Builder

Fatemeh Keshavarz

WHEN WE ARRIVED IN LUCKNOW in mid-January 2018, attacked by an unfriendly virus and trying to be as affable as somebody that sick could be, I expected anything but what we found. Our small team of six consisted of academics in love with Persian literature, history, and manuscript studies. Our mission was to build bridges with the family of Raja Suleiman Khan, the Raja of Mahmoudabad, and to do our best to prepare the family's prodigious collection of Persian manuscripts for restoration and digitization. To be sure, the size and scope of the collection testified to the family's dedication to learning. Nonetheless, a good part of the collection had been assembled by earlier generations. In our electronically connected world, communities and their priorities can change rapidly. Having read about the surge of nationalism in India, I was not sure how receptive the household milieu would be to the country's Persian/Islamic heritage. Would the Raja's sons not be indifferent to nuances of their heritage tradition under assault by the ever-encroaching global markets? Would they not feel that caring for the fragile Persian manuscripts they had in the library was a waste of time? Would they perceive us as outsiders?

Upon our arrival, however, we found gracious hosts and discovered a deep connection between our group and the Raja's family. A bridge connected our mutual ways of being in the world—one in Lucknow and one in the United States. More interestingly, the bridge had been built by the centuries-old figures of the global Middle East, whose voices continue to echo in a multitude of places in the East and the West. In this shared space, we spoke a hybrid language enriched by multiple cultures and interconnectivity. The environment was alive with imagination, love of learning, and critical thought. The Raja himself was a global figure at ease in five different languages and literary traditions—Arabic, English, French, Hindi, and of course Persian. So impressive was his command of Persian language (and literary tradition) that I felt compelled to ask the mediocre question: "Had he been born of and raised by a Persian mother?" The answer was "no," which he offered graciously.

It is not unusual for affluent families to give their children a good education. But the global nature of the Raja's learning and that of his two adult children was so compelling that one had to ask the oft ignored question: "What is it that infuses Eastern learning traditions with an insatiable thirst for the rest of the world?" I must revive a metaphor to make sense of the depth and breadth of the Raja's learning (and others like him). As silk, jade, spices, and other goods traveled along commercial highways such as the Silk Road in various parts of the Middle East and Central Asia, so too did the poetic voices along the myriad large and small conceptual roads that we may call the Persian poetic tradition. The cultural habit of memorizing and internalizing this poetry, as well as the robust manuscript production in a variety of subjects including poetry, created a shared language, the bridges between many major cities in the region.

Kashgar, Balkh, Herat, Samarqand, Shiraz, Isfahan, Tabriz, Baghdad, and Lucknow were among such cities. It was not just commercial goods that traveled across and between these cities that populated the Silk Road. These centers of culture and learning were connected to each other with golden threads of poetic, scholarly, and creative voices. The poets were often recognized by many, and their voices were cherished because they spoke of shared experiences. The poems themselves had multiple social uses. They were anthologized in books and in artful works of calligraphy that decorated walls. They were sung to music and chanted as tools for spiritual meditation. Sometimes they were even carved on the walls of important buildings. In these ways these poems helped create new communal and shared experiences.

In those short few days, when the Raja and I sat to eat, shared a car ride, or discussed the goals of our visit, poets of the classical Persian tradition—Sa'di, Attar, Rumi, and other—were present. Sitting in a circle with our friends and companions, we recited short verses, recalled their witty exchanges with friends and rivals, and referred to playful anecdotes from their books. It all gushed forth from memory. There was laughter, thought, awe, and sometimes even a teardrop. It was impossible not to feel each other's pain or sense each other's joy. A medieval poet in the Persian tradition would have referred to this event as Halgheh ye Ahbaab, "the circle of companions" who shared a sense of safety in a space that encouraged emotional tenderness and generosity.

Among poets whose voices connect major communities, Rumi now enjoys a special status. He continues to encourage unique "circles of companions" by bridging the poetic spaces of the East and the West. In fact, in the life story of the Jalal al-Din Mohamad Balkhi Rumi (d. 1273), known in the West simply as Rumi, there are incidents that exemplify intense cultural connectedness. Such connections enabled Rumi's family (and educated Muslims in general) to travel from one corner of the Muslim Middle East to another and to communicate with many a seeming stranger who shared their cultural and intellectual heritage. No doubt, the family's economic strength was crucial to their decision—and ability—to travel. But so was the knowledge that upon arrival in their new home, the family could find a welcoming community familiar with their cultural, religious, and literary experiences. Just as in the twenty-first century, I found myself at home in the presence of the Raja of Mahmoudabad who adorned his every sentence with a quote from Rumi or Hafez, Rumi's migrating family found that cultural bridges had been built prior to their arrival. In their case, the exchanges must have involved a special focus on religious and mystical learning.[1]

A GLOBAL START

Rumi was born in the city of Vakhsh in 1207, near the river Vakhshab just outside the major city of Balkh in present-day Afghanistan. He left with his family in search of a new home around the age of nine. There is much speculation as to why his father, Baha' Valad, a distinguished Sufi scholar in the court of the Khwrazm Shah, the royal ruler of Balkh, made that life-changing decision. Whatever the reason, Rumi and his family were on the road, probably for about two years, traveling through many major urban centers and finally settling in the city of Konya in Central Anatolia in present-day Turkey.

As a result, our poet was given an early global upbringing that spanned the Afghan, Persian, and Turkish cultures. To his father's credit, Rumi and his brothers were later sent to the city of Aleppo in present-day Syria to complete their education—adding the riches of another multicultural hub of learning to what Rumi had already collected. At the age of twenty-five, he replaced his father as a respected teacher of Islamic and Sufi learning. The cosmopolitan milieu of Konya kept Rumi aware of three overlapping cultural traditions: Turkish mostly spoken by the general public, Arabic centered on religious learning and practice, and Persian as the medium for poetic expression. Poetry itself served a wide range of purposes from spiritual and ethical teaching to entertainment, expressing political affiliation, making complex philosophical ideas accessible to the public, even as a tool for teaching subjects such as science or grammar.

The Sufis, the Muslim mystics, believed in the human potential to directly connect with God and eventually become one with the divine. They regarded this great human privilege as forgotten by humanity under the pressure of daily concerns and distractions. Most Sufis were practicing Muslims, some even qualified as religious scholars. At the same time, they did not believe bookish religious learning would revive one's lost memory of closeness to God. Neither did they use the overtly technical and ambiguous language often used by religious experts. What the Sufis believed was needed was a language capable of conveying beauty, sincerity, simplicity, and the natural human longing for being close to God. Rumi, a learned scholar, had a penchant for lyric poetry, which was fresh, lively, enticing, and accessible to ordinary readers. Even when he discussed theology, he used a language that connected with a wide range of readers. His poetry would help overcome such artificial barriers as ethnicity, gender, and religion, which continue to separate human beings and pit them against one another.

At the same time, it would be misleading to suggest that Rumi did not consider Islam as the right religion. Nonetheless, he viewed honesty, devotion, and longing for the divine as characteristics that took precedent over a seeker's religious affiliation. This conviction became stronger particularly after his encounter with a wandering Dervish by the name Shams of Tabriz who came to the city of Konya in 1244 AD and became the strongest inspiration in Rumi's life. Rumi's encounter with Shams compelled him to ask many important questions such as, "What is the point of intellectual knowledge if it does not alter a seeker's life?" This and similar questions ignited a rebellious mood in Rumi against laws and conventional regulations that in his opinion built mental barriers stealing one's ability to explore. Ignited by Shams's teachings, Rumi spent a lifetime breaking every breakable rule in any tradition that he worked with, whether poetic or religious. His goal was simple: to speak through a language that transcended such barriers as class, ethnicity, culture, and religion that would reach Hindus,

Muslims, Christians, Jews, and atheists alike. This was Rumi's "language of companionship":

> To speak the same language is to share the same blood, to be related.
> To live with strangers is the life of captivity.
> Many are Hindus and Turks who share the same language,
> Many are Turks who may be alien to one another.
> The language of companionship is a unique one,
> To reach someone through the heart is other than reaching them through words.
> Besides words, allusions and arguments,
> The heart knows a hundred thousand ways to speak.[2]

There are few poets/thinkers whose wish has so fully come true. Rumi's language of companionship continues to be heard and embraced around the globe, more than eight hundred years after his death in the city of Konya in 1273. What is at the root of Rumi's potential to speak with a global voice that has captured the attention of a world barely patient to listen to poetry? Imagine the multilingual and multireligious community of Konya during Rumi's lifetime. Those Turkish, Persian, and Arabic speakers were also aware of Greek speakers as well as the Central Asian Mongol conquerors of the region. In this complex environment, Sufis performed their ritual worship, which included chanting God's name, singing sacred poetry, playing instruments, and even dancing.

Rumi contributed to this practice as well. One day, as he walked through the goldsmiths' market, he started turning to the sound of the hammers and chisels that the artisans used in their shops to put the finishing touches to their handicrafts. Rumi's turning practice known as whirling became a new communal tradition, which attracted people of different backgrounds and persuasions. Without overromanticizing people's appreciation for each other's differences, or pretending that division and discord did not exist, it is possible to imagine the need for a poetry that tried to connect these diverse people. The whirling to music in an orderly fashion could also be viewed as a way to bring order to an ecstatic communal practice. While rebelling against tradition was built into Sufi thinking and practice, so too was creating a safe conduit for expressing it. In this way the Sufis were able to question some of the basics of Muslim belief. For example, they thought that faith was not true if not subjected to genuine doubt and disbelief. Mahmoud Shabestari (b. 1288), a well-respected Sufi master born a decade after Rumi's death, wrote:

So often belief is born of disbelief,
Such a disbelief cannot be called infidelity.

Sufis did not view rebellion, doubt, and disbelief as grave sins but rather as faith-building tools, even tests that proved the believer's devotion and steadfastness. The doors were kept open to many who would have otherwise remained outsiders. In the thirteenth century, Konya had its reasons (such as war and turmoil) to strive for forms of inclusivity and tolerance. People in the twenty-first century have reasons to find openness and inclusivity attractive. The geographical borders of the world have crumbled in the face of electronic communication tools. Rights groups remind us of the fact that marginalized others need to become real players in the global community. At the same time, the world's expanding economies seek inclusivity to access new markets. In short, we cannot remain isolated from the rest of the world. A compassionate global vision will help us embrace the world for the right kind of reasons. The Sufis' openness to the inner freedom to cross the borders between certainty and doubt, infidelity and faith, appeals to our global sensibilities. That also explains why some lovers or scholars of Rumi detect an opportunistic note in the West's total infatuation with Rumi's rebellious instincts. Whatever the reason, it is not hard to see why his desire to break out of traditional molds could appeal to almost any reader. He wrote:

Tell me what to do o Muslims! I do not know who I am,
Not a Zoroastrian, nor a Muslim or a Jew, neither am I a Christian,
Not of the East not of the West, neither of the sea nor of the land,
I don't belong to natural substances, nor do I come from the heavenly sphere.

There is an overabundance of such poetic proclamations in Rumi's vast collection of lyrical poems, which number more than thirty-five thousand verses. It is important to look at each defiant poem individually and not place them all in one category. Some verses clearly reflect a moment of inner turmoil. Others betray a sense of shock and discovery even as he writes them. In yet others, Rumi is mapping a way of life encouraging his readers to question the superficiality of their identity and revert to their deeper connections with other human beings. There are clearly different ways to approach his poetry depending on the reader's linguistic, social, and cultural understanding of his work. As if pointing to the significance of each reader's aptitude, Rumi once wrote:

If you try to pour the sea into a jug,
It will only take enough for a day's use (no matter how large the sea).

In other words, we are personally responsible for a good deal of meaning that we attribute to any text we read. Poems that downplay our differences are extremely inviting to our current fragmented identities caught in a web of division and discord. Rumi's vibrant voice resonates with our need for hope and healing.

THE PHYSICAL IS SPIRITUAL

It is fascinating to explore how Rumi considered human beings as malleable and having an expansive presence in the world. He often objected to creating rigid boundaries between the various aspects of our life experiences to avoid fragmenting or compartmentalizing our humanity. "The physical is spiritual" addresses Rumi's approach to the question of the human body and soul—another reason why he is globally popular. This is a complicated thought. Let me explain. Our cultural and ethical habits and traditions—even those of which we are not conscious—frequently teach us that the soul is exulted, light, and heavenly while the body is clumsy, subject to aging, sinful, and tied to base desires.

Even Rumi himself has compared us to an angel and a donkey, tied together with the angel trying to pull us in the direction of the heavens and the donkey's massive weight keeping us on Earth. Upon further examination, however, we find that the donkey does not denote ugliness and disdain but merely the instinctual weight of bodily needs and desires. We must ride the donkey toward better places in our life's vast meadow rather than be carried by it to wherever it chooses to go. In essence, there is nothing ugly or unseemly about our physique and its urges. For Rumi, human beings are one large continuum of living, learning and experience, body and soul. In this continuum of human existence, the body plays a role as vital and effective as any other component of our being. When we enjoy the beauty of nature, or desire another human being, our longing reflects the divine force of desire for the entire universe. It teaches and trains us for bigger and more inclusive desires, including our longing for the force of goodness that infuses all existence.

The celebration of the beauty and sacredness of the physical being must not be interpreted as a lack of ethical principles or physical discipline with regard to earthly desires. We must, according to Rumi, not be greedy with possessions or use excessive physical force just because we are able to. We must honor our human dignity by not overeating, for example, or by living a sexually promiscuous lifestyle. Rumi, in the tradition of the Sufis, calls us to live a balanced and dignified life. Indeed, in his lyrical poetry Rumi makes a point of molding together the human and the divine beloved—two forces that cannot be fully separated:

> If anyone asks you about the heavenly beauties, show your face, say: like this!
> If anyone asks you about the moon, climb up on the roof, say: like this!
> If anyone seeks a fairy, let them see your countenance,
> If anyone talks about the aroma of musk, untie your hair, say: like this!
> If anyone asks: "How do the clouds uncover the moon?"
> Untie the front of your robe, knot by knot, say: like this!
> If anyone asks: "How did Jesus raise the dead?"
> Kiss my soul on the lips, say: like this!

The use of sensual imagery in mystical poetry of a lyrical nature is common in many languages. However, the tone is often vague, and vivid erotic details are avoided. In Rumi's poetry these two manifestations of love, humanness and the divine, frequently change place with each other. They are not opposites and do not cancel out each other. Nor does he refer to erotic love reluctantly or just as an allegory for love of God. Rather, the love that Rumi speaks of is vast and complex. It embraces a panorama of human experience: physical, spiritual, and divine. For example, in the line where the disrobing of the beloved is compared to the clouds uncovering the moon, the first thing that comes to mind is the physical beauty and brilliance of the moon alluding to the beloved's bare skin. At a more mystical level, the celestial majesty and draw of the moon and the enticement of the beloved's disrobed body match each other's strength. All the while, we are aware that these two facets of beauty are not only inseparable but also interdependent.

A POET OF CHANGE, A POET OF HOPE

Similar to the Raja of Mahmoudabad in India, I too experienced poetry as a vital part of my childhood as I grew up in Iran. I had read Rumi's poetry from an early age and had always wondered why his thoughts and words felt so fresh. Carefully researching these poems, I began to see multiple indications of Rumi's search for new and dynamic ways of seeing the world and speaking about it. Although he used a familiar poetic form known as ghazal dedicated to love poetry, Rumi broke all the literary rules while composing his ghazals. For example, while a standard ghazal was expected to have six or seven to twelve or thirteen lines, Rumi's were sometimes as short as three or as long fifty verses. Also, with regard to their content, ghazals had a limited range of allowable topics to discuss. The lover was always sorrowful and abandoned by the cruel beloved, exemplified by a bright candle attracting the love-crazed moths to its flames and burning them to ashes. The love story of the rose and the nightingale was not that different either. The befuddled bird would sing to a coquettish rose that only responded with thorns of rejection.

For Rumi, however, there were lovers of all stripes and beloveds who were not cruel or aloof. Usually the spring had arrived, everything was coming to life, and all kinds of creatures were invited to join the festivities, starting with bees, flies, and grasshoppers and welcoming even camels, donkeys, and elephants. To get a concrete sense of this transformation, during my research on his lyrics, I did a brief quantitative study. I picked the Persian verb *shudan*, which means "to become." It could also mean moving from place to place, often resulting in a full change in one's state of being. So *zendeh shudan* means "coming to life," and *buzurg shudan* denotes "maturation." I searched a hundred *ghazals* randomly to see how often Rumi uses this verb to speak of transformative changes in our lives. The result showed the topic to be one of his favorites. The following poem is an example:

> I was dead, I came to life. I was a cry, I turned into laughter.
> The fortune of love fell upon me and I turned into everlasting fortune myself.
> He said: you are not crazy, you do not deserve to live in this house.
> I became crazy, I put myself in chains.
> He said: you are not drunk enough, give up this pretense,
> You are not the right type!
> I became drunken, I became full of enchantment.
> He said: you are not dead, you are not smeared with joy!
> Before his life-giving face, I died and fell.

As usual, each poem is packed with possibility. Is this a description of Rumi's personal transformation as a result of falling in love? Is it a philosophical glance at the story of the human struggle for growth and maturity? Or is the ghazal a panorama of flashbacks to personal experiences of which Rumi can speak only in abstract and metaphorical terms? What does it mean to us, the readers? Once again, we are standing on the seashore with our personal jugs ready to be filled. What we take away depends on our personal choices and the capacity of our vessels.

No matter what we take away from the sea, however, it will not dry up as long as we have the desire to return to it. It will not be low-spirited or devoid of surprising gifts either. This continued vibrancy is not just a result of literary genius of the work. Rumi makes a point of connecting it with the ever presence of the divine vibrancy in the universe. As such, it is also a fountain of continuous hope in his perception of the cosmic order. This sea is hiding pearls of hope in its depths. For the sea, this uninterrupted liveliness, is physically manifested in the shape of waves that never tire of dancing on the face of the ocean. For us human beings, what reflects liveliness and vibrancy is our kindness, our urge to be dynamic, or the inexplicable desire to run and dance to music. That is why the natural movement in Rumi's lyric poetry is often described metaphorically as laughter or dance. He wrote:

> If the flowers of His face, from the garden they are in, burst into laughter
> The spring of life would be renewed, the tree of body would burst into laughter

CONCLUSION

There is a story among Rumi scholars that goes like this. In the final days of Soviet Union, the thought-police were working hard to arrest a Muslim author called Rumi. This author's God-conscious writings sold like hot cakes in Russian translation and threatened their communist principles. It is not easy to determine the veracity of this story, but in a way that does not matter. Truths have many varieties including nonfactual ones. The particular truth in this story speaks to the enthusiasm among some Russian readers for Rumi's poems in translation.

But there is another relevance to this story: Rumi's yearning to break all barriers and speak to people of different cultures and backgrounds. He expresses yearning for a multilingual global world in a very simple story, the story of grapes. Four men of modest means are together: a Persian, a Turk, an Arab, and a Greek. Somebody gives them money to spend on anything they like. The Persian says, I want *angur*; the Turk opts for *uzum*; the Arab desires *'inab*; and the Greek insists on buying *estafil*. As the four fight over what each wants, Rumi observes: "If only there was a translator among them!" The reason is simple. They all want the same thing—grapes.

NOTES

1. Franklin D. Lewis, *Rumi Past and Present, East and West: The Life, Teachings and Poetry of Jalâl al-Din Rumi* (Oxford, UK: Oxford University Press, 2000).
2. All translations of Rumi's poetry are by the author.

FURTHER READING

Attar, Farid al-Din. *Conference of the Birds*. Translated by Dick Davis. New York: Penguin Classics, 1984.

Keshavarz, Fatemeh. *Jasmine and Stars: Reading more than Lolita in Tehran*. Chapel Hill: North Carolina University Press, 2008.

———. *Reading Mystical Lyric: The Case of Jalal al-Din Rumi*. Columbia: University of South Carolina Press, 1998.

Moyers, Bill. Interview with Coleman Barks. "The Language of Life: Love's Confusing Joy, March 16, 1995." https://billmoyers.com/content/loves-confusing-joy-coleman-barks-poet-jelaluddin-rumi/.

Rumi, Jalal al-Din. *The Masnavi, Book One*. Translated by Jawid Mojaddedi. Oxford, UK: Oxford World's Classics, 2004.

Safi, Omid. *Radical Love: Teachings from the Islamic Mystical Tradition*. New Haven, CT: Yale University Press, 2018.

Schimmel, Annemarie. *I Am Wind, You Are Fire: The Life and Work of Rumi*. Boston: Shambhala, 1992.

FIVE

On Nations without Borders

Hamid Dabashi

I am from Kashan—My lineage
May go back to a plant in India,
To a broken clay pot
From the ancient archeological site
Of Tepe Sialk—
My lineage may go back
To a prostitute
In the city of Bukhara.[1]

SOHRAB SEPEHRI (1928–1980)
"The Echo of the Footsteps of Water"

WHERE DOES ONE COUNTRY START and where does it end for another country to start? How much do the current maps of the globe, with various countries having emerged in the aftermath of the collapse of empires and their colonies, correspond with the lived experiences of people on two sides of a fictional frontier? The fabrication of such fictive frontiers for specific postcolonial nation-states—Iran is here, there is Afghanistan, and then India over there, and back here is Iraq, and so on—are today exposed for the fetishized mythologies that have historically informed and animated their colonial experiences with European empires. In no particular terms, political or cultural, are postcolonial nation-states, thus carved out of an enduring geography of non-European worlds, anywhere in the world hermetically sealed or claustrophobically spaced within and unto themselves. All these nation-states are deeply informed by and in turn widely influenced in regional and global developments outside their recent and entirely porous borders. These nations informed the world and the world informed them beyond the artificial borders of their postcolonial predicaments—there only for them to be divided in order to be ruled better.

The idea of a "global Middle East" reveals in its innate and barely contained paradoxical tensions the colonial context in which the very regional designation of "the Middle East" was conceptually carved out and violently partitioned and sequestered from the multiple global contexts in which the region has always existed. What today is called "the Middle East" was integral to three global Muslim empires that ruled half of the civilized world: the Mughals, the Safavids/Qajars, and the Ottomans. That long global history and the multiple worldly cultures it entailed is now categorically repressed under the colonially concocted rubric of "the Middle East." The Persian Gulf, as the epicenter of this colonial designation, has historically been linked to the Arabian Sea, the Indian Ocean and beyond into Asian, African, and Latin American worlds entirely independent of the Euro-American imperial dominations.

In the colonial geography called "the Middle East," countries like Egypt, Iran, or Turkey were epistemically violated and carved out of their own natural habitat. The Persian Muslim mystic poet Rumi, for example (see chapter 4 in this volume), was already global in his own multiple imperial worlds long before he was translated into English in sunny and beautiful California and given a renewed life halfway around the globe from where he was born, where he lived, where he composed his poetry, and where he was deeply loved and revered. The severity of the epistemic violence perpetrated from the deepest Orientalist delusions to the widest reaches of Cold War area studies, to the innate prejudices of "Western media" (itself a fetishized commodity) is hard to exaggerate. The task at hand is to retrieve the multiple worlds that the colonial geography of "the West and the Rest" has violently superimposed on our global memories.

WHERE IN THE WORLD?

"The Middle East," "the Arab World," "the Muslim World," "the Orient"— all such terms have deeply and violently distorted the historic continuity and varied complexities of worlds homogenized to cross-corroborate the illusion of "the West." "The West" is an ideological proposition, not a geographical designation. "The West" is white. "The Rest" is colored. The twain is ideologically contingent on each other. If these allegorical otherings were to be rehistoricized back to their worlds, the thing called "the West" would not know what to do with itself and implode. The global map on which the current geographical stretch called and categorized as "the Middle East" is the result of an entirely colonial, Eurocentric, and racialized imagination. When Xenophon (circa 430–354 BC) wrote his *Cyropaedia*, he did not think of the Persian emperor to have come from "the Middle East." When the Persian queen Esther appears prominently in the Hebrew Bible, she was not an Iranian version of a Saudi princess. When Persian Alexander romances were lovingly written and widely read, the Macedonian warrior was not considered a champion of "Western civilization" for the very idea did not exist.

When libraries of scientific works from Arabic were translated into Latin, when Ferdowsi's *Shahnameh* (completed circa 1010) was translated into French, when Montesquieu wrote his *Persian Letters* (1721), when Goethe named his collection of poetry after Hafez's Diwan (1814–19), and notably, when the German philosopher Fredrich Nietzsche (1844–1900) named his revolutionary prophet Zarathustra. The prophet Zoroaster (lived circa 1000 BCE) had established the dominant religion in ancient Iran until the Muslim conquest, with a widespread presence of his teachings available in Greek and Roman sources long before Nietzsche chose his epithet for the iconoclastic prophetic hero in his groundbreaking philosophical treatise.[2] By the time Nietzsche used the figure of Zoroaster as his post-Christian prophet, the figure of the Persian sage was widely known in Europe and had even been featured as a character in Mozart's *Magic Flute* (Die Zauberflöte), which premiered on September 30, 1791. As an enlightened sovereign priest, Mozart's Sarastro in many ways anticipates Nietzsche's Zarathustra. But the text of *Thus Spoke Zarathustra* and its famous phrase "God is Dead" became iconic to a postmodernist, poststructuralist philosophy in Europe that the German subversive philosopher anticipated by decades.

To overcome fictitious domains such as "the Middle East," or "Near East," or "Far East," all as the doppelgänger of "the West" or any other variation of it, we must shift to major loci of travel and trade, exchange of goods, services, labor, capital, and therefore cultures—for that is where the palpable realities and their corresponding concepts emerge. The Persian Gulf, the Arabian Sea, the Indian Ocean, the Mediterranean Sea, the Caspian Sea, the Black Sea, the Volga River, the Transatlantic trade, the Pacific rim, the Caribbean Sea: these are far more accurate loci of trade and travel, capital, labor, and cultures than the imaginative delusion of "East and West" or even more generically, "The West and the Rest." The global circulation of labor and capital went circular, not vertical or diametrical. Manufacturing the imaginative geography of "East and West," however, is not entirely the handiwork of colonialists and their Orientalist ideologies. Arabs, Iranians, Indians, Turks, and others are equally if not even more responsible for cross-authenticating such falsifying fantasies. For they have readily yielded the enduring complexities and proximities of their own geographies to the overpowering topography of their colonial conquers.

Arabs know more about Europe than they do about Iran, India, Africa, or Turkey, as do Iranians, Indians, and Turks know more about Europe than they care to know about their own neighbors and the alternative geographies they have historically formed, informed, animated, peopled, and enabled. The problem therefore is not global but culture-specific, epistemological rather than merely political. To overcome this falsifying geography, we need to rehistoricize and not merely engage in political disputations.

PERSOPHILIA: THE GENEALOGY OF AN IDEA

Both Edward Said (1935–2003) and Frantz Fanon (1925–1961) confronted and sought to reverse the condition of coloniality, each in their own ways— Said by his critique of the modalities of knowledge production and Fanon by his critique of the violence at the root of colonization. Orientalism, as Said argues in his influential book by the same name, was something larger and more upstream in European consciousness than its specific gestation at the service of European colonialism. To the degree that Fanon and Said both paid attention to the larger bourgeois frames of literary or cultural productions, they saw them as entirely subservient to state purposes. Just like Said, but in a different register, Fanon's poignant critique of violence was equally geared toward the formation of a postcolonial state.

The postcolonial struggles since Fanon's death, and particularly in the aftermath of the Arab revolutions, are rooted in the calamities of postcolonial tyrannies in Asia, Africa, and Latin America. The myth of the postcolonial state has resulted in the postpartum blues of the Arab revolutions. The postcolonial state perpetuates the colonial condition of epistemic violence on alternative worlds. Critique of the condition of coloniality must therefore transcend the critique of violence—physical or epistemic—definitive to the formation of the state power and their ideologies of state-formation, from Islamism to Zionism to imperialism. There is a paradox in the domain of cultural production that extends from the European bourgeois public sphere to postcolonial parapublic spheres that we must recuperate and theorize.

In *Persophilia: Persian Culture on the Global Scene* (2015) and subsequent works on Iran and Palestine, I map out the transnational public sphere and the formation of the postcolonial subject over the past five hundred years from the waning of the last three Muslim empires to waxing of European colonial powers.[3] I bring a global perspective to the bourgeois public sphere of which the German social theorist Jürgen Habermas had only seen its European transformation in his groundbreaking book *The Structural Transformation of the Public Sphere: An Inquiry into a Category of Bourgeois Society.* I look at the rise of nations (without states) as the simulacrum of those particular locations where the postcolonial person is formed. Nations become nations independent of the states that lay false claims on them.

My primary concern in *Persophilia* is not to trace varied aspects of Persian "influences" on European culture in juxtaposition to the usual argument of the so-called "Westernization" of non-European cultures. To me "Westernization" and "modernization" have a much simpler and more straightforward name: "colonization" of people and their cultures and resources and the abuse of their labor. My concern is with the changing contours and parameters of bourgeois public spheres, in what particular manner they appropriated non-European cultures—Chinese, Indian, Persian, African, and so on—to manufacture the semblance of a worldly consciousness, now that the exchange of labor and capital had already created a global condition of production and consumption.

The evidence for transnational public spheres is of course not limited to Iran or any other particular postcolonial nation-state. It was the very conception of the limited space of the postcolonial nation-state, the aftershock of the colonial mapping of the world, that concerns me. Perhaps best evidenced in the case of South Africa divestment movement and now the Boycott, Divestment and Sanction (BDS) movement for Palestine, we see the transnational public sphere generating and sustaining modes of polity (through active solidarity) that are no longer limited to any particular nation-state, or a state apparatus, or nonstate actors. Predicated on a transnational public sphere over which no state has any enduring power, this active and agile transnational public sphere constitutionally compromises the power of the state over its immediate subjects.

I propose a reconsideration of the whole idea of "sovereignty" to be predicated on national and not state formations; I suggest the very idea of "the national" to be ipso facto transnational or even postnational. If we were to read the formation of *the nation* as a mode of "collective consciousness" predicated on particularly traumatic shared memories (think of *Nakbah* in the case of Palestine), both the transnational public sphere on which this conception of the nation is formed and the postnational polity toward which it is directed are the compelling parameters of knowledge production, of being, and perforce of consciousness. It is imperative that we look at the transnational public sphere on which such manifestations of *Persophilia* point to the allegorical circulatory of cultural registers around the globe—and not just in and around Europe. The case of *Thus Spoke Zarathustra* offers a perfect example of the posthumous adventures of the Persian prophet, long after and far beyond his birth and habitat, in a primarily philosophical domain with profound implications for the twentieth- and twenty-first-century European philosophy.

One particularly powerful gestation of Nietzsche's Zarathustra is via Walter Kaufmann's groundbreaking translation into English. It came to North America and eventually found its way to an utterly brilliant postcolonial novel, *United States of Banana* (2011), by the Puerto Rican poet/novelist Giannina Braschi. The story takes place at the Statue of Liberty in Staten Island in New York in post–9/11 America. Hamlet, Zarathustra, and Giannina (the persona of "the author") have gathered to put their minds together to free the Puerto Rican prisoner Segismundo, who has been jailed there for more than a hundred years by his father, the king of the United States of Banana. Segismundo is ultimately freed, Puerto Rico becomes the fifty-first state of the United States, and all Latin American nationals receive US citizenship and a US passport. With a sublime sense of sarcastic humor and replete with the active anxieties of all immigrants, the novel is a scathing critique of capitalism and its miserable consequences. Hamlet, Zarathustra, and Giannina are on a quest not just to liberate the allegorical figure of Segismundo but also to stage the endemic problems of Puerto Rico as a de facto colony of the United States. The novel became highly successful and appeared in multiple other mediums, including film and a graphic novel in Swedish.

Now put Mozart's *Magic Flute*, Nietzsche's *Thus Spoke Zarathustra*, and Braschi's *United States of Banana* together over the expanse of more than two hundred years and something utterly remarkable appears. *Magic Flute* was the opera Mozart composed based on a German libretto by Emanuel Schikaneder against the tradition of dominant Italian librettos. *Thus Spoke Zarathustra* is arguably the most subversive philosophical text of the most iconoclastic European philosopher of the past two hundred years. Braschi's *United States of Banana* is one of the most brilliant postcolonial works of fiction in the immediate aftermath of 9/11, savagely critical of the predatory capitalism and its ravages in Puerto Rico and around the globe. What emerges here is that in the most subversive moments of a transnational public sphere that includes Europe but is not limited to Europe, the figure of the Persian prophet is potently portrayed as an icon of wise deliverance. This figure could have been Buddha, Laozi, or any other non-European sage. The question here is not the Iranian provenance of Zoroaster but the manner in which subversive ideas find their way upon the global scene.

Why would a Puerto Rican poet/novelist, you may ask, writing in English and living in New York early in the twenty-first century opt for the ancient Persian prophet as a character in her decidedly postcolonial, postmodern, and poststructuralist novel—or *why not* perhaps is a more potent question. Zoroaster is as definitive to her creative imagination as the other character she invites from Shakespeare's *Hamlet*. From his origin in ancient Iran to his Greek and Roman gestations and finally in the aftermath of his active resuscitation on the bourgeois public sphere in Europe by Mozart and Nietzsche, Zoroaster had become a global metaphor by virtue of the very global circulation of labor, raw material, and capital that has set the engine of human consciousness on a new speed. Allegories travel. They don't stay home. The world is their home, and allegories mix and match and marry and divorce and live and die and are born again in multiple and unpredictable gestations.

POETICS OF TRANSCENDENCE

If we are to transcend the violent provincialization of multiple worldly cultures around the globe, all set under the colonial shadow of one particularly provincial allegory called "Europe" and mapped out as European culture over the past two hundred years or so, we need to ask a simple question: How do cultures, polities, and societies transcend themselves to reach self-universalization? Every single worldly culture that has come under colonial domination has been robbed of its own innate worldliness, cosmopolitan disposition, and organic links to other worlds surrounding it. How did European culture become so successful at universalizing itself and repressing the equally universal dispositions of other worlds it so successfully subjugated to its economic interests and cultural hegemony? The task at hand is not simply to argue that regions and cultures branded as "Middle Eastern" or "Arab" or "Islamic" are organically linked to other cultures. The task is to retrieve and decipher the worlds such worldliness necessarily entailed and is now repressed under the show of the allegory of "the West."

Over the second half of the twentieth century and well into twenty-first century, this transnational space has had varied manifestations, of which cinema is one particularly poignant example. The global success of Iranian cinema over the last quarter of the twentieth century and beyond was precisely because of the enduring presence of all the world's masters gathering in the formation of this national cinema. The two towering figures of Abbas Kiarostami and Yasujirō Ozu—from two ends of Asia, from Iran and Japan—are the exact cases in point where visions meet and insight mirror each other. Kiarostami was far more influenced by Ozu than by any of his Iranian contemporaries—except the poet/painter Sohrab Sepehri. If Ozu from Japan, Vittorio De Sica from Italy, and Satyajit Ray from India gathered to give birth to Kiarostami in Iran, then the political boundaries manufactured in the course of the colonial and postcolonial history of the past few centuries are rather superficial and entirely porous.

Yes, colonialism was integral to a circularity of culture and capital, but the imperial confidence with which Europe built itself on the fragments of other cultures worked beyond the economic forces of colonialism. A perfect example is the attention that Henri Matisse (1869–1954), among other leading European artists, paid to Persian art. As art curator and historian Lawrence Gowing has put it:

> He [Matisse] spoke of a painter's need for whatever "will let him become one with nature—identify himself with her, by entering into the things … that arouse his feelings.".… It is significant that the subjects should be domestic, for conditions of living concerned Matisse deeply, but the way in which the subject is transcended is quite outside the specific reference of European painting. In 1910 Matisse had just been to see a great exhibition of Islamic art at Munich. He said that "the Persian miniatures showed me the possibility of my sensations. That art had devices to suggest a greater space, a really plastic space. It helped me to get away from intimate painting." Yet he was always clear that it was his own sensations that chiefly concerned him. His interest in everything else was strictly limited. Years later, when he was considering visiting a great exhibition of Chinese art he suddenly realized that he did not wish to: "Je tie m'interessequa moi." [I interested myself.] He confessed it "with a curious and almost disarming mixture of shame and pride."[4]

FIGURE 5.1 Henri Matisse, *Sculpture and Persian Vase*, 1908. Nasjonalgalleriet, Oslo, Norway.

This is the perfect example of how the European artists' attention to Persian art on one day, or the lack of it to Chinese art on another, which preference might have been reversed of course, were entirely contingent on the particular artist's "own sensations"—as indeed it should be. The key for the artist is "the way in which the subject is transcended...quite outside the specific reference of European painting." Once that reference and allusion are detected and mapped out back onto the artist's own world, the deed is done. "It helped me," Matisse says, "to get away from intimate painting." He needed some Persian distance from his Parisian subjects. After which the artist is back to his self-universalized Europeanism—as indeed he must.

The "influence" of Persian art, as a result, is only to the degree it seasons the European artist's creative soul. The quintessence of that "soul" remains incessantly "European"; it is indeed made even more "European" by the exercise even, or particularly, when he ventures into non-European domains. Aspects of other aesthetic cultures are abstracted, disposed of their own particular worldliness, rendered elemental and allegorical, for the use of the European artist at the most creative, the most effervescent, moments of his artistic creativity. That does not make his art Oriental, or Persian, or exotic. It makes it in fact decidedly more European, as the very notion of the European continues to conquer more emotive territories. The globalization of European capital on the broken back of colonial labor and raw material required and exacted the universalization of European aesthetics in particularly similar manners.

Let's jump from a European to an Iranian artist, from Matisse early in twentieth-century Europe to Kiarostami early in twentieth-first-century Iran—almost exactly one century apart. As Matisse built his own aesthetic world, from Fauvism to neo-Impressionism and beyond, with elements borrowed from anywhere and everywhere freely, with the imperial confidence of a European artist, Kiarostami built his universe rooted in his own homeland but branched out around a globe equally his—as he saw the world through his lenses, photographic or cinematic. To that worldliness Kiarostami was born as an artist and to that worldliness he submitted his own aesthetic intuition of transcendence in his own unique and inimitable way—as indeed all artists do. But the predominance of "Europe" as a metaphor overshadows and eclipses other worlds, such as the one evident in Kiarostami's art, effectively turning it into an appendix, a sideshow, an Oriental accident to that European essence.

The point here is to dismantle and overcome that center-periphery binary that cross-authenticates Matisse as universal and provincializes Kiarostami as "Iranian"—and thus open up our horizons for alternative worlds enabled by that very transnational public sphere upon which Matisse shined one day and Kiarostami on another. Kiarostami was as much "Iranian" as Matisse" was "French." Matisse was not universal, Kiarostami or Satyajit Ray or Diego Rivera Iranian, Indian, and Mexican, respectively, in contradistinction to Matisse's "universalism." The world would be richer and more enabling if seen through such multiple worlding of the world.

Seen in this way, there is an uncertainty and a promising vision in Kiarostami's art that has remained anticipatory, lurking, shadowy, misty, and mystical not just in his photography and poetry but perhaps most pointedly in his cinema, in his suspected aesthetic promises, suddenly placing Matisse in a framing he would not, he could not, have known by a visit to an "Islamic art exhibition" to look at some "Persian miniatures." The abstract realism that thrives in Kiarostami's artwork is at once factual and fictive, real and unreal, evident and suggestive. That abstract realism was waiting to happen

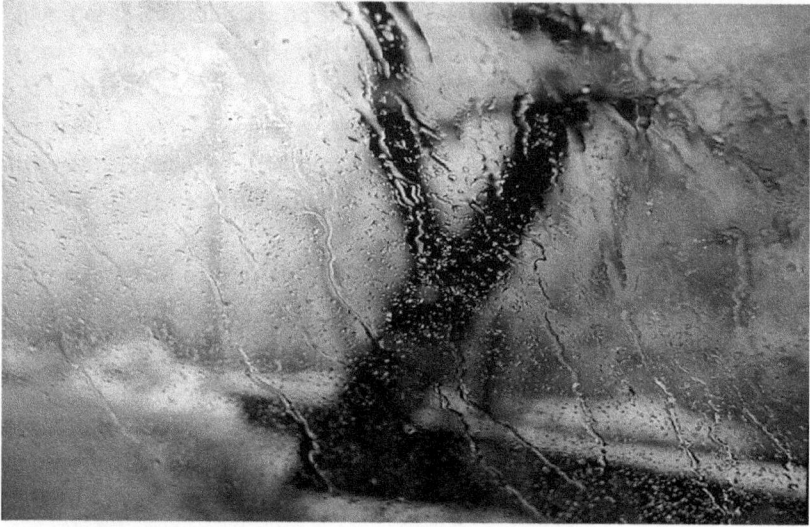

FIGURE 5.2 Abbas Kiarostami, *Wind & Rain*, 2007. www.artsy.net/artwork/abbas-kiaro stami-wind-and-rain-56.

in Kiarostami, although traces of it can be seen from Ozu to Ray. The point here is not to map out a visual or cinematic genealogy of "influences." The point is the manner in which a plurality of worldly consciousnesses always awaits its aesthetic realization.

The closest visionary to Kiarostami's cinematic vision of transcendental transparency of existence was his contemporary Iranian poet Sohrab Sepehri for whom the matter and metaphor of poetry were predicated on a translucent exposure to naked truth. Sepehri was, in his poetry, the naked truth, as later Kiarostami became in his cinema. Even before Sepehri, the inaugural moment of Nima Yushij (1897–1960) had reached an archetypal intuition of transcendence in a poetry that became definitive to an entire generation. If we look at yet another Iranian poet of the period, Ahmad Shamlou (1925–2000), we see the cross-mobilization of metaphors from the poetry of a whole spectrum of poets from Pablo Neruda from Chile to Vladimir Mayakovski from Russia to Nazim Hikmet from Turkey to Mahmood Darwish from Palestine to Faiz Ahmed Faiz from Pakistan. This overarching spectrum of poetic intuition expanding countries, climes, and continents is precisely the evidence of the multiple worlds that have all been hiding under the false delusion of "the West and the Rest." What becomes evident in the poetry of these towering figurers from around the globe is the fact that over the course of postcolonial histories, nations have accrued collective consciousness of their own. If we were to decouple the myth of "the nation-state," the transnational disposition of nations would emerge more pronouncedly.

The ruling postcolonial states—whether procolonial or anticolonial— have been a controlling device, a regulatory and stabilizing mechanism preventing and preempting their nations from reconnecting with the world they barely lost but always falsely remembered before their encounter with European colonial modernity. By falsely claiming "their" nations on the skeletal blueprint of "the nation-state," states as monopoly of violence have thwarted the organic growth of nations to full self-consciousness by manufacturing a linear, state-sponsored "history" for themselves to legitimize themselves. To the Pahlavi dynasty of Iran (1925–79), the entire course of Iranian history from the time of Cyrus the Great was monarchical. To the Islamic Republic (1979 to present), history has been reinterpreted as one long heroic epic of Shi'i clerics saving the nation from the time of Prophet Muhammad. Whether revolutionary or reactionary, states have been the terror of the nations they have exclusively claimed for themselves, thus aborting these nations from normative self-transcendence.

My point of departure here is to see when nations enable their poets, artists, or philosophers to map the contours of their self-transcendence. There is a reason why at the height of European self-confident philosophizing, Heidegger could theorize "Being-in-the-World," speculate about the condition of "thrownness," of the "Dasein" as a precondition of fascination with the world. That philosophical confidence came from a normative claim on the world in its entirety—the way the Shi'i philosopher philosophized at the height of the Safavid empire. Heidegger towered over philosophical speculation of his and our times with his fascination with existence precisely at a moment when the postcolonial world was still trying to formulate a just and legitimate conceptions of the state for itself. From Weimar to the Nazis, those states were accidental to Heidegger's confident claims on "Being-in-the-World." This inevitably enables the European philosopher, thus self-declared, to understand what it means to be disclosed, to have an ontological structural wholeness. This opening onto temporality of Dasein for Heidegger enables the philosopher to claim a past (thrownness/disposedness), a future (projection/understanding), and a present (fallen-ness/fascination)—all denied philosophical conditions in the shadow of Western poststructuralism. We need to go back all the way to Mulla Sadra in the sixteenth century to encounter such colossal confidence in reading the world with imperial self-assuredness.

Today, for every confident Heidegger in Europe, we have had a Satyajit Ray in India, a Yasujirō Ozu in Japan, a Nuri Bilge Ceylan in Turkey, or an Abbas Kiarostami elsewhere—each one of them crafting a world, a worldliness, and a being-in-the world from the lived experiences of a marginality they overcame to make central to their own world. A poet, a filmmaker, an artist on the postcolonial site configures something more than their counterparts do in Europe or the United States. An artist like Kiarostami has an innate philosophical interlocutor, the way Ingmar Bergman or Jean-Luc Godard does not for the simple reason that these European filmmakers work against the background of a strong and pronounced philosophical presence that their audiences bring with them to their cinema. In the case of non-European filmmakers and artists, that "non-Europeanness" is carried forward as a philosophical burden—full of pain and perforce discoveries.

The case of Persophilia is the historic evidence of nations forming on a transnational public sphere beyond the fictive frontiers of their postcolonial destiny as occasioned by global operation of labor, capital, and raw material, all beyond any violently barb-wired borders. The term "global Middle East" contains precisely the conceptual paradox of colonially carving a region on the map of the global circulation of labor, capital, and raw material that in and of itself places peoples and cultures on an organic globality beyond the reach of any colonial designation. In the European fascination with things Persian, or Indian, Chinese, and so on, while the European bourgeois public sphere was transforming itself into universal vision of itself, it was also, though unbeknownst to itself, offering itself as the fragmented allegories of more expansive worlds and their opening horizons to come.

NOTES

1. *Epigraph*: Sohrab Sepehri, "The Echo of the Footsteps of Water," in *Hasht Ketab/Eight Book* (Tehran: Tahouri Publishers, 1976).

2. For a comprehensive treatment of the figure of Zoroaster, see various entries under "Zoroaster" in *Encyclopedia Iranica,* www.iranicaonline.org/articles/zoroaster-index.

3. See Dabashi, *Iran without Borders* and *Persophilia*; see also Ruba Salih and Sophie Richter-Devroe, eds., *Palestine beyond National Frames: Emerging Politics, Cultures, and Claims,* afterword by Hamid Dabashi, "Palestine without Borders," *South Atlantic Quarterly* 117, no. 1 (2018): 179–87.

4. Lawrence Gowing, *Henri Matisse: 64 Paintings* (1966, reprint: New York: Museum of Modern Art, 2017), 18.

FURTHER READING

Dabashi, Hamid. *Iran without Borders: Towards a Critique of the Postcolonial Nation*. New York: Verso, 2016.
———. *Persophilia: Persian Culture on the Global Scene*. Boston: Harvard University Press, 2015.
Fanon, Frantz. *A Dying Colonialism*. Translated from the French by Haakon Chevalier. New York: Grove Press, 1965.
Said, Edward. *Orientalism*. New York: Pantheon Books, 1978.

PART THREE

Home and the World

SIX

Reflections on Exile

Edward Said

EXILE IS STRANGELY COMPELLING to think about but terrible to experience. It is the unhealable rift forced between a human being and a native place, between the self and its true home: its essential sadness can never be surmounted. And while it is true that literature and history contain heroic, romantic, glorious, even triumphant episodes in an exile's life, these are no more than efforts meant to overcome the crippling sorrow of estrangement. The achievements of exile are permanently undermined by the loss of something left behind forever.

But if true exile is a condition of terminal loss, why has it been transformed so easily into a potent, even enriching, motif of modern culture? We have become accustomed to thinking of the modern period itself as spiritually orphaned and alienated, the age of anxiety and estrangement. Nietzsche taught us to feel uncomfortable with tradition, and Freud to regard domestic intimacy as the polite face painted on patricidal and incestuous rage. Modern Western culture is in large part the work of exiles, émigrés, refugees. In the United States, academic, intellectual, and aesthetic thought is what it is today because of refugees from fascism, communism, and other regimes given to the oppression and expulsion of dissidents. The critic George Steiner has even proposed the perceptive thesis that a whole genre of twentieth-century Western literature is "extraterritorial," a literature by and about exiles, symbolizing the age of the refugee. Thus Steiner suggests: "It seems proper that those who create art in a civilization of quasi-barbarism, which

This essay has been reprinted with permission from Edward Said's estate, from Edward Said, *Reflections on Exile and Other Essays* (Cambridge, MA: Harvard University Press, 2000).

FIGURE 6.1 "Palestinian Cultural Mural Honoring Dr. Edward Said," San Francisco State University. Artwork by Fayeq Oweis and Susan Greene, 2007. Wikimedia Commons, https://commons.wikimedia.org/wiki/File:Palestinian_Cultural_Mural_Honoring_Dr._Edward_Said.jpg.

has made so many homeless, should themselves be poets unhoused and wanderers across language. Eccentric, aloof, nostalgic, deliberately untimely…"
In other ages, exiles had similar cross-cultural and transnational visions, suffered the same frustrations and miseries, performed the same elucidating and critical tasks—brilliantly affirmed, for instance, in E. H. Carr's classic study of the nineteenth-century Russian intellectuals clustered around Herzen, *The Romantic Exiles*. But the difference between earlier exiles and those of our own time is, it bears stressing, scale: our age—with its modern warfare, imperialism, and the quasi-theological ambitions of totalitarian rulers—is indeed the age of the refugee, the displaced person, mass immigration.

Against this large, impersonal setting, exile cannot be made to serve notions of humanism. On the twentieth-century scale, exile is neither aesthetically nor humanistically comprehensible: at most the literature about exile objectifies an anguish and a predicament most people rarely experience first hand; but to think of the exile informing this literature as beneficially humanistic is to banalize its mutilations, the losses it inflicts on those who suffer them, the muteness with which it responds to any attempt to understand it as "good for us." Is it not true that the views of exile in literature and, moreover, in religion obscure what is truly horrendous: that exile is irremediably secular and unbearably historical; that it is produced by human beings for other human beings; and that, like death but without death's ultimate mercy, it has torn millions of people from the nourishment of tradition, family, and geography?

To see a poet in exile—as opposed to reading the poetry of exile—is to see exile's antinomies embodied and endured with a unique intensity. Several years ago I spent some time with Faiz Ahmad Faiz, the greatest of contemporary Urdu poets. He was exiled from his native Pakistan by Zia's military regime, and found a welcome of sorts in strife-torn Beirut. Naturally his closest friends were Palestinian, but I sensed that, although there was an affinity of spirit between them, nothing quite matched—language, poetic convention, or life-history. Only once, when Eqbal Ahmad, a Pakistani friend and a fellow-exile, came to Beirut, did Faiz seem to overcome his sense of constant estrangement. The three of us sat in a dingy Beirut restaurant late one night, while Faiz recited poems. After a time, he and Eqbal stopped translating his verses for my benefit, but as the night wore on it did not matter. What I watched required no translation: it was an enactment of a homecoming expressed through defiance and loss, as if to say, "Zia, we are here." Of course Zia was the one who was really at home and who would not hear their exultant voices.

Rashid Hussein was a Palestinian. He translated Bialik, one of the great modern Hebrew poets, into Arabic, and Hussein's eloquence established him in the post-1948 period as an orator and nationalist without peer. He first worked as a Hebrew language journalist in Tel Aviv, and succeeded in establishing a dialogue between Jewish and Arab writers, even as he espoused the cause of Nasserism and Arab nationalism. In time, he could no longer endure the pressure, and he left for New York. He married a Jewish woman and began working in the PLO office at the United Nations, but regularly outraged his superiors with unconventional ideas and utopian rhetoric. In 1972 he left for the Arab world, but a few months later he was back in the United States: he had felt out of place in Syria and Lebanon, unhappy in Cairo. New York sheltered him anew, but so did endless bouts of drinking and idleness. His life was in ruins, but he remained the most hospitable of men. He died after a night of heavy drinking when, smoking in bed, his cigarette started a fire that spread to a small library of audio cassettes, consisting mostly of poets reading their verse. The fumes from the tapes asphyxiated him. His body was repatriated for burial in Musmus, the small village in Israel where his family still resided.

These and so many other exiled poets and writers lend dignity to a condition legislated to deny dignity—to deny an identity to people. From them, it is apparent that, to concentrate on exile as a contemporary political punishment, you must therefore map territories of experience beyond those mapped by the literature of exile itself. You must first set aside Joyce and Nabokov and think instead of the uncountable masses for whom UN agencies have been created. You must think of the refugee-peasants with no prospect of ever returning home, armed only with a ration card and an agency number. Paris may be a capital famous for cosmopolitan exiles, but it is also a city where unknown men and women have spent years of miserable loneliness: Vietnamese, Algerians, Cambodians, Lebanese, Senegalese, Peruvians. You must think also of Cairo, Beirut, Madagascar, Bangkok, Mexico City.

As you move further from the Atlantic world, the awful forlorn waste increases: the hopelessly large numbers, the compounded misery of "undocumented" people suddenly lost, without a tellable history. To reflect on exiled Muslims from India, or Haitians in America, or Bikinians in Oceania, or Palestinians throughout the Arab world means that you must leave the modest refuge provided by subjectivity and resort instead to the abstractions of mass politics. Negotiations, wars of national liberation, people bundled out of their homes and prodded, bussed or walked to enclaves in other regions: What do these experiences add up to? Are they not manifestly and almost by design irrecoverable?

We come to nationalism and its essential association with exile. Nationalism is an assertion of belonging in and to a place, a people, a heritage. It affirms the home created by a community of language, culture, and customs; and, by so doing, it fends off exile, fights to prevent its ravages. Indeed, the interplay between nationalism and exile is like Hegel's dialectic of servant and master, opposites informing and constituting each other. All nationalisms in their early stages develop from a condition of estrangement. The struggles to win American independence, to unify Germany or Italy, to liberate Algeria were those of national groups separated—exiled—from what was construed to be their rightful way of life. Triumphant, achieved nationalism then justifies, retrospectively as well as prospectively, a history selectively strung together in a narrative form: thus all nationalisms have their founding fathers, their basic, quasi-religious texts, their rhetoric of belonging, their historical and geographical landmarks, their official enemies and heroes. This collective ethos forms what Pierre Bourdieu, the French sociologist, calls the habitus, the coherent amalgam of practices linking habit with inhabitance.

In time, successful nationalisms consign truth exclusively to themselves and relegate falsehood and inferiority to outsiders (as in the rhetoric of capitalist versus communist, or the European versus the Asiatic). And just beyond the frontier between "us" and the "outsiders" is the perilous territory of not-belonging: this is to where in a primitive time peoples were banished, and where in the modern era immense aggregates of humanity loiter as refugees and displaced persons. Nationalisms are about groups, but in a very acute sense exile is a solitude experienced outside the group: the deprivations felt at not being with others in the communal habitation. How, then, does one surmount the loneliness of exile without falling into the encompassing and thumping language of national pride, collective sentiments, group passions? What is there worth saving and holding on to between the extremes of exile on the one hand, and the often bloody-minded affirmations of nationalism on the other? Do nationalism and exile have any intrinsic attributes? Are they simply two conflicting varieties of paranoia?

These are questions that cannot ever be fully answered because each assumes that exile and nationalism can be discussed neutrally, without reference to each other. They cannot be. Because both terms include everything from the most collective of collective sentiments to the most private of private emotions, there is hardly language adequate for both. But there is certainly nothing about nationalism's public and all-inclusive ambitions that touches the core of the exile's predicament. Because exile, unlike nationalism, is fundamentally a discontinuous state of being. Exiles are cut off from their roots, their land, their past. They generally do not have armies or states, although they are often in search of them. Exiles feel, therefore, an urgent need to reconstitute their broken lives, usually by choosing to see themselves as part of a triumphant ideology or a restored people. The crucial thing is that a state of exile free from this triumphant ideology—designed to reassemble an exile's broken history into a new whole—is virtually unbearable, and virtually impossible in today's world. Look at the fate of the Jews, the Palestinians, and the Armenians.

Noubar is a solitary Armenian, and a friend. His parents had to leave Eastern Turkey in 1915, after their families were massacred: his maternal grandfather was beheaded. Noubar's mother and father went to Aleppo, then to Cairo. In the middle-sixties, life in Egypt became difficult for non-

Egyptians, and his parents, along with four children, were taken to Beirut by an international relief organization. In Beirut they lived briefly in a pension and then were bundled into two rooms of a little house outside the city. In Lebanon, they had no money and they waited: eight months later, a relief agency got them a flight to Glasgow. And then to Gander. And then to New York. They rode by Greyhound bus from New York to Seattle: Seattle was the city designated by the agency for their American residence. When I asked, "Seattle?," Noubar smiled resignedly, as if to say, better Seattle than Armenia —which he never knew, or Turkey, where so many were slaughtered, or Lebanon, where he and his family would certainly have risked their lives. Exile is sometimes better than staying behind or not getting out: but only sometimes.

Because nothing is secure. Exile is a jealous state. What you achieve is precisely what you have no wish to share, and it is in the drawing of lines around you and your compatriots that the least attractive aspects of being in exile emerge: an exaggerated sense of group solidarity, and a passionate hostility to outsiders, even those who may in fact be in the same predicament as you. What could be more intransigent than the conflict between Zionist Jews and Arab Palestinians? Palestinians feel that they have been turned into exiles by the proverbial people of exile, the Jews. But the Palestinians also know that their own sense of national identity has been nourished in the exile milieu, where everyone not a blood-brother or -sister is an enemy, where every sympathizer is an agent of some unfriendly power, and where the slightest deviation from the accepted group line is an act of the rankest treachery and disloyalty.

Perhaps this is the most extraordinary of exile's fates: to have been exiled by exiles—to relive the actual process of up-rooting at the hands of exiles. All Palestinians during the summer of 1982 asked themselves what inarticulate urge drove Israel, having displaced Palestinians in 1948, to expel them continuously from their refugee homes and camps in Lebanon. It is as if the reconstructed Jewish collective experience, as represented by Israel and modern Zionism, could not tolerate another story of dispossession and loss to exist alongside it—an intolerance constantly reinforced by the Israeli hostility to the nationalism of the Palestinians, who for forty-six years have been painfully reassembling a national identity in exile.

This need to reassemble an identity out of the refractions and discontinuities of exile is found in the earlier poems of Mahmoud Darwish, whose considerable work amounts to an epic effort to transform the lyrics of loss into the indefinitely postponed drama of return. Thus he depicts his sense of homelessness in the form of a list of unfinished and incomplete things:

But I am the exile.
Seal me with your eyes.
Take me wherever you are—
Take me whatever you are.
Restore to me the colour of face
And the warmth of body
The light of heart and eye,
The salt of bread and rhythm,
The taste of earth…the Motherland.
Shield me with your eyes.
Take me as a relic from the mansion of sorrow.
Take me as a verse from my tragedy;
Take me as a toy, a brick from the house
So that our children will remember to return.

The pathos of exile is in the loss of contact with the solidity and the satisfaction of earth: homecoming is out of the question.

Joseph Conrad's tale "Amy Foster" is perhaps the most uncompromising representation of exile ever written. Conrad thought of himself as an exile from Poland, and nearly all his work (as well as his life) carries the unmistakable mark of the sensitive émigré's obsession with his own fate and with his hopeless attempts to make satisfying contact with new surroundings. "Amy Foster" is in a sense confined to the problems of exile, perhaps so confined that it is not one of Conrad's best-known stories. This, for example, is the description of the agony of its central character, Yanko Goorall, an Eastern European peasant who, en route to America, is shipwrecked off the British coast: "It is indeed hard upon a man to find himself a lost stranger helpless, incomprehensible, and of a mysterious origin, in some obscure corner of the earth. Yet amongst all the adventurers shipwrecked in all the wild parts of the world, there is not one, it seems to me, that ever had to suffer a fate so simply tragic as the man I am speaking of, the most innocent of adventurers cast out by the sea."

Yanko has left home because the pressures were too great for him to go on living there. America lures him with its promise, though England is where he ends up. He endures in England, where he cannot speak the language and is feared and misunderstood. Only Amy Foster, a plodding, unattractive peasant girl, tries to communicate with him. They marry, have a child, but when

Yanko falls ill, Amy, afraid and alienated, refuses to nurse him; snatching their child, she leaves. The desertion hastens Yanko's miserable death, which like the deaths of several Conradian heroes is depicted as the result of a combination of crushing isolation and the world's indifference. Yanko's fate is described as "the supreme disaster of loneliness and despair."

Yanko's predicament is affecting: a foreigner perpetually haunted and alone in an uncomprehending society. But Conrad's own exile causes him to exaggerate the differences between Yanko and Amy. Yanko is dashing, light, and bright-eyed, whereas Amy is heavy, dull, bovine; when he dies, it is as if her earlier kindness to him was a snare to lure and then trap him fatally. Yanko's death is romantic: the world is coarse, unappreciative; no one understands him, not even Amy, the one person close to him. Conrad took this neurotic exile's fear and created an aesthetic principle out of it. No one can understand or communicate in Conrad's world, but paradoxically this radical limitation on the possibilities of language doesn't inhibit elaborate efforts to communicate. All of Conrad's stories are about lonely people who talk a great deal (for indeed who of the great modernists was more voluble and "adjectival" than Conrad himself?) and whose attempts to impress others compound, rather than reduce, the original sense of isolation. Each Conradian exile fears, and is condemned endlessly to imagine, the spectacle of a solitary death illuminated, so to speak, by unresponsive, uncommunicating eyes.

Exiles look at non-exiles with resentment. They belong in their surroundings, you feel, whereas an exile is always out of place. What is it like to be born in a place, to stay and live there, to know that you are of it, more or less forever? Although it is true that anyone prevented from returning home is an exile, some distinctions can be made among exiles, refugees, expatriates, and émigrés. Exile originated in the age-old practice of banishment. Once banished, the exile lives an anomalous and miserable life, with the stigma of being an outsider. Refugees, on the other hand, are a creation of the twentieth-century state. The word "refugee" has become a political one, suggesting large herds of innocent and bewildered people requiring urgent international assistance, whereas "exile" carries with it, I think, a touch of solitude and spirituality.

Expatriates voluntarily live in an alien country, usually for personal or social reasons. Hemingway and Fitzgerald were not forced to live in France. Expatriates may share in the solitude and estrangement of exile, but they do not suffer under its rigid proscriptions. Émigrés enjoy an ambiguous status.

Technically, an émigré is anyone who emigrates to a new country. Choice in the matter is certainly a possibility. Colonial officials, missionaries, technical experts, mercenaries, and military advisers on loan may in a sense live in exile, but they have not been banished. White settlers in Africa, parts of Asia and Australia may once have been exiles, but as pioneers and nation-builders, they lost the label "exile."

Much of the exile's life is taken up with compensating for disorienting loss by creating a new world to rule. It is not surprising that so many exiles seem to be novelists, chess players, political activists, and intellectuals. Each of these occupations requires a minimal investment in objects and places a great premium on mobility and skill. The exile's new world, logically enough, is unnatural and its unreality resembles fiction. Georg Lukács, in *Theory of the Novel*, argued with compelling force that the novel, a literary form created out of the unreality of ambition and fantasy, is the form of "transcendental homelessness." Classical epics, Lukács wrote, emanate from settled cultures in which values are clear, identities stable, life unchanging. The European novel is grounded in precisely the opposite experience, that of a changing society in which an itinerant and disinherited middle-class hero or heroine seeks to construct a new world that somewhat resembles an old one left behind forever. In the epic there is no other world, only the finality of this one. Odysseus returns to Ithaca after years of wandering; Achilles will die because he cannot escape his fate. The novel, however, exists because other worlds may exist, alternatives for bourgeois speculators, wanderers, exiles.

No matter how well they may do, exiles are always eccentrics who feel their difference (even as they frequently exploit it) as a kind of orphanhood. Anyone who is really homeless regards the habit of seeing estrangement in everything modern as an affectation, a display of modish attitudes. Clutching difference like a weapon to be used with stiffened will, the exile jealously insists on his or her right to refuse to belong. This usually translates into an intransigence that is not easily ignored. Willfulness, exaggeration, overstatement: these are characteristic styles of being an exile, methods for compelling the world to accept your vision—which you make more unacceptable because you are in fact unwilling to have it accepted. It is yours, after all. Composure and serenity are the last things associated with the work of exiles. Artists in exile are decidedly unpleasant, and their stubbornness insinuates itself into even their exalted works. Dante's vision in *The Divine Comedy* is tremendously powerful in its universality and detail, but even the beatific peace achieved in the *Paradiso* bears traces of the vindictiveness and severity of judgment embodied in the Inferno. Who but an exile like Dante, banished from Florence, would use eternity as a place for settling old scores?

James Joyce chose to be in exile: to give force to his artistic vocation. In an uncannily effective way—as Richard Ellmann has shown in his biography— Joyce picked a quarrel with Ireland and kept it alive so as to sustain the strictest opposition to what was familiar. Ellmann says that "whenever his relations with his native land were in danger of improving, [Joyce] was to find a new incident to solidify his intransigence and to reaffirm the rightness of his voluntary absence." Joyce's fiction concerns what in a letter he once described as the state of being "alone and friendless." And although it is rare to pick banishment as a way of life, Joyce perfectly understood its trials.

But Joyce's success as an exile stresses the question lodged at its very heart: is exile so extreme and private that any instrumental use of it is ultimately a trivialization? How is it that the literature of exile has taken its place as a topos of human experience alongside the literature of adventure, education, or discovery? Is this the same exile that quite literally kills Yanko Goorall and has bred the expensive, often dehumanizing relationship between twentieth-century exile and nationalism? Or is it some more benign variety?

Much of the contemporary interest in exile can be traced to the somewhat pallid notion that non-exiles can share in the benefits of exile as a redemptive motif. There is, admittedly, a certain plausibility and truth to this idea. Like medieval itinerant scholars or learned Greek slaves in the Roman Empire, exiles—the exceptional ones among them—do leaven their environments. And naturally "we" concentrate on that enlightening aspect of "their" presence among us, not on their misery or their demands. But looked at from the bleak political perspective of modern mass dislocations, individual exiles force us to recognize the tragic fate of homelessness in a necessarily heartless world.

A generation ago, Simone Weil posed the dilemma of exile as concisely as it has ever been expressed. "To be rooted," she said, "is perhaps the most important and least recognized need of the human soul." Yet Weil also saw that most remedies for uprootedness in this era of world wars, deportations, and mass exterminations are almost as dangerous as what they purportedly remedy. Of these, the state—or, more accurately, statism—is one of the most insidious, since worship of the state tends to supplant all other human bonds. Weil exposes us anew to that whole complex of pressures and constraints that lie at the center of the exile's predicament, which, as I have suggested, is as close as we come in the modern era to tragedy. There is the sheer fact of isolation and displacement, which produces the kind of narcissistic masochism that resists all efforts at amelioration, acculturation, and community. At this extreme the exile can make a fetish of exile, a practice that distances him or her from all connections and commitments. To live as if everything around you were temporary and perhaps trivial is to fall prey to petulant cynicism as well as to querulous lovelessness. More common is the pressure on the exile to join—parties, national movements, the state. The exile is offered a new set of affiliations and develops new loyalties. But there is also a loss—of critical perspective, of intellectual reserve, of moral courage.

It must also be recognized that the defensive nationalism of exiles often fosters self-awareness as much as it does the less attractive forms of self-assertion. Such reconstitutive projects as assembling a nation out of exile (and this is true in this century for Jews and Palestinians) involve constructing a national history, reviving an ancient language, founding national institutions like libraries and universities. And these, while they sometimes promote strident ethnocentrism, also give rise to investigations of self that inevitably go far beyond such simple and positive facts as "ethnicity." For example, there is the self-consciousness of an individual trying to understand why the histories of the Palestinians and the Jews have certain patterns to them, why in spite of oppression and the threat of extinction a particular ethos remains alive in exile.

Necessarily, then, I speak of exile not as a privilege, but as an alternative to the mass institutions that dominate modern life. Exile is not, after all, a matter of choice: you are born into it, or it happens to you. But, provided that the exile refuses to sit on the sidelines nursing a wound, there are things to be learned: he or she must cultivate a scrupulous (not indulgent or sulky) subjectivity. Perhaps the most rigorous example of such subjectivity is to be found in the writing of Theodor Adorno, the German-Jewish philosopher and critic. Adorno's masterwork, *Minima Moralia*, is an autobiography written while in exile; it is subtitled *Reflexionen aus dem beschädigten Leben* (Reflections from a Mutilated Life). Ruthlessly opposed to what he called the "administered" world, Adorno saw all life as pressed into ready-made forms, prefabricated "homes." He argued that everything that one says or thinks, as well as every object one possesses, is ultimately a mere commodity. Language is jargon, objects are for sale. To refuse this state of affairs is the exile's intellectual mission.

Adorno's reflections are informed by the belief that the only home truly available now, though fragile and vulnerable, is in writing. Elsewhere, "the house is past. The bombings of European cities, as well as the labour and concentration camps, merely precede as executors, with what the immanent development of technology had long decided was to be the fate of houses. These are now good only to be thrown away like old food cans." In short, Adorno says with a grave irony, "it is part of morality not to be at home in one's home." To follow Adorno is to stand away from "home" in order to look at it with the exile's detachment. For there is considerable merit in the practice of noting the discrepancies between various concepts and ideas and what they actually produce. We take home and language for granted; they become nature, and their underlying assumptions recede into dogma and orthodoxy.

The exile knows that in a secular and contingent world, homes are always provisional. Borders and barriers, which enclose us within the safety of familiar territory, can also become prisons, and are often defended beyond reason or necessity. Exiles cross borders, break barriers of thought and experience. Hugo of St. Victor, a twelfth-century monk from Saxony, wrote these hauntingly beautiful lines:

> It is, therefore, a source of great virtue for the practised mind to learn, bit by bit, first to change about invisible and transitory things, so that afterwards it may be able to leave them behind altogether. The man who finds his homeland sweet is still a tender beginner; he to whom every soil is as his native one is already strong; but he is perfect to whom the entire world is as a foreign land. The tender soul has fixed his love on one spot in the world; the strong man has extended his love to all places; the perfect man has extinguished his.

Erich Auerbach, the great twentieth-century literary scholar who spent the war years as an exile in Turkey, has cited this passage as a model for anyone wishing to transcend national or provincial limits. Only by embracing this attitude can a historian begin to grasp human experience and its written records in their diversity and particularity; otherwise he or she will remain committed more to the exclusions and reactions of prejudice than to the freedom that accompanies knowledge. But note that Hugo twice makes it clear that the "strong" or "perfect" man achieves independence and detachment by working through attachments, not by rejecting them. Exile is predicated on the existence of, love for, and bond with, one's native place; what is true of all exile is not that home and love of home are lost, but that loss is inherent in the very existence of both.

Regard experiences as if they were about to disappear. What is it that anchors them in reality? What would you save of them? What would you give up? Only someone who has achieved independence and detachment, someone whose homeland is "sweet" but whose circumstances make it impossible to recapture that sweetness, can answer those questions. (Such a person would also find it impossible to derive satisfaction from substitutes furnished by illusion or dogma.) This may seem like a prescription for an unrelieved grimness of outlook and, with it, a permanently sullen disapproval of all enthusiasm or buoyancy of spirit. Not necessarily. While it perhaps seems peculiar to speak of the pleasures of exile, there are some positive things to be said for a few of its conditions. Seeing "the entire world as a foreign land" makes possible originality of vision. Most people are principally aware of one culture, one setting, one home; exiles are aware of at least two, and this plurality of vision gives rise to an awareness of simultaneous dimensions, an awareness that—to borrow a phrase from music—is contrapuntal.

For an exile, habits of life, expression, or activity in the new environment inevitably occur against the memory of these things in another environment. Thus both the new and the old environments are vivid, actual, occurring together contrapuntally. There is a unique pleasure in this sort of apprehension, especially if the exile is conscious of other contrapuntal juxtapositions that diminish orthodox judgment and elevate appreciative sympathy. There is also a particular sense of achievement in acting as if one were at home wherever one happens to be. This remains risky, however: the habit of dissimulation is both wearying and nerve-racking. Exile is never the state of being satisfied, placid, or secure. Exile, in the words of Wallace Stevens, is "a mind of winter" in which the pathos of summer and autumn as much as the potential of spring are nearby but unobtainable. Perhaps this is another way of saying that a life of exile moves according to a different calendar, and is less seasonal and settled than life at home. Exile is life led outside habitual order. It is nomadic, decentered, contrapuntal; but no sooner does one get accustomed to it than its unsettling force erupts anew.

SEVEN

Mo Salah, a Moral Somebody?

Amro Ali

THE ASTONISHING RISE, impact, and reception in Egypt and around the world of Egyptian football player Mohamed Salah has largely transpired amid a moral crisis in sports. Comedian James Corden captured this demise in 2010 when he addressed the British sport elites at the BBC Sports Personality of the Year award: "I don't see a room full of sporting legends here, I see a room full of people looking for their next sponsorship deal, book deal, TV series.... You lot need to get back to basics, remember who you are, what you are, what you stand for."[1] Six years later, at the funeral of boxing legend Muhammad Ali in 2016, reverend Dr. Kevin Cosby of Louisville drew on African-American theological discourse to crystalize an athlete's quest for dignity: "Before James Brown said 'I am black and I am proud,' Ali said 'I am black and I am pretty.' Black and pretty were an oxymoron. Blacks did not say pretty... but Muhammad Ali said, I am proud, I am pretty, I am glad of who I am. And when he said that, that infused in Africans, a sense of somebodiness."[2] It was Martin Luther King Jr. who initially coined the term "somebodiness." He believed that "without a deep sense of somebodiness, a person would be incapable of rising to full maturity."[3] Comparisons between Salah and Ali are not unusual, and may at first appear disingenuous. Some would say that it is unfair to compare Ali's fifty-five years of public life to Salah's public beginning. Ali rose to fame in the United States in the 1960s and 1970s, an age of political change and disruptions. He had a wider space for political articulation to flourish. Salah heralds from a despotic environment in which he has to carefully calculate his every word and move as well as navigate the treacherous digital terrain of hypervisibility, instant gratification, and mass reactions.

However, if Salah is yet to be on par with Ali, he is certainly already evincing social effects comparable to Ali. Salah has risen as a sports figure who internalizes this somebodiness and delivers a model for Arabs and Muslims to feel a sense of self-determination, self-acceptance, self-definition, and to be a person of worth on an equal footing with others. For Egypt, Salah is the hero that unsettles the authoritarian system and acts as an antidote to unhappiness. For the Arab and Muslim world he is a redemption of something lost, a substitute in an era devoid of real Muslim leaders. For the rest of the world, particularly Europe, he is the disrupter of the secular realm and obstacle to bigotry who can jam the wires of Islamophobia. Salah encodes the somebodiness that restores a sense of dignity to the Egyptian at home, and to Arabs and Muslims abroad, while delivering a reckoning for which the West has to deal.

To witness the motion of Salah's body is to witness the creation of empirical data. The concealed lightness in his chest, fast pulse, dry mouth, heightened senses, breathlessness, and laser focus swirl into his formidable goals. Each one unleashes the spirit—everything expressive in-between his upward glance to the heavens and prostration to the earth. The smiles, cries, inner glow, holding his arms out wide as if to hug the arena, the world, among the chorus of squealing, screaming, shouting, whooping, and hollering—all entering a vortex that makes the man mythic. It is from here that the ordinary becomes inscribed with deeper meanings. On any given day, the most stunning of athletes elicit common tropes of success, fame, riches, and gossip. Salah goes further because people take him further with their projections. Salah invokes hope, justice, kindness, dignity, and faith, among other attributes.

The risk that accompanies such exaltation means the actual human Salah will inevitably violate the public-constructed Salah. This was seen in February 2019, when following a train crash in Cairo that left twenty-five dead and more than forty injured, Salah tweeted a smiling selfie, raising the ire of Egyptian social media for his bad timing. In addition, in June 2019, Salah ignited anger when he defended his teammate Amr Warda after he had been expelled from the Egyptian soccer team during the Africa Cup because of accusations, with some damning screenshots, of online sexual harassment cases. In defense of his teammate Salah tweeted: "We need to believe in second chances…we need to guide and educate. Shunning is not the answer." This provoked a furious backlash, especially on social media from many who argued with good reason that Warda had been given numerous chances and yet continued to harass women online and had yet to apologize to his victims.

Salah was viewed as complicit in exonerating Warda and of being insensitive to the problem of sexual harassment in Egypt (although that was clearly not Salah's intention). These social media storms showed just how consequential the figure of Salah, the "fourth pyramid," had become. Why does he mean so much for so many?

YEARNING FOR ANOTHER EGYPT

While Salah may have risen to national fame when he helped defeat Congo in October 2017, propelling Egypt into the World Cup, his astonishing football talent alone cannot explain his rising star. Nor did his story of humble beginnings take hold in that moment. Rather, it happened barely two weeks after this victory when Salah was offered a luxury villa by entrepreneur Mamdouh Abbas. Salah politely declined the gift and suggested that a donation to his village Nagrig in the district of Gharbia would make him happier. His refusal of the villa was a significant breach in the business-as-usual patronage and wheeling-and-dealing circles. If Salah was loved for his victory over Congo, he was now respected more for this move and his many acts of charity, including the building of a school in his home village and donating or upgrading new facilities at Basioun hospital. Salah embodied a sudden assertion of human values within a dehumanizing system. His rejection of the villa pierced a culture that celebrates material wealth, consumer culture, and individual advancement.

At the same time, Salah has not shunned commercial opportunity. His appearances in Vodafone and Uber commercials, among other lucrative contracts that are symbols of global capitalist consumption, are usually treated as a sideshow or accepted as the norm that comes with football stardom. People would rather associate him more with refusing the villa and his other charitable acts, and for good reason. Egyptians have long missed looking up to someone who commands respect, at least someone who is not in exile, in prison, or long dead, and Salah has helped restore meaning to terms that had become scrambled: dignity became dignity again; principles became principles; kindness became kindness; and happiness became happiness.

There is an epidemic of unhappiness in Egypt. Young people often express a pervasive sense of hopelessness and an extreme desire to leave the country. A male body builder tells me of a new prayer in his social circles: "We say to each other: 'I pray that you leave this country.'" A young female health worker laments she wants to leave Egypt because "to give birth to a baby here feels morally wrong." A juice seller sarcastically quips, "We no longer have time to think of anything else but survival, we don't even have time to contemplate suicide." It has become commonplace to argue that such unhappiness in Egypt is caused by high unemployment, poverty, dysfunctional education, or crackdowns on independent voices. But there is something worse and pathological: the grim reality that new possibilities no longer emerge on the horizon.

The January 25, 2011, revolution in Egypt generated a political language of binaries that polarized Egyptians: revolutionary versus counterrevolutionary; secular versus Islamist; civilian versus military; pro- and anti-Brotherhood, among others. Such binaries still contained an element of the possible, yet many of them have diminished under the shadow of the generals, who launched a coup in 2013 under Abdel Fattah el-Sisi, dealing a blow to regenerative politics. The unity that has come in its place is a negative unity; it is almost always against something, such as terrorism. And when it stands for something, let us say Egypt, it is a nationalist straitjacket that is imposed, with no room for plurality of voices. Salah might just be the first figure in a while behind which pro- and anti-regime supporters can unite. The young Egyptian footballer has galvanized a number of his country's youth to abandon drugs. Salah was able to inspire calls to a drug user helpline to shoot up by 400 percent. Salah posters, cardboard cutouts, graffiti, and sculptures greet people at countless Egyptian social spaces, making him akin to the patron saint of coffeehouses, schools, and walls. Something interrupted the despotic drive to stamp out the uniqueness from the flow of Egyptian life and partially reversed the Arab and Muslim world's despondence with Egypt after the 2013 coup.

Salah's stance to steer away from politics, or from inadvertently disclosing his political leanings, has given him an amplified united base. Nevertheless, during the presidential elections in Egypt in 2018, people wrote in Salah's name on their ballots as a form of protest, raising the unwitting candidate to third place.[4] Salah touched on another existential question within Egyptian state and society: the strong desire for international recognition. This phenomenon weaves its way through Egypt's modern history.[5] There have been concerted efforts to export el-Sisi's branded Egypt, for example, with the new Suez Canal project billboards doting New York's Times Square with the slogan "Egypt's gift to the world."

Salah, instead, lived up to fulfilling that slogan in a much more dramatic

FIGURE 7.1 Graffiti of Mohamed Salah at a Cairo cafe. Photo by Ibrahim, 2018. Wikimedia Commons, https://commons.wikimedia.org/wiki/File:Salah_Graffiti_in_Cairo.jpg.

and compelling way. In fact, the "King of Egypt" has arguably had more impact on the world's positive views of Egypt than all the post-2013 tourist campaigns, international conferences, and mega projects combined. As English comedian and television host John Oliver wrote on Salah for *Time* magazine's 100-most-influential people: "Mo Salah is a better human being than he is a football player. And he's one of the best football players in the world.... You'd be hard-pressed to find a professional athlete in any sport less affected by their success or status than Mo."[6] It is no wonder that mentioning Salah in conversation can give many Egyptians a feeling of tingling hands and weightlessness. It is not unusual to hear someone say they hate celebrity-worship, football, famous figures, "but I make an exception only for Salah" is the usual conditional clause.

The regime believes it can commodify happiness, order Egyptians to comply with being the world's happiest people. It has held discussions with the Ministry of Happiness of the United Arab Emirates to "export" some of their cool psychedelic juice to Egypt. Happiness is a question that spans a history of philosophical musings, from Aristotle's *Nicomachean Ethics*, to al-Ghazali's *Alchemy of Happiness*, to Nietzsche's *Twilight of the Idols*. All of them would shun the Anglo-inspired utilitarianism of John Stuart Mills that speaks of happiness as the ultimate net objective and has been largely repackaged for neoliberal modernity, rather than a meaningful higher life that produces happiness as a by-product. In other words, you cannot separate the attainment of happiness from respect for justice, dignity, and honor. It does not seem to faze the authorities that happiness is meaningless without rescuing vibrant citizenship, opening public spaces, providing fair trials, and preventing overall existential meaning from being fragmented.

Salah offers glimpses into the voids spawned by such fractures as he communicates not only on the instrumental level of football success but with meaningful and empathic qualities that come with an honorable character. As the sport historian Mike Cronin has written: "Followers want superb athletic performance, the hard-won victory, and the demonstration of the aesthetic beauty of the body in motion. But they want all this competition, even though it is now firmly allied with the force of global capitalism, to be fair, to mean something, and to offer them life lessons."[7]

THE SALAH EFFECT AND EUROPE

Salah falls into a long controversial tradition of athletes mixing religion with sports. Although the two are generally seen to be separate, particularly in the West, historically the opposite held true. In ancient Greece, the Olympic Games were performed in honor of Zeus.[8] In Christianity and Islam, sporting activities were seen as strengthening the believer in the service of God. Yet in the modern era "the bond between the secular and the sacred has been broken, the attachment to the realm of the transcendent has been severed. Modern sports are activities partly pursued for their own sake, partly for other ends which are equally secular."[9] So sports are played to honor our cities, countries, universities, ourselves, and global capitalism.

Not only has the link been broken, but the secular has long appropriated qualities of the sacred, and we see this with the extent that sport has become the world's so-called secular religion. As the philosopher and theologian Michael Novak has noted: "To have a religion, you need to have a way to exhilarate the human body, and desire, and will, and the sense of beauty, and a sense of oneness with the universe and other humans. You need chants and songs, the rhythm of bodies in unison, the indescribable feeling of many who together 'will one thing' as if they were each members of a single body. All these things you have in sports..., sports are a form of religion."[10] Hence, it is not unusual that an unease runs through believers when stadiums become the rival to houses of worship. Islamic jurists continue to be torn between viewing sports as a spearhead of moral corruption and one of elevation of the soul. A seminal book published in Riyadh in 1981 linked football zealotry of young Muslims to "a moral vacuum and degradation." Even if Muslims are unaware of the scholarly debates, there is often a quiet anxiety of seeing the hero-worship of football overtake the mosque.

In the West, a player like Salah makes a noticeable dent in this anxiety. Salah patches up the sacred with the secular and in fact "blasphemes" against the secular religion with deeds of the most arresting nature. From the forehead to the grass and the index finger toward the skies, hundreds of millions of Muslims are drawn to this well-understood language of piety, and suddenly something feels redeemed. Like a spiritual wholesomeness was restored to the sport. Salah saw no need to dismiss or distill his Muslim identity, even after he achieved a turbo-charged social mobility and stardom—a point that is not lost on many. The sight of his veiled wife, Maggie, by his side on a green oval in a European city before the eyes of millions, is a hypnotic sight to Muslims (and the rest of the world) precisely because it is unusual, particularly because it occurs at a time of heightened anxieties toward Muslims in the West. In Europe, where Islamophobia is rife, imams entreat young Muslims to emulate Salah, and they return to the mosques with their heads held up high.

The stellar Muslim athlete in the West has long represented a sort of redemption of the Muslim world. At times it can feel that all the corruption, dysfunction, and poverty that characterizes much of the Muslim world can be offered a temporary reprieve by a sporting event. But a Muslim one in a former colonial power or country loathed for its foreign policy can invoke a sense of vindication. A compelling comparison can be made with Zinedine Zidane, the professional French football player who led France to victory in the 1998 FIFA World Cup and the 2000 European Football Championship, who is the current manager of the Real Madrid football club. The French footballer of Algerian descent was accepted by Arabs and Muslims but with much difficulty, let alone credibility. Zidane's ambiguous relationship to his heritage never made it any easier.

In an interview with *Esquire* in 2015, Zidane stated: "I have an affinity with the Arabic world. I have it in my blood, via my parents. I'm very proud of being French, but also very proud of having these roots and this diversity." The Muslim angle was of little use when the wine-drinking athlete states he is a non-practicing Muslim. Nor was the cultural ownership of Zidane straightforward. His Berber roots complicated the pan-Arabist appeal that does not offer much room for plurality or minority voices. In the end, Arabs and Muslims outside France had to settle for a superficial acceptance of Zidane's profile in order to be associated with the great Zizou.

Salah, however, came with little of the haziness that characterized Zidane. He was a village boy who was "truly" Arab from the Nile delta. Consequently, the Arab world's traditional idea of a leading, strong, vibrant, noble, and outward-looking Egypt—one that spearheads the arts, preserves the seat of intellectual Sunnism, champions pan-Arabism, and stands up for the Palestinian cause—was projected onto Salah with deafening force. An idea that was seen to be long perverted by successive Egyptian regimes was redeemed through Salah, the "pride of the Arabs" as he has been nicknamed from Casablanca to Baghdad. The Salah effect has been enough to rile up Moroccans to rally behind their departing team for the World Cup, demanding they venge Spanish player Sergio Ramos's arm grab that injured Salah, impacting his performance in the World Cup in Russia. This sparked an unusual international outrage that crossed boundaries, including a bizarre peaceful protest that was later aborted outside the Spanish embassy in Jakarta, and the Lebanese, similar to Egypt, writing Salah's name on ballots during Lebanon's 2018 parliamentary elections.

One of the most circulated videos regarding Salah was a chant sung by English fans in the Liverpool stadium.

Mo Sa-la-la-la-lah,
Mo Sa-la-la-la-lah!

If he's good enough for you,
he's good enough for me.
If he scores another few,
then I'll be Muslim too.

If he's good enough for you,
he's good enough for me.
Sitting in the mosque,
that's where I wanna be!

Mo Sa-la-la-la-lah,
Mo Sa-la-la-*la-lah*!

This song has been much interpreted along mainly two main views. On the one hand, Salah has been praised for his role in combating Islamophobia, and on the other, he has been derided as having no impact on the scourge of Islamophobia. Football writer Andi Thomas has nicely diffused the moral impasse: "Islamophobia...ends not with the valorization of exceptional Muslims—who are, by definition, exceptions—but in the acceptance of ordinary Muslims."[11]

This is not to dismiss the Salah effect. A Stanford University study highlighted that the football star has caused Islamophobic hate crimes to drop by 18.9 percent and anti-Muslim tweets to fall by half. "Positive exposure to outgroup role models can reveal new information that humanizes the outgroup writ large," the study noted. While the study was limited to Merseyside, the county that Liverpool is in, it is a curiosity of whether Salah can replicate such comparable effects beyond the county. The answer is not so simple. There is another space that needs some illumination, the gray areas where Salah operates. A hurricane is not simply viewed as favorable or unfavorable. Its impending arrival alone stirs up a mixture of fear, hope, wonder, and the sensation of things moving too quickly to process. Once it has passed, it leaves an indelible mark, more than just the trail of devastation. The residents start rebuilding, gain an appreciation for the importance of communal bonding, they become more conscious of the forces of nature, not to mention the gratitude felt for the lives and homes spared, prayers for the dead, and so forth.

Similarly, when the Muslim athlete in the West projects an athletic artistry and cultural firepower, she or he dislocates the arrangements that make the current state of merciless racism possible. In Salah's case, this could open up new conceptual pathways to dealing with Muslims and people of color, enable a young child to get exposed to an alternative Islam away from his or her parent's dogmatic views, or collapse sectarian divisions to allow Sunnis and Shiites to bond. Even if Salah falls out of favor down the track, the spectators' positions on Muslims may have long matured and predisposed them to sympathetic stances. This does not mean that none will return to former held prejudices, but just as many will be pushed along the track of reflection and reconsideration of previously held views. At the very least, it can be said that Salah makes the Islamophobia field more complicated to engender and triggers pores for alternative views to arise.

These pores are widened by global media and Salah's followers who pick up on some of his obscure noble acts. For example, when Salah went to greet his old Italian team in the Liverpool changerooms, he refused to celebrate his goals out of respect to his former comrades. He warmly welcomed a blind man for a private session who was filmed in the stadium cheering his goal. He affectionately hugged a boy who ran onto the field to reach him. These acts, while contingent on his goals, transcend culture and religion. The multilayered Salah—the intimately relatable footballer and loving father who kicks a ball with his daughter Makka—stands out like a moment of truth and living universality. A mammoth mural that went up in Times Square in the summer of 2018 reflects his larger than life image. Maybe Islamophobia is not the problem here, but that people forgot what it is like to be human. Throwing Salah into the equation makes xenophobic populism less appealing. Salah does not come with solutions but pries people to ask better questions.

The Salah effect has trickled down even to British children imitating Salah's prostration after scoring a goal in their backyard. We are no longer talking about another successful Muslim athlete, the likes of which are present in Liverpool and the other football's big leagues, but an extraordinary Muslim athlete who broke out of the sports arena and shook up the public sphere. Something happened that short-circuited a sport that is often treated by governments of all persuasions as a distracting bread and circus for the masses. Something torpedoed, even if temporarily, the xenophobic drive to tarnish Muslims in the West.

Salah, a heroic figure in contemporary culture, is armed with a moral code. He is seen to bring hope to many and is an unsettling specter that silently haunts the establishment. Football glory alone cannot make a compelling claim to heroism. Salah is a different sort of hero. He is a hero of disruption, a living paradox of a political voice without talking politics. Though his voice is rarely used to issue higher calls, Salah operates in a politics of juxtaposition in which his perceived immaculate persona is implicitly contrasted with the familiar polluted forces of high politics or scandal-ridden European athletes.

In his collection of essays and letters, *Resistance, Rebellion, and Death,* Albert Camus wrote to an estranged German friend in 1943: "I should like to be able to love my country and still love justice. I don't want any greatness for it, particularly a greatness born of blood and falsehood. I want to keep it alive by keeping justice alive." Overall, Salah perhaps embodies this ideal. That love of country does not require drums and chest-beating, but grace, sincerity, modesty, and charity. He is a reminder that there exists a better human nature in a landscape barren of prominent reverential role models. To Egypt and even the rest of the world, Salah is the outlier that proclaims the alternative to nationalism is not treachery but civic responsibility, the alternative to stifling religious conservatism does not always have to be apathy or mockery of the sacred, but breathing faith into a sound value system, and the alternative to injustice can be forgiveness. Ultimately, people had almost forgotten what humility among those with renown looks like.

This is not to say Salah will not disappoint—the Warda case clearly shows that Salah has yet to reach the golden threshold where global audiences can overlook his faults and see his myth solidified. Similar to the way Muhammad Ali's biographer described the boxer: "We forgive Muhammad Ali his excesses, because we see in him the child in us, and if he is foolish or cruel, if he is arrogant, if he is outrageously in love with his reflection, we forgive him because we no more can condemn him than condemn a rainbow for dissolving into the dark. Rainbows are born of thunderstorms, and Muhammad Ali is both." That level of mythological immunity is immensely difficult for most players to attain and perhaps for the better if it means an inability to escape from one's responsibility and accountability. Yet, as it stands, it could be said Salah is treated as the rare homecoming party for which Egyptians have long awaited. His face on dangling lanterns lights up dark alleyways, and his colorful posters germinate over the debris of fading election posters in a country that sees official and media-manufactured heroes reckon with publicly anointed heroes.

When Ali was still transitioning out of the Cassius Clay incarnation, he made a high-profile trip to Egypt in June 1964. Despite being well received, the *New York Times* reported, Egyptians at times could not understand Ali's confusing display of both humility and boastfulness. One office worker who met the boxer said: "A king would not say he is king of the world about himself—he'd leave it for others to say about him." Ali's religious practices confused them, like shouting "Allah Akbar" or raising his hands in prayer at inappropriate moments. Or when his piousness would suddenly take a break for a flirtation or two with Cairo's waitresses and young women in the host group, even during official processions. Nevertheless, Egyptians were forgiving of the young Ali and concluded that he may not always know what he is doing, but they admired his effort and fervor. Salah presents himself as a blank canvass to be painted on by everyone's politics, faith, and hopes. Where one's appropriation of Salah can help deflate the sense of nobodiness; he is declared "King of Egypt" by many except Salah himself.

NOTES

1. James Corden as quoted in Keith Duggan, "Comic's Speech Proves No Joke for Sports Stars," *Irish Times,* March 27, 2010.

2. WLKY News Louisville, "Muhammad Ali Memorial: The Rev. Dr. Kevin Cosby," *YouTube,* www.youtube.com/watch?v=YwFuQ-mGh6U (accessed June 10, 2016).

3. Phillip D. Johnson, "Somebodiness and Its Meaning to African American Men," *Journal of Counseling and Development* 94, no. 3 (July 2016): 333.

4. José Bourbon, "Elections in Egypt: How Salah Defeated One of the Candidates," *Sports Gazette,* April 2, 2018, https://sportsgazette.co.uk/elections-in -egypt-with-around-1-million-votes-salah-defeated-one-of-the-candidates/.

5. Ali, "What Would People Say?"

6. John Oliver on "Mohamed Salah," *Time,* April 29–May 6, 2019, https://time .com/collection/100-most-influential-people-2019/5567841/mohamed-salah/.

7. Mike Cronin, *Sport: A Very Short Introduction* (Oxford, UK: Oxford University Press, 2014), 118.

8. Allen Guttmann, *From Ritual to Record: The Nature of Modern Sports* (New York: Columbia University Press, 2004), 21.

9. Guttmann, *From Ritual to Record,* 26.

10. Novak, *Joy of Sports, Revised,* 31.

11. Thomas, "Soccer Star Mo Salah's Massive Popularity Is Changing Perceptions."

FURTHER READING

Ali, Amro. "What Would People Say? The Obsession with Public Image in Egypt." *Tahrir Institute for Middle East Policy*, March 5, 2014. https://timep.org/commentary/analysis/what-would-people-say/.

Johnson, Phillip D. "Somebodiness and Its Meaning to African American Men." *Journal of Counseling and Development* 94, no. 3 (July 2016): 333–43.

Novak, Michael. *Joy of Sports, Revised: Endzones, Bases, Baskets, Balls, and the Consecration of the American Spirit*. Lanham, MD: Madison Books, 1993.

Thomas, Andi. "Soccer Star Mo Salah's Massive Popularity Is Changing Perceptions of Muslims in the Uk." *Vox*, June 19, 2018. www.vox.com/world/2018/6/15/17433822/mo-salah-liverpool-injury-egypt-2018-world-cup-muslim-islam.

EIGHT

Gamal Abdel Nasser

Khaled Fahmy

AT 7:30 P.M. ON FRIDAY, June 9, 1967, millions of Egyptians turned on their TVs to watch their president deliver what they expected would be a momentous speech. Gamal Abdel Nasser was no stranger to them, for they had heard and watched him on countless previous occasions, always charismatic, always upbeat. But this speech was unlike anything they had heard from him before. Nasser's face was ashen, the mesmerizing spark in his eyes gone. With a sorrowful voice, he struggled to explain the magnitude of a crushing defeat his army had suffered at the hands of Israel over the previous few days. Only a few days earlier, on Monday, June 5, Israel had launched an air and ground attack that destroyed the entire Egyptian air force and decimated the land army in Sinai. Having absorbed the scale of the defeat, Nasser decided to confront his people, and in that fateful speech on TV he admitted complete responsibility for this catastrophe. He announced his resignation from all public duties he had held over the previous fifteen years.

Three things stand out in this dramatic speech. To begin, this was the first (and last) time an Arab leader had the moral courage to face his people and admit responsibility for his shortcomings. Second, in declaring his willingness to pay the price of his failures, Nasser did not tender his resignation to any public institution—for example, the sitting parliament, the cabinet, or the Court of Cassation, the highest court in the land. Rather, Nasser announced his resignation live on national TV and presented it to the Egyptian people directly, telling them that he was ready to return to the masses and to stand shoulder to shoulder with them as a normal citizen. Third, the reaction to this dramatic declaration was equally stunning. Even before the speech was over, millions took to the streets in Cairo and throughout the country in a mixture of shock and grief, asking not for Nasser's life or for him to face trial but for the exact opposite: they beseeched him to rescind his resignation and to stay in power to fight another day. By midday on June 10, 1967, Nasser answered the plea of his people and returned to office to pick up the pieces of a defeated army and a grieved nation.

Nasser lived for only three more years, but his influence far outlived his life. He is arguably the most influential Arab personality in the twentieth century. During his sixteen-year reign (1954–70), the entire Arab world witnessed many momentous events. Yet the events of June 1967 hold the key to unraveling this very colorful period of not only Arab history but world history as it unfolded with the rise of postcolonial states. For much of the world, Nasser was identified with postcolonial and nonaligned movements of the Global South.

POLITICAL LIFE

Gamal Abdel Nasser was born on January 15, 1918, in Alexandria, Egypt's second largest city. His father was a postal clerk, and his mother the daughter of a successful coal merchant. The father's job took him to different postings, and the young boy received his primary and secondary education in schools throughout the country. Like many of his schoolmates, Nasser became deeply involved in street politics. Cairo and Alexandria were teeming with political demonstrations, chiefly around problems connected to the military occupation. Britain had invaded Egypt in 1882, and despite the fact that the ruling local dynasty headed by the Khedive or the Sultan was maintained, Britain held all real power.

Following the nationwide revolution in 1919, Britain had to concede some ground, and in 1922 Britain granted Egypt a truncated independence that left foreign policy, military defense, and protection of foreign minorities within British hands. Significantly, Britain retained the right to keep troops in the Suez Canal area. This truncated independence coupled with a constitution that gave enormous powers to the King, resulted in a political system wherein political power was divided between three centers that were at loggerheads with each other: the British, the palace, and the Wafd Party, which was the most popular political party that had been behind the 1919 revolution.

In addition to the pressing need to end the occupation, the nationalist movement was also seeking an answer to Egypt's deep economic problems. Despite heavy investment in infrastructure, the agricultural sector was

FIGURE 8.1 Second Lieutenant Gamal Abdel Nasser (center) with fellow members of his army unit in Egypt, 1940. Biblioteca Alexandria. Wikimedia Commons, https://commons.wikimedia.org/wiki/File: Nasser_with_comrades,_1940.jpg.

closely tied to cotton cultivation and was thus vulnerable to the fluctuations in world prices (see chapter 15 in this edited volume). Despite some inroads in industry and an expansion in education, unemployment rates were high and poverty levels abysmal. The massive maldistribution of income was most glaringly obvious with respect to landownership: roughly 6 percent of landowners possessed 65 percent of the cultivated area, while 94 percent of landowners possessed only 35 percent of the land.

Because of a clogged political system and an acute economic and social crisis, the streets of Cairo were abuzz with demonstrators during Nasser's youth. He was so embroiled in street politics that during his last school year he spent only forty-five days in school. Eventually he had to decide what career to pursue, and after enrolling in the Faculty of Law for a month, Nasser decided to apply for, and was admitted to, the Military Academy in March of 1937. He seemed to have found his calling. On graduating, Nasser received his first assignment in Upper Egypt and was later posted in Sudan, Alamein, and Cairo, where he was appointed as an instructor in the staff college.

From the very beginning of his military career, Nasser built on his prior experience as an organizer and agitator. Together with fellow young officers, he engaged in heated conversations about the country's economic, social, and political problems and how these problems were mismanaged. In due time, Nasser and his comrades formed a secret organization that they called the Free Officers. For a while they contemplated assassinations, but they soon realized that the problems their country confronted could not be solved by simply getting rid of some key figures. Eventually, the idea of a coup dominated their secret meetings, and they started plotting concrete plans to take over the government.

Two developments influenced their thought, the first being the disastrous performance of the Egyptian army in the 1948 war against Israel. Under Arab pressure, and despite lack of proper training, equipment, or clear offensive plans, King Farouk sent his army to Palestine to join Syrian and other forces. Nasser and some of his close comrades served in this war. They returned with a deep conviction that the military defeat was ultimately a reflection of the corrupt political system. The second development was the bloodless coup in Syria in March of 1949 led by the chief of staff, Husni al-Za'im. The Syrian coup illustrated to the Free Officers how easy it was to stage a coup—so easy, in fact, that al-Za'im's coup was only the first of three coups in Syria in that year alone.

Since the end of the Second World War in 1945, the regime seemed incapable of dealing with the deepening political crisis, which included armed resistance against the British military base in the Suez Canal area. On January 25, 1952, British troops in Ismailia opened fire on the Egyptian police garrison in the city, killing dozens of policemen and officers. When news of the massacre reached Cairo the following day, Black Saturday, the city was set ablaze with mobs attacking foreign businesses, department stores, cinemas, and night clubs. For the following six months, four successive prime ministers came and went, all failing to pacify the restive streets or to contain the simmering violence. Nasser and his comrades in the Free Officers brought forward their planned coup and decided to strike on the evening of July 23, 1952. The coup turned out to be bloodless, and Egyptians woke to news that their country was now in safe hands. A new dawn of sound democratic principles had begun.

The Free Officers had to act swiftly to consolidate their control. But before they could do so, a crisis suddenly developed that required decisive action. Workers in the Kafr al-Dawwar industrial town in the Delta struck. Believing the new regime would stand by their demands for better wages and shorter hours, these workers beseeched General Muhammad Naguib, a high-ranking officer whom the Free Officers had chosen as their figurehead, to intervene on their behalf. But after consulting with his junior partners, Naguib turned down the workers' request, ordered the army and the police to descend on the town, and arrested the strike leaders. A military tribunal was set up, severe prison sentences were passed, and two workers hanged—all within four weeks of the strike.

The Free Officers sent a clear signal of their firm intention to control the communist and labor movement and, more generally, of their determination to stamp out the wave of popular discontent that, paradoxically, had been instrumental in bringing them to power. But they also had to prevent the ancien régime from regaining its balance. On September 9, 1952, they passed a land reform law that put a limit of two hundred feddans (one feddan is approximately one acre) on land ownership. In a big fanfare the Free Officers announced that expropriated land was to be distributed to landless peasants. In fact, the land was distributed to middle-ranking peasants, who now had to get their seeds and fertilizers from government-controlled cooperatives. The law dealt a serious blow to the landed aristocracy that had dominated the political class for generations.

Before year's end, the 1923 constitution was suspended, and a few weeks later all political parties were abolished. The Free Officers, now reconstituted as the Revolutionary Command Council (RCC), gave itself the right to pass a plethora of laws that significantly reduced public freedoms and fundamentally changed the nature of the Egyptian state. With the successive Syrian coups fresh in his mind, Nasser had to coup-proof the army. He purged the high brass officers and entrusted the army to a close friend, Abdel Hakim Amir. By early 1954 there were widespread calls in the streets and in the press for the army to return to its barracks and for the constitution to be restored. A new wave of purges cleansed the universities, trade unions, newspapers, and professional organizations of all opposition. By November 1954, even Naguib was dismissed from the presidency and put under house arrest, where he remained until 1971.

Nasser now appeared as the most prominent leader of what started to be termed the "revolution." He planned to reach a new treaty with the British that would replace the 1936 treaty that the Wafd Party had abrogated in 1951. He allowed the British to reactivate the Canal base. Using the media that was now firmly under his control, Nasser presented the treaty as a great diplomatic victory. However, only five days after signing the treaty, and while delivering a speech in Alexandria, there was an attempt on Nasser's life. Eight shots were fired, but they all missed their target. The assailant turned out to be a member of the Muslim Brotherhood, which had earlier denounced Nasser for not being firm enough in his negotiations with the British.

The assailant and five leaders of the Brotherhood were sentenced to death by military tribunal. The regime used the incident to try to completely destroy the Brotherhood: the group's assets were confiscated, and thousands of members were rounded up and subjected to indescribable torture in police dungeons. With the Brotherhood decimated, the last source of opposition was silenced. In a little over two years Nasser's regime had managed to consolidate its hold over the country and had succeeded in putting a lid over the spirited popular movement of the previous decade that had threatened to take Egypt along the path of a radical social revolution.

INTERNATIONAL INTRUSIONS

Two developments unfolded in rapid succession in 1954–56 that catapulted him to world fame and put him on the pantheon of Third World leaders alongside Tito of Yugoslavia, Nehru of India, Nkrumah of Ghana, and Sukarno of Indonesia. The first of these two alarming developments was Israel's belligerent activities on the borders with Egypt, and the second was the West's insistence on drawing Egypt into a military pact that was hoped to be a bulwark against Soviet global expansion.

Ever since the end of the first Arab-Israeli War in 1948, the meager Egyptian force in the Gaza Strip could not prevent tensions at the Gaza border between Palestinians and Israelis. Exacerbating Nasser's frustration was a tripartite declaration of arms control that the United States, Britain, and France (1950) aimed at maintaining the military balance between Israel and the Arab states. In reality, Nasser knew that Britain, the United States, and later France were selling sophisticated weapons to Israel at such a scale that the balance was decisively tipped in Israel's favor. Israel disproportionately asserted its military might against Palestinians and also hatched an infamous plot known as "The Lavon Affair"—so named after the Israeli defense minister, Pinhas Lavon, who had authorized the plot, to attack British and American targets inside Egypt so that the British would rethink the withdrawal of their troops from the Suez Canal region.

With his inability to deter Israel due to the Western arms embargo, Nasser appeared vulnerable and his young regime looked shaky. He set out to acquire weapons with which to deter Israel. However, not only did he fail to secure weapons from the West, Nasser also found himself under relentless pressure to join a military pact that Britain had been planning as a bulwark against Soviet expansion. Much to his chagrin, Britain cobbled together the "northern tier" (which included Middle Eastern countries, Pakistan, Iran, Iraq, and Turkey) to form what came to be known as the "Baghdad Pact," whose formation was announced on February 22, 1955. Nasser was particularly furious that Nuri al-Said, the prime minister of Iraq, agreed to join the pact, and a serious rift ensued between the two leaders. Nasser thought al-Said had been undermining his efforts to exploit Arab aggregate bargaining powers. Al-Said, however, thought that Nasser was unrealistic and that the West would never sell arms to the Arabs without the Arabs making some defense commitments. To make things worse, only a week after the signing of the Baghdad Pact, the Israelis launched yet another raid, this time against the Egyptian military camp in the Gaza Strip. Thirty-six Egyptian soldiers, twenty-nine Palestinian soldiers, and two civilians were killed.

Six weeks later, Nasser finally found a solution to his deep sense of vulnerability in the face of Israeli aggression. From April 18 to 24, 1955, the first Afro-Asian Conference convened in Bandung, Indonesia. This conference was comprised of twenty-nine countries, many of whom had recently gained their independence from European colonial rule. Their leaders gathered to promote Afro-Asian economic and cultural cooperation. Nasser was greeted with exceptional warmth and respect due to his firm stance against colonialism and his pledge to support independence movements, most notably the struggle of the Algerians to end the French occupation of their country that had lasted for more than 120 years. Bandung offered Nasser the opportunity to make his first contact with a communist leader in the form of Chou En-lai, the Chinese prime minister. Nasser asked Chou En-lai if China could supply Egypt with weapons, a request passed on to the Soviets. In due time, the Soviets agreed to supply Nasser with weapons, albeit under Czech cover. The "Czech arms deal" was announced on September 24, 1955, and Egypt received advanced Soviet planes, tanks, and guns that seriously challenged Israel's superiority and promised to redress the imbalance of power in the region.

But the significance of Bandung was not limited to the arms deal. Fellow leaders of newly independent states echoed Nasser's deep hostility to Western colonialism and the polarization brought about by the Cold War. They supported Nasser's reluctance to enter into military pacts with Britain and the United States. On his trip back home, Nasser stopped in India and received a warm welcome from the Indian prime minister, Jawaharlal Nehru. On his return to Egypt, Nasser received a rapturous welcome. He later remarked: "My visit to India was the turning point in my political understanding. I learned and recognized that the only wise policy for us consisted in adopting positive neutralism and nonalignment. On my return home, the reception that greeted this policy convinced me that it was the sole possible policy that could attract the broadest support of the Arab people."[1]

Feeling increasingly confident after Bandung, Nasser appeared to have come up with a formula to bolster his young regime: a domestic policy built on social and economic reform, political repression coupled with tight media control, and a foreign policy built on opposition to old imperial powers, resistance to military pacts, and strong support of independence and anticolonial movements. However, with the land reform of 1952 affecting only 10 percent of cultivated land and having little or no impact on Egypt's landless peasants, Nasser felt the need to launch a more drastic policy, which culminated in the Aswan High Dam project. Building a high dam across the Nile in the south of the country, it was believed, would not only harness the destructive impact of the annual floods of the Nile but significantly increase the area of cultivatable land. Moreover, it would generate electricity to Egypt's four thousand villages that lacked basic amenities like potable water, lighting, and sewage, while allowing for the industrialization of the entire country. It was hoped that the High Dam would transform the economy from being an agrarian one shackled by feudal relations to a modern industrial economy.

Egypt could not finance this ambitious project alone. The Soviet Union presented an offer to finance the project in 1955, but Nasser preferred to negotiate with the United States and the UK for a loan from the World Bank. However, the United States withdrew its offer, hinting at the weak creditworthiness of the Egyptian economy, but it was deeply suspected that the main reason was the Czech arms deal of the previous fall. Nasser received the US withdrawal as a personal snub. Just one week later, he retaliated in a grand manner. In a speech on July 26, 1956, he announced the nationalization of the Suez Canal company. The Canal had always been a sensitive point in Egypt and a rallying cry for Egyptian nationalism. Although the Canal Company was at least nominally an Egyptian company, most of the proceeds were invested in Britain and France. Nasser thought that nationalizing the Suez Canal company would both answer the insulting US message and also raise enough funds to finance the High Dam project.

Legal nationalization was seen in the West as a challenge to its economic dominance and a defiance of its political influence and invited the possibility of retaliation. Nasser was well aware of the risks involved. Only three years earlier, in 1953, Mohammad Mosaddegh, Iran's democratically elected prime minister, had nationalized his country's oil industry only to be forcibly removed from power by a coup planned and executed by the US Central Intelligence Agency (CIA) and the UK Secret Intelligence Agency (MI6). The West's retaliation to the nationalization of the Suez Canal Company came with a fury and wrath that left an indelible mark on Nasser's legacy and the history of European imperialism. What gave this retaliation a peculiar twist was Israel's central contribution to it.

Anxious about the rising star of Nasser within the Arab world and the possibility of rallying support behind the Palestinians, and alarmed by the Czech arms deal that had challenged Israel's considerable military advantage, Israeli prime minister David Ben Gurion was determined to strike at the Egyptian military before Egyptian officers and pilots had had time to absorb the new military technology they had just acquired. He opened negotiations with France, first, to buy extra arms to regain the edge Israel had enjoyed and, second, to coordinate a possible joint military attack on Egypt. The request fell on receptive ears given that France had been deeply irritated by Nasser's support of the Algerian War of Independence that had been launched two years earlier.

Both countries approached British prime minister Anthony Eden to join the planned military operation against Egypt. Without consulting parliament, informing his American allies, or seeking authorization from the UN Security Council, Eden joined the conspiracy. In a secret meeting in a villa near Paris, the three governments conspired to launch military operations against Egypt with the aim of bringing down Nasser and installing a friendly regime in Cairo. Military operations started according to plan on October 29. The picture looked very grim, especially after the Israelis managed to capture the entire Sinai Peninsula and join British and French troops at the Suez Canal.

Nasser's response was firm and defiant. He delivered a resounding speech in Cairo's thousand-year-old mosque, al-Azhar, declaring that he would not surrender. Nasser asked for popular resistance against the invaders. Diplomatically, he came out victorious. The British and others publics were enraged at this "Tripartite Aggression," as the Suez campaign came to be known in Egypt. The United States and the Soviet Union were also strongly opposed to the joint Israeli-British-French action that raised the possibility of a clash between the two nuclear superpowers. A UN General Assembly resolution set up a special force, the United Nations Emergency Force (UNEF), and both superpowers put pressure on all three invading countries to withdraw their troops. Britain and France soon complied, with the British prime minister ultimately forced to resign. Israel procrastinated but finally withdrew its army from Sinai in March 1957 after the United States guaranteed free navigation through the Gulf of Aqaba.

Despite this important diplomatic victory, Nasser retained a firm grip on political life in Egypt. If anything, political repression got worse. The state of emergency that the Wafd government declared in 1952 was lifted only briefly during Nasser's eighteen years in power. Security agencies proliferated and competed with each other. Exceptional courts were established, and opponents of the regime ended up receiving prison sentences, their property confiscated, and their political rights stripped away. Basic freedoms were severely curtailed, and the rights of free expression, of assembly, of free movement, and of industrial action and collective bargaining were drastically reduced. In a single-candidate referendum held in June 1956, Nasser was elected president of the republic with a 99.99 percent majority.

ENTERING THE GLOBAL STAGE

Globally, the Suez crisis catapulted Nasser to world fame given his defiant posture as well as his skill and tenacity during the long diplomatic negotiations that followed the withdrawal of the invading armies. His reputation skyrocketed across the Arab world in particular. Many in the region viewed him as the only leader capable of bringing about Arab unity. In this context a group of Syrian army officers who feared a communist takeover in their own country flew secretly to Cairo in January 1958 to urge Nasser to form a union with Syria. Nasser initially resisted, but he finally agreed to merge the two countries. On February 22, 1958, the United Arab Republic was formed with

Nasser as its president. But this union was short-lived, for only three years later a group of Syrian army officers staged a coup against Nasser's authority. They were backed up by a large segment of the Syrian middle classes who were hard-hit by Nasser's land reform and other economic policies. The breakup of the union was, by Nasser's own admission, a serious blow. While he enjoyed overwhelming popularity among Arab masses, the monarchical regimes in Saudi Arabia, Jordan, Yemen, Libya, and Morocco, as well as the republican regimes of Iraq and Syria, resented his domineering character and revolutionary fervor.

An auspicious event in September 1962 promised to reverse Nasser's fortunes and restore his injured pride. A group of army officers from Yemen staged a coup against the theocratic ruler Imam Ahmed and declared a republic. The Imam fled to the mountains and sought financial and military assistance from Saudi Arabia. The coup leaders sought assistance from Nasser, who was only too eager to lend a hand. He tried to regain in Yemen what he had lost in Syria, and was aware that southern Arabia was a new regional frontier in the struggle against Western imperialism. After losing the Suez Canal base, Britain had been bolstering its presence in Aden, a port the country had controlled since 1838 which protected Britain's interests in the Persian Gulf. Since the early 1950s, the United States had been establishing stronger ties with the Saudi monarchy, both to secure a cheap and steady supply of oil and as a bulwark against Soviet expansion in the region.

Nasser found himself embroiled in a messy and costly civil war that soon developed into a war by proxy. The new revolutionary regime confronted the Yemeni royalists who were backed by Saudi Arabia, Britain, the United States, and even Israel. Over the following five years, more than seventy thousand Egyptian troops were sent to that quagmire, ten thousand of whom died in what was seen as Nasser's Vietnam. To make things worse, the economic and political situation in Egypt was deteriorating. Following the Suez crisis, British-, French-, and Jewish-owned property was confiscated. A large number of private firms, banks, and insurance companies were nationalized, and the public sector was tasked with leading the much-needed process of economic development, but with disappointing results.

The lack of a viable political system made matters worse. With no permanent constitution, and with a parliament that sat for no more than five of his eighteen years of rule, Nasser ruled mostly by decree. He personally presided over many of his cabinets, doubling as prime minister. Despite his overwhelming popularity, he never trusted the people nor allowed them to participate in any meaningful process of self-rule. Furthermore, not only did he ban political parties, but he failed to establish a state-controlled political organization that would galvanize his popular support. Instead, Nasser was behind the secret body the Vanguard Organization to spy on his rivals in both the government and the army.

By the mid-1960s, his regime was under enormous strain. His autocratic rule had deprived him of effective mechanisms to deal with the growing domestic, regional, and global problems. Even with a growing cadre of detractors, it was the army that caused the most ominous threat to his regime. When Nasser entrusted the army to his close and loyal friend, Abdel-Hakim Amir, he did not anticipate that Amir would use the army to build a base for his own power and seal off the army from any form of supervision or oversight, including by Nasser. The army had slipped out of Nasser's control, and Amir effectively created what was referred to as "a state within a state."

This rivalry between these two power centers within Egypt led to the disaster of June 1967. Without Nasser's authorization, Amir undertook a series of escalatory measures against Israel that dramatically increased the possibility of military confrontation. Following an aerial battle over Damascus in April in which Israel downed six Syrian fighters, Amir mobilized the Egyptian army and ordered it into Sinai on May 14. Two days later, Nasser, under pressure from Amir, ordered the UN peace-keeping troops, UNEF, which had been stationed in Sinai since 1956, to be redeployed. Amir deliberately manipulated the English translation of Nasser's letter to the UN replacing the word "redeployment" with "withdrawal." Most dangerously, on May 22, in response to Amir's accusation of being weak, Nasser announced the closure of the Gulf of Aqaba to Israeli navigation, something that Israel took to be a casus belli. Finally, Amir drafted a hasty offensive plan to attack the Negev and capture the southern Israeli port of Eilat. When Nasser got wind of this plan, he reprimanded Amir and scrapped the plan.

Amir was playing with fire, determined to avenge his 1956 defeat by Israel (he once said that he had a personal vendetta with his Israeli counterpart, General Moshe Dayan). Nasser's old buddy had now turned rival. In the meantime, Israel saw this reckless escalation as a golden opportunity to deal Nasser a death blow. Its military had been armed to the teeth, and the generals were confident that they could finish off Nasser's army within a week. However, the army first needed the green light from Israel's civilian cabinet headed by Prime Minister Levi Eshkol and the United States to avoid the scenario of 1956 when, they believed, the United States interfered diplomatically to deprive Israel of military victory. Meir Amit, the chief of the Mossad (Israel's military intelligence), flew to Washington and met senior military and intelligence officials. While not exactly giving Amit a green light, they gave an amber one. Back in Israel, Amit reported to a small group at the Israeli prime minister's house that he had the impression "that the Americans would welcome an operation if we succeed in smashing Nasser."

Nasser, however, proved to be difficult to smash. Even when his air force was wiped out on June 5, his army was destroyed two days later, he admitted responsibility for the crushing defeat and announced his resignation to the Egyptian people, the genuine outpour of solidarity and support he received on June 9 and 10 from the masses in Egypt and many other Arab countries prompted him to rescind his resignation and return to office to fight another day. General Dayan is reported to have said that he was waiting for a phone call from Nasser, ostensibly to receive terms of capitulation and defeat. Nasser, however, never made that call. Instead, Nasser finally got rid of Abdel Hakim Amir (who on September 13 committed suicide, or "was suicided" as the joke went in Egypt), mended his ways with other Arab leaders (and thus received desperately needed funds), and started the arduous processes of rebuilding his shattered army. However, despite calls for a political opening to allow Egyptians a say in ruling their own country, Nasser was adamant to undertake the herculean task single-handedly. On September 28, 1970, he died from a severe heart attack.

Nasser was only fifty-two years old, and news of his sudden death drove millions (some say up to seven million) to march in his funeral. His remarkable achievements—toppling the corrupt monarchy, ending the seventy-year-long British occupation, championing the rights of the poor and the needy, establishing an Arab regional order, defying imperialism in Suez, and advocating Third Worldism—secured him a place in the hearts of millions of Egyptians, Arabs, Africans, and others worldwide. However, his serious shortcomings—curtailing basic democratic rights, eroding the institutions of the state, failing to resolve Egypt's economic problems, and, above all, losing his confrontation with Israel—meant that his legacy remains contested among Egyptians even today. It is no accident that no statue of Nasser exists in Cairo, and it is telling that any suggestion to name Cairo Airport after him would prove divisive and controversial. Nearly fifty years after his death, Nasser remains a uniquely inspiring leader to many Egyptians, while many of their fellow compatriots see him as a deeply flawed and detested tyrant.

NOTE

1. Kristin S. Tassin, "'Lift up Your Head, My Brother': Nationalism and the Genesis of the Non-Aligned Movement," *Journal of Third World Studies* 23, no. 1 (Spring 2006): 157.

FURTHER READING

Aburish, Saïd K. *Nasser: The Last Arab.* London: Duckworth, 2005.

Beattie, Kirk. *Egypt during the Nasser Years: Ideology, Politics, and Civil Society.* Boulder, CO: Westview Press, 1994.

Gordon, Joel. *Nasser: Hero of the Arab Nation.* Oxford, UK: Oneworld Publications, 2006.

Kandil, Hazem. *Soldiers, Spies, and Statesmen: Egypt's Road to Revolt.* London: Verso, 2012.

Nutting, Anthony. *Nasser.* London: Constable, 1972.

Stephens, Robert. *Nasser: A Political Biography.* London: Penguin, 1971.

Younis, Sherif. *Nida' al-Sha'b: Tarikh Naqdi lil-Idologiyya al-Nasiriyya.* Cairo: al-Shoruq, 2012.

PART FOUR

Food, Film, Fashion, Music

NINE

Circuits of Food and Cuisine

Sami Zubaida

CULINARY CULTURES, INGREDIENTS, methods, and tastes are shaped by global processes of exchange, mixing, and technical innovations. Globalization is not peculiar to the modern age. Empires from the most ancient times were instrumental in bringing together and mixing different regions and cultures. The production, commerce, consumption, and art of food have all been linked to imperial power—from the Roman, the Byzantine, the Persian, then successive Muslim empires, culminating in the Ottomans, and most spectacularly, the capitalist empires of which the British was the most thorough. What distinguishes the global in our own time is the speed and scope of diffusions and transformations.

The complex, stratified societies engendered by empire include elites of consumption to whom luxuries and refinements, notably of food and drink, become markers of distinction and status. These elites sharpen the drive for innovation and the quest for rare ingredients. Historically, spices became valued ingredients in the consumption patterns of the rich in most regions, and as such valuable commodities fueling trade and navigation, from Roman times and into early modern Europe and the Middle East. The Muslim conquests, starting in the seventh century, established a succession of dynasties and empires which at first unified this region and connected it to far-flung parts of the Old World by conquest and trade. The formation of a "global Middle East" (with the caveat that the term "Middle East" is a construction of the nineteenth-century colonial period) started before this date in the preceding empires but was spectacularly enlarged and complicated with the Muslim empires. I use the term "Muslim empires" uneasily. They comprised many peoples who were not Muslim, and many Muslims who did not participate in their religious capacity. Even more category problems would arise if

FIGURE 9.1 Abbasid chicken, detail from *'Aja'ib al-Makhluqat*, thirteenth century. Smithsonian Institution, 1954.

we called them "Arab," however, given that the Persian element was a prominent constituent, as was Syriac, Greek, Berber, Jewish, and later Turkish. On balance, the designation "Muslim" refers to the rulers and institutions.

The dynasties of the Muslim empires dominated the lands of the preceding Byzantine and Persian empires and incorporated many elements of their institutions and cultures as well as personnel. They further extended their territories, east as far as India (Muslim incursions into Sind in the northwest in the eight century) and west into North Africa and Spain (conquered 711–56, then ruled and settled, in various parts till 1481). Baghdad, the center of the Abbasid Empire (750–1258), had an estimated population of a million people at the height of its "golden age" in the eighth through the tenth century. This cosmopolitan center comprised many ethnicities and cultures and was a hub for wide-ranging trade of arts and crafts as well as ideas and intellectual currents. The Caliphal court was modeled in many respects on that of the preceding Sassanid Empire (224–651 AD). This included food and drink.

Baghdad, like other urban imperial centers in later centuries, was the beneficiary of circuits of ideas and goods—including food ingredients—which qualify as "global." Rice, hard (durum) wheat, sugarcane, citrus fruit, spinach, and aubergine were just some of the food items brought into the Middle East region from further east, mostly from India, Assam, and Southeast Asia. Rice, for instance, probably originated in China, Burma, and Thailand, and was diffused through India. It was likely known in parts of the Middle East, such as Sassanian Iran, before Islamic times. But with limited areas of cultivation, its widespread and expanded use happened under the Abbasids and subsequent times. Rice was then carried by the Muslim expansion into Europe, Iberia, and Sicily.

We have manuscripts of treatises on food and medicine, including a courtly recipe manual, *Kitab al-Tabikh* (The book of cookery), reputedly written by a prince of the Abbasid house. Elaborate recipes abound with luxurious ingredients that include a diversity of meats in stews, dumplings and oven (*tanur*) cookery, amply seasoned with a wide variety of spices and sauces, oils and fats (olive, sesame, rendered sheep tail, and clarified butter). Dough and meat combinations are made into different bread and pastry concoctions. Descriptions of opulent banquets are plentiful in literary texts; the food and drink are interlaced with music, song, and poetic recitations describing and extoling the food.[1]

LANGUAGE AND LINEAGE

We find the names of ingredients and dishes traveling over wide areas, often from original Middle East locations. When it comes to dishes, the same label may slip from one designation to another. Examples of diffusion of names of ingredients include rice, *arruz* in Arabic, *arroz* in Spanish, *riso* in Italian; sugar, *sukkar, shaker, azucar, zucchero, sucre*. Aubergine, probably deriving from the Indian *brinjal/bengan*, in turn coming from a Sanskrit origin, is rendered *badinjan* in Arabic and Persian, *patlican* in Turkish, *berenjano* in Spanish, *melanzana* in Italian.[2]

The association of aubergine with Arabs in Spain is illustrated by a "moor" character in *Don Quixote* (the seventeenth-century Spanish classic) with the name "Sayed Hamid the aubergine eater!" (Cide Hamete Beningeli). There are many other examples of food designations diffused through Muslim expansion, such as that of citrus fruit, from *narinj*, bitter orange, and *limu* for lime, to *naranja, limon* and lemon; the sweet orange was a much later introduction (mid-sixteenth century) from China or India, and its name in all Middle Eastern languages associate it with Portugal: *burtuqal* in Arabic, which may indicate Portuguese diffusion from the east.[3]

The wide diffusion of the designation *burani/borane* and its variants illustrates the globalization of elements of food culture from Medieval times.

Food historian Charles Perry has traced the origins of the designation to the princess Buran, daughter of the vezir al-Hassan ibn Sahl and her lavish wedding party to the Abbasid Caliph Al-Ma'mun (son of Harun al-Rashid) in 825. There is no contemporary record of the food eaten at this feast. The designation *burani*, then *buraniyya*, is spread to all parts of the Medieval Islamic world, into Spain, then to Ottoman lands including the Balkans and the Caucasus. It starts appearing in cookery recipes in the tenth-century *Kitab al-tabikh* (The book of cookery) by one Al-Sayyar, from the Abbasid house, and relating the recipes, banquets, and anecdotes of Abbasid princely and high society. *Burani* appears in this work as a simple dish of fried aubergine.

Perry speculates that aubergine, new to the Muslim world in the ninth century, may have been an item in the wedding feast, thus giving the recipe name the honorific reference to Buran. This is especially significant in a context in which the vegetable received a largely hostile reception at its inception, due to its bitter taste and suspicion of poisonous content. Al-Sayyar's recipe was the first to require that the cut aubergine is first salted, drawing out the bitter juices—a procedure that became standard till recent times and the breeding of new varieties without the bitterness. Subsequent recipe books, in the thirteenth and fifteenth centuries, contain ever more elaborate dishes involving aubergine in various combinations with meat and stuffing. Dishes labeled a version of "*burani*" are currently found in the Arab world, Iran, Turkey, Central Asia, and Bulgaria, among other places.

A regular item in the medieval cookery manuals is a dish called *sikbaj*, basically of meat cooked in vinegar, with various additions of vegetables, spices, dried fruit, and honey. Its origin is attributed to the preceding Sassanid court, where it is claimed was a favorite of the king Khosrau I Anushirvan, continuing to be in royal favor under the Arab dynasties.[4] The word is Persian, consisting of *sirke* for "vinegar" and *bag/baj/ba* for "stew." The rich ate a sumptuous *sikbaj* with meat and all the luxurious ingredients, but the poor had their own austere versions. In his *Book of Misers* (ninth century), Al-Jahiz relates that Khorasani workers in Basra (Khorasan province in northeast Iran) would club together to buy meat and vegetables, which they would boil in vinegar, then proceed to eat one ingredient each day: onions, leeks, carrots, and save the meat for Friday. Part of these innovations was to substitute meat for fish among sailors and coastal communities as well as Christians adapting it for fasting days. Fish *sikbaj* recipes appear in later (thirteenth century) cookery manuals, some specifying fish, dragged in flour, fried, then marinated in vinegar, vegetables, and aromatics, which would also preserve the fish for later consumption.[5]

Sikbaj disappears from the Middle Eastern food scenes in later centuries: it is now only known in dictionaries and histories. The Spanish *escabeche*, established in Iberia by the fifteenth century, is most likely a descendant of *sikbaj*. It is typically fish, often fried, marinated in a sweet vinegar, onion, and aromatics, eaten cold. Fish/vinegar combinations are also recorded in Italy, France, and even further north in Europe with labels resembling *escabeche*, such as *scabeg* and *scabeccio*. There is speculation that the word "aspic," fish in jelly, is similarly derived.[6] When Sephardic Jews settled in England in the eighteenth century, they introduced a fish dish similar to *escabeche*. Hanna Glass's 1796 cookery manual, *The Art of Cookery, Made Plain and Easy*, includes a recipe on the "Jews Way of preserving salmon," which directs dipping the fish in eggy batter, frying it in oil, then preserving it in vinegar for later consumption. By the mid-nineteenth century there are accounts of Jews selling cold battered fried fish in London's East End, then later in the century combined with fried potatoes. However, no mention here of vinegar, except perhaps as a condiment. It is well attested that the Japanese tempura (fish, seafood, and vegetable fried in crisp batter) was introduced by the Portuguese in the mid-eighteenth century.[7] Can we, however, reasonably attribute all battered fried fish to the *sikbaj/escabeche* lineage? From ancient Sassanid Persia, through the Muslim empires, into Iberia and further in Europe, then into the New World, and possibly contributing to the ancestry of fish-and-chips, *sikbaj* is a spectacular example of the global Middle East in food and gastronomy.

The commonly related story that pasta originates in Chinese noodles carried to Italy by Marco Polo is apocryphal, not being supported by any evidence. "Pasta" is a modern category, the word derived from the word for "paste" or "dough," which comprises diverse dishes of different forms and provenance. Hard wheat (durum), as distinct from the soft bread wheats, probably originated in Abyssinia (current-day Ethiopia) but was widely diffused in the Middle East and the Muslim Mediterranean, including Spain, by the tenth century. It was also established in Sicily, from whence it and its pasta products spread north to the rest of Italy. It is a basic ingredient of many of the dishes in the region and around the Mediterranean: semolina, couscous, burghul/bulgur (cracked wheat), and ultimately so-called *pasta secca*, dry pasta such as spaghetti/macaroni.[8]

Sicily was ruled by Muslim dynasties from 902 to 1061. It then fell to

Norman kings, who, for the subsequent century or more, retained a strong Muslim presence in the court and in society, profiting from their skills in arts and crafts. One prominent intellectual in the service of the Norman Roger II was Muhammad Al-Idrisi (1100–1165), traveler, geographer, and cartographer, who plotted a map of the world on a silver disk, commissioned by Roger, and authored a book of geography, *Pleasant Journeys for Him Who Longs to Cross the Horizons* (Nizhat al-mushtaq fi-ikhtiraq al-afaq). It is in this book that John Dickie, the historian of Italian food, found an indication of the manufacture and export of dry pasta. Idrisi wrote on the town of Trabia, with flowing streams driving a number of mills: "Here there are huge buildings in the countryside where they make vast quantities of *itriya*, which is exported everywhere: to Calabria, to Muslim and Christian countries. Very many shiploads are sent."[9]

Itriya or *alitriya* is an Arabic word for long thin strands of dried dough that were boiled in soups and paired with other ingredients in various preparations. Although the word was in use in earlier sources of cookery and medical manuals, it is not clear when it was made from hard wheat. But it certainly was in Idrisi's Sicily where hard wheat culture had been established for some time, and one that the island eventually exported to the rest of Italy and further afield. Derivatives from the word *itriya*, such as *tria*, survive in Italy, with other variants in Spanish. Other words used for pasta in the Middle East also survived in Spain and elsewhere, most notably *fidawsh*, now *fideos*, a kind of vermicelli cooked in Spain. The Persian *rashta* for types of pasta in soup is still in use.

MOVEMENT TO THE EAST

The Middle East was connected to India, Central Asia, and China by networks of empire and trade, and food and drink cultures and vocabularies traveled on these axes. The Mongolian invasions and conquests, starting in the thirteenth century, wreaked much destruction, notably the sack of Baghdad in 1258, which ended the Abbasid Caliphate. Once settled, however, the connections between the different outposts acted as conduits for trade and cultures as well as war. Branches of the Mongol khanates established their rule in the old imperial centers in China, Persia, and Central Asia, adopting the courtly cultures of the conquered empires, including sophisticated cuisines. Ingredients, methods, and labor were moved across these regions. Tea, for instance, is thought to have been first carried to the Middle East along these routes. The *tannur/tandur* clay oven—now familiar in India/Pakistan, Turkey (tandir), Iran, Central Asia, the Caucasus, and much of the Arab world—most probably originated in ancient Mesopotamia, the word traced by linguists to the Akkadian *tinuru*, indicating clay and fire.

The Mughal Empire in India (1526–1857) created cultural syntheses, including food and drink, which contained many Middle Eastern elements. The Mughals came from Central Asia, Samarkand to be precise. They spoke a Turkic dialect, but the language of culture and refinement was Persian. This language remained dominant in Indian courts, and among aristocracies and intellectuals till the twentieth century. What may be discerned as a Turko-Iranian world was bringing together what are now Iran, Afghanistan, and parts of India and Central Asia in common cultural and linguistic themes, under diverse dynasties that combined these elements.

The culinary style of the Mughals had much to do with the nomads and the steppes, highlighting meat cooked simply by grilling and boiling. The refinement came mostly from Persian sources, especially after the long exile of Humayun, the second emperor, in Kabul and the Safavid court in Iran (1540–55). He returned with an entourage of Persian courtiers, craftsmen, and cooks. The elaborate rice cookery of Safavid courts enriched the much simpler Indian styles. The fusion that followed combined Indian spicing with Persian arts, giving rise to the rich Pulaos and Biryanis. Korma, a rich stew of meat in cream/yoghurt sauce with ground almonds, is one of the stars of the North Indian kitchen. The word "korma" originates from the Turkish *qawurma*, which designates a number of meat dishes, but most notably of meat (typically mutton) salted, cooked, and conserved in its fat (much like the French confit), stored in jars or goat skins for winter consumption, added to various concoctions for richness. This is prepared and consumed to the present day in Anatolia, the Arab Levant, Kurdistan, and northern Iraq. The word emerges in Iran as *ghorma*, as in the much loved *ghorma sabzi*, the green stew of mutton cooked in butter fat with minced aromatic herbs and dried limes. The word "korma" shifted its meaning in travel across the regions but retained the connotation or rich meat stew in fat, butter, or cream.

The food historian Rachel Laudan has offered an intriguing map of the distribution of one genre of food, the dumpling of wheat dough stuffed with meat mixtures, boiled or fried, mapped onto the extent of the Mongol empire: the *manti* of Central Asia and Turkey, the *burek* family (Turkey and the Arab Levant), the samosa/*sanbusak* of Middle East/India, the *chuch-*

vara of Central Asia becoming *shish-barak* in modern-day Arab Levant, the Pelmeni of Russia; and their descendants, the ravioli, the kreplach (Ashkenazi Jewish), and the gyoza (Japan). This is an ambitious and speculative map but suggestive.[10] It does not, of course, imply a single origin but a pattern of diffusion and influence.

DRINK

Despite the well-known religious prohibition or discouragement of alcoholic drink in Islam, it is a central feature of the Middle East's contribution to world consumption and civilization. The word "alcohol" derives from the Arabic *al-kuhl* (antimony eyeliner), perhaps because spirits were used as solvents for the material, as for other medicinal uses, or as a metaphor for purity. The tension between commandment and practice offered a fertile theme for poetry, narrative, mysticism, and humor. Alcohol and the imagery of intoxication are common elements in the lore of Sufi mysticism. Classical belles-lettres narratives and essays feature tales and humor about drink. A whole genre of poetry, known as *khamriyyat*, after *khamr* for wine, appears throughout Muslim history. The poetry of Abu Nuwas (d. 815) is but one prominent example of the wine literature genre. Books of etiquette (*adab*) elaborate the arts of good company of boon companions, as books of medicine specified the health benefits of moderate drink and its place in the humoral balances of body and diet.

From earliest times, beer was a central element of Mesopotamian diet and culture. It was a regular item of diet, as well as of recreation and intoxication, much celebrated in poetry and song, and part of religious rituals and temple offerings to the gods. Beer featured prominently in the first written records on clay tablets in Sumerian and Akkadian from the fourth millennium BCE. In the Mesopotamian epic of Gilgamesh, considered the earliest work of literature, the character Enkido starts as a wild creature, at one with nature and the animals, but becomes human after getting drunk on beer. Grains, wheat, and barley were central to this culture that produced a variety of breads and porridges. Beer was made from fermented barley and flavored with various sweeteners of fruit, honey, and aromatics. The materials and methods for making beer spread widely in the ancient world. It may have been developed independently in ancient Egypt. The Akkadian word for beer was *shikaru*. The linguist Dan Jurafsky has traced the mutations of this word through the

Hebrew biblical *sheker*, also meaning flavored beer, used as libations in rituals, then the Latin *sicera*, defined as beer, mead, or fruit ciders, and ultimately the French *cidre* and English cider.[11]

The origins of grape wine are traced to the Caucasus, Georgia, and Armenia, where the wild grape was first domesticated. The earliest chemical traces were found on sites in the Iranian Zargos mountains, dating to 5000 BCE. The region also contributed to many aspects of the creation and consumption of distilled spirits. The earliest clear record of distilled spirit from wine date to the ninth century in Abbasid Iraq, first by the alchemist Jaber ibn Hayan (721–815), known in Medieval Europe as Gebr. He produced flammable vapor from a distilling pot called *al-imbiq*, a word of Greek origin, subsequently "alembic" in Europe. It is not clear at what point this pure "spirit" was drunk recreationally, as distinct from being used in alchemical procedures and for medicines. There is a possible indication of recreational drinking in one anecdote from the aforementioned poet Abu Nuwas: calling for ever stronger drink in a Baghdad tavern, he ends up with a liquor that was "as hot between the ribs as a firebrand." Otherwise, there is little indication of widespread spirit drinking till later centuries, across much of the old world, including Europe. Sicily was probably the entry point of distillation under Arab rule in the eleventh century.

The Arabic word *araq* (which means "sweat") was used to designate spirituous drink. It is an apt metaphor for the process of distillation, referring to the condensation of the vapor into spirit. That word spread in many parts of the world to describe various local distillations, from fermented mare's milk in fourteenth-century Mongolia to distilled palm wine in many parts of South Asia to fermented dates in parts of Africa and the Middle East. The personnel of the British East India Company in India were drinking "arak" distilled from palm wine, and the British and Dutch seafarers were drinking it from the seventeenth century, before rum and gin. Jurafsky relates an interesting story of the invention of arak in Southeast Asia and its transmission to the British and the Dutch.

Chinese settlers in Java established factories for making sauces (the origins of soy sauce, fish sauce, and ketchup), by fermenting red rice, molasses, and soy. Some had the good idea of distilling this fermented combination into drinkable spirit. This was eventually discovered by British and Dutch merchants who thought it a brilliant substitute for the wine and beer then drunk on ships, which spoiled and soured in hot weather: the arak was stable. While distilled spirit, such as whiskey, existed in Britain at the time especially on the Celtic fringes, it was not widely known or drunk. Arak became a favored drink for the seafarers and was enhanced as a cocktail mixed with the lemon that was supplied against scurvy.[12]

The Arabic designation "Arak" may have been carried by Arab and Muslim merchants and dhows that traversed many parts. The spread of the word and its derivatives survives to the present time. "Arak" in the Arab world now designates the well-known aniseed-flavored, grape-based spirit, with Lebanon as the major producer of increasingly refined brands. The Turkish word *raki* is derived from *araki* and is the national drink of the country and the favored tipple of Mustaf Kemal Ataturk (1881–1938), founder of the modern republic. The word *raki* becomes *rakia* in Balkan and East European countries, designating a variety of spirits, mostly fruit-based, like plum brandy. In Iran *arak* is a vodka-like drink. Arak then, the substance and the word, are among the notable global exports of the Middle East region. It is, perhaps, ironic that the words "alcohol" and "arak" originate in a region of Muslim-majority population, where the religious prohibition on alcohol had been widely bypassed, but where it is becoming for many today an identity issue.

Coffee, the now ubiquitous drink all over the world, probably originated in Ethiopia or Yemen. Its diffusion in the Middle East and Europe, from the sixteenth century, proceeded in Ottoman lands. Coffee and coffeehouses were at first viewed with suspicion by religious and political authorities. Coffee was thought to be an intoxicant, and the word *qahwa* ("coffee" in Arabic) was previously applied to wine. Coffeehouses were suspect because they offered free social spaces, considered subversive, a theme that persists into modern times. Nevertheless, coffee became a favored beverage, with many social rituals around its consumption. Coffeehouses are a prominent part of the landscape of Middle Eastern cities. They spread into Europe and have become important social institutions of the public sphere. Coffeehouses represent another crucial contribution of the Middle East to global developments.

THE GLOBALIZED CULINARY CULTURE

Over the past decades we have observed a veritable revolution in the spheres of food and drink in the West and beyond. Food has become a major sphere of recreation and spectacle. Cook books, TV shows, social media blogs, Instagram posts, and much else have become regular features of the gastronomic sphere. What were exotic ingredients and dishes until recent times have become banalized. Supermarket shelves and specialist purveyors have kept pace with ever novel offerings. Part of this transformation has been the subordination of traditional European patterns of the restaurant meal, of three or more courses, in favor of variety of tastes presented in small plates often shared by the table.

This is where *mezze* comes in, alongside the Spanish tapas. *Mezze*, the repertoire of small dishes and tastes that accompany drink, is a Persian word meaning "taste." Not only the ubiquitous hummus but many other items—falafel, tabbouleh, foul, bourek, kebab, and more—are now offered not only in Middle Eastern eateries but in many others and by groceries and supermarkets, stimulated by cookery columns in newspapers, magazines, TV, and social media. Picking at snacks with drink is, of course, a common practice in many places. What is particular and special is the development of a specific repertoire and etiquette and the specialized institutions offering it—bars, cafés, and restaurants (such as the Turkish *meyhane*). The *mezze* repertoire and the ideas behind it extend at least to the nineteenth century in the Ottoman world, including the Balkans (the Greek *mezides*). The most notable centers were the Turkish cities with prominent Greek, Armenian, and Jewish populations, notably Istanbul itself and the Aegean/Mediterranean Coast, as well as the cities of the Arab Levant, Syria/Lebanon/Palestine, and into Iraq. Maghreb regions had their own traditions, there called *kemia*, not *mezze*.

"Kebab" has also became routinized in many European and American cities and their ethnic enclaves as a common item on diverse menus, not just in Middle Eastern eateries. More prominently, kebab has become a favored fast food, in wraps and sandwiches and with various garnishes, to rival hamburger and fried chicken, often offered from the same outlets (and, in Britain, with fish-and-chips). Doner kebab, with meat or chicken, is a particular favorite. In France and Holland you can now buy ready-meal packets of "kebab," meaning doner-style shavings of meat (including pork) and chicken. A drive to innovation and discovery imbues this dynamic gastronomic sphere and a foodie public. Middle Eastern food has become a central component of this now globalized interest.

"The Mediterranean" is a ubiquitous presence in the vocabulary of this gastronomic effervescence. There is an assumption of common culinary themes around its basin, built around characteristic ingredients of its ecology, such as the olive and the vine. The now common stereotype of "Mediterranean cuisine" hides great diversity between the different shores, however. The Mediterranean is more significant as the "middle sea," the medium for the movement of populations, artifacts, and ideas over the centuries, starting perhaps with the trade and conquest networks of the Phoenicians, from the shores of Lebanon to North Africa, and further into France and Spain, and are credited with introducing wine to what became Marseille, thus establishing it in that part of France. Much later, after the discovery and conquest of the New World, food products from that continent—notably the tomato, the pimento, the haricot bean (*fasoulia*), and maze—were diffused and traded in movement from Spain to Ottoman lands.

One particularly pertinent set of movements was the Sephardic migrations, following the expulsion of Jews from Spain in 1492. Jewish networks of trade, migration, and family dispersion were already established for much of the Islamic middle ages between Iberia, North Africa, and the Middle East. The expelled Jews dispersed at first to proximate destinations of Portugal, Morocco, Provence, and Italy. Further persecutions and expulsions from some of the European destinations pushed many Jews to Ottoman lands, settling in Istanbul, Salonika, and eventually into Arab cities in Egypt and the Levant. These movements left many culinary traces in recipes and vocabularies.

CONCLUSION

This chapter has surveyed the many routes of the spread of food and drink elements, ingredients, combinations, technology, and vocabularies, from and through the Middle East region to other parts of the world, including Europe and India. That was part of the movements and cultural syntheses enabled and stimulated by empires. It was "slow" globalization, affecting mainly urban and maritime centers. Modern globalization, starting with capitalist markets and imperialism, and accelerating at a great pace in more recent times, has ushered in novel aspects to the food system, both in terms of production and distribution, but crucially in the sociocultural fields. The movements of population have created wide diasporas and diasporic communities and cultures, especially in the West. Travel, tourism, trade, and media feed into a thriving consumer culture. Social media have vastly reinforced those trends.

All these elements feed into an ever expanding and diverse "foodie" milieu, in which food and gastronomy become spheres of recreation and spectacle.

Middle Eastern foods and cultures, their mutations and reconstructions, feature prominently in these mostly Western foodscapes: kebab, hummus, falafel, baklava, mezze, and many other items have become part of common repertoires and vocabularies. Bewildering varieties have emerged, from frozen packets of doner kebab (some with pork meat), to pesto hummus, to couscous tabbouleh. The mezze mode of serving fits in with the current fashion for "small plate" service in many bars and restaurants. This globalized space, with diasporic, cultural, and commercial elements, encourages constructions and inventions of traditions and claims to "ownership" by national, ethnic, and regional advocates. Elements of common repertoires become subject to contention: Who "owns" baklava, lahmajun, or hummus? The globalized space, the foodie culture, and the diasporic presence encourage these claims of particular appropriations of a common geographical heritage.

NOTES

1. Muhammad B. al-Husan, *A Baghdad Cookery Book*, translation by Charles Perry (Petits Propos Culinaires) (London: Prospect Books, 2005).

2. Andrew M. Watson, *Agricultural Innovation in the Early Islamic World: The Diffusion of Crops and Farming Techniques, 700–1100* (Cambridge, UK: Cambridge University Press, 1983), 15–71.

3. Watson, *Agricultural Innovation in the Early Islamic World*, 49.

4. Dan Jurafsky, *The Language of Food: A Linguist Reads the Menu* (New York: Norton Ludan, 2014), 35–49.

5. Jurafsky, *Language of Food*, 40–41.

6. Jurafsky, *Language of Food*, 41–45.

7. Jurafsky, *Language of Food*, 46.

8. Watson, *Agricultural Innovation in the Early Islamic World*, 20–23.

9. John Dickie, *The Epic History of the Italians and Their Food* (New York: Free Press, 2008), 21.

10. Laudan, *Cuisine and Empire*, 145.

11. Jurafsky, *Language of Food*, 72–75.

12. Jurafsky, *Language of Food*, 55–60.

FURTHER READING

Colas, Alejandro, Jason Edwards, Jane Levi, and Sami Zubaida. *Food, Politics, and Society: Social Theory and the Modern Food System*. Oakland: University of California Press, 2018.

Hattox, Ralph S. *Coffee and Coffeehouses: The Origins of a Social Beverage in the Medieval Near East.* Seattle: University of Washington Press, 1996.

Laudan, Rachel. *Cuisine and Empire: Cooking in World History.* Berkeley: University of California Press, 2013.

Perry, Charles, A. J. Arberry, and Maxime Rodinson. *Medieval Arab Cookery: Papers by Maxime Rodinson and Charles Perry with a Reprint of a Baghdad Cookery Book.* London: Prospect Books, 1998.

Tapper, Richard, and Sami Zubaida, editors. *A Taste of Thyme: Culinary Cultures of the Middle East.* New York: Taurus Parke Paperbacks, 2000.

TEN

Pictures in Motion

Kamran Rastegar

ONCE UPON A TIME, CINEMA (1996), a film by the Iranian director Mohsen Makhmalbaf, takes an ingenious approach to celebrating the history of cinema in Iran up until the time of its making. The story is set in the late nineteenth century and through a time-travel narrative device imagines that the Iranian ruler Nasir al-Din Shah (reigned 1849–96) obtained an early cinematographic camera from Europe. Instead of attending to Iran's pressing economic and political needs, the Shah ensconces himself in his palace with his new camera, making films and employing his courtiers and courtesans as actors, along with himself, in his films. The film is a brilliant homage to, but also a critique of, cinema's role in Iran. While cinema offers a powerful vehicle for illustrating social and political realities, it also serves as a form of commercial mass entertainment, a form of cultural production that distracts and entertains rather than motivates its audience to change the world. While Makhmalbaf's film is distinctly Iranian—there are no gestures or references made to non-Iranian cinemas—much of what lies at the heart of *Once Upon a Time, Cinema*, resonates with the histories of other global cinema cultures.

Makhmalbaf's film offers us a window into the rich and varied history of cinema in Iran. Despite revolutions and significant social changes over the course of the twentieth century, cinema arguably came to be the most important cultural form in Iran. While experiences with cinema in other Middle Eastern countries differ, sometimes greatly, from that of Iran, what can be said is that the Middle East is no less a fertile region for cinema culture than any other region in the world. To better understand the commonalities and differences in the historical experiences of cinema across the region, I will first briefly summarize the history of the major or film cultures that exist in the region and their place on the global stage.

FIGURE 10.1 *Once Upon a Time, Cinema*. Photo by Mitra Mahaseni, 1992. www.makhmal
baf.com/?q=Photo-Gallery/once-upon-a-time-cinema-photo-gallery.

GLOBALITY OF CINEMA

Cinema is perhaps the first truly global art form. Although cinema is not
produced in equal measure around the world, whether in terms of quantity or quality, it has become a form of cultural production that is global in
terms of its aesthetics, consumption, and circulation. Another way to say this
is that cinema, as a global art form, has developed in ways that mirror the
asymmetries and hierarchies that have structured global relations over the
course of the twentieth and twenty-first centuries. While regional cinemas,
especially non-Western ones, on the whole bear the marks of their original
cultures, the narrative feature film, despite its origins in early twentieth-century Hollywood, remains a remarkably durable form that retains a broadly
coherent structure and set of aesthetic conventions in its various regional
forms.

The reasons for the global nature of cinema culture are many, but central
among them are the facts that cinema came of an age during the height of
European colonialism and matured during a period of increasing American/
Western global hegemony. Cinema first arrived in colonized societies as a
venue for the animation of the colonial imaginary, through narratives that
cast European adventurers, soldiers, and missionaries as heroes, often bat-

tling indigenous forces that resisted their benevolent attempts to introduce modernity to ostensibly savage or barbaric societies. The colonial adventure film, among the most popular of cinematic genres in the early twentieth century, was central to the establishment of film industries in France, Britain, and the United States.

Despite the power of these Western film industries, two major non-Western cinema industries emerged nearly simultaneously during the colonial period, in India and Egypt. Although both industries were deeply entangled with British colonial interests, each came to develop successful commercial film industries that effectively married the conventions of the feature narrative film as popularized in the West, to stories, symbols, and songs rooted in their own cultural histories. For example, the Egyptian film *The White Rose* (1933), one of the first sound films in Egypt, told the story of a young hard-working and enterprising man who falls in love with the daughter of an upper-class man. The theme of cross-class romance was also common in British and American films of the period. However, the star of *The White Rose*, Muhammad Abd al-Wahab, was a rising star of Egypt's music industry, and the musical numbers in the film are unmistakably innovations in Egyptian popular music.

Throughout much of the twentieth century, the Egyptian film industry remained the dominant national cinema of the Arab world while also exporting to other regions. By the 1960s other countries like Iran and Turkey began to develop dynamic and productive film industries. By the 1970s a variety of noncommercially oriented filmmakers across the region, most often supported by nationalized film industries of the largely socialist postcolonial governments, sought to practice forms of filmmaking that would operate outside of the dominant Hollywood mold. In countries like Syria and Algeria, small but highly creative filmmaking took place, sometimes but not always in some relation to the forms of filmmaking that Soviet and other Eastern Bloc countries had developed. During the same period, a vital Palestinian resistance cinema also emerged, institutionally set within the organs of the Palestine Liberation Organization (PLO). This genre of cinema was inspired by, and sometimes benefitted from, direct training by figures in the internationalist leftist current resisting neocolonial subjugation. They linked Palestine to resistance struggles in South Africa, Angola, Latin America, and Vietnam, among other sites of struggle. Even Egyptian cinema of the 1960s and early 1970s bore hallmarks of the Arab socialist vision of Nasserism, despite also retaining elements of its commercial and popular heritage.

By the 1990s the socialist projects of postcolonial states were largely replaced by forms of neoliberal economic "reform," which dramatically affected the role of filmmakers of the region. Increasingly, domestic film production was brought into global financial arrangements wherein local filmmakers entered "co-production" contracts with Western film financiers to produce films that would often find larger audiences in the West than at home. At the same time, the "democratization" of filmmaking, through the availability of cheap cameras and editing technologies as well as overall lower production and distribution costs such as Internet distribution, has decentralized filmmaking. These changes will affect the industry for years to come. The fruits of this new form of what would properly be termed "digital video making" rather than "filmmaking" were observable in major cultural and political upheavals such as the Iranian Green Revolution of 2008, the Arab Spring revolutions of 2011, and the ongoing Syrian war.

The global aspects of cinema in the Middle East may best be illustrated by encountering three major regional figures: Youssef Chahine (Egypt), Abbas Kiarostami (Iran), and Nadine Labaki (Lebanon). While not necessarily comparable in terms of their influence and impact, the careers of these three filmmakers illustrate the degree to which the cinemas of the Middle East have always had global reflections and continue to play a significant role in the global cultures of cinema.

YOUSSEF CHAHINE

Youssef Chahine's career spanned from the 1950s through the first decade of the 2000s, nearly up to his death in 2008.[1] Chahine's youth coincided with the establishment and expansion of Egypt's successful commercial cinema of the 1930s through the 1950s, and his first films were produced within this very context. Chahine's earliest works were dramas that fit perfectly within the domestic commercial cinema, while subtly weaving political and social themes into the entertainment formula (as did many other directors of this same period). *Bab al-Hadid* (Cairo Station, 1958), perhaps the best example of this earlier style, is regarded as one of Chahine's most memorable works. Chahine's maturity as a filmmaker coincided with the aftermath of the 1952 revolution, when Egypt's cinema came to be transformed into a cinema with strong nationalist and overtly political currents. For good or for bad, the state supported and became more heavily involved in film production.

Chahine's political ideals assumed a fuller voice in the post-1952 period, a social climate energized by the socialist ambitions of Nasserism and political issues such as pan-Arabism and the confrontation with Israel. It was in such a context that Chahine accepted a proposal to direct the state-sponsored Crusades epic, *Salah al-Din the Victorious* (Nasir Salah al-Din, 1963), a clear parable for the rise of Gamal Abdel Nasser and the aspirations of Arab nationalism. It must be said, though, that Chahine was one of many Egyptian filmmakers to also address the limitations of Egypt's postrevolutionary idealism, by critiquing Nasser's authoritarianism and by examining the wound of Egypt's spectacular defeat in the 1967 war with Israel. In *The Sparrow* (Al-Asfour, 1972), Chahine juxtaposes hyperbolic governmental announcements about the war with the slow realization by ordinary Cairenes that the fight was in fact lost. The last scene of the film remains one of the most poignant exemplifications of the confusion and disillusion the defeat brought to Egypt.

By the 1970s, when Sadat's free-market policies (*infitah*) and other factors led to a collapse of Egypt's film industry, Chahine reinvented himself again, this time by working with European (largely French) producers. He produced a string of works that remained relatively little known in Egypt, despite receiving many awards in top international film festivals. The three films of his *Alexandria Trilogy* delighted European viewers and catapulted Chahine to international attention, often garnering him with the title of the "best" Arab filmmaker (a distinction that often grated on other Arab filmmakers and critics who saw this as a kind of tokenism). The trilogy wove the personal and autobiographical with the historical and social, challenging taboos. For example, these films sympathetically addressed bisexuality and homosexuality.

In the 1990s, Chahine once again changed direction and began to produce works that—often to the dismay of his prior champions in Europe and the United States—used popular commercial idioms to explore sociopolitical themes. In his film *Destiny* (Al-Masir, 1998), set in middle ages Andalusia, Chahine cast popular singers and TV soap stars in a musical melodrama addressing religious extremism and pluralism. In *Silence, We're Rolling* (Sukut h'nsawar, 2001) the same casting formula was used in another song-and-dance melodrama about corruption and consumerism in contemporary Egypt. Chahine never concerned himself with offering apologies to his confused arthouse supporters for this shift, and directly aligned himself with popular sentiments in Egypt not only in his filmmaking but also in his public comments. He voiced angry criticism at the effects of US policies in the Arab world and appeared on the shoulders of students at public (and often banned) demonstrations against the Iraq War among other causes.

In October 2008, just months after Chahine's passing, Abu Dhabi inaugurated the lavish Middle East International Film Festival, on the heels of the competing and no less opulent Dubai International Film Festival. These two festivals have dramatically redrawn the map of Arab cinema, tearing the focus away from Egypt, where the Cairo Film Festival, once the apex showcase of the Arab film industry and one of the most important festivals in Africa, became greatly diminished in significance to new geographical and economic arenas in the oil-rich Gulf countries. Many Arab filmmakers view these new developments with some trepidation, while still hoping that new opportunities will emerge. The United Arab Emirates, rarely mentioned in histories of Arab cinema production, are now pouring immense resources into developing an infrastructure for cinema production. Production companies in the Gulf are looking for "crossover" opportunities, working on Arab stories with Hollywood technicians and stars.

More significantly, these festivals are looking beyond Hollywood to Bollywood, Beijing, and other regions in the world of cinema, placing their own production ambitions into a new transnational framework. The economic contexts within which Chahine flourished—first, a local commercial cinema, then a nationalized and nationalist cinema, then as a client of European production funds, then finally back to a more domestic and populist idiom of filmmaking—speak to the varied ways by which the global and local interplay in his cinema. In the post-Chahine period, institutions in the Gulf have emerged as key players in the production of Arab cinema. In the process they are creating new political and economic norms for the industry, which is orienting more toward Asian markets.

ABBAS KIAROSTAMI

Born in 1940, Abbas Kiarostami's rise to the global filmmaking stage took a determinedly different course from that of Chahine. Where Chahine's career reflected the diversity and multiplicity of forms and approaches that characterized Egyptian cinema of the twentieth century, Kiarostami began as a peculiar and somewhat singular figure in Iranian cinema. He began with a small but dedicated audience among Iranian artists and cultural figures, and grew to become the most celebrated figure of Iranian cinema for more than twenty years. He later turned his attention to making films outside of Iran, with little direct reference to his homeland.

In the 1970s, as one of the founding filmmakers affiliated with the Kanun, the Institute for the Development of Children and Young Adults, Kiarostami made several films. These films were presumably envisioned as works for an audience of children, either to be screened in special events (the Kanun sponsored a mobile cinema screening unit that would travel to provincial towns and villages to screen works for children in different areas of Iran) or on television, where they would be part of children's programming. Prior to 1960, Kiarostami worked in television advertising, but his visual language in the films he made with the Kanun in 1970s was decidedly noncommercial. His work resonated with trends in what is usually called the "First Iranian New Wave" of cinema, which had been initiated, for example, by the poet Forough Farrokhzad's short film *The House Is Black* (Khaneh Siyah Ast, 1963) and Daryush Mehrjui's first film, *The Cow* (Gav, 1969).

At this stage in his career, Kiarostami was not considered a global filmmaker in any significant way. His early films such as *Bread and Alley* (1970), *Recess Bell* (1972), or *The Traveler* (1974) often ironically or playfully interrogated the lives of children. These films seemed to exemplify a distinctly hermetic vision that had little reference either to the conventions of Hollywood or the broader global popular forms of cinema, nor did they harmonize with the austere social realism or experimental approaches of Eastern Bloc cinema. At most, one might have found some resonance with certain European neorealist approaches such as that found in Italian cinema of the 1950s, but this analogy would only partially illuminate the kind of cinema Kiarostami came to develop.

Unlike some of his peers who had established careers in Iran's film industry, Kiarostami did not leave Iran in the direct aftermath of the 1979 Iranian Revolution. During the initial upheavals after the revolution, and then as a result of the destructive war between Iran and Iraq (1980–88), commercial filmmaking in Iran all but went into hiatus for several years. The Kanun, however, remained an active organization in the postrevolutionary period, and through his role there Kiarostami continued making short films and documentaries throughout the war years, including a feature documentary, *The First Graders* (Avvali-ha) in 1984. Nonetheless, his work continued to be directly oriented to a domestic audience. It was only with his feature fiction film, *Where Is the Friend's House?* (Khaneh-ye doost kojast?, 1987), that Kiarostami began to enjoy international attention, by having won an award at the Locarno Film Festival. His 1990 semidocumentary film *Close Up* brought further international accolades and sharpened international interest in what came to be called "New Iranian Cinema," which included younger filmmakers such as Mohsen Makhmalbaf, Jafar Panahi, as well as others from Kiarostami's generation such as Bahram Bayzaei. From among the denizens of the New Iranian Cinema, Kiarostami came to be viewed increasingly as the most refined, sophisticated, and innovative director—in many ways, the intellectual heart of the movement.

From the late 1980s on, Kiarostami's career took an increasingly global aspect, even as for many years he remained committed to a narrow focus on certain aesthetic approaches and certain themes rooted to his Iranian context. With his "Kokar" trilogy (three films all shot in a remote northwestern Iranian village called Kokar), beginning with *Where Is the Friend's House* (1987), then with two additional films, *Life and Nothing More* (1991) and *Under the Olive Trees* (1994), a small but influential set of film critics in Europe and then in the United States took note of Kiarostami's work. His subsequent films catapulted him to global recognition. *Taste of Cherry* (1997) won the prestigious Palme d'Or at the Cannes Film Festival, while his next film, *The Wind Will Carry Us* (1999), won the Silver Lion award at the Venice Film Festival. Both films were distributed commercially by major film distributors and enjoyed wide international releases.

Kiarostami then adopted a new and even more radical filmmaking approach, which he outlined in detail in his auto-documentary *Ten on Ten* (2004), a companion piece to his 2002 feature film *Ten*. The latter film takes place entirely in a car and was shot with two video cameras but with the director absent from the shooting. The actors would drive in the car and improvise a scene that Kiarostami had very generally sketched out for them, and Kiarostami used the footage from each scene without edits or alterations. Beyond his unquestionably compelling aesthetic approach, what makes the last stage of Kiarostami's work "global" is his turn away from solely using state or private funds from Iranian sources to working with European producers, in particular in France. As a result of this move, Kiarostami was able to more effectively distribute and promote his works outside of Iran, to the extent where his film *Ten*, while shot on the streets of Tehran, was never officially released in Iran.

One may say that Kiarostami's ultimate aim was to achieve a form of "pure" cinema, beyond national borders or identities. Between 2004 and

2016, he taught a series of master classes around the world to share the philosophy behind his technique. Kiarostami traveled to Doha, Barcelona, Toronto, Marrakech, Havana, Sao Paolo, and many other locations. These classes, and the dozens of filmmakers trained by Kiarostami in them, perhaps will serve as the capstone testament to the global nature of his cinematic vision, cut short with Kiarostami's untimely death in 2016. Nonetheless, he came to be viewed within a fairly rarified sphere of filmmakers that are often considered by critics and audiences alike as having transcended national origin to being a practitioner of "world cinema" in a more essential form. Kiarostami's films are taught in film studies courses around the world, and he is known perhaps less for his identity than for the aesthetics of his works, even if they are films that never garnered truly mass audiences.

NADINE LABAKI

Born in 1974 in Beirut, Lebanon, Nadine Labaki represents a generation of filmmakers that came of age in the early twenty-first century and whose global vision of cinema has been shaped by the social, political, and economic realities that govern the region. Labaki's career follows the rise of a number of women filmmakers from the Arab world into a global stage for filmmaking. Filmmakers such as Leila Marrakchi (Morocco), Raja Amari (Tunisia), Jehane Noujaim (Egypt), Annemarie Jacir (Palestine), and Haifaa al-Mansour (Saudi Arabia) are among the most celebrated of a thriving generation of twenty-first-century Arab women who are shaping the future of cinema in the region. Building on the efforts of previous generations of Arab women filmmakers who often struggled to find prominence within the field, the current generation has made notable gains in their achievements, with recognitions that have found them audiences far beyond the borders of their homelands.

Labaki's career as a filmmaker began in 2007 with her feature film *Caramel*. Set in a women's hair salon in Beirut, the film staged a women's space that allowed for the exploration of experiences and forms of relation that often fall outside of the frame of conventional, male-oriented, filmmaking. In addition, Labaki's work is informed by her earlier experiences as a director of music videos, a genre that also fluctuates between perceived global and local aesthetic and formal conventions. In that sense her work is as much informed by the new media landscapes of the period, with satellite TV channels and Internet streaming of video, as it is in conversation with the legacies of Chahine, Kiarostami, or other greats of world cinema.

In considering Labaki's emergence as a filmmaker, it is important to recognize that her film career has also been defined by what is termed the "coproduction model." Rather than emerging from a strong national film context, as in the cases of both Youssef Chahine and Abbas Kiarostami, Labaki has had to work in an environment dominated by transnational coproduction. Although Lebanon has an extensive history of cinema, Lebanese filmmakers have long had to look outside of their borders for support and funding. For these reasons, *Caramel* and Labaki's subsequent films were all produced with the involvement of European film producers and funds. The allegorical comedy *Where Do We Go from Here?* (Halla la'Wayn?, 2011) uses local dynamics and themes from Lebanon in a way that resonates with a broader audience. Labaki's third work, *Capernaum* (2018), which explores the traumas of Syrian refugees in Lebanon through a story of a Syrian refugee boy, catapulted her further into international recognition with prizes from the Cannes Film Festival, the Asia Pacific Screen Awards, the British Film Institute, and the first Oscar nomination ever for an Arab woman in the category best foreign language film in 2019. Purely on the basis of these accolades and numerous other awards, the film may arguably qualify as the most critically successful film made by an Arab filmmaker in history.

That Labaki's films are all made with (largely European) coproduction funding says more about the prevailing economic pressures that filmmakers from non-Western societies face than about the nature of the films or the disposition of their director. The coproduction model brings tremendous opportunities for filmmakers who may not have access to necessary funds or production support to make films, but it has certain dangers as well. The coproduction relationship invites comparisons to the former colonial model, whereby regional cultures were treated as subservient or in need of support from an advanced European metropole. Also, there are built-in parameters in terms of what kinds of films are attractive to decision-makers who hold the purse strings for coproduction—one may go so far as to speak of a "coproduction aesthetic" that defines many (but certainly not all) coproduced films. This aesthetic may have more to do with the perceived desires of European and other international audiences than to what the domestic audiences in the Middle East may be seeking in their own cinema cultures.

Nonetheless, successful contemporary filmmakers from the region find ways to work within these constraints to develop their projects and to tell stories that they find compelling. These tensions speak of the nature of "the global" in the twenty-first century where, at its origins, cinema's global nature was entwined with the global project of colonialism. As the global begins to be redefined by new economic and political models—for example, neoliberalism—at the end of the twentieth century, so too has the global nature of cinema been defined by its imbrication within these economic projects.

CONCLUSION

Middle Eastern cinema cultures have a long and rich history. For much of this history they have generally been focused on regional or national contexts. Youssef Chahine's career, which spanned much of the twentieth century, exemplified the ways by which Egyptian cinema circulated around the Arab world but exceeded regional boundaries to achieve global recognition. Abbas Kiarostami exemplified the ways by which Iranian cinema of the 1970s began to develop what may be termed an indigenous cinematic language, which reemerged among an entire generation of filmmakers in the late 1980s and 1990s. What is remarkable about Kiarostami and other Iranian filmmakers of that period is their success in achieving global audiences despite the "national" consistency of their aesthetic approach.

However, by the end of the twentieth century, regional cinemas underwent significant changes, and other newer cinemas have increasingly been drawn into global cultural currents, as exemplified by such filmmakers as Nadine Labaki. While these fresh currents have opened up new venues and audiences for Middle Eastern films, they evoke much of the ambivalence that surrounds the idea of "the global." Does "global" mean a world of cultural and economic flows defined by hierarchies of richer and poorer, more industrially advanced and less industrially developed societies? Or can "global" be reimagined as a more revolutionary possibility, a world of new connections and opportunities that surpass the limits of nationalism and regionalism? The current state of the cinemas of the region reflects these very tensions.

NOTE

1. Portions of this section appeared in an earlier form in Kamran Rastegar, "Arab and African Cinema's Uncertain Future," *Vertigo Magazine* 21 (November 2008),

www.closeupfilmcentre.com/vertigo_magazine/issue-21-november-2008/arab-and
-african-cinema-s-uncertain-future/. These portions are reprinted with kind permission of the publishers.

FURTHER READING

Khatib Lina. *Lebanese Cinema: Imagining the Civil War and Beyond.* London: IB
Tauris, 2008.
Khouri, Malek. *The Arab National Project in Youssef Chahine's Cinema.* Cairo:
American University in Cairo Press, 2010.
Naficy, Hamid, editor. *Home, Exile, Homeland: Film, Media, and the Politics of
Place.* AFI Film Readers. New York: Routledge, 1999.
Rastegar, Kamran. "Film Studies." In *Women and Islamic Cultures: Disciplinary
Paradigms and Approaches: 2003–2013.* Edited by Suad Joseph, 87–102. Leiden:
Brill Press, 2013.
Saeed Vafa, Merhnaz, and Jonathan Rosenbaum. *Abbas Kiarostami.* Expanded
second edition. Urbana: University of Illinois Press, 2018.

ELEVEN

Musical Journeys

Michael Frishkopf

IN 2000 A NEW YORK LAW FIRM representing the famous rapper Shawn Carter (aka Jay-Z) sought my advice as a Middle Eastern music consultant. They informed me that their client had released a hit song, "Big Pimpin'" (1999), produced by Timothy Mosley (aka Timbaland), sampling a short Middle Eastern–sounding melody. The global record company EMI claimed copyright and demanded compensation. The lawyers were wondering if the tune wasn't simply Egyptian folklore, not subject to copyright. Could I please listen and offer my expert opinion?

I listened. I had been living in Egypt for most of the 1990s, immersed in Arabic and Sufi music, and was completely out of touch with hip-hop. But to my surprise, the producer's melody was the instrumental introduction to a famous Egyptian film song "Khosara" ("What a pity," 1957), composed by Baligh Hamdi (1932–1993) and sung by Abdul Halim Hafiz (1929–1977). The rights were indeed owned by EMI. The parties settled out of court for $100,000.

Always flowing, music is continuous, unbounded, unboundable... uncountable. Unlike language, music knows no impassable social barriers; being intangible and semantically ambiguous, it is the globalizable expressive substance par excellence. "Middle Eastern music" doesn't imply the "Middle East" any more than "Middle East" implies "Middle Eastern music." Rather, such music, along with its poetry and dance, extends weblike around the world, its dynamic filaments branching, and sometimes reconnecting, through multiple pathways. The idea of discrete, bounded "musics" is a convenient conceit that doesn't hold up to scrutiny. The stories in this chapter trace these crisscrossing filaments, through media, marketing, and fusions; via Orientalism, tourism, and migration; Islam, conflict, and commerce.

FIGURE 11.1–11.2 Abdul Halim Hafiz (left), 1955, and Shawn Carter aka Jay-Z (right), 2011. Creative Commons.

Throughout I draw on personal experiences, across years of encountering and traversing these filaments myself.

RECORDINGS OF "WORLD MUSIC"

I grew up listening to my parents' collection of Folkways records (now Smithsonian Folkways), a label founded by Moses Asch in 1948 and an important vehicle for global dissemination of traditional Middle Eastern music. Most of these recordings were produced by ethnomusicologists or collectors and catered to a niche North American market. Decades later, as professor of ethnomusicology at the University of Alberta, I co-founded folkwaysAlive!, a partnership with the label, and got to know their Middle East catalog more thoroughly.

As a graduate student studying Middle Eastern music at UCLA, I discovered Rashid Sales, founded in 1934 in Detroit by Albert Rashid. Since the early twentieth century, the Detroit-Dearborn region has been a magnet for Middle Eastern immigrants, many seeking work in the automotive sector. Rashid's was the first American company to import Arab music for Arab Americans. During World War II, records could not be imported, and so in 1943 the company moved to New York City, where they began recording Arab American artists, helping forge an Arab American identity.

The origins of "world music" as exotic spectacle trace to nineteenth-century world expositions, such as the Exposition Universelle in Paris (1889) and the World's Columbian Exposition in Chicago (1893). American interest accelerated with immigration, tourism, and the rise of mass media, especially films. At first, record stores' "International" bins stocked Middle Eastern discs mainly for immigrants and connoisseurs. Starting in the late 1980s, the industry marketed Middle Eastern (along with other non-Western) music to a broader audience as "World Music," hailed as "authentic," "traditional," "ancient," "exotic," "sensual," or "spiritual"—qualities often played up by artists themselves, a kind of self-Orientalization.

Middle Eastern stars could extend their reach via fusions and collaborations. While living in Cairo, I researched shifts in Arabic music styles. Since the late 1970s, popular music ensembles westernized, adding trapset, keyboards, bass, and guitar, though elements of older Arab orchestras were often retained (especially percussion and the *kawala*, or reed flute). In the 1990s, Amr Diab, Egypt's biggest star, incorporated Latin and Mediterranean sounds, paving the way for global distribution. His biggest hit, "Habibi ya Nur al-'Ayn" (1996), featured the Gipsy Kings, whose salsa-flamenco chords and rhythms propelled its circulation throughout Europe, Latin America, and South Asia. Diab is recognized by the *Guinness Book of World Records* for "Most World Music Awards for Best Selling Middle Eastern Artist" (1996, 2001, 2007, 2013). Many other Arab artists imitated his formula for global pop appeal, although the Arab-Latin mix had been anticipated by composers such as Mohammed Abdul Wahab since the 1930s. Scholars rightly view Spanish (and hence Latin) music as already informed by the Middle East, via Arabic kingdoms of medieval Andalusia, accounting for the compatibility of Arab and Latin styles (discussed in detail later in this chapter).[1]

NIGHTCLUBS, ORIENTALISM, AND INTERVALS

The Averof nightclub, formerly located at 1924 Massachusetts Avenue in Cambridge, Massachusetts, is the site of my earliest aural memory of Middle Eastern music, circa 1981. "Oriental Nightclubs" emerged in North America in the 1950s, and the Averof instantiated the usual Orientalist stereotypes. But it was a key node for cultural creativity as well. Growing up in a Boston suburb, I had passed by the Averof for years. Finally, one evening in 1981, I stepped inside with a friend for dinner. The venue compressed a potpourri of Middle Eastern sounds, performers, images, and foods—Greek, Syrian, Turkish, Armenian, Egyptian, even Israeli—into a unified "Oriental" presence, while affirming "authenticity." The food was delicious, but the highlight was the Middle Eastern orchestra with singer and belly dancer. Afterward, what reverberated in my head most tenaciously—I can conjure the sonic memory to this day—was an unfamiliar musical interval. Much later, I learned that what I'd heard was the "neutral third," an interval occurring in various guises throughout the Middle East, whose power seems to inhere in the tonal ambiguity of its upper note, called *sikah*. For me, that upper note simply cried out with emotion.

Orientalism's quintessential musical interval is not the neutral third but the augmented second, easily performed on Western instruments and widely deployed by film composers, along with stereotypical timbres and ornaments, to signal the Middle East. Hollywood soundtracks—from Maurice Jarre's epic score for *Lawrence of Arabia* (1962) to Alan Menken's whimsical songs for *Aladdin* (1992), burnish demeaning Orientalist stereotypes. More sinisterly, the same intervals and sounds accompany villains—for example, Brian Tyler's soundtrack to *Ironman 3*, where the evil terrorist Mandarin is accompanied by a breathy flute resembling the Middle Eastern *nay*.[2] By contrast, the neutral third, occurring in various guises throughout the Middle East, is absent in Western music. Falling between major and minor thirds, it can't be located on the piano. *Sikah* is also continuously variable, and personally expressive—placement dependent on musical and social contexts, and individual expression, evading the small-integer fractional representations proposed Greek theory, such as Ptolemy's 5:4 for the major third, and 6:5 for the minor one.

In 1992, shortly after arriving in Cairo for dissertation research, I attended a rehearsal of the famous *Firqat al-Musiqa al-'Arabiyya* (Arab Music Orchestra). One elderly violinist proudly told me, "I'm famous for my *sikah*." My inner eyebrow rose. No violinist could be known for a single note! Or could they? Perhaps, I mused, *sikah* is something like a "blue note," a unique musical cry. As we shall see, there may well be a deep historical connection between *sikah* and the blues. The augmented second and the neutral third are (respectively) characteristic intervals of two widely known Middle Eastern modes, *hijaz* and *rast*. Dozens of such modes, known as *maqamat*, exist, similar to Western scales but more numerous, featuring microtonal intervals and implying melodic patterns.

Genealogically connected to Western music from medieval times, they have also provided an exotic palette for modern composers and performers living in the West. Examples include world music pioneer (and Folkways artist) Henry Cowell (1897–1965), who described his impressionistic *Persian Set* (1957) as "a simple record of musical contagion," and Hafez Modirzadeh (b. 1962), a contemporary Iranian American saxophonist from North Carolina, who has synthesized a cross-cultural tonal sensibility centered on jazz and Iranian music, treating the neutral third within what he calls "chromodal discourse."[3]

At the time of my visit, the Averof represented a long tradition of Middle Eastern music in North America. The ethnomusicologist Anne Rasmussen has performed the seminal research in this domain, showing how sounds of the Arab world arrived through immigration, resulting in community performances—*mahrajanat* and *hafalat*—resembling those of the "old world" from the 1930s.[4]

A few decades later, Middle Eastern music diffused into the broader society, whose appetite had been primed by extravagant Orientalist images combining divergent cultural signs: harems and "harem" pants; veiled faces and unveiled bodies; turbans and bikini tops; minarets and *mashrabiyya*; gardens and deserts; opulence and austerity; brass urns in ancient souks; genies and snake charmers; ornate rugs and flying carpets... all well-lodged in the public imagination thanks to Western art: translations from *1001 Nights*, novels, poetry (Lord Byron's *Turkish Tales*), plays (Oscar Wilde's *Salome*), operas (e.g., Mozart's *The Abduction from the Seraglio*), paintings (Delacroix, 1798–1863), and films (e.g., Valentino in *The Sheik*, 1921). Seeking audience and sales, some musicians of Middle Eastern extraction were all too willing to cater to expectations and combine, distort, or exaggerate Middle Eastern traditions. Thus was an "Oriental" music—fusing Syrian, Egyptian, Turkish, Persian, Greek, and Armenian—born in the Oriental Nightclub and expressed in LP recordings with evocative covers. Self-parody was rampant. Perhaps none sampled all the stereotypes as thoroughly as the Lebanese American musician Mohammed el-Bakkar, who moved to the United States in 1952, where he performed and recorded until his death in 1959.

THE DANCE

The global diffusion of the Middle Eastern dancer is older than that of the musician. Indeed the "belly dance" (from the French *danse du ventre*) was (and continues to be) a co-creation of Middle East and West. In Egypt, what later became "Oriental" dance was first performed by professional singer-dancers known as *'awalim* ("learned women") in private, elite contexts, or by dancing girls known as *ghawazi* ("invaders" of hearts—a tribe of dancers banished to Upper Egypt in 1834) in more public ones. Exposed to European observers, the dancer's image developed through representations by nineteenth-century Orientalist painters whose fanciful images featured scantily clad women. By contrast, the actual dancers, as depicted in more "scientific" period works, appear to have been relatively covered.

But the erotic imagination of the painters was soon realized in practice. With the stationing of British soldiers in Egypt in the late nineteenth century, a public dance style emerged as *raqs sharqi*, translating "Oriental dance." During the same period, with the advent of world fairs and exhibitions, Middle Eastern dancers appeared in Western cities, performing according to Orientalist expectations, to the combined satisfaction and horror of Western audiences accustomed to a Victorian morality. This *danse du ventre*, "Oriental dance," or "hoochie coochie" was welcomed and condemned, all in one breath, linked (in the Western imagination) to the contemporary as well as the biblical Middle East: Salome's dance of the seven veils, as imagined by Oscar Wilde. Thus the *Chicago Daily Tribune* noted that in the Rue de Cairo concerts of the 1889 Paris exposition "there may be seen a dance which in all probability is much the same as that which Salome danced before Herod. It is the danse du ventre . . ."[5]

Introduced to North America at the 1893 Chicago World's Fair, the dance caused a stir. Subsequently performed at New York's Grand Central Palace, "men scrambled and fought, elbowed and crowded" to enter. As "lissome" dancer Ferida was "working her abdominal muscles with a vigorous, throbbing motion" and "200 pairs of eyes looked on with intense interest," the show was abruptly shut down for indecency by one Inspector Williams.[6] Here is an instance of that strange double reflection so characteristic of Orientalism—the "East" as imagined by the "West" is simultaneously celebrated and censured, and ultimately reincorporated into the "East" as a global phenomenon. Later, belly dance was widely accepted in America, both as spectacle and as practice. Increasingly participants were American women of all ethnicities, attracted to this dance as exotic femininity, exercise, or (occasionally) vocation. Meanwhile, both dance and music evolved in its new land.

One of the first professional American stars was Vietnam-born Nai Bonet, who debuted in 1957 at the age of thirteen. For her 1966 Karate single "Jelly

FIGURE 11.3 "Jelly Belly" by Nai Bonet, Karate Records, 1966.

Belly" she dances to rock and roll accessorized with Middle Eastern sounds
(augmented second; reedy timbres), purporting to "teach you how to do the
jelly belly." (A Scopitone film begins: "In New York City, where there are
more belly dancers than all of Egypt," then offers dance instructions, reinforced in the liner notes.)

By the 1970s, American women were flocking to learn belly dance.
Record labels like Monitor (now Smithsonian Folkways) released instruc-
tional belly-dance hits, featuring Arab American artists such as George Abdo
and his Flames of Araby orchestra. Subsequently, the belly dancer became
a sign of female empowerment, linked to a supposedly matriarchal prehis-
tory, dominated by fertility Earth Goddesses and a pre-Abrahamic "gyno-
centric" culture celebrating the hips and belly—far from her meaning in the

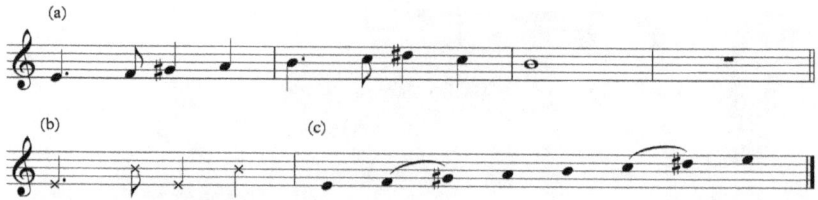

FIGURE 11.4 "Misirlou": (a) opening phrase, (b) *Ayyub* rhythm, (c) *Hijaz Kar maqam*; slurs indicate augmented seconds. Prepared by the author.

Muslim Middle East. New styles developed, incorporating elements from the "Orient," Spain, and India (e.g., "Tribal Fusion"). Today, women from around the world gather for Cairo's dance festivals, where they study with the world's top professionals—many of whom may hail from Eastern Europe!

MUSICAL ADAPTATIONS AND FUSIONS

Global circulation of Middle Eastern music exhibited its own tortuous trajectories and transformations, intertwined with those of dance. Perhaps the most famous instance is an auditory filament deeply woven into pop culture, "Misirlou" (Turkish for "Girl from Egypt") in *maqam Hijaz Kar* (containing not one but *two* augmented seconds), carrying the *Ayyub* rhythm. Both *maqam* and rhythm are widespread in the Middle East.

"Misirlou" probably circulated throughout Ottoman lands, adapting to local lyrics, instruments, and contexts. From Greek *rebetiko* music, it traveled to America, recorded by Tetos Demetriades in 1927. Successive versions appeared as "Eastern exotica," varied in covers by Woody Herman (1941), Arthur Lyman (1958), Martin Denny (1961), and Yacoubian & Company (*The Glorious Greeks*, 1963, featuring a belly dancer on the cover). Anton Abdelahad (1915–1995), a celebrated Arab American singer and oud player from Boston, recorded it in the 1940s. A belly-dance version by George Abdo appeared on *The Art of Belly Dancing* (1973).

But its biggest boost came with a 1962 warp speed rock and roll cover by Lebanese-American Dick Dale (1937–2019). Born in Boston as Richard Monsour, Dick Dale and his group the Del Tones were progenitors of "surf rock." An uncle taught Dale *darabuka* (Middle Eastern goblet drum). He played at local fairs or *mahrajanat,* where his uncle performed "Misirlou" on the oud. Transferring the melody to guitar, Dale gained wide exposure

FIGURE 11.5 Anton Abdelahad, photo by Ron Wahl, March 1, 1964, at the Al Kareem Club, Saint Petersburg, Florida. Photo courtesy of the Abdelahad family.

performing it on *The Ed Sullivan Show*, and in the film *A Swingin' Affair!* (1963). Known for his trademark rapid-fire picking style, Dale once said it represents "the power of Mother Nature, of our earth, of our ocean." But it is the oud's basic tremolo technique. Subsequently, "Misirlou" spun through popular culture, accelerated by the Beach Boys (1963) and even performed by Pete Seeger (1989) of Folkways fame. Dale's version was the principal theme for the movie *Pulp Fiction* (1994) and has even been used in advertising (e.g., Domino's Pizza). The Kronos Quartet recorded "Misirlou Twist" in 2000, and The Black Eyed Peas sampled it on "Pump It" (2006). Spotify lists more than a thousand different versions!

MIGRATING MUSIC AND MUSICIANS

A few months after moving to Cairo in 1992, I began to hear a new hit song everywhere. Egyptian music dominates the Arab world, but this song was not Egyptian. No one seemed to understand the words, but they loved it just the same. It was "Didi," by Algerian singer Khaled, and most Egyptians' first exposure to Algerian *rai*, an earthy, bluesy, uninhibited musical genre, expressing stories straight from the street and the heart, in colloquial Algerian Arabic. But ironically enough for such a localized genre, "Didi" did not arrive in Cairo straight from Algeria.

Rooted in the old *malhun* vocal tradition, *rai* emerged in cosmopolitan, colonial Oran, resonating with Algerian, Egyptian, French, American, and Spanish sounds. After independence in 1963, Algerian authorities deplored *rai* as subversive and immoral; it was banned from the airwaves from the early 1970s to the mid-1980s. *Rai* nevertheless flourished, thanks to the global rise of cassette production, synthesizers, and drum machines. Meanwhile, *rai* the genre took root in France, home to thousands of Algerians—and many *rai* fans. Subsequently, Algerian Islamists violently persecuted *rai* artists. The great Cheb Hasni was tragically assassinated in 1994. Many artists, including Khaled, "King of Rai," emigrated to France. In Europe, *rai's* popularity grew, attracting Western producers, incorporating Western lyrics and styles like rock, reggae, and funk, along with Western instruments and musicians. *Rai* ultimately exploded on the world music scene, catapulting its stars to unprecedented fame. "Didi" arrived in Cairo via Paris.

In 1998, following my long Cairo sojourn, I too emigrated west—settling in Edmonton, Canada, for a new job teaching Middle Eastern music at the University of Alberta. A group of semiprofessional belly dancers asked if I could teach them outside the university. Taking up the challenge, I developed a Middle Eastern music program for dancers. We covered basic rhythms (*iqa'at*) and *maqamat*—including that slippery *sikah*. I began to accompany belly-dance performances on *nay* and *org* (synthesizer), along with local Arab musicians.

Years later, in 2014, the proprietor of Bedouin Beats, an Edmonton belly-dance studio, proposed collaborating with four phenomenal London-based artists for a series of dance workshops and concerts: Brazilian belly dancer Serena Ramzy and three Egyptian musicians: percussionist Hossam Ramzy, violinist Emile Basili, and keyboardist El Gamal El Kordi. I enthusiastically agreed.

Ramzy developed his career in synergy with global belly dance and popular music scenes, occupying a singular role as musical mediator. Growing up in a wealthy Egyptian family who expected him to become a doctor, Ramzy was passionately drawn to Arabic percussion, receiving his first *tabla* (*darabuka*) at age three. After finishing school, he moved to London in the mid-

1970s, becoming a highly successful jazz, rock, Latin, and Arabic drummer. He has produced some fifty albums for the global belly-dance community, including percussion music; instrumental versions of classic songs by Egypt's greatest singers, such as Mohammed Abdel Wahab, Farid Al Atrash, and Abdel Halim Hafiz; and Middle Eastern folk musics. All the dancers I've met know Hossam Ramzy's recordings intimately; it is their connection to the Middle East. Across that region he has helped artists achieve global recognition. He worked with Turkish singer Yeşim Salkım, produced an album by acclaimed Egyptian Sufi chanter Shaykh Mohamed Al Helbawy, and directed the orchestra for *1, 2, 3 Soleil* (1998), a live album featuring three of *rai*'s greatest stars—Khaled, Faudel, and Rachid Taha—in a sold-out Paris concert.

Hossam Ramzy has also introduced Middle Eastern music to popular stars of Europe and North America who incorporated it (and him) in their recordings, across a range of genres: Peter Gabriel (*Passion*), Led Zeppelin (*No Quarter*), Loreena McKinett (*The Book of Secrets*), Ricky Martin (*Life*), Chick Corea ("The city of brass"), Shakira, Sting, Gypsy Kings, Joan Armatrading, Electric Light Orchestra, Debbie Harry…the list is distinguished, and long. In Edmonton we featured the four visiting artists in two concerts to thunderous applause, performing music of Umm Kulthum, Mohammed Abdel Wahab, and Abdel Halim Hafiz, with the student dancers, and my Middle Eastern and North African Music Ensemble (MENAME), a university-community hub. Ramzy told me that his goal is to spread Egyptian culture through music, rhythm, and dance. There has never been anyone better situated—via talent, dedication, location, and connections—to make that happen.

ISLAMIC CONNECTIONS

Another bundle of sonic paths from the Middle East to the world is catalyzed by Islam. Many African American artists profess Islam, particularly via Black Muslim movements such as the Moorish Science Temple, the Nation of Islam, and the Five Percenters, as well as the Ahmadiyya, and mainstream Sunni Islam. Direct influence appears primarily in lyrics, although Brand Nubian's "Allahu Akbar" (1993) opens with a sampled call to prayer. Even non-Muslim rappers include Arabic lyrics, testimony to the centrality of Islam in their community. There is also overtly Islamic hip-hop. One exceptional female artist is Syrian American Mona Haydar, who expresses Middle Eastern, Muslima, and American identities in "Hijabi" (2017), featuring sounds of the Middle Eastern *rabab* (ancestor of Europe's rebec and violin) and celebrating the headscarf as female liberation and empowerment against Western Orientalism, Islamophobia, and dehumanization.

Such music may be loosely classified as *nashid*—Islamic song, carrying Middle Eastern elements. Having studied *nashid* in Cairo with Shaykh Mohamed Al Helbawy, Shaykh Yasin al-Tuhami, and others, I began to investigate the broader phenomenon after moving to Canada, surprised to discover its global scope, from Britain (Yusuf Islam—aka Cat Stevens—and Sami Yusuf) to Sweden (Maher Zain), from Macedonia (Mesut Kurtis) to South Africa (Zain Bhikha), to Malaysia (Raihan). For that matter, the Middle East's global sonic impact is ubiquitous in the Muslim call to prayer (*adhan*) and Qur'anic recitation (*tilawa*). In 2005, I invited Shaykh Al Helbawy to Edmonton, to perform *nashid* with MENAME, for a diverse Canadian audience. He also taught us how to perform the *adhan* in six different *maqamat*!

SAMPLING

Long before I met him, I knew Hossam Ramzy through his recordings and also from the aforementioned Jay-Z court case. I'd discovered that Timbaland hadn't sampled the original Egyptian song, but rather an instrumental version from Ramzy's *The Best of Abdul Halim Hafiz*. Hossam later told me he had no idea how Timbaland got hold of his album, only that it was widely available thanks to the thriving belly-dance scene. Timbaland claimed to have heard it at a "carnival," saying, "It makes me think about summertime, a bunch of girls and king cobra coming out of a genie bottle"—a wonderful jumble of Orientalist images cut/paste straight out of the closing scenes of Disney's animated *Aladdin*.[7]

A decade after the out-of-court settlement in 2000, I received a message from a Los Angeles law firm, responding to another lawsuit, this one brought by Baligh Hamdi's nephew and heir, Osama Ahmed Fahmy, who claimed infringement of the composer's "moral rights" through addition of lewd lyrics. In fact, the two songs have something in common beyond the melody: both are about women. But the similarities stop there. While Abdel Halim's conveys romantic Arabic clichés ("What a pity.... My eyes are crying for you with bitterness....My days, my nights, Searching for you....My eyes are sleepless, My tears are confused"), Jay-Z's is misogynistic and "explicit" ("You know I thug 'em, fuck 'em, love 'em, leave 'em / 'Cause I don't fuckin' need 'em / Take 'em out the hood / keep 'em lookin' good / But I don't fuckin' feed 'em"). Nevertheless, Fahmy lost his suit, the federal judge ruling that moral rights could not be asserted outside Egypt.

Ramzy, as well as the dance community, served as key mediators in this melody's tortuous path. The anecdote shows that such global musical pathways—here, from romance to dance to gangsta rap—traversing radically contrastive cultural worlds, entail equally radical transformations of meaning.

Middle Eastern music has been sampled in other controversial cases too, resulting in cultural incongruities, ethical improprieties, and thorny issues of appropriation. Madonna's sexually explicit "Erotica" (1992), centering on BDSM with flashes of Christian symbolism, samples (at 3:50) Lebanese diva Fairouz's rendition of a Christian hymn (*tarnima diniyya*), "Ana al-Umm al-Hazin" ("I am the sorrowful mother," from her 1962 album *Good Friday: Eastern Sacred Songs*), whose lyrics evoke the original Madonna mourning her son. The contrast is heightened by Fairouz's own Virgin Mary image— three madonnas.

DEEPER HISTORICAL LINKS

Watching the 2018 breakout film *Black Panther*, I was struck by the opening vocal, "Wakanda," performed by the legendary Senegalese singer Baaba Maal. I sensed a hidden connection. In a CBC interview, the film's Grammy and Academy Award–winning composer Ludwig Göransson recounted his adventures seeking "authentic" African music. Traveling overland from Dakar for hours, he finally reached Maal's ancestral home in the remote village of Podor on the Mauritanian border. There Maal recorded the striking vocal solo, about an elephant—metaphor for a king—that had just died. I managed to find the unedited solo on YouTube, and analyzed it.

It was just as I suspected: knowingly or not, Maal was effectively singing in the Arabic *maqam* of *rast*, featuring *sikah*! But the recording's significance extends beyond Hollywood Orientalism. Podor may be remote today, but this trans-Saharan trading city on the Sénégal and Doué rivers was once the capital of an African kingdom called Takrur (800–1285), fusing North African Berber/Arab and sub-Saharan Serer cultures, that had mediated

Middle Eastern–African exchanges for centuries. Through Takrur and other West African kingdoms, Islam diffused along the Sahel, providing a pathway for interaction with Middle Eastern sonic practices. Takruri Muslims studied in Egypt as well as the Maghreb.[8]

Takrur was also a significant source of enslaved Africans traded to the Americas; Podor itself was a slave trading post. Enslaved Muslims were captured from riverine communities along the Sahel, then transported to slave forts on the coast, as portrayed in the acclaimed 1977 television series *Roots*.

Forcibly transported to North America in horrific conditions, disconnected from their traditions, and dehumanized as chattel, enslaved African Muslims lost much of their religious and cultural identity. But many scholars believe that music of Muslim West Africa, linked through Islam to the Middle East, was preserved in vocal style and tonality. Some even hear echoes of the *adhan* in African American field hollers. The historian Sylviane Diouf has speculated that with the banning of collective drumming, singing, and dancing—the typical style in non-Muslim coastal West Africa—musical features of Muslim West Africans, relying more on solo singing and stringed instruments, and more compatible with European types, flourished.[9]

Thus the banjo (perhaps related to the West African *banza*, *ngoni*, or *xalam*), bowed fiddle (analogous to the *goge*, *gonje*, or *riti*), distinctive guitar techniques, a plaintive, ornamented solo singing style, and use of widely intoned blue notes appear to derive from Muslim West Africa, having emerged in interaction with North Africa.[10] Enslaved Muslim musicians could adapt their skills to plantation owners' desire for fiddle and guitar music. While historical links cannot be unequivocally established, it seems likely that a West African Muslim musical style and instrumentarium, shaped through interactions with North Africa and the Middle East, forms one root of African American as well as Latin American musics.

But why were Muslim West African and European instruments compatible? Because they were genealogically connected! Islam helped catalyze north-south trade routes and kingdoms, linking sub-Saharan Africans to North African Arabs and Berbers, to southern Europeans. Following the Arabo-Islamic conquest of North Africa, the Berber Umayyad general Tariq ibn Ziyad (670–719) crossed the Strait of Gibraltar ("Jabal Tariq") in 711 CE and conquered Spain. Al-Andalus—harmonizing Europe, North Africa, and the Middle East—would endure until 1492 with the fall of its last dynasty in Grenada. However, the impact of the Middle East over nearly eight centuries was indelible. Many scholars believe that the European tradition of courtly love poetry, along with numerous musical instruments—including the *laúd* or lute (*al-ʻud*, or oud); the rebec (*rebab*); the kettledrum or naker (*naqqara*); the snare drum or tabor (*tabl* or *tabir*); the frame drum, *adufe* or *pandero* (*duff, bendir*); and the guitar—likely entered from Middle Eastern civilizations via Al-Andalus or interactions during the Crusades (1096–1291). Furthermore, it was precisely 1492 when Columbus set sail to "discover" the Americas, conveying the Andalusian instrumentarium to the New World.

Somewhat later, the Ottomans impacted Europe, particularly in areas of conquest—Greece, the Balkans, and Hungary. In 1529 and 1683 they even reached the gates of Vienna. The famous military band music (*mehter*) of the *yeniçeri* (Janissaries, the Sultan's Elite Guard) featured oboes, trumpets, bass and kettle drums, triangle, and cymbals, inspiring European military bands, and *alla turca* movements among Viennese composers. Ottoman musical influence in Greek and Balkan traditional music remains palpable today.

The upshot is that most European instruments arrived from the greater Middle East during the period 700–1700 CE. As the musicologist Curt Sachs has written: "Nearly all the musical instruments of medieval Europe came from Asia, either from the southeast through Byzantium, or from the Islamic empire through North Africa or from the northeast along the Baltic coast," spreading from there to the New World, and thence the entire world.[11] Indeed, the standard percussion ensembles of the West—from classical to rock and jazz—are derived from *mehter* music. Zildjian, the world's premier cymbal manufacturer, traces to early seventeenth-century Istanbul, when the Ottoman Sultan invited Avedis, an Armenian metallurgist, to craft cymbals for his Janissaries, bestowing the name Zildjian, "son of cymbal maker." In 1929 the family business moved to Quincy, Massachusetts, to better serve the larger Western market. Thus, whether playing his Egyptian *tabla* or a Western drum kit, Hossam Ramzy is sounding the Middle East.

A broader historical picture thus emerges. The Middle East developed two-pronged channels of musical interchange—one toward Europe and the other toward West Africa—later converging on the New World, crucible for new Afro-Euro musical forms. Musician Gunther Schuller termed this phenomenon the "Third Stream."[12] Although he did not note Middle Eastern contributions, later scholars—notably John Storm Roberts—did.[13] Coming to pervade nearly all Western musics, colonialism and imperialism projected these new musical forms to global proportions, including the Middle East itself, where blues, jazz, funk, rock, hip-hop, and Latin genres are all heard today. Imported wholesale or harmoniously fused with local forms, they are but a distant echo of something already familiar.

NOTES

1. See Michael Frishkopf, "Some Meanings of the Spanish Tinge in Contemporary Egyptian Music," in *Mediterranean Mosaic*, edited by Goffredo Plastino, 199–220 (London: Routledge, 2002).

2. David Lean (director), *Lawrence of Arabia,* 1962; Ron Clements and John Musker (directors), *Aladdin,* 1992; and Shane Black (director), *Iron Man 3,* 2013.

3. David Nicholls, Review of "Persian Set," by Henry Cowell. *American Music* 16, no. 2 (1998): 251–53; and Hafez Modirzadeh, "Chromodality and the Cross-Cultural Exchange of Musical Structure," PhD dissertation, Wesleyan University, 1992.

4. See Anne Rasmussen, "The Music of Arab Americans: Aesthetics and Performance in a New Land," in *Images of Enchantment: Visual and Performing Arts of the Middle East*, edited by Sherifa Zuhur, 135–56 (Cairo: American University in Cairo Press, 1998).

5. *Chicago Daily Tribune*, September 29, 1889, p. 25.

6. *St. Louis Post—Dispatch*, December 3, 1893, p. 11.

7. Timbaland also claimed to have "hired an old guy to play it on an Arabian flute," which is certainly not true: the sample is an exact copy of Ramzy's recording, featuring modern Egypt's greatest *nay* (reed flute) player, Mahmud Effat (1935–1994).

8. In Arabic *takrur* came to refer to West Africans generally—hence Cairo's neighborhood of Bulaq Dakrur, where some of them had settled.

9. See Sylviane Diouf, *Servants of Allah: African Muslims Enslaved in the Americas* (New York: New York University Press, 2013), 270–77.

10. This is not to imply that Muslim West African instruments derive from Arab models. Rather, there was interaction across trade and migration routes.

11. Curt Sachs, *The History of Musical Instruments* (New York: Norton, 1940), 260.

12. Gunther Schuller, *Musings: The Musical Worlds of Gunther Schuller* (New York: Oxford University Press, 1989), chapter 18.

13. See John Storm Roberts, *Black Music of Two Worlds: African, Caribbean, Latin, and African-American Traditions* (1972; reprint, New York: Schirmer Books, 1998); and the re-released Folkways Records album, *Black Music of Two Worlds* (1977; reprint, Washington, DC: Smithsonian Folkways Recordings, 2007). From the latter: "The subject of this album-set is the meeting of three musical traditions—African, Arab, and European—to create a fourth tradition of great richness and international impact, that of the Black New World."

Charry, Eric S. 1996. "Plucked Lutes in West Africa: An Historical Overview." *The Galpin Society Journal* 49: 3–37.

Diouf, Sylviane A. 1998. *Servants of Allah: African Muslims Enslaved in the Americas*. New York: New York University Press.

Frishkopf, Michael. 2012. "Tradition and Modernity: The Globalization of Sufi Music in Egypt." In *Popular Culture in the Middle East and North Africa: A Postcolonial Outlook*, edited by Walid El Hamamsy and Mounira Soliman, 162–82. London: Routledge.

———. 2009. "Globalizing the Soundworld: Islam and Sufi Music in the West." In *Sufis in Western Society Global Networking and Locality*, edited by Ron Geaves, Markus Dressler, and Gritt Maria Klinkhammer, 46–76. London: Routledge.

———. 2008. "Music." In *The Islamic World*, edited by Andrew Rippin, 510–26. London: Routledge.

McMurray, David, and Ted Swedenburg. 1991. "Rai Tide Rising." *Middle East Report*, no. 169 (March): 39–42.

Rasmussen, Anne. 1998. "The Music of Arab Americans: Aesthetics and Performance in a New Land." In *Images of Enchantment: Visual and Performing Arts of the Middle East*, edited by Sherifa Zuhur, 135–56. Cairo: American University in Cairo Press.

Storm Roberts, John. *Black Music of Two Worlds*. Liner notes. Washington, DC: Smithsonian Folkways Recordings, 2007.

TWELVE

The Kufiya

Ted Swedenburg

EVER SINCE THE RISE of the armed Palestinian resistance movement in the late 1960s and early 1970s, the kufiya has been a key symbol of the struggles of the Palestinian peoples and an item adopted as a sign of solidarity by sympathizers around the world.[1] In the course of its transnational dissemination, the kufiya's uses have undergone many permutations, as it has appeared variously in the form of everyday streetwear, as high fashion, as a signifier of cool, as a bone of controversy, while still retaining its function as a badge of resistance. Even in the United States, where official and public support for Israel are probably stronger than anywhere else on the planet, kufiya wearing has been significant, if highly contested.

Elsewhere, and especially in countries of the Third World, where popular solidarity with Palestinians is much more deeply ingrained in the political culture, kufiya wearing has been considerably less controversial. Stories and arguments over the kufiya's uses in the United States, where the Palestine issue is controversial and disputed, have been much more charged than elsewhere. In other parts of the globe, the appearance of the kufiya as a political signifier in the public sphere is mostly taken for granted and normalized. This account therefore mostly focuses on the kufiya in the United States and its relation to Palestine, with additional examples drawn from other places. We begin with a discussion of what one observer has termed the US "kufiya craze" of the mid-2000s.

KUFIYA CRAZE

In January 2007 an "anti-war woven scarf" was the featured men's accessory in the early spring online catalog of youth-targeting US clothing outlet

Urban Outfitters. What was on offer, in fact, was the kufiya, in both traditional black-and white and red-and-white versions as well as in turquoise, green, and brown—the latter, colors that had been popular for several years on streets in the West. Unsurprisingly, given the scarf's associations, the announcement triggered protests—whether organized or spontaneous is unclear—and so, just days after it had launched the accessory, the company deleted the line. CEO Dick Hayne even apologized to an Israeli activist that Urban Outfitters had not intended "to imply any sympathy for or support of terrorists or terrorism."

Shortly after the Urban Outfitters controversy, French designer Nicholas Ghesquière introduced a series of kufiya-based designs at luxury outfit Balenciaga's February fashion show in Paris. (Fashion is a transatlantic enterprise, and so it makes sense to discuss fashion trends in Europe as having effects on the United States and vice versa.) Ghesquière took distinctive black-and-white–patterned kufiyas (not named as such), added embroidered red patterns, and festooned them with antique-looking coins. Worn on the runway by Brazilian supermodel Flavia de Oliveira, the accessories sold for a reported £3,000. The kerfuffle over Urban Outfitters's "anti-war scarf," the appearance of kufiyas in high-fashion outfits, and the accessory's visibility on city streets soon piqued mainstream media interest. Perhaps the most high-profile of many reports was one that appeared on page 1 of the *New York Times* Sunday Style Section on February 11, 2007. Titled "Where Some See Fashion, Others See Politics," the piece credibly discussed both dimensions of kufiya wearing but concluded with a statement from a Parsons School of Design student who declared that the fashion was now "dead."

But deceased it was not. Kufiyas continued to be sported by many urban youth in the United States, especially those following "alternative" styles. The years 2007 and 2008 saw frequent comments in the mass media about celebrities sighted in kufiya scarves—actors such as Diane Kruger, Mary-Kate Olsen, Kirstin Dunst, Colin Farrell, and Taylor Momsen as well as musicians Justin Timberlake, Pete Wentz (of Fall Out Boy), and the Jonas Brothers. Other public figures spotted in kufiyas included LA soccer star David Beckham, President George W. Bush's niece Lauren, and senator John McCain's daughter Meghan.

Meanwhile, kufiyas were marketed in a variety of high fashion as well as mass style venues. Kufiya scarves appeared in ensembles displayed at Paris Fashion Week in October 2007 and in March 2008. After Ghesquière, probably the most prominent designer to employ kufiya motifs was John Galliano, when he unveiled his Spring 2008 Menswear collection, "Road Warriors on Venice Beach," in Paris in June 2007. Some of Galliano's male cigar-puffing models in fancy suits strutted the runway wearing traditional kufiya head-dresses, held in place by a cord known as an *'igal*. Another model, resembling an anarchist street fighter, appeared in a kufiya face mask. Others looked like soldiers of the future, clad variously in kufiya-patterned vests, pants and jackets, khakis and body paint, and kufiya headdresses.

Mainstream outlets marketed the item as well. Urban Outfitters continued to offer kufiyas at many outlets and in a multitude of colors but now not marketed as "anti-war" scarves. In winter 2009 the company introduced another kufiya, under the name "Houndstooth Scarf." Other retailers sold a trompe l'oeil version, a T-shirt with a scarf printed on it in the triangle pattern typical of kufiya streetwear. Some mainstream shops sold kufiyas, in multiple colors, employing anodyne names such as "Tablecloth," "Riviera," and "Euro," or exotic ones like "Kashmere." Still other retailers marketed the item as a *shemagh*—the name for the scarf more commonly employed in Britain and Canada, a product of the fact that the item was adopted and worn by British forces stationed in the Middle East during World War II. Some outlets were more daring: Studiohomme, a high-end online European shopping site for men, offered a "Leather keffiyeh" for 546 euros, while the more down-market US company David & Young, supplier to Nordstrom and Macy's, marketed a much cheaper kufiya in 2008 as a "peace scarf." In May 2007 the men's fashion magazine *DNR* (*Daily News Record*) named the kufiya, which it identified with Palestine, as the "Most Provocative Fashion Trend" of the year, but it was careful to add that the trend was mostly *not* a "fervent political statement."

Predictably, heightened public visibility provoked objections from the right-wing/Islamophobic set. In May 2008, Rachael Ray appeared in an advertisement for Dunkin' Donuts on her syndicated Food Network show, wearing a black-and-white scarf, triangle in front. Right-wing commentators launched a barrage of criticism, the most vehement coming from Michelle Malkin, the ultra-conservative Fox News commentator and syndicated columnist. Malkin asserted in her column that kufiya wearers were part of a "jihadi chic" trend and that wearing the scarf "symbolize[d] murderous Palestinian jihad." Malkin explained that the scarf had been "popularized by Yasser Arafat" and a "regular adornment of Muslim terrorists appearing in beheading and hostage-taking videos, the apparel has been mainstreamed by both ignorant (and not so ignorant) fashion designers, celebrities and left-wing icons."[2] Dunkin' Donuts hastily pulled the ad and apologized to anyone who might have been offended, asserting (correctly) that the design on Ray's scarf was paisley and so it was not a kufiya. Malkin responded: "It's refreshing to see an American company show sensitivity to the concerns of Americans opposed to Islamic jihad and its apologists." The hubbub received considerable mainstream media attention, most of it sharply critical of Malkin, while *People* magazine named the Rachael Ray kufiya brouhaha as one of the year's most memorable *fashion* moments.

MEANINGS

These controversies were chiefly based on the kufiya's close association with Palestine. Known as the *hatta* in Palestinian colloquial Arabic, the kufiya emerged as a national sartorial symbol of Palestinian resistance during the 1936–39 revolt against Britain's colonial occupation of Palestine and its support for Zionist colonization. It was the mostly peasant armed guerrillas of the revolt who regularly wore the kufiya into battle against the British occupiers and who mobilized it as a national symbol. Prior to the rebellion, the kufiya (in those days usually pure white), worn as headgear, marked its user as a *fallah* (peasant) or a Bedouin—that is, as a man who occupied an inferior position on the Palestinian Arab sociocultural hierarchy, below that of educated, middle- and upper-class urbanites, known as *effendiya*.

The latter distinguished themselves from those lower down on the social scale either by wearing the tarboosh (fez) or, if more modern-minded, by going bare-headed. During summer and fall of 1938, Palestine's guerrilla bands, based in the countryside, mounted a major offensive against the British forces and began to take control over a number of Arab urban centers. As they did so, they launched a campaign to force the urban *effendiya* to replace their tarbooshes with kufiyas, so as to impose national unity in matters of dress as well as to compel a symbolic inversion of the social hierarchy. The British defeated the revolt by late 1939, but the sartorial symbol of armed peasants doing battle with colonial occupiers remained alive in popular memory. During the 1960s and 1970s, the Palestinian resistance movement revived the kufiya as a symbol of national struggle and unity, but now in a black-and-white– or red-and-white–checkered or fishnet pattern. (Some claim that the distinctive pattern of this updated version of the kufiya in Palestine has its origins in the fishing culture of Mesopotamia.) In recovering the kufiya as signifier to deploy as the iconic headwear for the armed *fedayeen*, the resistance movement invoked the memory of the 1936–39 rebellion and its peasant roots. At the same time, the mainstream of the movement mostly elided the centrality of the kufiya to the events of 1938, when national unity was momentarily imposed by Palestine's lower orders. Yasir Arafat, leader of the Palestine Liberation Organization (PLO) and head of the largest resistance organization, Fateh, was famous for appearing in a kufiya arranged to appear like a map of Palestine.

The resistance movement, as it surged to prominence after the 1967 war, keenly sought international solidarity, and so it welcomed numerous progressive international visitors to the refugee camps and movement offices in Jordan and Lebanon. Thus it became common for US, European, and Third World leftists to don kufiyas, usually worn as scarves around the neck, in solidarity with the Palestinian struggle. In Sweden the kufiya's use was so widespread that the item is known there as a *Palestinasjal*, a "Palestinian scarf." In the United States during the 1970s, by contrast, left and progressive organizations were slow to take up support for Palestinian rights, but as the issue gained wider sympathy throughout the 1980s, many activists would put on the kufiya while going out to demonstrate in the decade's most important left mobilizations: the Central America solidarity movement, the antinuclear campaign, and the antiapartheid struggle. So conventional had it become for US progressives to wear a kufiya that cartoonist Jennifer Berman featured it in a 1987 cartoon, "The American Leftist (*Progressivus Sandinistis Supportoris*)," published in lefty weekly *In These Times*. The sketch poked gentle fun at the era's stereotypical male progressive activist, fitted out in "shapeless" wool cap and old overcoat, a "Guatemalan bag," and a "Palestinian style scarf."

Around the same time, kufiya style was crossing over from progressive circles into urban bohemia and came to be widely worn, especially in New York City, by trendy youths in mostly black outfits. Writer Nina Lalli recalled in the *Village Voice* in 2005 that during the 1980s "the scarves seemed to be for sale on almost every city street"—usually sold by street vendors, rarely in shops, and never by name-brand retailers. By the late 1980s the scarf was so ordinary that the Melissa character (played by Melanie Mayron) appeared with one in ABC television drama *Thirtysomething*'s first season, in March 1988. That same month, and shortly after the eruption of the first Palestinian intifada in December 1987, both *Time* magazine (March 21) and CBS News (March 18) reported on this local urban fashion phenomenon when they noticed that modish US urbanites were garbed in the very same scarves worn by the Palestinian youths throwing rocks at Israeli soldiers, at a time when that image dominated TV news. *Time* concluded that most kufiya wearers were ignorant of the scarf's political—that is, Palestinian—connotations and considered it "just" fashion or thought it cool because it was "ethnic."

The 1990s witnessed no progressive mobilizations in the United States comparable to those of the previous decade, but the kufiya remained in common use in leftish as well as with-it circles, and the kufiya was now also sold in some local boutiques featuring "ethnic" wear and used by some minor designers. In June 2001 the kufiya made its first appearance as high-profile Western designer wear, when Belgian designer Raf Simons launched a "Sometimes You Have to Fight for Your Freedom" men's fashion line, featuring kufiyas, balaclavas, and partially hidden faces. Simons's fashion line drew explicitly on the distinctive look of the era's global justice movement protesters, like the November 1999 Seattle demonstrators against the World Trade Organization (WTO), militant environmental activists, and anarchist streetfighters. Another sign of the conventional nature of the kufiya in that period was the appearance of Carrie Bradshaw (played by Sarah Jessica Parker) in a kufiya tank top on *Sex and the City* in February 2002.

A wave of post 9/11 hyperpatriotism rendered kufiya fashion initiatives unthinkable for a time in the United States. But as sentiment turned against the 2003 invasion of Iraq, kufiyas started to make a comeback, in the streets, in large antiwar mobilizations, and in fashion. In 2005 Keira Knightley, playing bounty hunter Domino Hardy in the film *Domino*, sported a purple kufiya scarf, whose presence around her neck seemed to underscore her super-tough qualities as a tracker of fugitives. In winter 2005–2006, designer Jon Audarson released a kufiya-patterned "Arab cowboy shirt," adopted by director Quentin Tarantino, and so in January 2006 the Fashion & Style pages of the *New York Times* took note of the kufiya's growing presence in street and fashion.

POLITICS OR FASHION?

How did US commentators understand this wave of public visibility of kufiyas between 2006 and 2009? One common claim—made both by activists and more dispassionate observers—was that a scarf that once had signified support for Palestinians had been turned into a commodity and a fashion item, that its political significance had thereby been neutered, and that it was now worn by ignorant legions and celebrities who had no inkling of its subversive meanings.

The case for the kufiya's demise as a political signifier was frequently argued by associating it with hipsters, conventionally described as young urban followers of the latest trends in fashion, ready to abandon a "dated" style for a new one at a moment's notice. Not a rubric that sophisticated young urbanites actually identify with, "hipster" is a stereotype, a term of ridicule used to mock someone engaged in a vapid search for the most recent fad. A classic example of the use of kufiyas to hipster-mock is *Paste* magazine's November 2009 decade retrospective titled "The Evolution of the Hipster, 2000–09," where we find year 2005's representative "Ms. fauxhemian," who "suffers for fashion, wearing a furry hat, boots and keffiyah even during the warmest months." Meanwhile Douglas Haddow, in a 2008 cover story for culture-jamming magazine *Adbusters*, titled "Hipster: The Dead End of Western Civilization," charged that among the many ways in which hipsters led Western youth to political defeat and vacuous consumerism was by turning the kufiya into a "completely meaningless hipster cliché fashion accessory."

As we have seen, the historical evidence suggests that the scarf was in fact embraced as trendy urban street fashion well before what Arab-American blog *Kabobfest* dubbed the "Kuffiya Kraze" in the mid-2000s. Already by the early 1980s, and in subsequent decades, the kufiya had served *both* as a sign of support for Palestinian causes and, in somewhat different contexts, as a sign of cool. Moreover, "kufiya as style" and "kufiya as politics" are not necessarily mutually exclusive phenomena. Rather, in the case of the kufiya there is a dynamic relation, rather than an absolute opposition, between politics and commodification, militancy and fashion, cultural appropriation and political solidarity. The first deployment of kufiya as trendy urban style in the early 1980s emerged at the same time that US progressives were donning the scarves while marching for nuclear disarmament and in solidarity with the struggles in El Salvador, and it is reasonable to suppose that hip urban youths in all-black were among the marchers. The period from 1983 to 1986, moreover, was an era when official circles made great efforts to foster public panic over Middle Eastern terrorism. So it is also likely that some youthful US kufiya wearers used the scarf to express their dissent, in somewhat oblique fashion, from the relentless media and government rhetoric that associated Palestinians with terrorism and justified the US government's steadfast refusal to grant official recognition to the PLO. Trendsters in kufiyas may also have imagined their neckwear as a kind of ironic embrace of a signifier of so-called terrorism.

When Urban Outfitters's 2007 catalog marketed the kufiya as an "antiwar scarf," this was clearly an attempt to cash in on widespread popular dissatisfaction with Bush's war in Iraq by marketing an accessory plainly associated with the ostensible Middle Eastern "enemy." Although the name "anti-war" suggests no connection to Palestine, many consumers would have been aware of that association and would also have seen the kufiya widely worn, as a show of solidarity, at the numerous demonstrations that mobilized hundreds of thousands in the United States and Europe in the run-up to the Iraq War in 2002 and 2003 as well as in the large-scale protests demanding an exit from Iraq that gained traction in the United States in 2005 and 2006. Moreover, all celebrity and fashion mobilization of kufiyas should not be dismissed out of hand as expressions of suave stylishness. When Steve McQueen, the British director of the 2008 film *Hunger* about Irish Republican prisoners' 1981 hunger strike (and the director of the 2013 film *12 Years a Slave*) appeared in the *New York Times Style Magazine* in March 2009 in a Galliano designer kufiya, we might imagine this signaled solidarity with Palestine. When Trent Reznor appeared in a kufiya in Nine Inch Nails's 2007 video "Survivalism," a sharp critique of state surveillance and "homeland security" in the United States, it is not reasonable to think that wearing the scarf was linked to the clip's political commentary?

When Sri Lanka–born singer M.I.A., daughter of a Tamil militant and known for her embrace of progressive causes, uses kufiyas in her "Born Free" (2010) music video, the case is clearer still. The near nine-minute short film shows highly militarized security forces, in what looks like the US Southwest, rounding up gingers and carting them away by bus. Red-headed lads in red kufiyas attack the convoy with rocks and Molotov cocktails but fail to stop it, and so the gingers are driven on to meet their deadly punishment in the desert. The video allegorizes Western states' targeting of ethnic minorities in the name of post-9/11 "security," whether they be undocumented Mexican immigrants in the United States or Muslim refugees in Europe. One could argue that celebrities sighted in kufiyas in the mid-2000s might have donned the accessory as a backhanded expression of dissent from the US invasion of Iraq or sympathy for the Palestinian plight. And even if a particular star were clueless about the radical political meaning of the accessory, could her stylish act of donning a kufiya even so have helped spread a message of dissent?

Since the high point of "kufiya craze," the item has continued to be worn in the United States and elsewhere, variously as political emblem—often to express Palestine solidarity or affiliation to left-wing political causes—as well as in new fashion lines and in everyday contexts. Two other recent trends are of interest. The first is that several Israeli fashion designers have embraced—or perhaps it is more correct to say, *appropriated*—kufiya motifs. Award-winning Israel-born, New York-based designer Nili Lotan used the kufiya pattern in silk dresses for her spring 2008 fashion line. However, Lotan insisted that the dress design was "related to conflict" but "not a political statement."

Other Israeli designers have since followed suit, including actress and self-styled style icon Dodo Bar Or, who launched a successful fashion line and shop in Tel Aviv and whose brand has been available in the UK since 2016. Dresses, tops, kaftans, and skirts in kufiya designs featured prominently in Bar Or's 2016 collections, and according to *Vanity Fair* UK, they drew "inspiration from traditional Israeli [*sic*] dress." Israeli designer Yaron Minkowski introduced a line of day and evening-wear dresses using kufiyas at Tel Aviv Fashion Week in October 2015. Unlike Bar Or, Minkowski acknowledged the Palestinian origin of his designs, stating that the kufiyas were purchased from factories in Hebron and that they were "symbols of coexistence"—but thereby elided the unequal nature of "coexistence" between occupied and occupier.

Another significant trend is the military or tough-guy kufiya. This style is largely the by-product of US military deployments that date back to the first Gulf War of 1991 but became more widespread in wake of the invasions of Afghanistan (2001) and Iraq (2003). This style also was notable in European NATO countries that contributed soldiers to the Iraq and Afghanistan invasions, such as Norway, Denmark, and the UK. While not standard military issue, kufiyas (or *shemaghs*, as they are also often called in these circles) are available at exchanges on US military bases, and they were and continue to be routinely worn on mission by US troops as well as troops from Europe, largely for the same practical reasons as locals: to protect against sun, wind, sand, and cold. Some in the US military claim that the practice was initiated by US Special Forces units, as an insignia of military expertise. The item's adoption by US soldiers in the Middle East helps explain why kufiyas routinely show up in a range of Hollywood movies, often to index wildness, recklessness, and the need to break rules in order to defend civilization. In mainstream discourse the kufiya typically signifies the bad guy, the Arab terrorist, or to use US soldiers' term for their Iraqi opponents, the "*hajji*," which often functions in Hollywood to lend potency, through a kind of sympathetic magic, to the virile American hero.

A wide range of movies have used "tough guy" kufiyas: Matthew McConaughey as a dragon fighter in the fantasy action film *Reign of Fire* (2002); John Travolta as a rogue CIA agent deploying a variety of "nonconventional" methods in order to blow away "bad guys" in *From Paris with Love* (2010); and Denzel Washington as a Bible-carrying wanderer and a master of all weapons in a postapocalypse United States in *The Book of Eli* (2010). Kufiyas and their arrangements have also served to denote a difference in character types. In Kathryn Bigelow's *The Hurt Locker* (2008), for example, the scarf of the "rational" member of the bomb-defusing team in Iraq (played by Brian Geraghty) blends neatly with his uniform, while the reckless freelance military contractor (portrayed by Ralph Fiennes) sports a kufiya as a headscarf, nonregulation. Likewise in *Green Zone* (2010), the sharply dressed chief warrant officer (played by Matt Damon) wears a tidily arranged khaki-colored kufiya scarf, whereas his wayward lieutenant antagonist (portrayed by Jason Isaacs), who is seeking to assassinate one of Saddam's generals in order to stamp out the potential for scandal regarding the absence of Iraqi WMD's, sports a nonofficial blue, sloppily arrayed scarf.

The rough-and-tumble, martial side of kufiya wearing has also been embraced by some on the far right in the United States. Kufiya wearers could be seen among the armed Patriot Militia members who patrolled the streets during the August 2017 pro- and anti-Confederate monument demonstrations in Charlottesville, Virginia, and among the Ammon Bundy–led antigovernment militants who occupied an Oregon nature refuge in January and February of 2016. Kufiyas are routinely sold in US stores and online outlets that stock military surplus, sometimes described as a "tactical desert scarf," and khaki scarves are frequently featured in gun catalog advertisements.

Beyond the United States, kufiya wear in solidarity with Palestine is more common and widespread, and so its uses are less remarked upon. At the same time, trends toward commodification and fashion have been at play as well. In South America, for instance, the kufiya was often put on as a statement of solidarity by activists of the left, and Venezuela's late president Cesar Chavez sometimes appeared in public wearing a kufiya scarf. In July 2014, Bolivia's representative, Sacha Sergio Llorenty Solíz, appeared at the

UN General Assembly wearing a kufiya, in solidarity with Gaza Palestinians who were being pummeled by Israel's military in Operation Protective Edge. "Fashionable" kufiyas are found in Latin America as well. Reinaldo Zevarce ("Alex") of the Venezuelan bubblegum pop group Isa TKM, and the popular Nickelodeon Latin America teen telenovela of the same name, appeared wearing a kufiya trompe l'oeil T-shirt in the 2009 video for the group's whimsical, upbeat song "Ven a bailar" (Come Dance).

According to anthropologist Roxanne Varzi, in Iran the kufiya was first donned by Islamic revolutionaries to show support for Palestine and resistance to Westernization; later, it became a symbol of the volunteer soldiers fighting for Islam in the Iran–Iraq War. Supreme Leader and former Iranian president Ali Khamenei is almost invariably seen wearing a black-and-white kufiya as a neckscarf. In South Africa, a country where popular solidarity with Palestinians is pervasive, the late president Nelson Mandela also at times put on the kufiya. In August 2014, at the opening ceremony of the World Debating Championships in Thailand, the South African team donned kufiya scarves and Palestinian flag badges to express their protest of the Israeli assault on the Gaza Strip.

In the Arab world, globalization and commodification have impacted kufiya uses. Multicolored kufiyas have been adopted there as well and could be seen for sale in the markets of Beirut and East Jerusalem in recent years. Palestinian designers and entrepreneurs, both in the homeland and in the diaspora, have used kufiya patterns in the production of all sorts of commodities, such as sneakers, hoodies, belts, neckties, women's tops, belts, ties, hair bows, earrings, handbags, and so on. During the January–February 2011 uprising centered on Tahrir Square in Cairo, one could spot kufiyas of many colors and worn by protestors in various ways, and also sold by vendors—visible signs of opposition to Egypt's authoritarian state.

CONCLUSION

Today the kufiya is one of most notable and visible signs of Middle Easternness circulating the globe today. Kufiya patterns are the main motif used by the Copenhagen women's fashion designer Cecille, who launched her line in 2011, and her apparel is sold in retail stores worldwide. One might spot a US right-wing militiaman wearing a khaki kufiya scarf together with his military gear, a young woman in Rio using a pink fishnet kufiya as a wrap, or a middle-aged Londoner protesting Britain's support for the Saudi-UAE war against Yemen, her neck protected by a black-and-white kufiya. In some cases it is hard, even well-nigh impossible, to discern what the precise meaning of kufiya wearing might be. In others cases it clearly signals solidarity with Palestine. But in whatever context and whatever form, as it continues its transnational migrations and transfigurations, the kufiya in some manner or the other usually refers back to Palestine and its struggles.

NOTES

1. Alternative spellings for the item are *keffiyeh* and *kaffiyeh*.
2. Michelle Malkin, "The Keffiyeh Kerfuffle," syndicated column, May 28, 2008, http://michellemalkin.com/2008/05/28/the-keffiyeh-kerfuffle/.

FURTHER READING

Renfro, Evan. "Stitched Together, Torn Apart: The Keffiyeh As Cultural Guide." *International Journal of Cultural Studies* 21, no. 6 (2018): 571–86.
Stein, Rebecca, and Ted Swedenburg, editors. *Palestine, Israel and the Politics of Popular Culture*. Durham, NC: Duke University Press, 2005.
Swedenburg, Ted. *Memories of Revolt: The 1936–1939 Rebellion and the Palestinian National Past*. Fayetteville: University of Arkansas Press, 2003.

PART FIVE

Geopolitics of Goods

THIRTEEN

Water of Vulnerability

Jeannie Sowers

DEMAND FOR WATER in the Middle East and North Africa (MENA) is rapidly increasing. Projected population growth in the MENA region through 2025 will likely lower per capita water availability by 30 percent to 70 percent over the next few decades, assuming that renewable water supplies remain constant, which is unlikely.[1] Demand for energy has also been rising quickly across the region. As with water, energy demand is driven not only by population increase but also by energy-intensive industrialization, desalination plants, and changing lifestyles.

This vast and ecologically diverse region is often characterized as oil-rich and water-poor. This generalization erases not only the significant variation in natural resource endowments but also obscures the social, political, technological, and environmental factors that determine whether and how well communities access water and energy. Rather than focusing on resource scarcity, however, it is more useful to think about vulnerability and risk in relation to the basic uses of energy and water. That is, what factors determine whether individuals and communities can access sufficient, decent quality water and energy, to meet basic needs, sustain livelihoods, and conduct economic activity? When shortages in both occur, as they regularly do in the Middle East and North Africa, why is this the case and what can be done?

Water and energy flows depend on government policies and infrastructure, economic purchasing power, and other factors not reducible to physical scarcity. The countries most vulnerable to lack of water and energy often suf-

This chapter is adapted from Jeannie Sowers, "Water, Energy, and Human Insecurity in the Middle East," *Middle East Report* 271 (Summer 2014), https://merip.org/2014/07/water-energy-and-human-insecurity-in-the-middle-east/.

fer from wars, civil conflict, or occupation—all of which render energy and water systems vulnerable to disruption and destruction. At present, water and energy shortages, as well as water contamination, contribute to human suffering most in Sudan, Iraq, Palestine, Syria, and Yemen. Another set of countries are at risk because they rely on water from a single river or shared aquifer. The yield from these water sources is vulnerable to appropriation by other states and to decreased water availability from changing rainfall patterns associated with climate change. Egypt, with its dependence on the Nile, and Iraq vis-à-vis the Tigris and Euphrates, face water risk from these factors. Where countries use river flows for hydropower, water scarcity also means potential energy shortages.

These kinds of dependencies and interlinkages between the provision of water and energy highlight what some have termed the water-energy nexus. Alleviating water scarcity through desalination or large-scale conveyance schemes, found in many of the Persian Gulf states and Libya, requires considerable energy for construction and operation. These costs are often out of reach for countries in the region without access to oil and gas revenues or foreign assistance. In Egypt operation of the Aswan High Dam has to balance needs for hydroelectric power with strategic storage and releases for agriculture and other uses downstream. Using dams for hydropower further entails water losses from evaporation in large reservoirs. A related consideration is the water or energy footprint, which seeks to capture the total amount of a resource consumed during the lifecycle of a product or activity. The extraction and processing of fossil fuels—whether coal, oil, or natural gas—has long been water-intensive, as is the production of biofuels. Different technological processes have differential consumptions of water and energy, which firms typically take into consideration only when public policies provide appropriate regulatory and pricing incentives.

Understanding human security and well-being through the prism of water and energy becomes all the more important in the Middle East given the effects of human-driven climate change. Climate change models predict greater warming in the southern and eastern Mediterranean than for the world as a whole, with a predicted increase of 2.2 degrees to 5.1 degrees Celsius (4 degrees to 9.2 degrees Fahrenheit), combined with an expected reduction in precipitation of 10 percent to 30 percent in parts of the region by the next century.[2] In the first decade of this century, the eastern Mediterranean and Iraq experienced persistent and severe drought conditions. The effects of anthropogenic climate change are already evident. Summer and winter temperatures have become more extreme. Rain and snowfall are less predictable, varying dramatically from historical patterns in timing, form, and intensity. Less frequent but more intense rain has contributed to unprecedented floods, landslides, and mudslides. Drought and dust storms are more frequent and severe, while the wildfire season has grown longer and more deadly. Rising sea levels have threatened coastal communities and resources, as inland water catchments and reservoirs have plummeted at times to record lows.

MEASURING WATER STRESS

That water and energy vulnerability is not simply equivalent to scarcity of the resource is well-known in the development world. Both policymakers and development agencies, however, routinely invoke indices of water stress that simply compare annual renewable water resources with population statistics to yield estimates of water availability per person. According to these criteria, most countries in the region have less than 1,000 cubic meters of water available per person per year. Using Israel as the reference case to determine how much water is needed per person in a developed economy in an arid region, Swedish hydrologist Malin Falkenmark argued that water availability of less than 1,000 cubic meters per year per person limits economic development and hurts human health. Similarly, the Water Stress Index, developed by the risk analysis firm Maplecroft so that multinational firms can "identify risk of water interruptions to supply chains, operations, and investments," assesses risk by comparing water consumption across all sectors against renewable water supplies in rivers, groundwater aquifers, and rainfall.[3] These indices all classify the oil-exporting countries of the Persian Gulf as the most "water stressed." Water consumption in every Gulf country outstrips renewable water supplies by several orders of magnitude. Saudi Arabia, for instance, consumes 936 percent of its total renewable water resources every year. In Maplecroft's ranking of 186 countries, the top five water-stressed states are Bahrain, Qatar, Kuwait, Saudi Arabia, and Libya. The next five are Western Sahara, Yemen, Israel, Djibouti, and Jordan.

Yet trying to capture water risk by comparing renewable water resources with population immediately poses problems. What does it mean to assert that states like Saudi Arabia, Qatar, and Israel are "water stressed" in comparison with conditions in Yemen, Jordan, and Djibouti? Qatar, for instance, ranked as the second most water-stressed country, also has the third highest GDP per capita in the world in 2012, after Norway and Luxembourg, at more than $93,000 per national.[4] Yemen, in contrast, has a GDP per capita of less than $1,500. With the third highest known reserves of natural gas in the world, and 68 percent of government revenues from the export of hydrocarbons, Qatar invests in expensive desalination plants and water reuse infrastructure, and imports many water-intensive food and goods. Yemen has far fewer options.

National aggregate figures overlook important inequalities within states, particularly for minority, refugee, nomadic, and noncitizen populations. Looking again at Qatar, while Qatari citizens are among the world's wealthiest (in terms of GDP per capita), the vast majority of the 1.5 million people living in the country are noncitizens. Although 1 percent of Qatari citizens were estimated to live below the government's poverty line, one study found that 40 percent of expatriate workers fell below the poverty line. Many of these workers reside in labor camps, with inadequate access to potable water, sanitation, and solid waste collection and without basic political or civil rights.

A more adequate measure of water risk, especially in terms of human security and well-being, is provided by programs like the Joint Monitoring Programme for Water Supply and Sanitation (JMP), administered by UNICEF and the World Health Organization (WHO). The JMP tries to assess whether households have access to improved water sources and sanitation infrastructure—that is, systems that prevent fecal and other contamination—using household surveys, questionnaires of experts, and direct sampling of water sources and sanitation facilities. Treating wastewater is crucial to safeguarding water supplies, as inadequate or no treatment contaminates shallow groundwater aquifers and rivers, thereby exacerbating problems of scarcity. In some countries, such as Egypt, Lebanon, Jordan, and others, wastewater facilities have been overloaded, inadequately maintained and poorly monitored. Water pollution is estimated to cost between 0.5 percent to 2.5 percent of GDP annually in the region as a whole, with Iran, Morocco, Jordan, the Gaza Strip, and Lebanon among the most severely affected.[5]

As of 2006, the JMP estimated that thirty million people remained without access to safe drinking water in the Middle East and North Africa, and sixty-nine million people without adequate sanitation services. Some countries—Egypt, Oman, Tunisia, and Turkey—improved access to water supplies between 1990 and 2008, while access declined in Algeria, Djibouti, Palestine, and Yemen. The JMP monitoring programs, while more robust than water stress indices, still fail to adequately account for water pollution, frequent cuts in service, and lack of quality standards for drinking water.[6]

WATER USES AND MISUSES

Most of the water used in the Middle East and North Africa, as in other regions, does not go to household or industrial uses but to agriculture. State policies focused, until recently, on augmenting water supplies primarily to supply agricultural constituencies and pursue food cultivation. Cheap fuel and new drilling technologies enabled a massive expansion in tapping groundwater aquifers globally over the past fifty years. In the Middle East, while shallow renewable aquifers along river basins and coasts had long been accessible, these changes prompted a rush to access "fossil" water stored in deep underground rock aquifers, remnants of an earlier geologic period when rainfall was plentiful. This groundwater revolution propelled the industrialization of agriculture during the 1960s and 1970s. The amount of land brought under cultivation expanded, and policymakers provided subsidies to keep the costs of energy and water low to encourage further agricultural expansion. Subsidized pricing of water and energy have become difficult to change even as resources become more scarce.

Mining of fossil groundwater reserves was accelerated by the construction of massive conveyance and pumping infrastructures to supply water to growing urban populations. The regime of Col. Muammar al-Qaddafi used Libya's oil revenues to build the Great Man-Made River, pumping water from the Nubian Sandstone Aquifer, the largest known fossil aquifer in the world, which spans portions of Libya, Chad, Egypt, and Sudan. The project, begun in 1986 and with a second phase completed in 1996, cost an estimated $25 billion and includes thirteen hundred wells and an extensive network of underground pipes and aqueducts. These water networks have have sometimes been targeted by warring parties in Libya's civil war. Jordan built the Disi Aquifer Conveyance Project to bring water to Amman and other areas from the Disi/Saq aquifer, which spans the Jordan–Saudi border, resulting in tension between the two countries over groundwater extraction. Over the past two decades, clear evidence has emerged of the overextraction of groundwater—aquifers are being drawn down faster than they are replenished through percolation from rain and surface flow. Springs and wells long used by local communities have dried up in Algeria, Yemen, the Palestinian territories, and Jordan, among others. In Jordan the rate at which principal aquifers could be used and adequately replenished was estimated at 275 million cubic meters per year in the early 2000s, while the extraction rate was 520 million cubic meters per year, resulting in depletion and salinization.

One of the most effective means of addressing water scarcity is also the most invisible. Since water consumption in many countries in the Middle East and North Africa, particularly in the Gulf, exceeded renewable water resources some decades ago, these deficits are largely made up by importing cereals and other foods. This trade in what British geographer Tony Allen has termed "virtual water" allows countries with limited water resources to feed their populations, provided they can find the hard currency required to purchase food on international markets. The economic risk to food-importing countries, such as Egypt, is that their economies will not generate enough foreign exchange to purchase food from agricultural exporters such as the United States, Russia, the European Union, and Australia. To offset this risk, and in the face of volatile and often speculative swings in food prices over the past decade, the Persian Gulf states in particular have joined China, India, and other countries in trying to obtain rights to agricultural land and harvests elsewhere. So-called land grabs by the Gulf states have targeted countries, such as Sudan and Ethiopia, with ample renewable water resources and large territories, but whose populations have regularly experienced famine and malnutrition, due to war, drought, and widely dispersed rural populations. Few of these agricultural projects have proved successful enough to alleviate vulnerability by food-importing states. Even with the virtual water embedded in food, the agricultural sector consumes approximately 85 percent of annual renewable water resources in the Middle East and North Africa.

Oil-exporting states—including Saudi Arabia, the smaller Gulf states, Israel, and Algeria—have had the economic clout to invest extensively in desalination to augment water supplies. Saudi Arabia's twenty-seven desalination plants produced more than 70 percent of municipal water and also provided water for industrial use and electricity generation in 2014.[7] The kingdom generated more than 10 million cubic meters of desalinated water per day, while the next largest producer, the United States, produced around 6 million cubic meters. (Unlike the Gulf plants, which desalinate seawater, most plants in the United States draw on brackish water.) In June 2014, Saudi Arabia announced plans for the world's single largest desalination plant.

Attempts to augment water and energy supplies, however, often obscure the most cost-effective and much-needed strategies: to conserve resources by managing demand, limiting pollution, and upgrading infrastructure. Some Middle Eastern states have moved toward reusing agricultural and municipal wastewater for industrial processes, irrigating parks and landscaping, and, to a lesser extent, for irrigation. Egypt, for instance, built a number of plants to mix freshwater from the Nile with drainage water from irrigation. Problems with polluted Nile water and the increasing salinity of drainage water, however, limited the quality of the mixed water and in some cases rendered the plants inoperable. International donors and NGOs have begun to promote the reuse of water within households—what is known as greywater. Water planners also seek to factor in "green water," or the water stored in soil and plants through rainfall and condensation, but this consideration has not yet figured in state policies on water.

ENERGY AND WATER

A growing concern for Middle Eastern policymakers and citizens is not just water, but energy supplies and how these affect water consumption. More than half of the electricity generated in the region is used for air conditioning, given that daytime summer temperatures regularly exceed 100 degrees Fahrenheit in some places. For oil- and gas-exporting countries, rapidly rising demand for fossil fuels at home cuts into rents accrued from selling hydrocarbons globally. In 2013 hydrocarbon revenues accounted for 90 percent or more of government revenues in Bahrain, Iraq, Libya, and Saudi Arabia; between 60 percent and 80 percent in Algeria, Qatar, Oman, the United Arab Emirates, Kuwait, and Yemen; and 50 percent in Iran.[8] For countries with limited or no energy exports, rising oil prices pose serious challenges in meeting domestic energy needs.

Middle Eastern states are thus actively exploring diversifying energy supplies to include nuclear, coal, and renewables. The water footprints of different energy infrastructures are of increasing concern to policymakers, yet plans for coal and nuclear do not adequately reflect water scarcity concerns. Nuclear power plants require significant amounts of water, particularly for cooling, as do commonly used wet-cooling process for coal plants and for some technologies used in concentrated solar arrays. Every country in the region has expressed interest in nuclear power; most have created state-owned authorities to develop the regulatory and financial instruments to move ahead. The United Arab Emirates leads the pack. In 2009 it contracted with a South Korean consortium to build four nuclear power plants, with another thirteen planned. The UAE has indicated it will use both seawater and treated wastewater in its plants. Egypt, which selected the northern coastal site of El-Daba'a for construction of its first nuclear plant, faced local opposition from displaced residents and tourism developers citing environmental and safety concerns. Egypt's President Al-Sisi nevertheless signed a contract with Russia's Rosatom State Atomic Energy Corporation, financed to the tune of $25 billion in loans from Russia, in 2015. Turkey has also contracted with Russia to build a nuclear plant.

Renewables are an increasingly dynamic part of the energy sector, particularly in the non-oil-exporting countries of the region. Every country has adopted targets for renewable energy production, and most have moved to enact concrete policy incentives as well. Wind energy requires no water to generate electricity once installed, and between 2008 and 2011 the average contribution of wind to electricity production increased 27 percent per year, led by turbine arrays in Egypt, Tunisia, and Morocco. Large-scale concentrated solar plants (CSP) have come online in Algeria, Morocco, Egypt, and the United Arab Emirates, while a few countries are exploring small waste-to-energy projects.

In 2013 renewables produced 3.3 percent of the total electricity produced in the Middle East and North Africa, but this share is set to increase in the coming years.[9] The majority of financing for renewables projects comes from state-owned utilities, government ministries, and international development institutions. These funders may continue to push renewable energy development toward large-scale, centralized projects, rather than encourage decentralized, small-scale installations that could directly address water and energy insecurity in marginalized regions. Several programs in Morocco and Tunisia have successfully promoted the use of solar photovoltaics (PV) and solar hot water for residential consumption and rural electrification. These programs offer models that could be rapidly diffused throughout the region, alongside investments in large-scale renewable energy projects. The greatest challenge ahead will be generating the political will to do so.

NOTES

1. Jeannie Sowers, Avner Vengosh, and Erika Weinthal, "Climate Change, Water Resources, and the Politics of Adaptation in the Middle East and North Africa," *Climatic Change* 104, nos. 3–4 (2011): 599–627.

2. J. P. Evans, "21st Century Climate Change in the Middle East," *Climate Change* 92 (2008): 417–32.

3. See "Water Stress Index," Verisk Maplecroft, http://maplecroft.com/about/news/water_stress_index.html (accessed July 15, 2020).

4. See "Level of Water Stress: Freshwater Withdrawal as a Proportion of Available Freshwater Resources," World Bank, https://data.worldbank.org/indicator/ER.H2O.FWST.ZS.

5. World Bank, *Making the Most of Water Scarcity: Accountability for Better Water Management Results in the Middle East and North Africa* (Washington, DC: World Bank, 2007).

6. Neda Zawahri, Jeannie Sowers, and Erika Weinthal, "The Politics of Assessment: Water and Sanitation MDGs in the Middle East and North Africa," *Development and Change* 42, no. 5 (2011): 1153–77.

7. See "About Saudi Arabia: Agriculture and Water," www.saudiembassy.net/agriculture-water (accessed July 15, 2020).

8. Data compiled from the National Resources Governance Institute and the US Energy Information Agency.

9. All data on renewables from International Renewable Energy Agency, "MENA: Renewables Status Report," 2013, www.ren21.net/Portals/0/documents/activities/Regional%20Reports/MENA_2013_lowres.pdf.

FURTHER READING

Davis, Diana K., and Edmund Burke III, eds. *Environmental Imaginaries of the Middle East and North Africa*. Athens: Ohio University Press, 2011.

Jones, Toby Craig. *Desert Kingdom: How Oil and Water Forged Modern Saudi Arabia*. Cambridge, MA: Harvard University Press, 2010.

Mikhail, Alan. *Nature and Empire in Ottoman Egypt: An Environmental History*. Cambridge, UK: Cambridge University Press, 2012.

Sowers, Jeannie. *Environmental Politics in Egypt: Activists, Experts, and the State*. New York: Routledge, 2013.

Verhoeven, Harry, ed. *Environmental Politics in the Middle East*. Oxford, UK: Oxford University Press/Hurst Publishers, 2018.

FOURTEEN

Cycle of Oil and Arms

Timothy Mitchell

Editors' note: Middle Eastern oil and its vital role in the Western economies has had a tremendous impact on domestic developments in the countries of the region. A long-standing view has deemed oil as a "resource curse," which has led to rentier state and dependence on big powers and their corporations. Government control of massive oil revenue enable them to forgo heavy taxation of the population while providing them with public provisions such as education, health, and handouts of various sorts. Altogether, these dynamics appease the local populations and buy off their dissent, thus rendering the regimes unaccountable and authoritarian.

Timothy Mitchell, however, has argued that far from being a source of under-development or authoritarianism, oil has in fact played a significant part in eco-nomic development and democratic demands in oil-producing nations. In fact, oil has underscored a drive for democracy, what Mitchell calls "carbon democracy," by providing the necessary infrastructure—industry, modern work relations, organiza-tion, and disruptive capacity of working people—making it possible for ordinary people to demand accountability and democracy. Yet from the very moment of its discovery, oil has also been intertwined with geopolitics and international power relations. Intense interest in oil as a vital source of energy has instigated foreign cor-porations and states to maintain influence in oil producing nations through market, or political maneuvering, resulting in regime change, massive arms sale, or wars.

This chapter shows how Western governments, notably the United States, pro-mote arms sale to the Middle East as a way to recycle back the money they pay to purchase oil. They can export unlimited amounts of arms, not only because arms do not have the same kind of limited use as, say, shoes or shirts, but also because the pro-motion of the discourse of "insecurity" and "instability" in the region instigated the urge for sophisticated weaponry. Whether such large-scale armament has brought

This chapter is an edited excerpt from Mitchell's *Carbon Democracy: Political Power in the Age of Oil* (London: Verso, 2011).

"security" remains questionable, but it has certainly escalated regional conflicts and instability.

. . .

IN 1964 THE BRITISH GOVERNMENT had tried to encourage the new military government in Baghdad to settle the dispute with the foreign owners of the Iraq Petroleum Company by offering it something in exchange: weapons. At a meeting with the Iraqi prime minister to discuss the oil law passed by the Qasim government before its overthrow the previous year, the British ambassador "took the opportunity of making a reference to our supplying Iraq with arms and equipment." Reporting that he "merely juxtaposed the two things," he told London that its plan to use the sale of military equipment to gain concessions in the oil dispute was unlikely to succeed, since "they are really doing us a favour in buying arms from us." The Iraqis were supporting Britain's weakening trade balance by "paying large sums in sterling," he explained, and at the same time were "well aware of our desire that they should not seek alternative sources of supply." A month later the Foreign Office noted in the same file that Iraq was now purchasing arms from the Soviet Union, and that partly as a result of poor after-contract performance by major British firms, Britain would "have to fight hard to persuade the Iraqis to continue to buy British."[1]

Although the ambassador pretended that oil and weapons were merely juxtaposed, in fact the two fit together in a particular way: one was enormously useful, the other importantly useless. As the producer states gradually forced the major oil companies to share with them more of the profits from oil, increasing quantities of sterling and dollars flowed to the Middle East. To maintain the balance of payments and the viability of the international financial system, Britain and the United States needed a mechanism for these currency flows to be returned. This was especially a problem for the United States, since the value of the dollar was fixed in relation to gold and provided the basis for the Bretton Woods financial system. Arms were particularly suited to this task of financial recycling, for their acquisition was not limited by their usefulness. The dovetailing of the production of petroleum and the manufacture of arms made oil and militarism increasingly interdependent.[2]

The conventional explanation for the rapid increase in arms sales to the Middle East, beginning in the mid-1960s, relies on the arguments offered by the arms salesmen and by the governments that supported their business.

Since the arms trade encouraged the militarization of Middle Eastern states, its growth shaped the development of carbon democracy. To understand this dimension of the relationship between oil and democracy, we need to unpack the justifications used for selling weapons and provide an alternative account.

The purchase of most goods, whether consumable materials like food and clothing or more durable items such as cars or industrial machinery, sooner or later reaches a limit where, in practical terms, no more of the commodity can be used and further acquisition is impossible to justify. Given the enormous size of oil revenues, and the relatively small populations and widespread poverty of many of the countries beginning to accumulate them, ordinary goods could not be purchased at a rate that would go far to balance the flow of dollars (and many could be bought from third countries, like Germany and Japan—purchases that would not improve the dollar problem). Weapons, however, could be purchased to be stored up rather than used and came with their own forms of justification. Under the appropriate doctrines of security, ever-larger acquisitions could be rationalized on the grounds that they would make the need to use them less likely. Certain weapons, such as US fighter aircraft, were becoming so technically complex by the 1960s that a single item might cost more than $10 million, offering a particularly compact vehicle for recycling dollars. Arms, therefore, could be purchased in quantities unlimited by any practical need or capacity to consume. As petrodollars flowed increasingly to the Middle East, the sale of expensive weaponry provided a unique apparatus for recycling those dollars—one that could expand without any normal commercial constraint.

Since 1945, the United States had relied on the "institutionalized waste" of peacetime domestic military spending to soak up surplus capital and maintain the profitability of several of its largest manufacturing corporations. It enhanced this mechanism of waste with spending on the Korean and Vietnam wars. When projections for expenditure on Asian warfare began to drop in the later 1960s, America's two dozen giant military contractors were in urgent need of new outlets for their hardware. No longer able to rely on increased purchases by the US government, they sought to transform the transfer of weapons to foreign governments, previously a relatively small trade financed mostly through US overseas development aid, into a commercial export business. In the 1950s about 95 percent of US arms exports were financed by government aid; by the 1990s the figure was about 30 percent.[3] The financiers concerned with dollar recycling now had a powerful ally.

Meanwhile, for the autocrats and military regimes of the Middle East, arms purchases provided a relatively effortless way to assert the technological prowess of the state. More important, once the West turned the supply of arms from a form of government-to-government aid into a commercial business, a space opened for middlemen to operate as brokers between the local state and the foreign firms. Members of ruling families, their in-laws, and their political allies were well placed to fill this role, allowing a part of the revenues from oil, recycled as arms purchases, an easy diversion into prodigious levels of private accumulation.

After 1967, Iraq turned to France and the Soviet Union for arms, rewarding the countries that were helping it develop a national oil industry. For Britain and the United States the main recycling point was Iran, which imported almost three times as much weaponry as Iraq in the decade after 1967. In 1966 the Shah of Iran agreed to a large purchase from General Dynamics of its new F-111 fighter-bomber, an aircraft that was over budget, failing to meet performance targets, and frequently crashing in test flights. He persuaded the Western oil consortium to increase production by 12 percent a year to finance this and future military spending. The following year, the companies increased production by double that amount, thanks to the Arab oil embargo during the June 1967 Arab–Israeli War, but in 1968 and 1969 Iran demanded even larger increases in revenue. As the supply of weapons and equipment accelerated, increasing numbers of arms contractors, bankers, construction companies, consultants, public relations firms, and military officers began to profit from the flow of finance, building themselves into the capillaries and arteries through which it flowed. US banks and arms manufacturers, aided by their British, French, and Italian counterparts, transformed the export of weapons into one of the West's most profitable export industries.

THE GUAM DOCTRINE

Since arms sales were useful for their uselessness, and there was no precedent for the volume of weapons sold, they needed a special apparatus of justification. The work of transforming the superfluous consumption of weaponry on a gargantuan scale into necessity was performed by a new rhetoric of insecurity and by a series of US actions to produce or sustain the required experience of instability and uncertainty. The old rhetoric of the postwar period about a communist threat to American interests in the Middle East was proving hard to keep alive. Having finally found a foothold in the oilfields of the Gulf, the Soviet Union had failed to threaten supplies of oil to the West, despite the warnings of Cold War experts. Soviet aid in exploiting the vast reserves of North Rumaila, offered in 1968, would allow Iraq to produce oil from a field whose development Western companies had spent four decades trying to delay (or seven decades, if one counts back to the days of the Baghdad Railway). Instead of threatening the security of the West's oil supplies, the Soviet Union was threatening to increase them.

The Arab defeat in the June 1967 war with Israel weakened Arab nationalists and strengthened the conservative, Western-backed regimes in the Gulf. The defeat also hastened a financial crisis in Britain. The brief Arab oil embargo and the closing of the Suez Canal interrupted the supply of Britain's sterling oil from the Gulf, creating a balance-of-payments crisis that forced the Labour government to devalue the pound and abandon its postwar effort to maintain sterling as an international trading and reserve currency. To address the financial crisis, Britain announced in January 1968 that it would end its role as an imperial power in the Middle East, withdrawing all military forces from the sheikhdoms of the Gulf within four years.

Militarists at right-wing think tanks in Washington, in particular the new Center for International and Strategic Studies, began to warn that the British withdrawal would create a "power vacuum" in the region. In reality, it was thanks to the creation of a vacuum, or at least a "deflation" in local power, that Britain could justify ending its military presence in the Gulf. Since the "revolutionary Arabs" had been "completely deflated" by the 1967 defeat, the Foreign Office noted, the sheikhdoms of the Gulf could survive without a British military presence.[4] The State Department official responsible for the Arabian Peninsula agreed, arguing that the claim of the US ambassador in Tehran that hostile forces were ready to fill "a vacuum" in the Gulf caused by the British departure was "overdrawn if not inaccurate." He pointed out that the major Arab powers—Egypt, Syria, and Iraq—"are pinned down elsewhere by the Israelis and Kurds" (whose rebellion in northern Iraq was funded by Israel), while the conservative Arab states saw an armed Iran "more as a threat than a reassurance."[5]

The Shah of Iran seized the opportunity of Britain's departure to portray the large Iranian military purchases already under way as a scheme to turn Iran into the region's policeman. The only significant threat the Shah faced was the growing number of domestic political opponents his government hunted down and imprisoned, a form of police work that had no need for most of the weapons he wished to purchase. He nevertheless demanded to buy ever more sophisticated and expensive arms and to be given the increased oil revenue and large US government loans to pay for them. The US ambassador relayed to Washington the arguments the Shah picked up from the American arms manufacturers, reporting his view that increased arms sales "would benefit US industry (he mentioned DOD [was] obliged to bail out Lockheed), substantially help difficult US balance of payments situation, and serve our own vital strategic interests in Gulf and Middle East."

The arms manufacturers helped promote the doctrines of regional insecurity and national military prowess, instructing their agents to discuss arms sales not as commercial arrangements but in terms of strategic objectives. In September 1968, Tom Jones, the chief executive of Northrop Corporation, wrote to Kim Roosevelt (the former CIA agent who had engineered the overthrow of Mossadegh in 1953 and whose consulting firm now facilitated arms sales to the Shah) about trying to sell Iran Northrop's P530 lightweight fighter, for which it had been unable to find buyers: "In any discussions with the Shah," Jones explained, "it is important that they be kept on the basis of fundamental national objectives, rather than allow it to take the appearance of a sales plan."[6]

In 1969 the newly elected administration of Richard Nixon inadvertently offered the arms manufacturers and their clients a new term for these "fundamental national objectives"—the so-called Nixon Doctrine. On a trip to Southeast Asia in July the president made some off-the-record remarks to the press at a stopover in Guam, intended to reassure the American-backed military dictatorships of the region that his promise to begin withdrawing forces from Vietnam did not imply any overall change in US policy, which would continue to rest on arming and assisting its client states to fight the threat of popular and democratic movements—or what Washington called "subversion"—with the United States intervening overtly only when local counterinsurgency programs failed. The remarks about the limited role of direct intervention also provided cover for the action on which the Nixon government was secretly embarking, behind its public promise—a large escalation of the war against Vietnam and its extension into Cambodia and Laos. Since the reassurance about continuing to arm client states was off-the-record and could not be quoted directly, the US press started referring to it in shorthand as the Guam Doctrine, then simply as the Nixon Doctrine—a term later adopted by Nixon's foreign policy team. This continuation of long-standing American military relations with client states was heralded in the American media as marking a new direction in US policy, a claim subsequently echoed in almost all academic scholarship on US foreign policy and the Middle East.

The advantage of turning existing US counterinsurgency policy into a "doctrine" was that rulers like the Shah of Iran, and his allies in American arms firms and think tanks, could now appeal to it and demand to be given the same role as the Southeast Asian dictatorships. Insisting that Washington either subsidize his weapons purchases with congressional loans or pressure the US oil companies to pump more Iranian oil to pay the arms bills, the Shah told the US ambassador "he could not understand why we did not want to help him implement [the] Nixon doctrine in [the] Gulf area where our and our allies' interests were also threatened."[7]

Deploying the Nixon doctrine enabled the Shah and his supporters to overcome opposition in the State Department and other parts of the US government. By 1972 the American ambassador to Tehran was writing to Henry Kissinger, the national security adviser, criticizing those in Washington who argued that the United States should do what was possible "to prevent Iran, in our studied wisdom, from overbuying." Using a back-channel communication to bypass the State Department, the ambassador warned that Britain, France, and Italy were competing for arms contracts and insisted that "there is no reason for us to lose the market, particularly when viewed over the red ink on our balance of payments ledger." In the margin of the message Kissinger added a handwritten note: "In short, it is not repeat not our policy to discourage Iranian arms purchases."[8]

Facing a collapse in the value of the dollar, and increased lobbying from the arms firms, the Nixon administration decided to sell the Shah all the weapons that he and his American lobbyists were demanding, allowing the sales to circumvent the normal governmental reviews and creating what a Senate report called "a bonanza for US weapons manufacturers, the procurement branches of three US services, and the Defense Security Assistance Agency."[9] Since Congress was unwilling to finance additional military sales credits, and the large New York banks were beginning to voice concerns about the Shah's ability to maintain payments on the money they were lending him to buy weapons, the US government also began to push for an increased price of oil to pay for them. The decision to weaponize the oil trade with Iran, and later other oil states, was announced as an extension of the "Nixon Doctrine" to the Gulf, supplying the extraordinary levels of arms transfers with the equipment needed to explain them. Subsequent histories of these events faithfully reproduce this apparatus of justification.

The Nixon administration also blocked the efforts of the UN and the Arab states, and at times even its own State Department, to settle the Palestine question, helping to maintain the forms of instability and conflict on which American "security" policy would now increasingly depend. In Kurdistan, the other conflict keeping Arab states "pinned down," Washington was unable to prevent Iraq from reaching a settlement with the Kurds in 1970 but responded to this threat of stability in the Gulf two years later by agreeing with Israel and Iran to reopen the conflict with renewed military support to one of the Kurdish factions. The aim was not to enable the Kurds to win political rights, according to a later congressional investigation, but simply to "continue a level of hostilities sufficient to sap the resources of our ally's neighboring country [Iraq]."[10]

The arms sales to Iran and their supporting doctrine played no important role in protecting the Gulf or defending American control of the region's oil. In fact, the major US oil companies lobbied against the increased supply of weapons to Iran and the doctrine used to justify them. They argued that political stability in the Gulf could be better secured by America ending its support for Israel's occupation of Arab territories and allowing a settlement of the Palestine question. The Nixon administration had also initiated a large increase in the sale of arms to Israel, although weapons sent to Israel were paid for not with local oil revenues but by US taxpayers. Arming Iran, an ally of Israel, the companies argued, only worsened the one-sidedness of America's Middle East policy. The oil companies also objected to the extraordinary level of weapons sales to Iran because the increased oil revenues Tehran required to pay for the weapons would force them to switch more production away from the Arab states, weakening the companies' relations with those states and benefiting the European oil firms and independent US firms that shared production in Iran. It might also lead Iran to demand an even higher share of profits.

The absurdity of the scale of arms sales to the oil states later became apparent, when the hyper-armed Iranian state was brought down by street protests and a general strike led by oil workers in the 1979 revolution, and when the tens of billions of dollars Saudi Arabia spent on weapons left it helpless in 1990 against Iraq's occupation of Kuwait. Whatever the excess, however, the arms sales also militarized the oil states, with continuing consequences for local populations. The Kurds of Iraq had already discovered this in the 1960s, when the government used its British-supplied weapons against them, and they would discover it again when Iran and the United States abruptly cut off support for the Kurdish insurgency in 1975. Protesters in Iran felt the consequences when the government deployed American-supplied helicopters to fire on political demonstrations in 1978–79 and in countless other episodes. The militarization also lined up numerous interests in the United States that preferred to see regional crises unresolved and wars in the Middle East prolonged.

NOTES

1. "Roger Allen, Ambassador in Baghdad, to Foreign Office," February 8, 1964, FO 371/175780; cover note added March 12, 1964.

2. Nitzan and Bichler, "Weapondollar-Petrodollar Coalition," 198–273.

3. Nitzan and Bichler, "Weapondollar-Petrodollar Coalition," 216.

4. Foreign Office Minutes, May 1971, FCO 8/1311, cited in William Roger Louis, "The Withdrawal from the Gulf," in Ends of British Imperialism: The Scramble for Empire, Suez and Decolonization: Collected Essays (London: I. B. Tauris, 2006), 877–903.

5. William D. Brewer, "Memorandum from the Country Director for Saudi Arabia, Kuwait, Yemen and Aden to the Country Director for Iran," February 27, 1970, Foreign Relations of the United States, Document 51; and Douglas Little, "The United States and the Kurds: A Cold War Story," Journal of Cold War Studies 12, no. 4 (2010): 71.

6. Tom Jones as cited in Sampson, Arms Bazaar, 48.

7. MacArthur, "Shah's Views on Procurement Military Equipment," US Department of State Telegram, Tehran 1019.

8. Harold Saunders, "Memorandum for Dr. Kissinger," July 14, 1972, Foreign Relations of the United States, Document 212.

9. As quoted in James Bill, The Eagle and the Lion (New Haven, CT: Yale University Press, 1989), 200.

10. Bill, Eagle and the Lion.

FURTHER READING

Mitchell, Timothy. Carbon Democracy: Political Power in the Age of Oil. London: Verso Books, 2011.

Nitzan, Jonathan, and Shimshon Bichler. "The Weapondollar-Petrodollar Coalition." In The Global Political Economy of Israel, 198–273. London: Pluto Press, 2002.

Sampson, Anthony. The Arms Bazaar. London: Hodder & Stoughton, 1977.

FIFTEEN

Cotton, Made in Egypt

Ahmad Shokr

WHAT MAKES EGYPTIAN COTTON EGYPTIAN? Is it the people who produce it? Or the place where it is produced? Or the distinctive physical properties that it bears? Are national products simply expressions of a particular society, culture, or territory that defines itself in national terms? Or does their existence depend on wider arrangements that transcend national borders? These kinds of questions came to light a few years ago in a controversy involving Egyptian cotton exporters, a major Indian textile manufacturer, and several American retail giants. In 2016, Welspun India—one of the largest suppliers of towels and bedsheets to the United States—was found to have falsely labeled 750,000 sheets as 100 percent Egyptian.[1]

In reality, the sheets were manufactured by mixing cheaper, lower-grade fibers from other countries into fabrics sold as Egyptian cotton. The scandal caused major US retailers like Walmart and Target to remove hundreds of thousands of bedding sheets from their stores, and Welspun later faced a series of consumer lawsuits. But the case of Welspun India was not unique. Textile manufacturers have long been known to seek economic gain by misrepresenting the origins of their cotton supplies. In the same year the Cotton Egypt Association (CEA)—an organization jointly formed by the Egyptian Ministry of Industry and Trade and Egyptian cotton exporters—estimated that 90 percent of global supplies were falsely marketed as 100 percent Egyptian.[2] Far from being an exception, the Welspun scandal demonstrates the complexities of managing a supply chain for a commodity with a global reputation that stretches across different parts of the world.

Led by the CEA, Egyptian authorities and exporters have made efforts to clamp down on what they consider to be marketing fraud. For example, the CEA now licenses the use of an Egyptian cotton logo to suppliers and manufacturers worldwide to certify the authenticity of their Egyptian cotton. Historically, the legal channels available to fight this battle have been limited. Other countries, like the United States and Sudan, produce cotton of similar quality to its Egyptian counterpart and manufacturers of those cottons have been legally entitled to call their finished product Egyptian regardless of the crop's origin. The reasons go back nearly a century when, in the 1920s, Egyptian officials did not defend the country's copyright to the term. As a result, courts around the world began ruling that Egyptian cotton was an acceptable label for fabrics made of any long-staple cotton as fine in quality as that produced in Egypt. In short, Egyptian cotton as defined in these rulings did not represent a place so much as a brand—a brand whose content was not bounded by any national borders but rather produced by specific transnational arrangements and relationships.

That courts in the 1920s, located thousands of miles away from Egypt, could pass verdicts on what defines authentically Egyptian cotton, raises important questions about where the boundary exists between national and transnational processes. While raw cotton is a commodity produced in Egypt, its existence is only made possible by an assemblage of networks and relationships that bind Egyptian producers and exporters to other parts of the world. For nearly two centuries most cotton produced in Egypt has crossed borders, weaving together dispersed sites around the world—for example, a village in the Nile Delta, a seaport in Alexandria, a cotton exchange in Liverpool, a factory in Lancashire, a retailer in America, and courtrooms in various major capitals—into various webs of interdependence and hierarchy.

This picture might encourage us to reconsider what we mean by the terms "national" and "global." In existing social scientific literature, there is a tendency to treat nations as entities that contain within them a defined set of human social relationships that are then privileged as units of analysis. This is what some critical scholars have called methodological nationalism. In reality, no nation is a discrete entity sealed off from the world around it; inside the borders of every nation exists human (and nonhuman) relationships and processes that are part and parcel of wider political, economic, and social dynamics on regional and/or international scales.

For historians, these sorts of dynamics have become increasingly visible since the nineteenth century—what historians refer to as the modern period in world history—as a result of economic, political, and technological transformations that have intensified human interconnection and interdependence across the globe and which developed with the spread of European imperialism. In particular, scholars have described the decades between 1870 and 1914 as a kind of golden age of imperial globalization characterized by a dramatic growth of world trade, the expansion of international finance, heightened migration, and massive overseas investments by European colonial powers in infrastructure to promote increased agricultural commodity production for European markets.

Of course, these same developments—building dams and irrigation canals in European colonies, introducing new methods of government, opening overseas markets, and reducing transportation and communication times through new technologies like railways, steamships, and telegraphs—also offered ways for European empires to acquire new powers. They could develop and expand their ability to access and exploit resources in their colonies, control overseas trade in valuable commodities, and gather and produce knowledge and information about colonized societies. The story of cotton in Egypt is very much a part of this history.

EGYPT'S "WHITE GOLD"

Egypt has long been famous for producing long- and extra-long-staple cotton—a crop with long individual threads that only exists in a handful of countries and that is used for the production of high-quality, silky fabrics. In Egypt most cotton has been historically produced in the Nile Delta, a fertile triangle located between the Mediterranean Sea and Cairo at its southern apex. In the nineteenth century this region was the site of the most transformative irrigation and public works projects in Egypt. As Egypt became incorporated into the world economy, its trade relations with the surrounding world underwent a significant transformation. In 1800 more than half of Egypt's trade was with the rest of the Ottoman Empire. By the end of the century, nearly 80–90 percent of Egyptian exports consisted of cotton for British and European textile mills. In less than one hundred years those regional networks that made up a vibrant world of commerce in the Mediterranean were displaced by new relationships of trade and dependency with Western Europe.

The story of Egyptian cotton began in the first half of the nineteenth century. As early as the 1820s, Egyptian modernizing reformers, led by Khedive Mehmed Ali Pasha, decided to promote the cultivation of long-staple cotton for commercial purposes—what scholars call cash cropping. Initially the state was heavily involved in producing and marketing cotton, but by the 1840s Egyptian rulers began to limit their involvement to building irrigation and transportation infrastructure to encourage cotton cultivation. The act of growing and trading cotton was left largely in the hands of new landowning classes and a network of mostly French, Italian, and Greek-speaking traders that formed a powerful mercantile bourgeoisie. In promoting cash crop cultivation, the goal of Egyptian rulers was to acquire revenue to build an army that would protect Mehmed Ali's autonomy from the Ottoman Empire and strengthen the Egyptian state in the face of growing Western power. This state-building imperative brought with it many other decisions too: The Egyptian government restructured its taxation system, introduced private landownership for village tax collectors to collect levies more efficiently, and built a vast network of canals, barrages, and railways, in part to enable the cultivation of cotton and its transportation from villages to local markets.

But this developmentalist project—initiated by Mehmed Ali and continued by his successors—soon began to reveal its large costs. First, turning Egypt into a supplier of cash crops with a subordinate status in the world economy exposed the country to global economic shocks, like the First Great Depression, that made life in the country more vulnerable to the volatilities of foreign markets. Second, the Egyptian government needed to borrow funds to push forward its modernizing program, including money for public works, urban development, and the construction of the Suez Canal. By the mid-nineteenth century, the Egyptian state was relying heavily on loans from European banks. These loans grew to the point where in 1876 the Egyptian government faced bankruptcy and European powers stepped in to take control of Egyptian state revenues through a financial commission known as the Caisse De La Dette Publique. Ironically, the move Mehmed Ali initiated toward specialization in cash crops, while intended to strengthen the Egyptian state on the world stage, ended up compromising the country's economic sovereignty in fundamental ways.

While Egyptian rulers helped transform much of the countryside into a vast cotton plantation, the impetus to continue growing that particular crop did not originate solely inside Egypt. Two crucial events in the nineteenth century encouraged a massive expansion of Egyptian cotton production for world markets, and both of them involved forces from outside of the Middle East: the US Civil War (1861–65) and the British Occupation of Egypt (1882–1956). Together, these two events served to further "globalize" the country's staple export. The American Civil War offers a prime example of how, in the emerging nineteenth-century world economy, events in one corner of the world could dramatically affect events in another part. Until the war the United States was by far the largest producer of cotton for European textile manufacturers who formed one of the dominant industries spawned by the Industrial Revolution.

When the war broke out, the Northern blockade of Confederate ports (which lasted from 1861 to 1865) prevented the export of American cotton, thereby creating massive shortfalls of cotton supplies to European markets. This encouraged British manufacturers to search for alternative suppliers in their overseas colonies (the British had not yet occupied Egypt). As a result, in the decades after the war, cotton production and trade intensified across different geographical sites, orienting places like the United States, Brazil, India, and Egypt toward the export of cotton for European industries. This global production complex created what historian Sven Beckert has called an "empire of cotton."[3] Within a few years, European involvement in Egypt reached its height with the British invasion of Egypt in 1882 and its subsequent occupation that lasted more than seventy years. In the first two decades of the occupation, the British did more to expand cotton production, leading one scholar to analogize British efforts in Egypt to a "green revolution."[4]

Although Egyptian cotton production were situated in a particular place—Egypt, especially the Nile Delta—their activities were firmly embedded in wider dynamics that connected them to far-flung regions of the world. These included transnational networks of trade, finance, and transport that connected Egyptian villages to textile factories in England; circuits of technical and agricultural expertise traveling between Europe and its colonies; and even the transnational movement of ideas and strategies for how to confront European imperialism and the turbulent and unequal world it had created. Moreover, the deepening incorporation of Egyptian producers into an imperial world economy introduced them to new kinds of market dependence whereby their everyday lives could be profoundly bound up with events happening far beyond Egyptian borders. A report in 1931 nicely captured the globally interconnected but highly unequal world in which Egyptian cotton growers now lived: "It is no exaggeration to say that the prosperity of the Egyptian peasant, working on his field many thousands of miles from the market where his product, or the finished article made from it, is bought and sold, can be sensibly affected by civil war in China, by political events in India, by labor disputes in England, by a stock exchange collapse in New York."[5]

FIGURE 15.1 "Arts et métiers. 1. L'arçonneur de coton; 2.3. Le fileur et la dévideuse de laine; 4.5. Le tourneur et le serrurier en bois." Rare Book Division, New York Public Library Digital Collections, http://digitalcollections.nypl.org/items/510d47e0-21bf-a3d9-e040-e00a18064a99 (accessed March 6, 2020).

By 1922, when Egypt gained its nominal independence from the British Empire, the country still exhibited many features of a plantation economy. Cotton accounted for the vast majority of Egyptian exports, between 75 percent and 90 percent. Egypt's dependence on cotton exports meant that farmers selling their products in international markets were increasingly vulnerable to price volatility, which became particularly extreme in the years after World War I. And the spread of cash crop cultivation went hand-in-hand with a growing disparity in landownership: By the 1920s a few thousand large landowners—who made up no more than 1 percent of the rural landholding population—owned more land than the country's two million smallholders, while many more remained landless.[6] This stark inequality would, at least in part, set the stage for the Free Officers Revolt in 1952, which overthrew the monarchy and established an independent republic.

Since the 1960s, the production and trade of cotton in Egypt has undergone several crucial moments of reorganization. While state involvement in cotton production and trade began to increase after World War I, by the 1960s most aspects of the cotton economy in Egypt were fully nationalized. Through the establishment of a countrywide agrarian cooperative system, the Egyptian state was able to control the provision of farming inputs, the coordination of cultivation across different villages, and the marketing of cotton. In place of the private merchants who dominated the cotton trade from the nineteenth century, a system of compulsory delivery to the state was instituted. This system of state control over cotton remained largely in place until economic liberalization efforts that began in the 1970s and accelerated in the 1990s. This new round of economic restructuring allowed cultivators to grow and sell crops outside of state supervision and enabled the reemergence of private traders. Over the last quarter century, this has caused many cultivators to move away from cotton toward more lucrative crops.

FROM FIBER TO FABRIC: THE JOURNEY OF EGYPTIAN COTTON

Apart from the United States, perhaps no country dominates the production of long-staple cotton on the global stage like Egypt. Egyptian cotton has a roughly two-year lifecycle. A bale of cotton planted in an Egyptian village this year will be sold as bed sheets or linens in a foreign retail store after two years. Along the way that bale of cotton goes through various stages of processing in which both the physical appearance of that cotton and the actors who handle it change several times.

Cotton production begins on the field where the plant is grown. Mahmoud is a farmer in the Sharqiyyah province of the Nile Delta. He grows cotton on three feddans (roughly three US acres) of land that he purchased years ago. He is one of a few remaining cotton growers in his village and its surrounding area, as the crop has undergone a significant decline in recent years. For Mahmoud, the lifecycle of cotton begins when he acquires the inputs he will need—usually on loan—to grow his crop. He gets seeds and pesticides from local government research centers and fertilizers from trading companies. Years ago, I met the son of one of the founders of Egypt's agricultural cooperative movement in the early twentieth century, and we discussed the historical relationship between finance and cotton cultivation. "Cotton necessarily means debt," he told me. "Without credit there is no cotton growing." Today this description continues to resonate with the lived experiences of cotton farmers in the Nile Delta. The cultivators in Mahmoud's village estimate that around half a farmer's income goes toward paying off debts.

Mahmoud begins to pick his cotton every season in September and October. However, it is a task much too big for one person. On average, picking one feddan of cotton in a day requires more than one hundred people. Where do cotton growers find the labor power to turn their crop into a saleable commodity? Many cotton growers initially resort to those closest to them. "Without a family, land is useless," one farmer told me. "The first step to growing cotton is having people to help." To save labor costs, many farmers rely on their family and children to help pick cotton. But picking a feddan or more of cotton often requires more hands than that. Other families combine their labor together in a pooling arrangement known as the *zimiil* system. Still others, like Mahmoud, turn to a local recruiting agent (*muta'ahid lam 'anfar*) in their village to hire more workers. In Mahmoud's case the agent charges him a commission of around 10 percent of a worker's daily wage: If Mahmoud hires a day laborer for 50 Egyptian pounds, he will pay the agent 5 Egyptian pounds. To pick an entire feddan, Mahmoud hires twenty or so laborers to work for him more than five days.

As I sat with a group of farmers and state-appointed engineers in Sharqiyyah, they explained to me the complicated factors that govern the profitability of a cotton field. They range from seasonal factors (weather, quality of inputs, etc.) to factors related to the land, like the elimination of crop rotations and the fragmentation of properties after inheritance that can allow pests to spread more easily from one plot of land to another. But above all, they blame the crop's recent decline on free-market policies implemented by the Egyptian state. Recently, subsidy cuts and a currency devaluation (which in 2016 caused the value of the Egyptian pound to crash almost 50 percent against the US dollar) have raised the costs of seeds, fertilizers, and pesticides. For example, farmers in Sharqiyyah told me that between 2015 and 2017 the price of fertilizers rose by 150 percent and pesticides they used to purchase for 17 Egyptian pounds cost 72 Egyptian pounds.

While these might be some of the proximate causes for the decline of cotton production, there is another longer-term cause that goes back more than twenty years: the entry of private trading companies that buy and sell in Egyptian cotton. Like the subsidies program, the number and composition of Egypt's cotton-trading companies have undergone a significant change since the 1990s. Until 1994, no cotton trading could happen outside the purview of public trading companies. That changed over the next decade as part of what scholars call Egypt's neoliberal transformation. After facing an external debt crisis only a few years earlier, the Egyptian government embraced policies of economic liberalization promoted by the United States and international financial organizations, which allowed dozens of private trading houses to open in Alexandria. Since 1994, peasants have been allowed to grow cotton without government quotas or restrictions and private traders have been permitted to buy, gin, and sell cotton to local manufacturers or to export it.

How does Egyptian cotton reach markets outside of Egypt? In answering this question, one should bear in mind that no global market exists as a coherent object or thing in a fixed location with defined boundaries. Rather, a global market for any commodity is an aggregation of many individual acts of trade. In that sense, a global market should be understood as a complex machine that cannot exist independently of its many moving parts. So what kinds of commercial encounters are involved in moving Egyptian cotton from a village where it is grown to a retail store where it is sold as a finished good?

Let us begin with those traders who purchase cotton from Egyptian villages. Today, most cotton grown in Egypt moves from villages to local and international markets through private traders. Farmers can sell their cotton either directly to private trading houses (usually through designated markets called *halaqas*) or to smaller local traders. In fewer cases, farmers sell their crop to state-run cooperatives who then resell it to public or private companies. Those private trading companies who buy the majority of the annual cotton crop typically operate a host of local offices in major cotton-producing regions across the country. For example, Modern Nile Cotton, one of the largest private trading companies in Egypt, maintains eight or so branches across the country and it both supplies Egyptian cotton to international markets and imports foreign cottons for Egyptian spinners.

How do private trading houses organize their activities? In the nineteenth century, Egypt had organized spot and futures markets (the latter being one of the oldest in the world) based in Alexandria. Both institutions were weakened and ultimately destroyed in the 1950s and 1960s as the postindependence Egyptian state constructed a centrally planned system to extend its control over important sectors of the economy. While Egyptian authorities have reverted to free-market policies over the past few decades, cotton trading today is still different in some fundamental ways than it was in the nineteenth century. One of the biggest differences is that there exists no institutionalized commodity exchange—like the Chicago Board of Trade (CBOT) or the New York Mercantile Exchange (NYMEX)—that brings traders of Egyptian cotton into one physical place. Instead, there are two main institutions that organize cotton trading inside Egypt. The first is the Alexandria Cotton Exporters' Association (ALCOTEXA), a nonprofit organization that produces market information and statistics, approves export contracts, helps set prices, and represents merchant interests.[7] Most private trading companies, like Modern Nile Cotton, are members of ALCOTEXA. The second is the Central Arbitration and Testing General Organization (CATGO), which arbitrates disputes between traders.

Many cotton farmers are circumspect in their dealings with private traders. Some farmers accuse local trading agents of trying to cheat them into lower prices. For example, one farmer told me that agents often complain they have an inventory of unsold cotton from previous seasons that compels them to buy the present year's crop at a lower price. "The merchants ask for a low price," he said. "And I have to sell because my wife and kids need money to buy goods." Even when traders deal honestly, farmers still worry that the absence of government regulation means they cannot guarantee they will get a good price for the cotton they sell. A 2016 report by the US Department of Agriculture's Global Agricultural Information Network observed that "farmers are particularly wary of planting cotton without a strong government commitment to marketing the crop."[8]

How does cotton move from the hands of trading companies to the destinations where they are manufactured into sheets and clothes? That function is carried out by global shipping companies and banks. Almost all cotton exported from Egypt leaves the country by sea. Most of that cotton—an estimated 70 percent—is exported from Egypt's major port city, Alexandria. Trading companies, like Modern Nile Cotton, gather their cotton in Alexandria and arrange transportation with major European and American container shipping companies—like Maersk, CMA CGM, and American President Lines Ltd. But cargo shipments are not transactions that happen on the spot; they can take several days or weeks and carry risks. They are acts of exchange that require some guarantee that they will be carried out. Both carriers and banks are involved in this process. In order for an exporter in Egypt and a purchaser, say, in India, to ensure their transaction will be completed, their act of exchange must be secured by their respective banks—oftentimes major banks that are headquartered in Europe or the United States. When sending a container shipment, an exporter typically has their bank issue a letter of credit to the bank of the manufacturer purchasing the cotton in order to guarantee the buyer will receive their payment on time. For their part, the shipping companies provide a bill of lading—a detailed list acknowledging receipt of the cotton for shipment—to the exporter consigning the goods.

The cotton is then shipped in containers to its manufacturing destinations, mostly in Asia, where they are spun by some of the world's leading textile manufacturers, like Welspun India. In 2017–18 the top importers of Egyptian cotton were India (by far the largest), Pakistan, China, and Turkey. From those countries silky fabrics are then shipped overseas and sold at a variety of commercial outlets—from major American merchandise retailers, like Walmart and Target; to European luxury department stores, like Harrods; to online companies, like Amazon.

EGYPTIAN COTTON IN A GLOBAL WORLD

We return to the Welspun India scandal with which we began. This controversy is but one case that makes visible how Egyptian cotton is fundamentally constitutive of what this book calls the global Middle East. Over the past two centuries, the lives of cultivators, processors, traders, regulators, and manufacturers of Egyptian cotton have been and continue to be deeply embedded in a series of transnational dynamics, which we might call "global," without being reducible to them. Their stories provide useful insights into the workings of those processes that exist at once within national boundaries and across them.

Much conventional scholarship treats nation-states as units that are empirically different but analytically equivalent—what in the beginning we called methodological nationalism. According to this view, each nation might be different in substance from other nations (in terms of its particular cultural practices, social norms, economic performance, etc.), but their overall structures are the same (every nation has an economy, a national culture, etc.). From a methodologically nationalist standpoint, a global perspective is one that simply adds many national situations together into a global whole.

However, it is difficult to reconcile this approach with the history of Egyptian cotton for three reasons. First, those developments we often think of as national, like the growth of Egypt's cotton industry, include many processes that do not obey any national borders. The examples we discussed of how the British helped incorporate Egypt into a nineteenth-century empire of cotton or how exporters and manufacturers today struggle to regulate a global supply chain offer a case in point. What appear to be national processes are sometimes already transnational to begin with. Second, those dynamics we call global usually exist in particular sites—like fields, ports, container ships, commodity exchanges, offices—rather than evenly encompassing the entire world. They are better seen as processes that link together agents, institutions, objects, and ideas across national spaces, rather than as boxes containing the sum total of national situations. If human societies around the world are collectively akin to a pendulum clock, then the "global" refers to the particular ways in which the clock's constituent parts interact (its spindles, wheels, springs, hour and minute hands, etc.) rather than to the wooden case enclosing them.

Third, as we have seen, the transnational movements of goods, people, ideas, and institutions have constituted and continue to constitute the boundaries, shape, and character of national authority in a place like Egypt. As the story of Egyptian cotton illustrates, a truly global perspective does more than add up a multitude of national situations. It helps us to see how those dynamics we often call global can exist on many scales and how they profoundly shape our understandings of the political and economic geography of human societies and interconnections.

NOTES

1. Alison Moodie, "Those Luxury Egyptian Cotton Sheets You Own May Not Be Luxurious—or Egyptian," *The Guardian,* November 19, 2016, www.theguardian.com/sustainable-business/2016/nov/19/egyptian-cotton-sheets-luxury-controversy-target-walmart.

2. "Crackdown on Fake Cotton Helps Revive Egypt Crop," *Reuters,* February 13, 2017, www.reuters.com/article/egypt-cotton-idUSL4N1FQ0CT.

3. Beckert, *Empire of Cotton.* See also Jakes and Shokr, "Finding Value in Empire of Cotton," 107–36.

4. Roger Owen, "The Rapid Growth of Egypt's Agricultural Output, 1890–1914, as an Early Example of the Green Revolutions of Modern South Asia: Some Implications for the Writing of Global History," *Journal of Global History* 1 (2006): 81–99.

5. *National Bank of Egypt, 1898–1948* (Cairo: Cairo Printing Press, 1948), 55.

6. Abdel-Fadil, *Development, Income Distribution, and Social Change in Rural Egypt,* 4–5.

7. Çalişkan, *Market Threads,* 105–30.

8. US Department of Agriculture, "Beyond All Expectations: Egypt's 2016 Cotton Production Set to Plummet," Global Agricultural Information Network (GAIN) Report (June 7, 2016), 1.

FURTHER READING

Abbas, Raouf, and El-Dessouky, Assem. *The Large Landowning Class and the Peasantry in Egypt, 1837–1952.* Translated by Amer Mohsen and Mona Zikri. Edited by Peter Gran. Syracuse, NY: Syracuse University Press, 2012.

Abdel-Fadil, Mahmoud. *Development, Income Distribution, and Social Change in Rural Egypt: A Study in the Political Economy of Agrarian Transition.* Cambridge, UK: Cambridge University Press, 1975.

Beckert, Sven. *Empire of Cotton: A Global History.* New York: Alfred A. Knopf, 2014.

Çalişkan, Koray. *Market Threads: How Cotton Farmers and Traders Create a Global Commodity.* Princeton, NJ: Princeton University Press, 2010.

Davis, Eric. *Challenging Colonialism: Bank Misr and Egyptian Industrialization, 1920–1941.* Princeton, NJ: Princeton University Press, 1983.

Goldberg, Ellis. *Trade, Reputation, and Child Labor in Twentieth-Century Egypt.* New York: Palgrave Macmillan, 2004.

Jakes, Aaron G., and Ahmad Shokr. "Finding Value in Empire of Cotton." *Critical Historical Studies* 4, no. 1 (Spring 2017): 107–36.

Owen, Roger. *Cotton and the Egyptian Economy, 1820–1914: A Study in Trade and Development.* Oxford, UK: Oxford University Press, 1969.

Reynolds, Nancy Y. *A City Consumed: Urban Commerce, the Cairo Fire, and the Politics of Decolonization in Egypt.* Stanford, CA: Stanford University Press, 2012.

Richards, Alan. *Egypt's Agricultural Development, 1800–1980: Technical and Social Change.* Boulder, CO: Westview Press, 1982.

Tignor, Robert. *State, Private Enterprise, and Economic Change in Egypt, 1918–1952.* Princeton, NJ: Princeton University Press, 1984.

Waterbury, John. *The Egypt of Nasser and Sadat: The Political Economy of Two Regimes.* Princeton, NJ: Princeton University Press, 1983.

SIXTEEN

Ports of the Persian Gulf

Laleh Khalili

PORT CITIES LOOK OUT TO THE SEA, often having more in common with their sister cities across the deeps and less with their hinterlands. They are often worldly, not only because of goods transiting through their harbors but because of the flows of merchants and mariners, capitalists and colonizers, soldiers, sailors and spies, and adventurers and dreamers. The food in ports is flavored by the cargo of spices and herbs brought from afar; and the music of ports is as much about the joy of arriving in safety as it is about lamenting the departures into storms and uncertainties. War, work, and commerce all create a dense web of global relations in which ports are pivotally embedded.[1]

Today, even in the age of aerial travel and virtual transportation of bits, bytes, and value, maritime trade is still enormously important, as more than 90 percent of the world's goods travel by ship to get to their destination. The most recent estimates by the United Nations Conference on Trade and Development (UNCTAD) saw seaborne trade in 2018 as 10.7 billion tons. Given that today China is the factory of the world, 40 percent of the world's cargo are loaded in Asian ports, while the same ports receive the bulk of the world's petroleum and raw materials. Among the top ten container ports in the world, only one is not located in East or Southeast Asia: Jabal Ali port in Dubai. A handful of other Middle Eastern ports (Jeddah and Sharjah) appear on the list of top fifty container ports in the world, published annually by the *Journal of Commerce*. Others have dropped off the list recently (Bandar Abbas and Port Said). Salalah in Oman, which had fallen off the list for a time benefited from becoming the port of transit for Qatar (replacing Jabal Ali), when Qatar was boycotted by Saudi Arabia and the United Arab Emirates. Other ports still have never been on the list in the two or so decades it has been compiled (Aden, Basra, Beirut). The top terminals for the transport of crude oil are located in the Middle East, more specifically on the Arabian Peninsula.

HISTORICAL PORTS

Arab ports are not newcomers to the world of commerce, however. The great Arab ports on the Mediterranean, the Red Sea, and the Gulfs (Arabian/Persian, Aden, and Oman) have long histories that predate the birth of Christianity and Islam. The Phoenicians of what is today the port of Beirut sailed faraway seas and taught their shipbuilding and seafaring crafts to peoples of the Mediterranean but also the Red Sea. Alexandria in Egypt was, for millennia, a major hub of trade and an object of intense imperial rivalry in the Mediterranean. Only the advent of the Suez Canal diminished Alexandria's importance. In the early centuries of Islam, the port of Siraf, near present-day Bandar Abbas in Iran, was one of the great trans-shipment ports between Iran and Mesopotamia in west Asia and China in the east.

For millennia, the ports of the Arabian Peninsula—Muscat, Aden, Mukalla, and Mokha—acted as ports of transit, coaling or bunkering, watering and victualing between India and the far east and the overland route from Suez to the Mediterranean coast. After the coming of Islam, Jeddah became the port of Mecca and the entry point for pilgrims, all the way until the middle of the twentieth century, when aerial travel finally overtook overland caravans and ships of pilgrims. Sohar, Siraf, and Basra routed the Indian Ocean trade to the eastern coast of the Mediterranean through Mesopotamia on land or on the great rivers, the Euphrates and the Orontes. On the Mediterranean shores the great ports became strategic and commercial emporia for the expanding Ottoman Empire.

The cargo passing through all these ports included pepper and spices, cotton and silk, ceramics, wheat and rice, tea and coffee, teak, cedar, bamboo and other timbers, precious metals and stones, and perfumes and dyes. Later, ores and manufactured goods joined the list. The goods came from the ports' hinterlands, or from across the seas or along coastal routes, and could be conveyed to further destinations. Religious pilgrimage was a great occasion for trade and commerce, and the historian Fernand Braudel described the Hajj as "the biggest [trade] fair in Islam."[2] This great transit of humans and goods made for cosmopolitan and polyglot port cities in which foods, forms of dress, and modalities of leisure were all influenced by seafarers and merchants from overseas.

In more recent history, not only pilgrimage and trade but also technological transformations, capitalism, and colonialism have been enormously important in the emergence, decline, and transformation of the great Arab ports. By the time European colonizers arrived in the Indian Ocean, Arab seafarers had devised complex navigational techniques that facilitated their transoceanic travel (some of these methods were likely passed on to them by Melanesian seafarers who traversed the Indian Ocean for millennia using methods now lost to us). We know that they used sidereal roses, astronomical observations, measurement of solar and lunar location in the sky, magnetic compasses, intimate knowledge of coastal routes, winds, and currents, and familiarity with natural signs of proximity to shore (especially flora and fauna of different coasts).

The technological transformations that facilitated the colonization of Asia by European powers—first the Portuguese, followed by the Dutch and the British—included new methods of building ships that made them both swift and capacious as well as the addition of arms to cargo ships. As historical accounts of colonization of Asia show, at least in the earlier centuries, European powers were unable to penetrate the interiors of the places they conquered, and their power was very often limited to the littoral areas and ports of the Indian Ocean shores. With colonization came new forms of extracting taxes, customs, and fees, and new modalities of control over merchants, shipping agents, seafarers, and the like. In many cases the new colonial powers grafted their institutions and laws and commerce to that which existed before them. European colonial powers asserted their sovereignty over the sea-lanes, controlling passage and access, a method taken up and further strengthened—at the force of arms—by successive colonial powers.

MODERN PORT CITIES

But what transformed the *infrastructure* of the ports and radically changed how port cities were organized were the change from sail to steam in the nineteenth century; the shift from coal to petroleum as ships' fuel in early twentieth century; and the emergence of standardized shipping containers in the latter half of the twentieth century. Although the steam engine had been discovered in the eighteenth century, the shift from sail to steam was consolidated when the East India Company decided to change over their ships to steam in 1839. The dominance of steam meant that ships that depended on harnessing the energy of the wind and were at the mercy of currents, winds, and tides would now be dependent on coal. In the early decades of steamships, coaling was a frequent necessity, requiring access to refueling stations at regular intervals. The British Empire's dominion over vast numbers of ports in Africa and Asia gave it a particular advantage in the maritime milieu. Where the British did not have a convenient coaling station, they invaded strategically placed ports under specious pretexts and set up fueling depots.

Aden was one such port; by the end of the nineteenth century, it was the fourth largest coaling station in the world, after London, Liverpool, and New York. Lebanese-American traveler and intellectual Ameen Rihani described two crucial characteristics of Aden in 1923, its coal depots and its lighthouse: "The one consists of black piles rising in squares and pyramids near the water and adding a touch of realism to the inferno of Steamer Point, the other stands aloft, above all the heights, housed in a circular tower, protected with glass, and made articulate with colors."[3] The coming of oil did not diminish Aden's significance. British Petroleum put in place one of the largest oil refineries in the world in Aden in the early 1950s, guaranteeing the port's dominance as a major bunkering (fueling) station. Only the decolonization of Aden and the simultaneous eight-year closure of the Suez Canal after the 1967 war with Israel diminished Aden's geographic advantage and led to the decline of Aden as a major port in the Middle East.

The coming of oil had other effects on the geography and urban makeup of ports. Where coal-heaving was an important source of employment at ports, creating harbors teeming with workers shifting coal onto and out of ships, bunkering and loading tankers with a cargo of petroleum was far more mechanized, necessitating far fewer workers. In addition to a diminishing of the power of port workers by slashing their numbers, oil terminals' placement also affected port geographies. Oil terminals and bunkering stations were often placed at some distance from the city proper, very often a mile out to sea. The stated reason was often the flammability of the fuel. But the distance—and increasingly the offshoring—of the oil terminals also meant that more ships could be accommodated without there being a need for infrastructural changes onshore, and much of the work would be automated without interference from intransigent workers.

The port cities themselves grew around the harbors and teemed with languages, sounds, flavors, and smells from all around the Indian Ocean and even further afield. Aden hosted merchants and dockers and sailors from East Africa and Gujarat. Alexandria boasted Syrians and Greeks. Beirut flourished with Armenians and Jews and Turks. The port areas themselves were proximate to the markets and bazaars and souks that sold imported goods. Beyond the warehouses, customhouses, and quarantines at the ports, coffeehouses and teahouses flourished, where merchants, seafarers, and ships' captains would gather and exchange information about trade routes, conditions of travel, and the situation of trade near and far. Some ports also had discreet quarters where sex workers plied their trade. Alexandria, Aden, and Beirut all hosted brothels in the seedier neighborhoods near the port, where seafarers and itinerant merchants could visit regularly, if circumspectly. In many cities the more affluent residents lived further away from the port, while the port city geographies saw roads emanating away from the harbor in different directions and toward the hinterland.

The major changes brought about by the discovery of petroleum in the Arabian Peninsula—moving oil terminals away from city centers and the automation of port work—occurred as early as the 1930s. Container-shipping foreshadowed even more radical changes. Standardized twenty-foot containers (and later, forty-foot and forty-five-foot boxes) became the norm of palletized cargo transport from the 1950s onward in the United States. Container-shipping had a great many advantages for the businesses that adapted it. For instance, the US military was an early proponent of container-shipping for transport of materiel to the Vietnam War. Because containers require movement by crane rather than the manual labor of stevedores, containerization would radically reduce the number of port workers and their concomitant power to mobilize.

As container-shipping necessitated vast storage spaces for stacking and storing the containers, it pushed the ports out of city centers to areas with available land (or land expropriated by force or via land reclamation). Landscapes were bulldozed, earth reclaimed from the sea, and harbors were dredged to allow for ever-deepening ship drafts. Where, before containerization, the port would have been the lively fulcrum of city life and enmeshed in its brothels, gathering places, and coffeehouses, it became a stale and securitized industrial estate, hidden behind barbed-wire fences. As the great maritime photographer and essayist Allan Sekula has written, "harbors are now less *havens* (as they were for the Dutch) than accelerated turning basins for supertankers and containerships."[4]

These transformations are of course not just about how technological change remakes the contours of the world. In the case of the great Arab ports, colonialism and capital accumulation have been central in this task of remolding the world. Earlier in this chapter I wrote about the conquest of Aden in 1839 and its transformation into a coaling station for East India Company's naval and commercial vessels. The sudden promotion of certain harbors into global ports was not the only effect of colonialism on ports; British colonial officials could also decide whether a major port should be left to decline. Whether the British rewarded a port with dredging, deepening its harbors, or constructing wharves and docks had far more to do with whether a particular group of merchants or rulers was to be rewarded or punished. In the mid-twentieth century, for example, the British entered a number of conversations with local rulers, financiers (including rulers of Kuwait and Qatar), and engineering companies about whether to dredge the creeks of Dubai or Sharjah.

The decision was made to persuade the emir of Kuwait to pay for the dredging of the Dubai Creek, while Sharjah was told that "its present harbour facilities must continue to decline and in due course it will cease to exist as a 'deep sea' port."[5] The emir of Sharjah had not been as acquiescent or useful to the British as the emir of Dubai and the dredging of the creek was a reward given to the latter and withheld from the former. It took almost two more decades, the massive hike in the price of oil and Sharjah's independence, for Sharjah to be able to not only dredge its creek but also build new ports and harbors on both Persian/Arabian and Oman Gulf shores (today Sharjah remains on the *Journal of Commerce*'s list of top fifty container ports).

STORIES OF DECLINE AND RISE

The colonial officials' imperious decision-making processes that led to the rise of some ports and decline of others did not simply occur around the construction of breakwaters, piers, and wharves. New routes of trades, strategic placement of naval bases, declaring some ports "free ports," and the placement of factories (whether points of production or mercantile trade, as East India Company offices were called) could all influence the prosperity of ports.

Perhaps the most dramatic example is the effect of the Suez Canal on Arab ports. The canal itself was devised as a weapon in imperial competition between Britain (with its control of the overland route to Asia through Sinai) and France (which controlled both southern and northern Mediterranean ports). The canal, which brought together metropolitan capital, forced Egyptian labor through the barrel of the gun to dig a long trench through the desert. The Suez Canal proved a boon for Aden as a coaling and watering port at the entry to the Red Sea. Ports on either end of the canal and along its route—Port Said, Suez, and Ismailia—all benefited from the shift to maritime transport through them. Jeddah saw an increase in pilgrims arriving by ship from West and North Africa. Alexandria, however, which had been the primary Arab port on the Mediterranean and the terminus of the overland route from India, saw a decline in its traffic.

The closure of the Suez Canal during the Tripartite War on Egypt in 1958 and for a much longer period between 1967 and 1975 saw shipbuilders and shipping companies invest in much larger tankers and containerships. The companies aimed to take advantage of economies of scale when rounding the much longer route around the Cape of Good Hope in South Africa and thus ships grew in length and width. Meanwhile, the closure of Suez Canal also provided a windfall in transit and trade to South African ports. The larger ships required much deeper harbors and access channels through shallower seas; and those ports that did not have access to resources to accommodate such requirements saw their shipping traffic decline precipitously.

Other factors affecting the business of a port have to do with whether a given port or the terminals within it have been operated by states or private concerns. A great many terminals around the Middle East are operated by private firms that hold multiple simultaneous concessions to manage nearby container terminals. One such firm is Dubai Ports World, the fourth largest terminal operator in the world with scores of concessions around the globe. In a number of instances, ports near Jabal Ali—especially in Djibouti, Aden and Kochi—have seen their container traffic *drop* after DP World has taken over their management, with shipping likely diverted to Jabal Ali.

Wars have been another determinative factor in whether ports have flourished or ailed. While the Lebanese Civil War destroyed the port of Beirut, it encouraged the emergence of smaller ports controlled by sectarian militias up and down the coast. The port of Junieh served the Maronite militia of Lebanese Forces, while the ports of Saida, Sur, and Tripoli were used by other militias involved in the Civil War. Much of Beirut's transit trade and shipping finance, insurance, and other businesses shifted to the ports of the Gulf. The Iran–Iraq War saw Kuwait ports becoming entrepôts for Iraq, while

Dubai became Iran's primary transshipment hub. The war in Syria saw a shift in trade to Israel's Haifa, where Turkish shipping companies would deliver containerized goods to be unloaded in Israel and loaded onto Jordanian trucks for distribution throughout the Arab Middle East. The various wars the United States has waged against countries in the region have transformed numerous ports there into staging grounds for US military and naval deployment and drawdowns.

Over the course of the past century, British naval bases in Alexandria, Bahrain, Oman, and Aden, US naval bases throughout the Arabian Peninsula and in North Africa, as well as a Russian naval base in Tartus have all created opportunities for the growth of ports that serve these bases. Many contractors serving the logistical needs of the US military and its allies during their wars in the Middle East have transformed themselves into logistics security or maritime service companies after the wars. These new firms based their headquarters in places like Kuwait, Dubai, and Abu Dhabi, thus reconfirming these ports as one-stop shops for a range of finance and security facilities. It is instructive that the devastation of all infrastructure in Libya since the start of the Arab Uprisings in 2011 has not extended to its oil terminals, even if the latter are the object of regular militia skirmishes and threats of takeover.

LABOR PROTESTS AT PORTS

Ports have been fascinating arenas for understanding labor regimes and the politics of workers' mobilization. In countries where they were allowed to organize, unionized port workers took part in struggles not only around workplace rights and labor conditions but for decolonization, rights to citizenship, and against state tyranny. In Algeria, Bahrain, Egypt, Lebanon, Morocco, Syria, and Tunisia port workers engaged in both nationalist and leftist struggles against colonial powers. In Aden the port workers were at the forefront of the contestation against British rule for decades in the mid-twentieth century. In revolutionary moments, whether in the mid-twentieth century or in the early twenty-first, Yemeni and Egyptian port workers were among the most ardent demonstrators against government repression. During the Arab Uprisings of 2011, Bahraini, Egyptian, Kuwaiti, Libyan, Omani, and Tunisian dockers participated in strikes during widespread popular protests.

During the 1960s, even in places where unionization was illegal (like Abu Dhabi, Saudi Arabia, and Qatar), port workers very frequently took part in strikes, which troubled the colonial officials. Memoranda from British labor attachés in the Gulf, for example, clearly reveal their fear of the protests spreading to other sectors or cities. In many instances British officials feared revolutionary or nationalist sentiments from Egypt or Palestine or later Aden and South Yemen influencing local port workers. Partially in response to these fears of contagion, first the British colonial officials and later the independent Gulf emirates implemented major restrictions on unionization (with partial exceptions in Bahrain and Kuwait). In addition, both overt regulations and more opaque procedures limited the numbers of Arab workers in these sectors and encouraged the importation of laborers from South and Southeast Asia to work in construction and port operation. That these workers are not allowed to organize, are paid low wages, and are vulnerable to deportation aids the enrichment of both the construction companies that receive the contracts to build the ports as well as those parastatal companies that manage and operate them. The profits extracted from the exploitation of workers is invested in the acquisition of port concessions overseas. In a sense the ports become not only a place for circulation of goods but also of people and capital.

PORT OF JABAL ALI

Jabal Ali port in Dubai encapsulates all these characteristics. Dubai itself was designated as a free port in early twentieth century, and as such it was exempted from customs fees. The growth of its ports, and its transformation into a trans-shipment hub has been predicated on the concurrent growth of maritime finance, security, and insurance industries there that serve not only businesses headquartered in the emirate but also corporations from as far afield as China. Dubai has a relatively low-key foreign policy, especially as compared to its more belligerent neighbor, Abu Dhabi, which was called "Little Sparta" by a US general. This relatively circumspect foreign policy positioning has meant that Dubai can encourage commercial shipping links with Iran, while hosting US military logistics bases at Jabal Ali and even as Abu Dhabi ramps up anti-Iranian activities and rhetoric. Dubai is also quietly home and headquarters to the UK Maritime Trade Operation, which, despite its innocuous name, is a naval force that monitors piracy.

The growth of Jabal Ali port, some thirty-five kilometers southwest of Dubai city center, has been sustained by the gigantic warehousing complex and free zone that surround it. These warehousing complexes support Jabal Ali's commercial aim as a trans-shipment port, receiving the largest ships and rerouting some of their goods overland or via smaller feeder ships to neighboring states. The free zone, rising out of the haze of heat and humidity, includes refineries, smelters, cement factories, chemicals manufacturing facilities, automobile traders, and hundreds of production and service companies. The free zone is sheltered from customs, fees, taxes, and regulations, and provides efficient company registration services that fold in worker visas, access to utilities, and a range of other resources. Since the companies based in the free zone have easy access to transportation facilities and exemption from a range of quotas and regulations, they can trade easily with near and far markets, including especially China, Europe, and India. This trade is facilitated by quick access to shipping at the port. The port complex also includes a "humanitarian city" that enables the shipment of humanitarian goods for war-torn and disaster-hit areas in the region for the World Food Program and other United Nations agencies. Aid ships are often escorted by EU, UK, and US naval forces.

The port of Jabal Ali itself has a vast harbor. Dubai Ports World boasts that it is the largest human-made harbor in the world. The port includes petroleum and chemical loading terminals (with ten berths), bunkering facilities, general cargo berths (where noncontainerized bulk cargo such as wheat or ore are loaded and unloaded), three very large container terminals (with nearly thirty berths), as well as facilities for storing wheeled vehicles transported by ro-ro (roll-on/roll-off) vessels. The port also has ship repair facilities and berths where US warships can moor out of view. Dubai is the main R&R port for the US Navy. Very near Jabal Ali port, the construction of a new airport, Al-Maktoum International Airport, is near completion, which will connect the port to air cargo facilities. To transport materiel to Afghanistan that cannot be conveyed through land borders of Pakistan or Central Asian states because of distance, cost, or geopolitical considerations, the US military uses a combination of flights and shipping through the port of Jabal Ali.

Arriving in Jabal Ali is always startling. The scale of engineering works that have resulted in a deep-water channel through the shallow coastal waters of the emirate becomes clear when one views the naval charts that show the ease with which today's ultra-large tankers and container vessels can be grounded in mud if they veer a few dozen meters off course. The port itself is the result of a huge land reclamation project where thousands of tons of rocks, gravel, mud, and prefabricated concrete blocks were poured into the sea to allow for the construction of the breakwaters, piers, and moorings. Nearby, one can see the incomplete (and now abandoned) Jabal Ali Palm, one of three palm-shaped artificial islands visible from space which at the cost of environmental degradation, pollution of the marine environment, and the despoliation of mud flats and coral beds, create land ex nihilo that can be used for property speculation and development. The berths at the ports are often electronically controlled, and access to the port by those who do not have permissions is restricted and monitored. The port resonates with the sound of massive gantry cranes unloading the freight, what philosopher Walter Benjamin, who loved traveling by freighters, has called the "modernized music of the world."[6]

The port of Jabal Ali is in many ways a global port par excellence. The workers who keep the place humming hail from all corners of the world: western European executive officers; Lebanese, Syrian, and Indian mid-level administrators; Punjabi and Filipino/a clerks; Pashtun and Pakistani stevedores; Nepalese security workers; Southeast Asian crane operators; Yemeni and Egyptian pilots; and so on. The port's polyglot culture is echoed in the city itself. Dubai's earlier modern ports—first along the Creek and later at the current site of Port Rashid—were at the very center of or adjacent to the historic city. The location of the Dubai's historic gold, spice, and fish markets indicates the connection of the neighborhood near the harbor to the work of the port. The transnational character of the old ports is on display in the spice and gold markets in particular.

Most spice merchants seem to be of Iranian origin; while the gold souk is operated predominantly by South Asian traders. Even today, motorized dhows plying the trade across the Persian Sea and the Gulf of Oman berth along the Creek, where one can hear a dozen different Asian and Middle Eastern languages spoken by the weathered men often wearing shalwar kameezes or sarongs there. Today, their cargo is less frequently gold or spice, and more often electronics, plastic merchandise, and nonperishable foodstuffs. Jabal Ali is very different. Its vast scale and distance from the city mean that its influence on the city of Dubai is far more veiled. The effect of the port of Jabal Ali on Dubai is mediated through the goods and capital that it injects into the city and the transnational community of workers it brings to the Gulf, rather than via shaping the social life of its immediate surrounds.

The construction of the port of Jabal Ali began in the 1970s, after the oil boom of 1973 had exponentially increased demand for consumer goods and construction material in the Arabian Peninsula. The placement of the port, at some distance from Dubai city center, through what was then still uninhabited and undeveloped lands and very near the border with Abu Dhabi, consolidated Dubai's hold on the area, which had been under dispute with its more powerful, richer, and larger southern neighbor. The combination of the free zone and the port was from very early on a calculated move, and the free zone's first major customers were South Asian textile manufacturers who by locating their factories in Jabal Ali managed to avoid European quotas on textiles imported from India and Bangladesh.

Commercial considerations weren't the only determinants of the port's prosperity. Geopolitics also affect the work of Jabal Ali, even if Dubai's rulers try to remain aloof from Abu Dhabi's regional political maneuvering and its alliances and enmities. Regional wars have boosted the port's business and continue to do so. Where Beirut or Basra or Bandar Abbas has declined, Dubai has picked up their business. Dubai Ports World's concessions in a number of regional port cities—including Karachi, Mumbai, Kochi, Jeddah, and previously in Aden and Djibouti—has meant that ships could be diverted to Jabal Ali or be rewarded by receiving feeders and transshipments through that port. When in 2017, Saudi Arabia, the UAE, and their allies imposed a maritime, land, and aerial blockade on Qatar, the emirate had to scramble to find new trans-shipment hubs in order to receive consumer goods and foods. The beneficiary of the diverted trans-shipments from Jabal Ali were the ports of Sohar and Salalah in Oman, whose deep-water berths on the Gulf of Oman and the Arabian Sea are amenable to receiving the largest containerships. The blockade has also accelerated the opening of Doha's own new major container port, Hamad Port.

If Jabal Ali is at the center of the ebbs and flows of trade, transit, and conflict in the region, it is not the only modern port on the Arabian Peninsula, or in the whole of the Middle East, to be so affected. Ports have always been more susceptible to the tides of war and commerce and more vulnerable to external influences that can shape the flow of goods in and out of them and contour their cityscapes. Ports, cosmopolitan though they may be, also very often magnify local and global inequalities and the flux of workers, sailors, adventurers, and revolutionaries through them attests to the ports' sensitivities to both local and global movements and politics. Jabal Ali, the behemoth port of the Middle East, is perhaps the best exemplar of this conjunction of capitalism, conflict, cosmopolitanism, movement, and struggle.

NOTES

1. The research for this chapter was funded by a research grant from the Economic and Social Research Council of the United Kingdom (ES/L002833/1). The project aims to understand the mutual effects of politics and maritime trade on seaports of the Arabian Peninsula specifically and their broader history more generally.

2. Braudel, *Civilization and Capitalism, 15th–18th Century,* vol. 2, 127.

3. Rihani, *Around the Coasts of Arabia,* 311.

4. Sekula, *Fish Story,* 12 (emphasis in original).

5. W. H. Adams, "Minutes of discussion regarding Halcrow's survey of Dubai and Sharjah creeks," January 28, 1955, FO 371/114696, UK National Archives.

6. Quoted in Howard Eiland and Michael Jennings, *Walter Benjamin: A Critical Life* (Cambridge: Harvard University Press, 2014), 241.

FURTHER READING

Braudel, Fernand. *Civilization and Capitalism, 15th–18th Century, Volume 2: The Wheels of Commerce.* Translation by Siân Reynolds. London: Phoenix Press, 1967.

Hanieh, Adam. *Capital and Class in the Gulf Arab States.* New York: Palgrave Macmillan, 2011. www.palgrave.com/gp/book/9780230110779.

Khalili, Laleh. *Sinews of War and Trade: Shipping and Capitalism in the Arabian Peninsula.* London: Verso, 2020. https://www.versobooks.com/books/3172-sinews-of-war-and-trade

Ramos, Stephen. *Dubai Amplified: The Engineering of a Port Geography.* New York: Routledge, 2010. www.routledge.com/Dubai-Amplified-The-Engineering-of-a-Port-Geography-1st-Edition/Ramos/p/book/9781409408222.

Rihani, Ameen. *Around the Coasts of Arabia.* London: Constable & Co Ltd., 1930.

Sekula, Allan. *Fish Story.* London: Mack Books, 2018. https://mackbooks.co.uk/products/fish-story-br-allan-sekula.

Ziadah, Rafeef. "Constructing a Logistics Space: Perspectives Form the Gulf Cooperation Council." *Environment and Planning D: Society and Space* 36, no. 4 (2017): 666–82.

PART SIX

Human Flows

SEVENTEEN

Touring Exotic Lands

Waleed Hazbun

THE MIDDLE EAST AND NORTH AFRICA has long attracted global visitors to its pilgrimage locations, sunny beaches, ancient ruins, and cultural heritage sites. More recently in the twenty-first century, Dubai has emerged as a mega tourism destination. Across the region, policy makers, private firms, and various societal actors have promoted tourism as a means to meet the challenges and opportunities of globalization and global integration.

In the post–World War II period, as countries throughout the region gained national independence, international tourism was often viewed as an engine for economic growth. From the 1990s, tourism became a means to promote economic liberalization and global economic integration. By 2016 the region represented about 5.5 percent of both international tourism arrivals and tourist receipts, while the direct and indirect contribution of travel and tourism amounted to 8 percent of GDP and 7 percent of employment in the region.[1] Regional conflicts and political instability, however, often disrupt tourism flows across the region, while tourism spaces serve as contact zones between hosts and guests, where disparities in economic wealth, political power, and cultural differences are often on display. As a result, tourism is subject to political struggle and at times a target for violence. Taken together, these aspects of tourism allow it to serve as a lens to explore the region's political economy and geopolitics as well as the emergence of the global Middle East.

THE DEVELOPMENT OF TOURISM

The Jewish, Christian, and Islamic faiths have long drawn streams of pilgrims and travelers to the region that is rich in holy sites. However, it was not until Napoleon's invasion in Egypt in 1798, when tourism fundamentally changed. His team of savants produced the twenty-three-volume *Description de l'Égypte* (1809–28), a meticulous recording of Egyptian culture and monuments that made sites like the pyramids and temples of ancient Egypt famous. In the second half of the nineteenth century, elite European travel in the form of the Grand Tour of learning and discovery, was eclipsed by the rise of popular leisure tourism. Egypt played a key role in the rise of the international tourism economy.[2] It was the first major region outside of Europe to witness the transition from where travel to a distant, "exotic" territory was made convenient and increasingly affordable in the form of package tours.

Beginning in the 1840s, the British firm Thomas Cook & Son helped to convert travel across Europe, often undertaken for the purposes of business, pilgrimage, and education, into a leisure commodity. By prearranging the provision of transportation, accommodation, and other needs of many travelers as a group, Thomas Cook & Son was able to decrease the costs and uncertainties of leisure travel and lay the foundations for the rise of organized popular tourism. As more upper- and middle-class Britons and then other Europeans began to engage in tourism, Cook's efforts helped create a tourist market in the transportation and accommodation sectors, leading to the development of a global infrastructure for tourist travel.

Following the opening of the Suez Canal in 1869, Thomas Cook's son, John Mason Cook, led the company's expansion into the Middle East. He established a vertically integrated business based on the firm's control over Nile transportation, several hotels, and hundreds of agents, guides, porters, and servants across Egypt and the Holy Land. Cook's operations expanded along with increasing European economic influence and political control. In the 1880s his firm was contracted to transport British troops and supplies. Meanwhile, the rise of British occupation and indirect colonial rule over Egypt led to the expansion of foreign travel to the country, enabling Cook's business to take off.[3]

Cook built a hospital for Egyptians in Luxor and often suggested that his firm fostered prosperity for the Egyptians, but his business model was based on low-cost labor and the development of a sector organized as a foreign-owned enclave.[4] Moreover, although Muslims have a long tradition of travel for the purpose of learning—most famously represented by the fourteenth-century travelogue of Ibn Battuta—local Egyptians and other Arabs at the time were not viewed by most Europeans as interested or capable of being leisure "tourists." More broadly in the interwar period, as European

FIGURE 17.1 Cook's Nile and Palestine Tour advertisement, 1902.

colonialism stretched across North Africa and the Middle East, European states and their private firms promoted travel to the colonies to foster greater attachment to these domains. They also sponsored archeological excavations of classical-era ruins that they presented as foundations of their own civilizations.

In the decade after most states in the Middle East and North Africa gained independence, the global tourism economy underwent a vast expansion, opening new opportunities for economic growth. Between 1950 and 1965 international tourist arrivals expanded from 25 million to more than 112 million globally, while foreign travel expenditures grew at an average annual rate of 12 percent.[5] This rapid expansion at the global level was spurred on by industrial growth in the North Atlantic economies and the rise of international airline travel and hotel companies. In the 1960s and 1970s governments across the developing world, backed by the World Bank and US and European development agencies, promoted tourism as a means to encourage market-based economic growth and provide capital for industrialization. For example, in his 1962 autobiography, the young King Hussein of the Hashemite Kingdom of Jordan wrote: "I believe that when our tourist program really starts properly... the tourist income to Jordan may well equal the fabulous oil revenues of other Arab states."[6] Meanwhile, Tunisia's president Habib Bourguiba viewed tourism as a means to display his country's openness to Europe and aspirations for modernization. Promoting tourism served the interests of newly independent states seeking the trappings of modernity, including flag carrier airlines, modernist-style international hotels, and icons of national heritage.

The opportunities were not so easily realized, however.[7] European and American airlines and tour operators dominated the most profitable aspects of the international tourism economy. Launching state-owned airlines and hotel companies and building the infrastructure needed for tourism development was costly. The establishment of Israel and the rise of the Arab-Israeli conflict, along with geopolitical conflicts between rival Arab states, created new borders and limitations that destroyed old patterns of travel. During the regional turmoil of the 1950s and 1960s the small eastern Mediterranean republic of Lebanon emerged as a leading tourist and leisure destination. With diverse attractions including a lively cultural scene, Lebanon benefited from being a destination for European visitors as well as Arab tourists. And while other Arab states suffered military coups or experimented with socialist-style economic policies, Lebanon remained open to foreign capital, hosted regional headquarters for international firms, and became a regional hub for commercial aviation.

The era of Lebanon as a destination for the global jet set, however, was brought to a close by the encroachment of the Arab-Israeli conflict and by the outbreak of Lebanon's civil war in 1975. Tourism development played a role in exacerbating domestic political and economic inequalities. During an early phase of the civil conflict the once glamorous hotels of Beirut's downtown hosted dueling sniper outposts in the "battle of the hotels" (of which the former Holiday Inn still towers over the Beirut skyline, gutted and bullet-riddled). The 1950s and 1960s witnessed the rapid expansion of "sand, sun, and sea" leisure tourism around the shores of the Mediterranean. The rise of Europe-based charter airlines and tour operators brought down the cost of leisure vacations leading to the vast expansion of the market. Developers built large blocks of hotels and holiday villages across the northern shores of the Mediterranean. This rapid growth created opportunities for the states along the southern and eastern shores. Tunisia formed a state-run agency to build tourist hotels in its major beach areas. Local private entrepreneurs soon extended these efforts, often with assistance from multinational firms. Similar developments appeared in other Mediterranean regions. Soon this expansion led to "the rapid conversion of the whole of the Mediterranean coast into the Pleasure Periphery of Europe and, to a lesser extent, of oil rich Arabs."[8]

These processes established an "international division of leisure" in the global tourism economy into which territories like Tunisia as well as Morocco, Israel, and Egypt were easily incorporated.[9] Due to constraints on capital, technology, and marketing, however, local firms were unable to reap the majority of economic rewards from tourism development. When Tunisia opened its territory to mass beach tourism development, transnational firms from Europe and the United States came to dominate the most lucrative elements of the industry, such as airlines, hotels, and tour operators. As more territories around the Mediterranean opened, the bargaining power of local governments and firms decreased. Still, tourism brought many positive benefits by creating employment and entrepreneurial opportunities. In many coastal towns young people flocked to tourism sector jobs, which were viewed as "modern" sector employment. By the late 1970s tourism receipts amounted to 7 percent of GDP and covered half of Tunisia's trade deficit. [10]

At the same time, many Tunisians grew concerned about the social and cultural impact of foreign tourism. Critiques of the tourism industry, though generally unwelcomed by an authoritarian regime dependent on revenues from it, began appearing. Ridha Behi's film *Soleil des hyènes* (Sun of the Hyenas, 1977) explores the impact of tourism development on a rural North African fishing village as a German firm builds a tourism complex nearby.[11] In the film local villagers and most of their businesses are marginalized by the hotel and the local elites who collude with the Germans. Many of the economic benefits of the hotel, such as the construction jobs, are presented as minimal or short-term. More controversially, Nouri Bouzid's film *Bezness* (1992) explores the world of young male Tunisians who work as hustlers and prostitutes in Sousse, a major destination for European tourists. While exposing an underside of the sector, the film offers an allegory about the experience of a small developing state facing the economic and cultural challenges of globalization.

The early prospects of tourism as an engine for economic growth were challenged by ongoing geopolitical conflicts in the region. The 1967 Arab–Israeli War helped propagate images of the region as a dangerous, unstable zone. Such conflicts damaged tourism sectors across the Middle East and North Africa. Destinations distant from the conflict zones suffered from a very broad neighborhood effect. In the 1967 war Jordan, Egypt, and Syria lost valuable locations for tourism development (the Sinai, Golan Heights, West Bank) while the region suffered from increased instability and violence. The next few years compounded these effects with the rise of international airplane hijackings (the most famous played out in Cairo and Amman in September 1970) and civil wars in Jordan and Lebanon. New opportunities, however, followed the 1973 Arab–Israeli War. The mid- to late 1970s saw the rise of peace negotiations between Egypt and Israel, in addition to vast increases in wealth in the oil-rich states.

During this era, by contrast, Israel's tourism markets boomed. It greatly benefited from the capture of the Palestinian West Bank, including East Jerusalem and Bethlehem as well as the beaches of the Sinai and the slopes of the Golan Heights. While remaining isolated within the Middle East, the jet age opened new possibilities for Israel, especially as it came to cultivate a Holy Land pilgrimage market from North America and Europe. The 1973 oil price hike and the recession in Europe and the United States led to a sharp decline in the beach tourism market, but some states benefited from the rise of petrodollar wealth. In Tunisia, for example, investment and loans from the Persian/Arab Gulf helped finance a new wave of coastal tourism development. Investors supported large-scale planning to standardize the production of what was becoming a highly generic mass beach tourism product that could compete for global market share but with more limited revenue per visitor. At the same time, the vast oil wealth led to the rise of citizens in the oil-rich states who became major spenders on leisure tourism. Gulf states, including Iran, spent millions of dollars buying aircraft like the Boeing 747 jumbo jet.

By the late 1970s planners and developers in the tourism sector began to respond to the saturation of the beach tourism market and the rise of interest in heritage, cultural, and nature tourism. With help from international organizations such as UNESCO, regional governments became more interested in preserving cultural heritage sites, such as ancient ruins at Luxor in Egypt, Petra in Jordan, and Carthage in Tunisia. These states gained multimillion-dollar grants and loans to develop their heritage infrastructure and promote tourism development. Such efforts accelerated by the late 1980s, when the decline in oil prices led to a sharp reduction in the flow of worker remittances and foreign aid to states like Jordan, Egypt, and Tunisia. As part of structural adjustment programs, these states were required to liberalize their economies and promote hard currency–generating exports. One of the first sectors to face privatization was state-owned hotel and tourism firms. State officials viewed tourism promotion as the most feasible way to expand access to hard currency as well as (again) seeing it as an engine for economic growth.

THE "NEW MIDDLE EAST"

In the late 1970s, Egypt under President Anwar Sadat was the first Arab state to pursue a peace treaty with Israel. While Egypt was seeking aid and security with closer ties to the United States, Israel wanted the "normalization" of the relations between Egypt and Israel to include cross-border tourist traffic. But with the exception of Israelis continuing to visit the Sinai beaches and resorts established under Israeli occupation, the tourist flows across the newly opened borders between Egypt and Israel remained minimal and the peace a "cold" one.

A new era emerged in the mid-1990s, when the Middle East underwent a rapid transformation in the tourism sector corresponding to the global expansion of international travel unleashed by the end of the Cold War and the rise of globalization. While the idea of regional Middle East tourism was introduced by the Israelis at the multilateral peace talks that followed the

1991 Madrid Peace conference, it was the 1993 Oslo Accords that launched a new wave of planning and dreaming about the possibilities of tourism. Even though the path to Palestinian statehood remained unclear, the mutual recognition of Israel and the Palestine Liberation Organization (PLO) and the establishment of a Palestinian Authority ignited a revolutionary transformation of geopolitical imaginaries. One of the chief architects was Israeli foreign minister Shimon Peres, who outlined his vision in *The New Middle East*.[12]

Peres and Israeli officials extrapolated from the Accords, the end of the civil war in Lebanon, and the 1994 peace treaty between Israel and Jordan to imagine a future Middle East with open borders allowing for regional flows of people, goods, and capital as well as the openness of the region to Western flows of tourists and investment. US officials enthusiastically embraced this vision that would seemingly enable the incorporation of the Middle East into the trends of free-market globalization and neoliberal economic reform advanced by the US globally. Many Arab government officials and private businessmen in Jordan and the West Bank, and a few beyond, cautiously and even with some skepticism embraced the economic possibilities, which were widely understood to include regional tourism. The mid-1990s saw an explosion of cross-border tourism flows between Israel and Jordan as well as rapid hotel building and tourism development across the region. Israelis rushed to visit the rock-carved ancient city of Petra while international tourists from Europe and North America could now more easily visit Israel, Jordan, and the Palestinian West Bank as part of a single organized tour.[13] The United States, the EU, and Japan all assisted the process with official loans, private investment, architectural plans, and technical assistance for heritage preservation, tourism planning, and infrastructure development. Meanwhile, some North African and Arab Gulf States pursued commercial ties to Israel, and Sephardic Jewish communities sought to reopen tourist and pilgrimage connections between Israel and Tunisia.

The era of the "New Middle East" was short-lived, however. The cross-border flows diminished by the late 1990s as the "peace process" failed to realize security and prosperity for Israelis and Palestinians. Each state, nevertheless, sought its own path. While Israelis and international tour groups could still pass through the Israel-Jordan crossing points, large segments of Jordanian society vocalized their disappointment and opposition to the 1994 peace treaty through the antinormalization movement, which opposed ties and cooperation between Arab states and Israel. Jordan continued efforts to expand tourist facilities near Petra, the Dead Sea, and in the capital city Amman, and to diversify its tourism offerings and external image by developing ecotourism and religious tourism. Israeli tourism was hit by the rise of suicide bombing attacks launched by the militant Islamist movement HAMAS opposed to the peace process. Following the breakdown of US-brokered Israeli-Palestinian negotiations in 2000, Palestinians launched what became the second intifada (or uprising) against Israel. Since the 1990s, Palestinians saw the devastation of their tourism economy by a regime of Israeli checkpoints, occupation, and wall building as Israel came to focus on more ideologically motivated visitors such as pro-Zionist evangelical Christians, who often did not recognize the Palestinian right to self-determination.

Egypt also expected to benefit from regional peace, but in the 1990s, with the rise of militant extremist Islamist movements, suffered from attacks targeting foreign tourists and the general tourism sector. Nevertheless, Egypt continued to plan new tourism developments, especially along the shores of South Sinai, but often these enclave-oriented developments offered limited benefits to local communities.[14] Like other states in the region, Egypt learned to master the techniques of crisis and image management through new advertising campaigns and conspicuous patrols by police and army at airports and tourist sites.

Tourism sectors across the region steadily expanded in the late 1990s with more states seeking to develop their markets. Between 1995 and 2000 the Arab Middle East's share of global tourist arrivals grew from 2.5 percent to 3.5 percent.[15] By 2000 tourism receipts represented around 8 percent of GDP in Tunisia and Jordan, 6 percent in Morocco, 4 percent in Egypt, 3 percent in Israel and Syria.[16] Meanwhile, new global trends in the sector appeared across the region. Even as the demand for low-cost beach holidays declined in Northern Europe, new markets developed in the formerly socialist states of Eastern Europe and Russia. The post–civil war reconstruction of Beirut was beginning to encourage the return of Arab tourists and the Lebanese diaspora visiting from abroad. Across Syria, Jordan, and Egypt new domestic and regional flows of leisure tourists helped give rise to a seasonal demand for furnished flats, cafes, nightclubs, and family amusement parks. Petrodollar investments began flowing into Arab capitals, launching neoliberal urban restructuring dominated by high-rise office complexes, residential towers, and shopping malls that further marginalized the urban and disaffected poor.[17]

The September 11, 2001, al-Qaeda attacks in the United States led to a brief collapse of international tourist flows to the Middle East. Nevertheless, in a few years' time, tourism development across the region experienced dynamic transformations. The established leisure markets in Tunisia and Morocco suffered major declines and struggled to recover. The post-9/11 era saw the consolidation of new trends and patterns. Just as the price of oil was increasing with the US launch of its "War on Terror" in Afghanistan and then its invasion of Iraq in 2003, leisure tourists and investment from the oil-rich Gulf emerged as the most powerful force reshaping regional development patterns.

Due to new security procedures and societal attitudes, Arabs and Muslims found travel to Europe and the United States less welcoming. They soon redirected their leisure travel toward other regional Arab destinations.[18] Syria and Lebanon experienced growing waves of tourists from the Gulf states including Iraq. New shops, restaurants, and hotels appeared in Amman, Damascus, Beirut, and Cairo. Backed by Gulf investment and new waves of visitors, Beirut and Cairo regained their reputations as capitals of Arab culture and nightlife.[19] Arab family-oriented travel became a recognized feature of the tourism sector. Another major trend consolidated in this era was the rise of Islamic and Halal tourism. Jordan, Egypt, and Syria as well as several Gulf states made efforts to develop their sites for religious pilgrimage while hotels, restaurants, and leisure complexes began offering food and family-oriented entertainment catering to pious Muslims. With these new facilities, they could also begin attracting Muslim visitors from Turkey, South Asia, and East Asia in search of more culturally appropriate leisure.

Predating the rise of modern tourism, the annual Hajj is the largest single "tourist" event in the region. Around two million visitors travel to Islam's holiest sites in Mecca, Saudi Arabia, each year to perform a series of rituals alongside other pilgrims from almost every country in the world. While a major source of economic revenues before the discovery of oil in the kingdom, the Hajj now functions to showcase what the ruling al-Saud family views as its guardianship over Islam's holy places—and by extension over the community (*ummah*) of the faithful across the globe. In addition to annual Hajj pilgrims, the kingdom has long welcomed visitors conducting *umrah*, or pilgrimage, at other times of year. Such visitors often engage in leisure and shopping tourism. Saudi Arabia has recently sought to develop a limited international tourism sector by, among other methods, allowing an extension of the *umrah* visa.

By far the most substantial post-9/11 transformations in regional tourism were those taking place in the smaller Arab Gulf states. The UAE and Qatar only gained independence in 1971, but these oil-rich states emerged as major business centers by the 1990s. Dubai, a member of the UAE but an emirate lacking major oil resources, invested in a seaport and airport and launched its own airline that rapidly expanded its network to Europe, Asia, and Africa. Dubai exploited its role as an entrepôt to become a destination for shopping, leisure tourism, and nightlife. By 2001 the number of hotel rooms in Dubai alone amounted to more than a quarter of the total found in all of Egypt, while tourism accounted for 12 percent of the emirate's economy.[20]

Dubai's tourism sector is resilient because it is highly diversified. The city, for example, can offer Europeans a warm beachside vacation while serving as a medical tourism destination for travelers from Asia. Dubai has also benefited from regional instability and war; it serves as a trading, logistics, and business hub that helps supply multiple sides of regional conflicts, including the massive US military presence spread across the Gulf. In the wake of 9/11, as petrodollars continued to flow through the region due to high oil prices, Dubai witnessed a massive expansion of its hotel, leisure, and commercial infrastructure, including the building of the world's largest shopping mall and one themed on the travels of Arab explorer Ibn Battuta. Dubai worked to develop a global brand image with iconic architecture, such as the Burj Al Arab hotel shaped like a sail and the world's tallest building, the Burj Khalifa. Most dramatically, Dubai built a series of artificial islands in the shape of a palm tree and a map of the world. These terraforming projects led the *New Yorker*'s Ian Parker to remark: "Dubai...is smitten with the idea of its own aerial legibility."[21]

In the process Dubai has forged a new "global" model for urban development in the Middle East. Rather than build on its heritage and history or define a distinct "Arab" or "Khaliji" (Gulf) place identity, the Dubai skyline and urban form reflect the almost generically global features of late modernity—skyscrapers, gated communities, themed entertainment, and unrestrained consumerism. This capacity for constant reinvention is enabled by its ability to attract a constant stream of uprooted capital and labor that risks volatility and dislocation in order to gain access to economic opportunities.[22]

The global financial crisis of 2008 hit Middle East tourism hard and even dis-
rupted Dubai's development plans. Just as the Gulf economies were recovering, the Arab world entered a whirlwind of political, economic, and cultural
change beginning with the uprising in Tunisia in December 2010. The depth
of these transformations reflected the nature of the region's incorporation
into the flows and forces of the contemporary neoliberal global economy.
The increasing inequality and volatility brought about by these neoliberal
economic policies helped to foster the political dissent and social mobilization that produced the uprisings.

After the fall of regimes in Tunisia and Egypt and protests in Syria,
Bahrain, Yemen, and Libya, it was the Arab Gulf states that sought to shape
the region's geopolitical future. First, Qatar together with Turkey supported
the Islamists, but soon Saudi Arabia and the UAE launched a counterrevolution to suppress popular mobilization and political dissent. This shift in
the regional balance of power had been anticipated by the recent patterns of
tourism flows. With the rise of political disorder and violence, the prospects
for tourism development across the region declined.[23] The UAE remained
the exception. Tourist flows to Dubai expanded. In the process the Gulf-
led counterrevolution produced new political divisions combined with refugee crises, civil war, and humanitarian disasters in places like Yemen, Syria,
and Libya.

The "Dubai model" for tourism development functions through its global
connections but also its ability to partition and exclude. Tourism-related
development projects tend to be enclave spaces—such as airports, shopping
malls, hotels, and entertainment parks. The production of such spaces relies
on an insidious form of spatial segmentation. As the anthropologist Ahmed
Kanna has observed, beginning at Dubai's airport (DXB), the fluid movements of capital and citizens from affluent nations contrasts with the con-
stricted spaces of the largely invisible wage labor population predominately
from South and Southeast Asia.[24] This "jagged" view of Dubai hints at the
often overlooked territorial dynamics and geopolitics that undergird its rise
as a space of transnational flows and a node within global networks.

A close look around the region can identify new regional flows and border crossings. In Palestine, for example, local and international NGOs foster
political solidarity tourism. Even under the conditions of geopolitical hostility, there are Americans who seek to dispel stereotypes by visiting Iran.

Northern Iraq under Kurdish autonomy has sought to build a tourism sector as it benefits from the new mobilities for Kurdish communities long divided by national borders. Meanwhile, new low-cost regional airlines are seeking to provide a means of reconnecting families and communities dispersed across the region. Nevertheless, the dominant trends are increased partitions and fragmentation rather than openness. Since the late nineteenth century, tourism has played a critical role as a vehicle for fostering flows of people, goods, capital, and images between the Middle East and other global regions and more recently between different parts of the Middle East. Although the economic benefits from these flows have played a vital role providing jobs and sources of revenue, these benefits come with social, environmental, and political costs. Overdependence on tourism leaves many communities vulnerable to the volatile trends in the sector.

Moreover, the prominence of tourism has resulted in many parts of region being represented globally through the superficial images circulated by the tourism industry. Meanwhile, political regimes and economic elites have often exploited their country's tourism resources for short-term benefits ignoring the long-term costs. As a result, viewed through the lens of tourism, the future of the global Middle East is likely to be very jagged, connecting enclaves across the region into global flows and trends but maintaining ever more harsh partitions in order to shore up hierarchies and exclusion. These divisions may someday provoke another series of, likely more tumultuous, uprisings across the region.

NOTES

1. UNWTO, *Tourism Highlights 2017*; and WTTC, *Economic Impact 2017 Middle East.*
2. See Hazbun, "East as an Exhibit," 3–33.
3. Hunter, "Tourism and Empire," 44.
4. Hunter, "Tourism and Empire," 44. See also Hazbun, "East as an Exhibit," 26–29.
5. Waters, "American Tourist," 112.
6. Cited in Hazbun, *Beaches, Ruins, Resorts,* 84.
7. See Telfer and Sharpley, *Tourism and Development in the Developing World.*
8. Turner and Ash, *Golden Hordes,* 100.
9. Turner, "International Division of Leisure," 253–60.
10. Hazbun, *Beaches, Ruins, Resort,* 26.

11. Disney, "Review of Hyena's Sun (*Soleil des Hyenes*)," 22.

12. Peres and Naor, *New Middle East.*

13. Stein, "'First Contact' and Other Israeli Fictions," 515–43.

14. Mitchell, "Worlds Apart," 8–11.

15. Hazbun, *Beaches, Ruins, Resort,* 189.

16. Hazbun, *Beaches, Ruins, Resort,* xv. Figures rounded to nearest whole number.

17. See Daher, *Tourism in the Middle East.*

18. Al-Hamarneh and Steiner, "Islamic Tourism," 18–27.

19. See Wynn, *Pyramids & Nightclubs.*

20. Hazbun, *Beaches, Ruins, Resort,* 207.

21. Parker, "The Mirage," 136.

22. On the cases beyond Dubai, see Stephenson and Al-Hamarneh, *International Tourism and the Gulf Cooperation Council States.*

23. See Almuhrzi, Alriyami, and Scott, *Tourism in the Arab World.*

24. Kanna, "Dubai in a Jagged World," 23.

FURTHER READING

al-Hamarneh, Ala, and Christian Steiner. "Islamic Tourism: Rethinking the Strategies of Tourism Development in the Arab World after September 11, 2001." *Comparative Studies of South Asia, Africa and the Middle East* 24, no. 1 (Spring 2004): 18–27.

Almuhrzi, Hamed, Hafidh Alriyami, and Noel Scott. *Tourism in the Arab World.* Bristol, UK: Channel View, 2017.

Daher, Rami Farouk, ed. *Tourism in the Middle East.* Clevedon, UK: Channel View, 2007.

Disney, Nigel. "Review of Hyena's Sun (*Soleil des Hyenes*)." *MERIP Reports* no. 66 (April 1978): 22.

Hazbun, Waleed. *Beaches, Ruins, Resorts: The Politics of Tourism in the Arab World.* Minneapolis: University of Minnesota Press, 2008.

———. "The East as an Exhibit: Thomas Cook & Son and the Origins of the International Tourism Economy in Egypt." In *The Business of Tourism: Place, Faith, and History,* edited by Philip Scranton and Jan Davidson, 3–33. Philadelphia: University of Pennsylvania Press, 2007.

Hunter, F. Robert. "Tourism and Empire: The Thomas Cook & Son Enterprise on the Nile, 1868–1914." *Middle Eastern Studies* 40, no. 5 (2004): 28–54.

Kanna, Ahmed. "Dubai in a Jagged World." *Middle East Report* 243 (Summer 2007): 22–29.

Parker, Ian. "The Mirage." *The New Yorker* (October 17, 2005): 128–43.

Peres, Shimon, and Arye Naor. *The New Middle East.* New York: Henry Holt, 1993.

Mitchell, Tim. "Worlds Apart: An Egyptian Village and the International Tourism Industry." *Middle East Report,* no. 196 (September–October 1995): 8–11.

Stein, Rebecca L. "'First Contact' and Other Israeli Fictions: Tourism, Globalization, and the Middle East Peace Process." *Public Culture* 14, no. 3 (2002): 515–43.

Stephenson, Marcus L., and Ala al-Hamarneh, eds. *International Tourism and the Gulf Cooperation Council States.* London: Routledge, 2017.

Telfer, David J., and Richard Sharpley. *Tourism and Development in the Developing World.* London: Routledge, 2015.

Turner, Louis. "The International Division of Leisure: Tourism and the Third World." *World Development* 4, no. 3 (March 1976): 253–60.

Turner, Louis, and John Ash. *The Golden Hordes: International Tourism and the Pleasure Periphery.* London: Constable, 1975.

United Nations World Tourism Organization (UNWTO). *Tourism Highlights 2017.*

Waters, Somerset R. "The American Tourist." *Annals of the American Academy of Political and Social Science* 368 (November 1966): 109–18.

World Travel and Tourism Council (WTTC). *Travel & Tourism: Economic Impact 2017 Middle East, 2017.*

Wynn, L. L. *Pyramids & Nightclubs.* Austin: University of Texas.

EIGHTEEN

Outsiders of the Oil States

Ahmed Kanna

FOREIGN RESIDENTS IN THE ARAB GULF countries have played a central role in building and shaping the modern societies of the Gulf, yet rarely do they have rights of citizenship. The example of the Arab Gulf illustrates how histories of empire and capitalism impact ongoing contests over economic and political power, the deterioration of the environment, and workers' struggles for rights and social justice. It can also help us understand how states arbitrarily allocate categories of "citizen" or "immigrant" and the rights, privileges, and vulnerabilities that accompany different groups.[1]

ARAB GULF?

The term "Arab Gulf" refers to a collection of countries in Southwest Asia that border the western side of the Arab or Persian Gulf, namely Bahrain, Kuwait, Oman, Qatar, Saudi Arabia, the United Arab Emirates, and sometimes the southern part of Iraq. This term "Arab Gulf" is problematic for a number of reasons. Traditionally it has tended to impose a homogeneity, an Arabness, on a group of nation-states and societies that are belied by their diversity, both among each other and internally. For example, each of these countries is stratified and crosscut by differences of class, region, religion, gender, ethnicity, and language, which tend to be erased by the category of "Arab Gulf." Furthermore, this category is a product of twentieth-century and especially post–World War II geopolitical logics that view its contribution to oil/energy and finance in the global capitalist economy as the region's primary function.

Another reason that the term is problematic is that this region is not very obviously "Arab" at all.[2] Admittedly, all these countries except Iraq are governed by hereditary monarchies that trace their roots to the central Arabian Peninsula and identify as ethnically and linguistically Arab. While the stereotype of people from the Arab Gulf is that they are wealthy members of a homogeneous culture and linguistic community, in reality the populations of the Gulf countries are far more linguistically, religiously, and ethnically heterogeneous than the Gulf ruling families. With the exception of the regional giant Saudi Arabia, indigenous Arab populations constitute a disproportionately small percentage of each country, while immigrants from South and East Asia constitute a major proportion and often a majority of foreign workers in all Gulf Cooperation Council (GCC) states. Take, for example, the cases of Dubai and Qatar. Their ruling families are ethnically and linguistically Arab, but their populations are overwhelmingly foreign. In Dubai those who hold national citizenship are in the minority, and among this group a majority trace their roots to Iran. The majority of the population are foreigners, the bulk of whom are Indian. In the United Arab Emirates and Qatar, foreigners represent the overwhelming majority, accounting for approximately 90 percent of the population of both countries. Only in Saudi Arabia and Oman do national citizens outnumber foreigners, and in Oman just barely.

Historically, the GCC countries reflected a Muslim transnationalism common for centuries in all the societies of the Indian Ocean and Red Sea littorals. These regions were a mix of Arab, Persian/Iranian, African, and South Asian cultures. Even today, it is not uncommon for members of older generations to be trilingual. In Oman and the UAE, for instance, people might speak Arabic, Persian, and Urdu, and in the eastern Arabian Peninsula Swahili is widespread. The cultural mixes are also evident in clothing. Coastal Gulf Arabs born before the *tafra naftiyya* (oil boom) of the 1970s wore clothing and adopted styles derived from East Africa, India, and the Arabian Peninsula. Today these styles have been replaced by an explicitly self-described Arab nationalist idiom. The typical "Gulf Arab" attire usually consists of a white *thoub* (loose-fitting robe) and *shmagh* (checked or white headscarf) for men, and *abaya* (black cloak) for women. Generations born during and after the *tafra naftiyya* remember when the only movie theater in town was the Bollywood movie house, where you needed to understand Hindi or Malayalam or Marathi to follow the plot. Modern Gulf food, especially on the coast, is still a blend of South Asian, Iranian, East African, and Arab Middle Eastern influences. These cultural practices all tell the story of the deeper, centuries-old history of the Gulf Arab region as maritime littoral between Zanzibar in East Africa, Iran in the Middle East, and the Malabar coast on the Indian subcontinent.

Foreign residents in the Gulf region have existed in significant numbers since the early nineteenth century. In Bahrain, the UAE, and Oman, travelers and residents from the wider Middle East, especially Iran/Persian Empire and India, were among the most well-represented and visible members of society. Conversely, Bahrainis, Emiratis, and Omanis themselves traveled extensively in Iran, East Africa, and South Asia and, until the modern oil age of the post-1970s, regarded the latter as destinations for higher education, medical care, and extensive business contacts unavailable at home. However, since the 1960s, countries such as Saudi Arabia were positioned by anticolonial Arab nationalist movements as collaborators with Western—in particular British and American—imperialism. In response, the monarchies of the Gulf began emphasizing their "Arab authenticity," by offering citizenship to foreign residents of Arab origin and de-emphasizing the existence of large numbers of non-Arab foreigners, in addition to the aforementioned cultural politics of homogenizing their own citizen populations and national mythologies through practices of "national dress."

The stereotype of the homogeneous Gulf Arab culture is a very recent phenomenon, a product of the *tafra naftiyya* period and the geopolitics of Arab nationalism of the 1960s to 1970s. The six states of the Gulf Cooperation Council (founded in 1981)—Bahrain, Kuwait, Oman, Qatar, Saudi Arabia, and the United Arab Emirates—attempted to homogenize their culturally diverse populations and present them as carriers of authentic Arab identity, in response to often hostile secular Arab nationalist and anti-imperialist states such as Egypt, Syria, Iraq, and South Yemen. In actuality, the GCC countries have "the highest ratio of foreign residents in the world."[3] A closer look at statistics provided by each of the governments of the GCC states reveals the following: of Bahrain's total population of slightly more than 1.3 million, 52 percent, or 683,818 people, are foreign nationals (2014 figures); of Kuwait's 4.3 million residents, more than 69 percent are foreign nationals (2016 figures); for Qatar, almost 90 percent of its 2.4 million people are foreign nationals (2015 figures); of the UAE's 8.3 million people, almost 89 percent are foreign nationals (2010 figures). Almost 33 percent of Saudi Arabia's nearly 31 million people are foreign (2014 figures), as are 45 percent of Oman's 4.4 million people (2016 figures). *Overall, 49 percent of the GCC's total population of nearly 51.5 million people are foreign born* (table 18.1).[4]

TABLE 18.1 Foreign residents as proportion of total populations
of Gulf Cooperation Council (GCC) countries

Country	Total population	Foreign residents	Percentage (%)
Bahrain	1.3 million	.64 million	52
Kuwait	4.3 million	2.97 million	69
Oman	4.4 million	1.98 million	45
Qatar	2.4 million	1.94 million	90
Saudi Arabia	31 million	10.2 million	33
United Arab Emirates	8.3 million	7.4 million	89

SOURCE: Gulf Research Center, https://gulfmigration.org/gcc-total-population-percentage-nationals
-foreign-nationals-gcc-countries-national-statistics-2010-2016-numbers/ (consulted July 27, 2020).

MIGRATION

Waves of migration to the GCC occurred in four major phases: before the 1970s oil boom or *tafra naftiyya*; the oil boom years of the 1970s; the years after the 1979 Iranian Revolution to the early 1990s; and finally, the period since the early 1990s. Oil was first discovered in Bahrain in 1932 and a few years later in Kuwait and Saudi Arabia, initiating an era of oil exploration and imperial intervention leading to a sharp increase in demand for labor. As migration scholar Hélène Thiollet has noted:

> In Saudi Arabia, the first drilling camp was established in 1934 in Dhahran. Employment rose from less than 150 employees in 1935 to 3,641 in 1939 for the California Standard Oil Company (CASOC), later the Arabian-American Oil Company (ARAMCO). Between 1933 and 1936 gas production infrastructures were set up in Bahrain, generating a surge in employment from 610 to 5,038 employees for the Bahrain Petroleum Company (BAPCO).... The Kuwait Oil Company (KOC) under Anglo-US ownership and Qatar's PDQ (Petroleum Development Qatar) started exploring and then drilling and expanding slightly later, leading to massive employment only in the postwar period (KOC went from 266 employees in 1945 to 12,705 employees in December 1949).[5]

Ruling families of the coastal Gulf and Saudi Arabia collaborated with the British and Americans, respectively. They produced a colonial pattern of labor migration and recruitment management. In the British-dominated coastal Gulf, this system involved a continuation of the British indentured labor system, whereas Saudi Arabia applied a more US-influenced practice derived from Jim Crow labor segregation. In the British-dominated coastal Gulf, technical and so-called skilled workers were brought in from Europe and particularly Great Britain, whereas skilled and semiskilled artisans and clerical workers were from South Asia, which was still under British occupation. Unskilled workers came from local populations or neighboring Arab countries. In Saudi Arabia, founded in 1932, the Americans held sway. Up until the 1950s, Americans and Italians made up the skilled workers, and Eritreans the unskilled labor. After the 1950s the GCC states started more heavily recruiting workers from the Levant, especially Palestine.[6] By the time of the oil boom of the 1970s, foreigners made up more than 70 percent of the labor force in the GCC countries.[7]

Arab nationalism was on the rise across the Arab world during the 1970s, and the movement harbored hostility to monarchism (which was and still is the norm in the Gulf). Workers from throughout the Arab countries were encouraged to immigrate to lend the Gulf monarchies a veneer of Arab authenticity. In Kuwait and Saudi Arabia, Arab non-nationals became the majority of foreign workers during the 1970s. The 1979 Iranian Revolution brought another shift in which Arab non-nationals were suspected of being receptive to discourses of militant Islam and republicanism. By the 1980s, Asian immigrants were again favored and overtook Arab non-nationals as the majority among foreign workers in the GCC.[8] With the 1990–91 Gulf War, a large number of non–Gulf Arab countries either supported Iraq or did not come out in support of Kuwait, which increased suspicion of Arab immigrants to the GCC. Approximately three million non–Gulf Arab residents from countries whose governments sided with Saddam Hussein's Iraq in the war were expelled from the GCC during this time, among them 350,000 Palestinians and Jordanians residing in Kuwait and 800,000 Yemenis from Saudi Arabia.[9] By the 2000s the largest immigrant groups in the GCC, as indexed by remittance figures, were from India, Pakistan, and Egypt.[10]

The labor force in countries of the Arab Gulf has remained highly stratified, with middle-class professionals from Western Europe and North America (especially if they identify as white) receiving highly preferential treatment. While there are middle class, professional, and even wealthy non-nationals from South and Southeast Asia and the Arab countries, the majority among each group are members of the working class and barely earn a livable wage. This system has colonial roots. Under British and American imperial domination, states and oil companies privileged white European and North American immigrants over so-called semiskilled and unskilled

Asian and Arab workers. Today, Europeans, North Americans, and others who in the American context would self-identify as "white," tend to see the Gulf as providing opportunities for consumer well-being not available in their home countries. They can live in a comfortable home with luxurious amenities and expensive cars (often provided through expense accounts), staffed by domestic workers who cook, clean, and care for their children. They also tend to harbor colonial sentiments about the supposed racial inferiority and cultural backwardness both of non-European residents generally, and of Gulf Arabs specifically—a sentiment it must be said that is encouraged by the Gulf's ruling regimes. By contrast, European foreign workers of color, such as Muslims from Europe and North America, tend to have much more ambivalent, if not relatively positive, views of Gulf societies as more religiously and racially tolerant than their native countries.[11]

Although a minority of immigrants to the Gulf are middle-class professionals from Europe, North America, the Middle East, and Asia, most Gulf immigrants are workers who labor under conditions of severe capitalist exploitation. Information on the construction sector offers a case in point. In 2016, according to a GCC-based migrant workers' rights organization, 17 percent of Kuwait's migrant workforce (approximately 186,000 people) worked in construction. Migrant construction workers numbered 4.28 million out of a total population of 31 million in Saudi Arabia, 154,000 of a total population of 1.3 million in Bahrain, and 652,000 out of a total population of 4.4 million in Oman. In Dubai and Qatar, whose respective populations are approximately 3 million and 2.4 million, around 500,000 and 600,000 are migrant construction workers. In both places these workers are mainly from Nepal, India, and Bangladesh.[12]

To consolidate their influence in the region, the British and American imperialists cultivated as local collaborators the most pro-capitalist and right-wing tendencies in Gulf societies. These eventually became the ruling families of the GCC states. Their role over the past century has been to suppress any moves, however modest, to independent politics, dissent, or resistance. Rulers fabricated narratives about themselves as the only members of their societies capable of ruling over populations whom they portrayed as backward and susceptible to all forms of irrationalism. The irony of imperialism in the Gulf region is that the local rulers have been the most avid purveyors of Orientalist and racist slanders against their own people. One of these myths has been that their populations can be pacified by supposedly generous welfare handouts and the creation of favorable working conditions for foreigners. In these ways the ruling families' narrative perpetuates the idea that the Gulf is "exceptional." The ruling families "saved" their societies from conflicts and the supposed backwardness of other postcolonial/Global South societies (see chapter 14 by Timothy Mitchell in this edited volume).

EXPLOITATION AND RESISTANCE

Since the early twentieth century, the Gulf region has been a site of near-constant capital-versus-labor struggle in key sectors such as oil extraction and construction. In the history of the Gulf, as in other parts of the world, it has been movements from below and by workers in particular that have posed the question of who has the right to rule: the people or the ruling family? Gulf workers—both Arab and foreign—have been part of an international history of working-class exploitation and an international history of working-class resistance, even while they are often ignored in world histories of class struggle. Working conditions experienced by foreign workers in the Gulf are part of a larger international pattern of migrant labor hyperexploitation similar to countries of the north; parallels can be made with the experience of Mexican and Central American undocumented workers in the United States.

While organized protest movements go back to the 1920s and 1930s movements for political reform by Gulf citizens, proletarian resistance was not far behind. The most dramatic of these proletarian movements occurred in Saudi Arabia between March 1953 and June 1956, a time widely regarded as the most important round of working-class mobilizations against the Arabian American Oil Company known as ARAMCO (and now as Saudi ARAMCO). These mobilizations featured petitions, demonstrations, strikes, and boycotts and were perceived as a threat to property relations both by Saudi elites and their American patrons. Thousands of workers, most of ARAMCO's labor force, participated in these mobilizations.[13] As with previous protest movements in Bahrain, Kuwait, and Saudi Arabia, the workers were protesting against low pay and poor working conditions, the racism of the largely southern US employer class, and invidious practices of divide and rule based on ascribed religious differences. Agitation by Saudi workers continued well into the 1960s and was also occurring elsewhere in the region. Often these protests were interwoven with Arab nationalist sentiments and were led by organizers who were oriented to that form of politics, although the ARAMCO workers' movement tended in a more socialist direction. Either way, both the imperial British and American states and their local comprador indigenous collaborators viewed any such agitation with deep hostility and as a potential opening to communist influence.

Attempts by workers to resist or protest working conditions posed a threat not only to the local ruling class but also to the US-led agenda that viewed oil nationalization and worker militancy with deep hostility. The threat, as geographer Adam Hanieh has put it, was "of a potential link between the control of oil (and its revenues), and the ability to use this control to reshape the politics of the region as a whole—moving it out of the ambit of US power or the capitalist world market."[14] The story of labor militancy in the Gulf, which occurred throughout the past century and reached its height in the 1950s and 1960s, is an important corrective to the official state narratives about their history, of enlightened rulers giving the gift of modernity to their passive and grateful subjects.

The Gulf states deployed what Hanieh, following the geographer David Harvey, has called the "spatial fix" that would ensure pacific conditions of profit accumulation. That spatial fix was the (in)famous concept of citizenship based on Arab ethnicity or *asl*, which was in turn deployed by Gulf states to divide the national from the foreign working classes. Consider the following numbers: in 1958, Saudi nationals constituted more than 70 percent of ARAMCO's workforce, and in the early 1960s more than 90 percent of the workforce in Saudi Arabia were Saudi nationals. By 1980 migrant labor made up the majority of the Saudi workforce at 50.7 percent. In Kuwait a series of laws issued in the 1950s and 1960s deliberately aimed to differentiate Kuwaiti and expatriate labor. Across the region, writes Hanieh, "class congealed spatially around temporary migrant labor flows and was demarcated through the institution of citizenship."[15]

This spatial fix functioned in a number of ways to intensify profit accumulation. The structural reliance on temporary migrant labor, articulated politically in the form of the so-called *kafala* or work sponsorship system, increased the rate of exploitation, such that in Dubai, for example, construction workers earn between fifty and eighty cents per hour. They work ten-hour days six days a week, live in residential compounds that further entangle them in already hyperexploitative relations of debt, in conditions of particularly exploitative forms of bonded labor. Migrant workers in the Gulf are under constant threat of deportation and have few rights to contest breaches of labor contracts or arbitrary shortening of contracts.

So far, this story has been largely about male workers. What about female workers? If we consider the main sector in which foreign female workers are employed, work such as domestic labor, the numbers are also striking.[16] For example, more than one-fifth of all Kuwaiti workers are domestic workers, approximately 620,000 in total. They account for over 10 percent of the total workforce in Bahrain, and more than 30 percent of the female workforce. In the UAE they make up around 20 percent of the total foreign workforce, or a total of around 750,000 individuals. Almost all of the domestic workers in the GCC countries are migrant workers. They normally work sixty-hour weeks and earn between $80 and $100 monthly, less than 20 percent of the average wage in Kuwait and Saudi Arabia, and less than 30 percent of the average in Qatar. In the UAE they perform around 80 percent of parental duties and outnumber family members in more than 20 percent of Emirati (UAE national) families.

This extreme exploitation remains in place because female workers experience obstacles to their organizing of resistance that male workers do not. Both male and female foreign workers are subject to the visa sponsorship and residency system, known as *kafala*, which binds workers to their employer, permitting workers to change jobs only with their employer's consent and allowing employers to terminate sponsorship, and therefore right of residence, at will. However, domestic workers unlike other categories of worker are excluded entirely from labor law protections such as limits on working hours and overtime pay. Furthermore, the gendering of their labor allows them to be spatially segregated in ways that men are not. Male foreign workers and female foreign workers are both considered "threats" from the employers' perspective, but in different ways. Foreign male workers are considered a sexual threat in public, while female workers are associated with sexual threat in private spaces. Males are segregated off in collective spaces— for example, in residence compounds. Their work spaces, such as construction sites, are also collective spaces and these allow a certain escape from surveillance by the boss and a spatial proximity that enables coordinated, at times politicized, mobilization.

Female workers, by contrast, tend to be segregated in privatized domestic spaces that isolate them and bring them under the constant surveillance of the boss. Any exercise of mobility or attempt to secure another job not authorized by the employer casts the domestic worker into a status of illegality and therefore increased precarity and vulnerability. As the anthropologist Pardis Mahdavi has pointed out, some women workers turn to sex work to ameliorate or escape from hyperexploitative domestic work, which in turn further exposes them to accusations of immorality and moral panics.[17]

This does not mean that Gulf foreign women workers lack agency or do not take part in organized resistance. Although women domestic workers do not tend to resist abuse and exploitation through mass strikes, as has been the case with male workers, they have organized through other forms such as transnational volunteer associations and migrant alliance networks. Philippine nationals in Saudi Arabia, for example, rely on compatriots whose more privileged class position or higher income level offers them more security and who can provide support for workers who choose to leave undesirable jobs. A more common means by which women workers escape abusive or excessively exploitative work is through what the bosses term "absconding" and what workers term "freelancing." This means simply walking off the job and looking for a better one. While this does carry major risks, such as illegality and a heightened vulnerability to deportation, workers who freelance can improve their pay and working conditions.[18]

Labor protests, militancy, and more generally rebellion against the Gulf countries' capitalist order and class structure are still pervasive. Geographer Michelle Buckley has documented how in Dubai there have been dozens, perhaps hundreds, of labor actions such as strikes and demonstrations by construction workers since the mid-2000s.[19] Workers in these actions protested nonpayment of wages, living conditions at labor camps, and lack of a minimum wage. Unwittingly, the state's segregation of workers into work camps facilitated their efforts to organize, what Buckley describes as an emergent and militant shop floor labor politics. Such actions have been met with violent state repression: mass arrests, summary deportation of strikers labeled "instigators," planting plain-clothes police informants, beatings, and turning off air conditioning at night as a form of punishment. But such attempts at coercion have only emboldened workers, who mobilized a massive two-week strike of thirty thousand to forty thousand workers in November 2007. By 2008 the Dubai state began responding with a less coercive and ultimately more effective strategy: privatizing labor relations. From then on, labor conflicts were to be directed to the employer rather than to the Ministry of Labour. This both helped avoid the formation of unions and, by separating groups of workers from different companies, shrunk and defanged labor protests.

This narrative of organized labor resistance to exploitation that yielded improved conditions for workers and new capitalist strategies of labor discipline has been repeated throughout at least a two-hundred-year history of industrial capitalism. Not only are these events unexceptional in a historical sense but also in a geographic one. While labor exploitation, particularly in its more violent and coercive forms, has often been discussed as specific to the supposedly "illiberal" South, a growing literature is pointing out that it is also characteristic of the supposedly "liberal" North—from North America to Europe and even to the supposedly socialist Nordic countries.[20] These connections strongly suggest that we need to move beyond geographic imaginations limited by the simplifying logics of "area studies" let alone "cultural difference" where culture is understood to be geographically bounded and coterminous with particular linguistic or ethnic or religious communities. Rather, regions such as the Gulf, which might seem most exceptional or culturally distinct in comparison to the supposedly liberal North or West, are as much part of—indeed integral to—global histories of class struggle and capitalism more generally, histories and geographies deeply connecting West and East, North and South.

NOTES

1. I wish to thank Linda Herrera and Asef Bayat for their generous critical readings, which helped me significantly improve upon earlier drafts of this chapter. Amélie Le Renard and Neha Vora have been close collaborators on the larger project of which this piece is a small part and have provided much critical feedback and support.

2. I follow in this chapter the standard nomenclature for the Gulf region as followed in the Arabic-speaking countries of the Middle East, which use "Arab Gulf." The region is also called "Persian Gulf," which is the norm in most European-language maps as well as in Iran. The purpose of this chapter is, among other things, to engage and critique Arab discourses on the region and the ways they homogenize it.

3. Hélène Thiollet, "Managing Migrant Labour in the Gulf: Transnational Dynamics of Migration Politics Since the 1930s," University of Oxford International Migration Institute Working Papers 131 (July 2016), p. 4.

4. These statistics are reported by the Gulf Research Center, a prominent GCC think tank, at http://gulfmigration.eu/gcc-total-population-percentage-nationals -foreign-nationals-gcc-countries-national-statistics-2010-2016-numbers/ (accessed July 27, 2020).

5. Thiollet, "Managing Migrant Labour in the Gulf," 7.

6. Philippe Fargues and Françoise De Bel-Air, "Migration to the Gulf States: The Political Economy of Exceptionalism," in *Global Migration: Old Assumptions,*

New Dynamics, edited by D. Acosta Arcarazo and A. Wiesbrock (Westport, CT: Praeger, 2015), 142.

7. Thiollet, "Managing Migrant Labour in the Gulf," 9.

8. Fargues and De Bel-Air, "Migration to the Gulf States," 143.

9. Fargues and De Bel-Air, "Migration to the Gulf States," 143–44.

10. Fargues and De Bel-Air, "Migration to the Gulf States," 145.

11. See Ahmed Kanna, Amélie Le Renard, and Neha Vora, *Beyond Exception: New Interpretations of the Arabian Peninsula* (Ithaca, NY: Cornell University Press, 2020), 55–79.

12. See "Construction Workers in GCC: Debt, Death and Broken Dreams," Migrant-rights.org, September 11, 2017, www.migrant-rights.org/2017/09/construction-workers-in-gcc-debt-death-and-broken-dreams/ (accessed July 27, 2020).

13. John Chalcraft, "Migration and Popular Protest in the Arabian Peninsula and the Gulf in the 1950s and 1960s," *International Labor and Working Class History* 79 (2011): 28–47.

14. Adam Hanieh, *Capitalism and Class in the Arab Gulf States* (New York: Palgrave MacMillan, 2011), 60–61.

15. Hanieh, *Capitalism and Class in the Arab Gulf States*, 63.

16. Figures in this paragraph are taken from "Domestic Workers in the Gulf," www.migrant-rights.org/statistic/domesticworkers/ (accessed July 27, 2020).

17. Mahdavi, "Gender, Labor and the Law," 425–40.

18. Mahdavi, "Gender, Labor and the Law."

19. Michelle Buckley, "Locating Neoliberalism in Dubai: Migrant Workers and Class Struggle in the Autocratic City," *Antipode* 45, no. 2 (March 2013): 256–74.

20. See Natalia Ollus, "Forced Flexibility and Exploitation: Experiences of Migrant Workers in the Cleaning Industry," *Nordic Journal of Working Life Studies* 6, no. 1 (2016): 25–45; Richard D. Vogel, "Harder Times: Undocumented Workers and the U.S. Informal Economy," *Monthly Review* 58, no. 3 (2006), https://monthlyreview.org/2006/07/01/harder-times-undocumented-workers-and-the-u-s-informal-economy/ (accessed July 27, 2020); and Wise, "Migration and Labor Question Today."

FURTHER READING

Hanieh, Adam. *Capitalism and Class in the Arab Gulf States*. New York: Palgrave MacMillan, 2011.

Kanna, Ahmed. *Dubai, The City as Corporation*. Minneapolis: University of Minnesota Press, 2011.

———. *The Superlative City: Dubai and the Urban Condition in the Early Twentieth Century*. Boston: Harvard University Press, 2013.

Mahdavi, Pardis. "Gender, Labor and the Law: The Nexus of Domestic Work, Human Trafficking, and the Informal Economy in the United Arab Emirates." *Global Networks* 13, no. 4 (2013): 425–40.

Wise, Delgado Wise. "The Migration and Labor Question Today: Imperialism, Unequal Development, and Forced Migration." *Monthly Review* 64, no. 9 (2013), https://monthlyreview.org/2013/02/01/the-migration-and-labor-question-today-imperialism-unequal-development-and-forced-migration/ (accessed July 27, 2020).

NINETEEN

The Levant in Latin America

John Tofik Karam

MIGRANT FEVER HIT THE LEVANT in the late nineteenth century and early twentieth century. Hundreds of thousands of peasants and town-dwellers departed places like Jabal Lubnan (Mount Lebanon), Beit Lahem (Bethelem), and Halab (Aleppo), then part of the Ottoman Empire. Most headed to what they called Amrika (America), not a single country but rather an amorphous territory filled with possibility. Only a third settled in the United States, while the majority spread across Argentina and Brazil as well as Honduras and Mexico and nearly everywhere in between. "It was all America," once remarked a migrant in Brazil with relatives in Argentina and Canada.

Some main ports of entry were Buenos Aires (in Argentina) and Santos (in Brazil), Valparaíso (in Chile) and Veracruz (in Mexico). Upon admission, arrivés found themselves called turcos (Turks) by migration officials and everyday denizens. The moniker referred to anyone with perceived origins not in present-day Turkey but rather onetime Ottoman lands that are today Lebanon, Palestine, and Syria. With ideas of modern lifestyle, national liberation, and visions for development, some returned to their ancestral villages. But for most making their homes in the Spanish- and Portuguese-speaking Americas, they and their descendants continued as turcos—a term of insult as much as indifference and endearment.

So-called turcos are economic, political, and cultural protagonists in what is generally labeled "Latin America." They have distinguished themselves on the economic front as CEOs in industry, trade, and finance, and they work as shop owners and salaried employees. In the political sphere, turcos rise up as establishment politicians, grassroots activists, and voters on the political right and left. They endure, support, and resist authoritarian military regimes and liberal democratic governments. In popular culture they are fictional characters on the screen and in novels, movie stars and screen writers, and viewing audiences. By looking at the reach and influence of turcos in Latin American markets, politics, and cultures, this chapter reveals the Middle East's reach across a part of the world usually imagined as a separate or distant geography. Rather than solely concern a people or a region, or a set of them, this perspective provincializes North American and Western European metropoles that are usually presumed to be the transit points or destinations of farther-flung flows of persons, goods, and ideas.

MONEY, MONEY, MONEY

The quintessential image of turcos evokes money-handling. From early on, Lebanese, Palestinians, and Syrians were peddlers. Some farmed and worked the land. But it was their commercial networks across rural and urban spaces that since the late nineteenth century catapulted them into national public spheres. In Brazil they dominated textile wholesale markets, famously on the Rua 25 de Março in São Paulo, and the Saara district in Rio de Janeiro. In Mexico they first settled in the neighborhood of La Merced of the nation's capital. In Chile they concentrated in the Patronato neighborhood of Santiago's Recoleta district and the town of La Calera two hours north. The fortunes of the few gave the illusion that turcos as a whole were a highly prosperous community, but in fact the majority of them engaged in a broad range of money-earning activities and there was a great deal of economic diversity among them.

A family that exemplifies the successful migrant experience is the Jafet brothers from Choueir in the central mountains of Lebanon. They left for São Paulo, Brazil, in the late nineteenth century and opened a wholesale textile firm by the name Nami Jafet and Brothers (named after the eldest brother). In 1906 they founded the Ypiranga Jafet Spinning, Weaving, and Stamping Factory. Nami founded the Syrian Chamber of Commerce, which he hoped would defend the interests of "Syrian," as opposed to Turkish, merchants across Brazil. Cornering the domestic market in World War I, the Jafet conglomerate grew and employed more than three thousand workers by the mid-1930s. Their textile mills and residential mansions took up the entire neighborhood of Ipiranga in São Paulo. In the following decades, the brothers' investments and enterprises extended into mining, banking, transportation, and other sectors. Their prominence culminated in the appointment of Nami's son, Ricardo, to the presidency of the Banco do Brasil, the oldest bank in Brazil and the second largest bank in Latin America by assets. With the family conglomerate in mind, Ricardo Jafet supported the campaign of the dictator-turned-president Getúlio Vargas (1930–1945), dovetailing with his economic nationalist vision in 1950, although the Jafet family fell out of favor with subsequent Brazilian administrations.

In Mexico City the story of Julián Slim Haddad looms large. Slim, as he was later called, departed Jezzine, a town in southern Mount Lebanon, at the turn of the twentieth century and eventually set up shop in Mexico City. He and his brother owned a dry goods store, The Star of the Orient. Soon they began using their profits to buy downtown property. Over the next decades, Slim accumulated a great deal of wealth through a combination of trade and rents. He had his share of time in court, whether being taken to court by merchants, tenants, and others, or taking others to court. After the Mexican Revolution (1910–20) the new leaders saw agriculture and industry as the paths to development. The Mexican ruling class and workers viewed with suspicion the Middle Eastern nouveau riche like Slim who had amassed fortunes without planting fields or running factories. Consequently, in 1927 the Mexican state prohibited the entry of migrants "of Syrian, Lebanese, Armenian, Palestinian, Arab, and Turk origin." Slim personally wrote to Mexican president Plutarco Elias Calles in defense of his compatriots. "Lebanese," Slim wrote, "are known for being active in work, for their thriftiness." As president of the Lebanese Chamber of Commerce, Slim participated in a campaign to "buy Mexican." In ostensibly speaking for Middle Easterners and highlighting their Mexicanness, Slim not only elided economic inequalities among Lebanese, Palestinians, and Syrians but also folded Middle Eastern difference into Mexican economic nationalist agendas.

Hailing from Beit Lahem in Ottoman Palestine, Juan Yarur and his brothers did likewise. Following a short stint in Bolivia, they ended up in Chile when their industrial exploits drew the attention of a local power broker. They came to own one of the largest cotton manufacturing companies with some three thousand workers, thanks to state incentives that ensured the importation of capital goods at low tariffs and with lavish loans. With the democratic election of Salvador Allende (1970–73), the Yarurs were resented as "millionaire turcos," not only by the government but also among workers. Allende's agenda to make democracy work for "the people" lit the liberationist aspirations of the Yarur workers. They went on strike to "lib-

FIGURE 19.1 Carlos Slim Helú and family, 1950.

erate" the factory, which was eventually purchased by the state and nationalized. Allende counted on anti-turco sentiment, who the elite and workers decried as "Oriental despots," to justify the sequestration of Yarur's and other businesses. But instead, such acts contributed to the military coup led by General Augusto Pinochet (1973–91). General Pinochet denationalized and returned Yarur's factory, which itself eventually closed due to the Chilean dictatorship's economic liberalization that lifted the tariffs protecting national industry.

In Mexico the business magnet Carlos Slim Helu, the son of the aforementioned Julian, rode the wave of free-market policies. With the neoliberal economic turn that began in the 1970s, state-owned and -run utility companies were being nationalized. Such was the case with the privatization of Telmex, the once Mexican state-owned telecommunications enterprise that Slim and other investors purchased in 1990. Mexican President Carlos Salinas de Gortari (1988–94) allegedly underestimated Telmex's value and sought closer relations with Slim by appointing him to the Commission of Finances and Asset Consolidation of the Institutional Revolutionary Party (known by the acronym PRI) that governed Mexico for more than a half century. After acquiring Telmex, Slim ventured into energy, construction, and transportation. One of the richest men in the world with an estimated net worth topping $63 billion in 2018, Slim's wealth in Mexico is still seen "as a result of the favors granted by the state."[1] Slim identifies as Lebanese Mexican and maintains a political neutrality, denying political party affiliation and criticizing free-market policies. Slim's visibility has the effect, simi-

lar to that of his father, of concealing wider economic differences among turcos themselves.

In Chile, Palestinians reemerged in financial liberalization. Carlos
Abumohor Tuma (called Abumohor), a child of Palestinian parents from
Beit Jala, inherited the family's textile business, which closed down like that
of the Yarurs. Instead, Abumohor brought together a group of Chileans
of Arab origin and went into banking. Taking advantage of the economic
deregulation of the Pinochet era, the group acquired their first bank in 1986
and set up one of Chile's largest commercial banks, Corpbanca. The business
tycoon (and Abumohor's partner) Álvaro Saieh complained when, after their
first acquisition, Chile's main newspaper, *El Mercurio*, published a caricature
of Abumohor dressed as an Arab holding a huge bag of money. Saieh, himself a chairman of Corpbanca and one of the wealthiest Chileans today, criticized this "discriminatory attitude that we don't always realize we have as
Chileans."[2] At the same time, Abumohor's sister and Saieh helped to found
and sat on the board of the Bethlehem Palestine Foundation 2000, a non-
for-profit Chilean organization for Palestinian children. The fortunes of
Abumohor, Saieh, and others are usually attributed to Middle Eastern difference, not Chile's financial deregulation and elite philanthropy. Whether
the Yarurs in past, or Slim and Abumohor in the present, turcos shaped and
were shaped by Latin American economic orders.

LEFT TO THE RIGHT

Early Middle Eastern migrants in Latin America, though they were rooted
in the world of trade and industry, came to terms with the political status
quo. They tended to steer clear of pledging formal allegiances to any party
or platform. It was primarily their descendants who began serving in public
office during the second half of the twentieth century. This period roughly
corresponds to the rise and fall of authoritarian military governments, specifically in Argentina (1976–83), Brazil (1964–85), Chile (1973–90), and
Paraguay (1954–89), all with support from the United States in the context
of the Cold War. During that time, and after the return of democratic rule
in the late twentieth and early twenty-first centuries, Lebanese, Palestinians,
and Syrians mobilized on the left and right, but turcos gained greater visibility on the right.

Arabs both flourished and languished under authoritarian military leaders. In Paraguay, Humberto Domínguez Dibb was a key player in the dictatorship of General Alfredo Stroessner (1954–89). Dibb was born to parents of Syrian and Lebanese origins in Asunción in 1943. In the mid-1960s he wed Stroessner's daughter, Graciela. Having the ear of his father-in-law, Dibb expanded his land-holdings and investments through indiscretionary influence, even after divorcing Graciela. Meanwhile, turcos on the other side of the political spectrum endured and were persecuted by Stroessner's regime. Such was the case of Luís Alfonso Resck Haiter, the Paraguayan-born son of Felipe Resck and Maria Haiter. In Villarica, Resck accompanied his father on the lands where they grew Yerba Mate. A critic of Stroessner's human rights abuses, Resck founded a center-left political party that was banned. As Resck languished in jail or exile, Dibb garnered the attention of Syrians, Lebanese, and Palestinians. Dibb came to exercise influence in a country club that had hosted the Egyptian ambassador at the time of the rise of Gamal Abdel Nasser in Egypt (see chapter 8, this volume), and he later purchased two hundred copies of Nasser's *The Philosophy of the Revolution*. Indeed, Dibb's father-in-law at the time, General Stroessner, sent his foreign minister to personally deliver Paraguay's highest honor to the Arab nationalist icon. After Nasser's death in 1970, General Stroessner declared "three days of official mourning" in Paraguay. Arabs mobilized for and against the Paraguayan dictatorship, but for the most part they were associated with its right wing, reactionary rule.

So-called turcos likewise both accommodated and questioned the status quo in Chile. Sabino Aguad Kunkar, born to migrants from Ottoman-governed Palestine, was trained as a lawyer and since the 1940s directed the Chilean Olympic Committee and other sports venues. Aguad allied with President Allende whose coalition of left and center-left parties hoped to put Chile on a democratic road to socialism. Aguad's colleague, Alejandro Hales, was the son of migrants from Ottoman-governed Jordan. A lawyer turned government official, Hales was against Allende's vision and initially welcomed the aforementioned military coup led by General Pinochet. But living next to a stadium converted into a holding pen for political prisoners, Hales saw upclose the regime's violence and became an important figure challenging it. Regularly making headlines in the Arab Chilean press, Aguad and Hales had their political differences, but they collaborated to unsuccessfully influence Pinochet to recognize a Palestinian state. Pinochet sought rapprochement with Arab states not only for petrodollars but also votes in the UN General Assembly in order to defeat proposed condemnations of his regime's abysmal record of human rights. Ultimately, the Palestine Liberation Organization (PLO) became a symbol of liberationist struggle for the Chilean left and Pinochet's violent rule came to rely on Israeli military technology.

The idea of Palestine found fertile terrain on the left and right in Latin America. One figure who stands out in this regard is Souheil Sayegh. Born in Jaffa and arriving in Brazil in 1956, Sayegh founded in 1980 what became the Palestinian Arab Federation of Brazil (FEPAL). In 1982 he ran for a seat in the São Paulo State Assembly on the ticket of the Workers' Party (PT). That same year, Sayegh translated and published a letter exchange between Luiz Inácio "Lula" da Silva, president of the PT (and eventually of Brazil) and Yasir Arafat of the PLO. Writing from Brazil in the context of the Israeli invasion of Lebanon that struck PLO headquarters in Beirut, Lula expressed "shock," "indignation," and his "desire to transmit... in my name and in the name of the Workers' Party, our total and unwavering solidarity." He concluded: "I am ready to go to Beirut now to be a witness" of the atrocities against "the Arab peoples in Lebanon."[3] Some years before this pledge of solidarity, Brazil's military government, which persecuted Lula, voted in favor of UN Resolution 3379, "Zionism is Racism." A day after the vote, the newly appointed president in Brazil's military regime, General Ernesto Geisel (1974–79), allegedly expressed remorse. But when US pundits criticized the vote, the Brazilian foreign ministry publicly backed its position. Migrants, leftists, and autocrats in Brazil seized upon the question of Palestine in projecting ideas of belonging, liberation, and autonomy.

Nonetheless, so-called turcos became fairly synonymous with rightist politics, especially in presidential elections. In Colombia, Júlio César Turbay Ayala was elected and served his term as president (1978–82). Son of a migrant from Tannourine, Lebanon, and a Colombian mother, and nicknamed turco earlier in his career, Turbay was responsible for a security statute that gave indiscretionary power to military and paramilitary forces, leading to numerous human rights violations and the exile of intellectuals, including the celebrated writer Gabriel García Márquez.

Similar scenarios of the political rise and sometimes fall of turcos were repeated across Latin America. In Ecuador, Abdalá Bucaram of Lebanese descent was elected president in 1996 only to be removed a year later. He was succeeded by Jamil Jorge Mahuad Witt in 1998, also of Lebanese/Ottoman heritage. His spurious adoption of the US dollar as Ecuadorian currency put the domestic economy in chaos, and he too was forced to resign in 2000.

In Argentina, Carlos Menem, the son of migrants from the Syrian town of Yabrud, was elected president for two terms (1989–99). Menem privatized state-owned enterprises, pinned the Peso to the US dollar, and reintroduced the military into domestic security, putting Argentina into recession and crisis.

In El Salvador's 2004 presidential elections, a young Palestinian descendent in a center-right party, Antonio Saca (2004–2009), defeated an older leftist Palestinian descendent, Schafik Handal, who had gained prominence in a national liberation movement, the Farabundo Martí National Liberation Front (FMLN). In Honduras in 2009 the democratically elected Manuel Zelaya was removed and sent into exile in a coup aided by Miguel Facussé, a US-educated Honduran of Palestinian origins whose parents hailed from Beit Lahem. Everyday Hondurans faulted Facussé and other turcos, not US sway over the country that made the exception possible. To a large degree, as turcos gained greater recognition on the right, onlookers and pundits alike tended to fault their Middle Eastern traits, or "difference," rather than their neoliberal and conservative stances, absolving the political right itself.

Turcos continue to hold office across the political spectrum, especially in Brazil. Michel Temer, the youngest son in a migrant family from Koura, Lebanon, conspired as vice president in the impeachment of President Dilma Rousseff and became president in 2016. His older migrant brothers in trade and industry bankrolled Temer in law school and his early political career. Temer and the center-right coalition that supported him rolled back progressive gains. Meanwhile, a presidential hopeful of the Workers' Party for the 2018 elections is Fernando Haddad, former mayor of São Paulo and the grandson of migrants from Zahle, Lebanon. Carrying in his wallet to this day a picture of his migrant grandfather, who he himself never knew, Haddad rose as a student leader and served as minister of education under President Lula. Middle Easterners continue on both the left and the right amid institutional crises that they alone did not trigger and polarized politics that they too remain divided in.

THE DIFFERENCE WITHIN

In the Spanish- and Portuguese-speaking Americas, ideas of difference (or otherness), such as Arabness, Muslimness, or Middle Easternness, constitute the self, within the nation.[4] To a degree of contrast, in Western Europe and North America these groups would be considered "minorities," or as people with hyphenated identities such as "Muslim-American" or "Arab-American." Cultural producers of Lebanese, Palestinian, or Syrian origins tend not to hyphenate themselves, even when acknowledging or speaking to Middle Easternness in their novels, films, and other cultural productions.

For instance, the most influential contemporary writer in Brazil is Milton Hatoum, born to a Shia Muslim Lebanese father and a Maronite Christian Brazilian mother of Lebanese origin. While in the United States, Hatoum came upon an advertisement for his talk calling him as a "Lebanese-Brazilian writer." Hatoum told his host that a "Lebanese-Brazilian" category "makes absolutely no sense in Brazil," which he described as a country formed through "racial mixing." Drawing on Brazilian nationalist language, Hatoum "emphasiz(ed) the coexistence of different ethnicities and origins in Brazil, even at the risk of appearing utopian."[5] In his oeuvre, *Tale of a Certain Orient*, first published in 1989, Hatoum acknowledged the "presence of Arab culture" but characterized the novel as a universal "search for origins." After reading a review of that novel in the Lebanese newspaper *An-Najar*, Hatoum's father in Manaus remarked: "It's strange. I never thought I'd go back to Lebanon through a book written by my son." Through familial stories and trajectories, but refusing particular labels, Hatoum claims a universality usually reserved for Western European or North American writers.

A novelist whose reach has gone far outside the continent reaching corners across the globe is Gabriel García Márquez, Colombian Nobel laureate of literature (1982), known as Gabo. Characters who fit the profile of turcos permeate his writing. The plot in *Chronicle of a Death Foretold*, for instance, revolves around the killing of Santiago Nasar, the Colombian-born son of a "marriage of convenience" between his Arab father, Ibrahim, with whom he spoke Arabic, and his Colombian mother, with whom he lived. The plot is based on a murder that Gabo covered as a journalist in the actual city of Sucre, where he befriended Lebanese, Palestinian, and Syrian families. In the novel Gabo writes that "Arabs made up a community of immigrants... in the towns of the Caribbean... selling dyed rags and flea market trinkets."[6]

Arabs are marked by difference but within larger questions of narration, foretelling, what is not heard, and who bears accountability. Gabo's novel became a film in 1987 and a Broadway musical in 1995. In the interim, the character of Santiago Nasar was taken up by Lebanese writer Elias Khoury in the novel *Majmaʿal-asrār* (The collection of secrets). Khoury structures his novel around a letter Santiago Nasar allegedly sent from Colombia to cousins in Lebanon.[7] Constructed from within Colombia, this idea of Arabness was now imported back into the Arabic language to capture the multiplicity of origins.

Brazilian author Jorge Amado, whose novels have been translated into forty-nine languages, also casts a wide range of turco characters. In his novel *Gabriela, Clove, and Cinnamon*, a protagonist is Mister Nacib, a jovial tavern-owner whose father, Aziz Saad, arrived from Ottoman-governed Syria. Clients and friends called Nacib turco as an "expression of caring, of intimacy," writes Amado.[8] Invariably, Nacib took offense and corrected them: "Brazilian," he shouted, "son of Syrians." Nacib fell in love with Gabriela, a metaphor for the Brazilian nationalist ideal of miscegenation, or mixing across perceived racial and cultural lines. With Nacib renewing his romance with Gabriela as cook and mistress at the novel's end, Amado confirmed the place of Arab men in Brazil by reproducing the race, gender, and class hierarchies that entitle men of means to subjugate poor women of color. Amado's story was made into a soap opera in 1975, a film by Bruno Barreto in 1983, and a soap opera remake in 2012. This novel that features perhaps the most famous Arab character in contemporary Brazilian literature was translated into Arabic, Hebrew, Persian, and Turkish, among many other languages.

Miguel Littín is by far the most renowned filmmaker in Chile. Born south of Santiago to a father of Palestinian origin and a mother of Greek descent, Littín defined New Latin American Cinema characterized by grit, inequality, and struggle, against glossy Hollywood aesthetics. Littín's debut in 1969, *Jackal of Nahueltoro*, tells the story of an exploited farmer who is rescued by a poor woman with children that he ends up killing in a drunken stupor. Littín was appointed to Chile's state film bureau by President Allende and was forced to flee after the military coup led by General Pinochet. Clandestinely returning later, Littín filmed a documentary critical of the Pinochet dictatorship. This journey became the subject of a work by Gabriel García Márquez, *Clandestine in Chile: The Adventures of Miguel Littín*. Littín shot his most recent film, *The Last Moon*, in Jerusalem, Beit Lahem, and Beit Sahur. Having survived three shootings at the hands of Pinochet, Littín joked that Israeli attempts to cut the film's shooting failed to intimidate him. Making a film on the "Question of Palestine" resonated with Littín's own memories of such stories from his paternal grandmother as well as with being a Chilean director narrating struggles under Pinochet and similar violent regimes.

No review of turco cultural icons would be complete without the popular singer and dancer Shakira. Her paternal grandparents migrated from Zahle, Lebanon, to New York City, the birthplace of her father. From there the family moved to Barranquilla, Colombia, where Shakira was born as Shakira Isabel Mebarak Ripoli. It was her Lebanese grandmother who first taught her dance moves from what became called belly-dancing, *raks el-sharq*. Her father brought Shakira to listen to the beats of a doumbek, an Arab drum, in a Middle Eastern restaurant in the coastal Colombian town where she grew up. These shimmies and beats resound on Shakira's debut album *Magia* (Magic) with Sony Music Colombia, released in 1991, and continued through her transition from Spanish to English under the same label in the 2000s. One of the top-earning female artists for the past decade, Shakira draws upon Latin American, Middle Eastern, and other styles of music and dance. Her difference is as malleable as it is manageable among consumers as well as conglomerates of the global culture industry.

The Middle East is likewise a subject in Latin American universities. Since the 1960s, Argentine, Brazilian, Chilean, and Mexican universities have founded research centers or programs to study the Middle East.[9] Lebanese, Palestinian, and Syrian migrants or descendants were often involved in these undertakings. Sometimes non-Middle Eastern academic collaborators were motivated by the Moorish and Muslim legacies of the Iberian peninsula (called al-Andalus), imagined to have been transported to Latin America, linguistically and socially. Above all, it was the solidarity movements across what was denominated the "Third World" or what is today called the "Global South" that inspired academic programs for the study of the Middle East in Latin America. With fewer resources than European or US counterparts, these academic programs support language and area studies of the Middle East and North Africa as well as ethnic or migration studies of Middle Easterners and Muslims in Latin America.

CONCLUSION

The Levant in Latin America reveals that North America and Western Europe are not the centers of power but rather nodes of a global order with neither a core nor a periphery. Middle Eastern migrants and descendants are key players, presidents, and protagonists in Latin American economies, politics, and cultures. Whether in state-led development or market-driven reforms, so-called turcos founded firms, banks, and trading houses. Under authoritarian military regimes and democratic civilian rule, Latin Americans of Arab origin mobilized for and against political establishments. In novels, films, and pop culture in both Spanish and Portuguese, Arabs have been represented by others and represented themselves.

In closing, I return to the great Gabo. In his novel *News of a Kidnapping*, Gabo tells the story of the real-life kidnappings executed by drug traffickers that changed the face of Colombian politics and society. The story focuses on the case of Diana, the daughter of Colombian president Júlio Turbay. This novel was the basis for the wildly popular Netflix series *Narcos*. Gabo's novel gained perhaps even greater popularity in Iran after being evoked by Mir Hossein Moussavi in 2011. As a former presidential candidate and political opposition leader, Moussavi was placed under house arrest and likened his situation to the prominent figures sequestered in Gabo's novel. Within weeks, *News of a Kidnapping* boasted "phenomenal" sales in Tehran, according to the publishing house Nashr-e Cheshmeh. Iranian websites allegedly made an electronic version of the book available in Persian. The narrative of the kidnapping and murder of the daughter of the former Colombian president of Lebanese origin now circulates in Persian and has become an important metaphor in Iranian political life. This and countless examples illustrate how the circulation of people, life, and art of a global Middle East influence and are influenced by new publics in unexpected places and myriad ways.

The globality of the Middle East addressed in this chapter, however, focused on the circulation of neither images nor things but rather persons. Identified as Lebanese, Palestinians, Syrians, "Levantines," turcos, or otherwise, Middle Easterners undertake a global mobility best captured by the term *mahjar* in Arabic. The term stems from the Arabic root H-J-R (ه ج ر), which implies some sort of migration (as in *hijra*). With the prefix "m" (م) that denotes "place" at the start of the root, *mahjar* can refer to any "place of migration," whether one migrates to a city like Rio de Janeiro, a country such as Brazil, or a region like Latin America. As a term of reference, *mahjar* first gained popularity among early twentieth-century writers who migrated to and produced significant works in Argentina, Brazil, and the United States. But now in the early twenty-first century, it is the term of choice to speak of migrant and global connections among Middle Easterners.

NOTES

1. Carlos Martínez Assad, "Los libaneses inmigrantes y sus lazos culturales desde México," *Dimensión Antropológica* 44 (2008): 3.

2. Quoted in Alexis Jano Ros, *Inspiradores latinoamericanos: De emprendedores a líderes empresariales* (México DF: Ediciones Granica México, 2014).

3. Lula as quoted in "Opinião do Leitor," *Nova Escrita Ensaio* (October 5, 1982), 8–10, 221–22.

4. González Echevarría, *Myth and Archive*, 97.

5. Milton Hatoum, "Arabescos Brasileiros," trans. John Tofik Karam, *Mashriq & Mahjar: Journal of Middle East and North African Migration Studies* 1, no. 2 (2013): 3–13.

6. Gabriel García Márquez, *Crónica de una muerte anunciada* (Barcelona: Editorial Bruguera, 1981), 130.

7. Christina Civantos, "The View from Beyond: Diaspora and Intertextuality in Ilyās Khūrī's *Majma'al-asrār*," *Journal of Arabic Literature* 46, nos. 2–3 (2015): 193–215.

8. Jorge Amado, *Gabriela, Cravo e Canela*, 79th edition (1958; reprint, Rio de Janeiro: Editora Record, 1998), 61. For an insightful analysis of Amado's Arabness, see Waïl Hassan, "Jorge Ahmed," *Comparative Literature Studies* 49, no. 3 (2012): 395–404.

9. In Brazil see the Núcleo de Estudos Medio-Orientais coordinated by Paulo Gabriel Hilu da Rocha Pinto at the Universidade Federal Fluminense in Niterói, Rio de Janeiro, and the Biblioteca América do Sul-Países Árabes directed by Paulo Elias Farah in São Paulo. In Argentina see the Programa de Estudios sobre Medio Oriente coordinated by Juan José Vagni at the Universidad Nacional de Córdoba, and the Centro de Estudios del Medio Oriente Contemporáneo run by Paulo Botta. In Chile see the Centro de Estúdios Árabes of Eugenio Chahuan at the Universidad de Chile. In Mexico there is the Centro de Estudios de Asia y África at El Colégio de México in the federal capital. Although the centers in Chile and Mexico were founded in the 1960s, the others began in the 2000s.

It should also be noted that Lebanese, Israeli, Moroccan, and UAE universities have hired Latin American specialists and/or opened Latin American studies centers. In Lebanon the Center for Latin American Studies and Cultures was founded by Roberto Khatlab at the Université Saint-Espirit de Kaslik. In Israel the Institute for Latin American History and Culture is run by Raanan Rein at Tel Aviv University. In Morocco the Institut des Etudes Hispano-Lusophones is at the Université Mohammed V-Agdal. In the UAE, Federico Velez and others teach Latin American studies at Zayed University.

FURTHER READING

Garcia Marquez, Gabriel. *Chronicle of a Death Foretold*. Translated from the Spanish by Gregory Rabassa. New York: Vintage Books, 1983.

González Echevarría, Robert. *Myth and Archive: A Theory of Latin American Narrative*. Cambridge, UK: Cambridge University Press, 1990.

Karam, John Tofik. *Another Arabesque: Syrian-Lebanese Ethnicity in Neoliberal Brazil*. Philadelphia: Temple University Press, 2007.

Narbona, María del Mar Logroño, Paulo G. Pinto, and John Tofik Karam. *Crescent over Another Horizon: Islam in Latin America, the Caribbean, and Latino U.S.A.* Austin: University of Texas Press, 2015.

PART SEVEN

Politics and Movements

TWENTY

Global Tahrir

Asef Bayat

WHY AND HOW DID THE OCCUPATION of Tahrir Square during the Egyptian revolution of January 25, 2011, become a global meme? The story in some sense begins on December 16, 2010, when Mohammed Bouazizi, a poor street vendor from a depressed town of Sidi-Bouzid in Tunisia, set himself on fire after the police abusively confiscated his scale and vegetables because he lacked a permit. The news traveled rapidly in the town and brought relatives and local youths to the streets in outrage. The event exploded on social media and reached global news agencies.

Throughout the following three weeks, much of central Tunisia was engaged in what came to be a mass uprising, with the protestors demanding jobs, dignity, and freedom. As the uprising stretched northward to the capital Tunis, workers staged strikes and the professional middle classes joined the demonstrations. The protestors wanted the president to step down. When on January 14, 2011, demonstrators filled Bourghiba Boulevard in the capital city, and the army refused to shoot to kill, President Zine El Abidine Ben Ali and his wife Leila Trabelssi, who had ruled Tunisia through corruption, nepotism, and an iron fist for twenty-two years, left the country to Saudi Arabia for good. The uprising had paid off.

The events in Tunisia emboldened Egyptian activists. The two main youth groups of the time that organized through social media, "The April 6 Movement" and the anti-torture Facebook page "We are All Khaled Said," had already been planning an event for January 25 on the occasion of Police Day. They wanted to protest police abuse, the continuation of the Emergency Law, and more specifically the brutal torture and murder of a young man, Khaled Said, by the police for alleged cyber activism. In an astonishing and unexpected response, tens of thousands of people showed up on January 25.

Young and old, men and women, Christians and Muslims, marched from some twenty different points in Cairo, including poor neighborhoods, and flooded the iconic Tahrir Square. Similar uprisings spread in Libya and then Yemen, Syria, and Bahrain.

On the whole, nineteen Arab states experienced mass revolts; four dictators were toppled, one (Bashar al-Asad) came to the brink. And the rest, notably the monarchs and kings, apprehended by the tidal wave of revolutions, rushed to appease their own populations by an overture of political reforms (such as constitutional amendments) or dispensing economic packages while trying to sabotage, discredit, or influence the revolutions elsewhere in the regional neighborhood. For a time, brief but momentous, the region experienced the spirit of the Arab Spring, as protestors seized and occupied central urban spaces where they held monumental rallies, demonstrations, and prolonged sit-ins. Among them, Tahrir remained an extraordinary, and soon a globally iconic, symbol of place, public, and egalitarian self-rule.

Remarkable as it was, the occupation of Tahrir represented only a moment in the broader dynamics of the Egyptian revolution and the Arab Spring revolts. The revolution in Egypt was a response to some thirty years of social and economic change that involved growing urbanization, demographic shifts, higher literacy and educational attainment, and liberalization of the economy, combined with political stagnation. This combination created both dissent against the Mubarak regime and opportunities for its public expression. Expanding urban dwelling cultivated desires, demands, and entitlements such as paid jobs or urban services that the regime failed to fulfill for a large segment of the population. Demographic change made these societies exceedingly young, while expanding education created expectations; but the young people's dreams of stable jobs and decent living standards were frustrated by the regime's neglect. The free market it promoted failed to deliver to a wide section of the population. Opposition groups that had previously worked underground, burst into the public in the late 2000s in poor areas, factories, university campuses, and mosques. In many cases they spread via social media prior to the uprising. The landmark Tahrir protest on January 25, 2011, embodied a creative synergy of online activism and offline street mobilization that had been building up for nearly a decade.

In response, state security forces used tear gas, clubs, and rocks, and the government blocked the Internet. But the protests grew even larger in the following days stretching out to the provincial cities of Alexandria, Suez, Mahalla, and Mansoura, among others. On Friday, February 28, "the Day of

Rage," Egypt saw the largest crowds in the nation's streets. Protestors fought security forces, attacked police stations, burned government buildings, and chanted "Bread, Freedom, and Social Justice" (*aysh, huriyya, adala igtimaiyya*). When the police retreated from the streets in the night and failed to show up at their posts the following days, protestors occupied Tahrir Square and began to erect tents. Citizens formed popular committees to protect their neighborhoods from possible acts of crime. With the police gone from the public space, the military took to the streets but signaled neutrality.

Now grown into a full-fledged uprising, protestors demanded to end the thirty-year rule of President Mubarak. Eighteen days of spectacular uprising, with 841 dead, thousands injured, and a military that was clearly turning its back on Mubarak, forced the president to step down on February 11, 2011. Mubarak transferred power to the Supreme Council of Armed Forces (SCAF) to run the nation's affairs and preside over the "transition" process—to hold parliamentary and presidential elections, and prepare a new constitution. Even after the autocratic Mubarak surrendered, the occupation of Tahrir continued, this time against the new military rulers.

TAHRIR MOMENTS

During the spectacular uprising, the symbol of Tahrir inspired and animated the imagination of millions of people around the globe who led and participated in similar movements for social justice. Tahrir Square became a global emblem. The square traveled as a model for the global Occupy Movements that emerged in eighty countries and five hundred cities around the world, including New York, Madrid, Athens, and Tel Aviv. Why did the Tahrir repertoire exude such a remarkable global reception, especially when the idea came from a region, the Arab Middle East, that was deemed in mainstream media as a cultural backwater, if not outright backward? Of course, travel and adoption of ideas and cultural codes are key features of the globalized world. But flows of knowledge and cultural and political paradigms often remain a one-way street, usually moving from the rich countries of the Global North (the "center") to the poorer nations of the Global South (the "periphery")—a reality that has gained the description by some as "cultural imperialism."

The Tahrir moment worked against the current; it stirred millions of activists in the streets of the "Center" to forge their own Tahrir squares, to resist the staggering inequality of wealth (as captured in the slogan "We are the 99%"), precarious life, and governmental politics that had become subservient to corporate greed. Tahrir represented an extraordinary mix of a political space, "liberated street," and unparalleled political practice (these were noninstitutional, mass-based, and horizontal movements), making possible a sustained campaign of persistent protest until victory.

In contentious politics, space matters in at least two ways. First, it fuels the "political street" in that it serves as a physical locus in and about which contention is shaped, expressed, and communicated. When people lose trust in state institutions to respond to their claims, they resort to their own institutional power (like in a workplace or university) to put pressure on the authorities to address their grievances. So workers go on strike, or students disrupt classes. However, when people (such as the unemployed, youths, or homemakers) do not have such institutional power, or when they doubt the effectivity of such measures, they tend to resort to public spaces, streets, where they march, demonstrate, or hold rallies. Here, the streets or squares allow the protesting people to assemble and form a crowd, extend their network of solidarity, exhibit their numerical power to both friends and foes, and push for their claims by disrupting public order and challenging the authorities.

There is another way in which space figures in contentious politics, in the form of "liberated zones." Here, contenders exclusively use or deliberately seize control of certain spaces depriving adversaries of operating them. They occupy territories, villages, or towns to establish an alternative social order—an order they envision for their country's future. For instance, on January 1, 1994, when the Mexican government signed the North America Free Trade Agreement (NAFTA) with the United States and Canada, three thousand indigenous fighters from the Zapatista National Liberation Army (EZLN) seized control of six towns in central and eastern Chiapas in Mexico. The Zapatista movement established self-rule in the territories with alternative institutions of work, education, health, and justice system in which ordinary people played a central role. Similar examples of "liberated zones" can be found in the Paris Commune in 1781, or the Mozambican war of liberation (1964–75) against Portuguese colonial rule. The experience of popular self-rule in Rajova, a Kurdish territory of Syria, in 2016 is a more recent example of a liberated zone.

What transpired in Tahrir Square in Egypt's January 2011 revolution stood somewhere between the "political street" and the "liberated zone."

Tahrir represented a "liberated street" in the heart of a megacity, a new invention in contentious politics, and an improvisation in the absence of a revolutionary strategy to seize state power, to establish an alternative public order without the state. Midan Tahrir had a history and memory of occupation going back to 2003. During the height of the Israeli military incursion of the Palestinian West Bank and Gaza in 2003, and in the wake of the US invasion of Iraq, thousands of enraged Egyptians occupied Tahrir, where they assembled, held rallies, and chanted slogans against the United States and Israel. With the police standing aside, the crowd redirected the traffic to make space for the protesters to rally. As the night fell, they brought candles, books, and blankets, formed smaller groups, sat down on the ground, recited poetry, discussed politics, and fashioned a convivial community of affect and anguish. Once the protestors went home late at night, however, the police moved in to repossess the square. The occupation ended after only one day.

But during the January 25, 2011, uprising, when tens of thousands of protestors filled the vast Tahrir roundabout from every direction, activists decided to stay on until Mubarak was gone, thus giving the square and its politics a new life and meaning. With the square in its possession, activists held mass rallies, wrote tracts, hung banners, and erected stages, and before long set up makeshift tents to spend the nights. Then came medical teams, cleaning crews, and popular security groups. In the headquarters around the square, multiple leaders discussed strategies, assigned tasks, and allocated resources—food, resting locations, mobile phone charging stations, and other services. In residential buildings surrounding Tahrir, a number of apartments offered rest and respite, the places where revolutionaries would take breaks from the strain of the Midan, use lavatories, wash, rest, rejuvenate, and strategize next steps.

Young men and women spent nights together as comrades in the campsites; and Muslims and Christians assisted each other in their prayer services. Tech-savvy activists fed news to social media—mainly Facebook and Twitter at that time, while Al Jazeera television continuously transmitted the events and images of Tahrir worldwide. As days passed, ordinary Cairenes—men, women, children, the elderly—would join the revolutionaries turning Tahrir the battlefield into evenings of carnivalesque, fun, and picnics; their presence boosted the trade of street vendors who did not cease to shout out for hot tea, cold drinks, T-shirts, and protective masks, even in the midst of rallies, shooting, and tear gas. Travelers paid visits from provincial towns and villages, not missing the adventure of Tahrir moments; and young couples came to the square to exchange wedding vows and hold their wedding celebrations and honeymoons in that monumental arena.

Tahrir became a microcosm of the alternative social order for which the revolutionaries seem to aspire. During those eighteen days, it was a place of democratic governance, nonhierarchical organization, collective decision-making, self-help, and altruism—a liberated zone wherein differences across lines of gender, religion, region, and class seemed to fade. Intrigued by this display of democratic politics, some observers portrayed Tahrir as a "theater" that staged an egalitarian, affective, and cooperative order that the Arab Spring appeared to herald.[1] Enthusiastic by the appeal of agora in the eighteen days of Tahrir Square, philosophers Alain Badiou and Slavio Zizek saw in these revolutionary moments the promise of a new social order that could serve as the foundation for a different future. For others, it was something like the ancient Greek polis described by Hannah Arendt, as a form of government that relied on self-rule and commonsense initiative with no particular single ruler.[2]

The Tahrir moment evolved and was imagined as a model of radical democracy, an alternative to revolutionary organization, vanguard party politics, guerrilla tactics, or liberation war. It was this image, this new model of the "future in the present," that lay behind its global appeal in a disenchanted world where the idea of old-fashioned revolution was dead, while the liberal democracy enslaved by corporate interests had failed to address people's concerns for unemployment, precarity, and inequality. Inspired by the Arab Spring, the disaffected citizens around the world, chiefly in Europe and United States, drew on the Tahrir moment to build their own Occupy movements and liberated squares.

GOING GLOBAL

Only days after the fall of President Hosni Mubarak, when Tahrir was still in full swing, up to twenty thousand protestors in Wisconsin, in the United States, came out against Republican governor Scott Walker, who wanted to reduce social benefits and end labor collective bargaining. They carried signs and Egyptian flags as though this was their Tahrir Square. As they took to the streets, hundreds of people were arrested. In Spain an initial hundred-person encampment in Madrid's Puerta del Sol in May 2011 grew into tens of thousands of demonstrators who initiated what came to be known as Los

Indignados, the movement of the indignant people, to protest the staggering 20 percent unemployment (40 percent for youth), austerity, and precarious life; in total more than six million (of the total forty-six million) Spaniards joined in the protests.

Then came Athens, where one hundred thousand Greeks took to the streets, putting up tents in Syntagma Square for weeks. Their movement spread rapidly to others cities. The occupation of squares became the enduring feature of urban landscape in Greece, a country hardest hit by the Eurozone crisis, spending cuts, and higher taxes. "We Won't Pay, Let the Rich Pay," they shouted out. Protestors in Tel Aviv camped in Rothschild Boulevard dissenting joblessness and the high cost of living; the movement was marked by four hundred encampments along with four hundred thousand demonstrators marching throughout the country. In the United States, Occupy Wall Street (OWS) began with the occupation of the Zuccotti Park in New York in September 2011 and soon spread across hundreds of cities where encampments in the central squares spoke of the coming of a new form of popular politics. Within months, the occupy movements had spread into Britain, The Netherlands, then Mexico, Chile, Russia, India, Turkey's Gezi Park as well as Bangkok, Thailand, and Ukraine, where its central arena of the revolution in Kiev was named in the Arabic word "Midan" to invoke Egypt's iconic square, "Midan Tahrir."[3] Even in Brazil, a country that under a center-left government had enjoyed the lowest unemployment rate in its history, and unprecedented expansion of economic and social rights, a small increase in bus fares sparked a nationwide movement of one million protestors demanding an end to corruption, a low cost of living, and a decent education system.[4] Like others, this movement too, according to the *Guardian*, took its "inspiration from [...] the Arab Spring and the Occupy Movement."

But it was especially in Occupy Wall Street, Spain's Puerta de Sole, and Israel's Rothschild Corner that the Tahrir repertoire found much of its appeal. In early June 2011 the Canadian-based magazine *Adbusters*, with a circulation of seventy thousand, sent an email to subscribers proclaiming, "America needs its own Tahrir." Berkeley activist Micah White, anarchist theorist David Graeber, and other activists joined forces to begin a campaign to occupy lower Manhattan.[5] On September 12, *Adbusters* urged: "Let's learn the strategic lessons of Tahrir (nonviolence), Syntagma (tenacity), Puerta del Sol (people's assemblies) and lay aside adherence to political parties and worn-out lefty dogmas." In their call for action the initiators challenged

Americans, "Are you ready for a Tahrir moment?" urging the activists to articulate a clear demand with a nonstop occupation until victory.

On October 17, 2011, a thousand protestors poured into Zuccotti Park in the heart of Manhattan's financial district, where in 2007–2008 the corrupt banks and hedge funds had caused America's worst financial crisis since the Great Depression. Protests grew and spread to hundreds of other cities within the next few weeks. Protestors established "liberated streets" with tents, desks, kitchen supplies, wireless Internet, and formed a dozen working groups for tactics, supply, sanitation, medical care, finance, and the like. Thousands of protest actions took place with "occupation" as the key repertoire, as in Occupy Brooklyn Bridge, Occupy Port of Oakland, and Occupy the Stock Exchange. In these liberated urban zones, the crowd sat on the ground, ate together, discussed politics, prepared placards and banners, talked to the media, spent nights in tents, and lived an alternative life different from their daily routines. Activists made it clear in a leaflet that "we are using the revolutionary Arab Spring occupation tactics to achieve our ends and we encourage the use of nonviolence to maximize the safety of all participants."[6] However, the "ends" were never clearly articulated.

Public statements cited Tunisia and Egypt as models for action; and some wondered how they could attract the urban community to spend the night in the occupied squares as the community in Cairo gathered in Tahrir after every evening prayer. The *New York Times* reported from Zuccotti Park: "Here in Lower Manhattan, and around the country, protestors have embraced a movement springing from the Arab World as a model of freedom, democracy and nonviolence."[7] *The Week* magazine depicted OWS Occupy as a "US version of the Arab Spring."[8] This sense of transnational connection was most vividly expressed in the humor of the Egyptian street vendor at Zuccotti Park, Ehab Sami, who happened to be doing a thriving business there. He became a celebrity with New Yorkers who chatted with him as he traded his falafel and fried eggplants, and asked for his thoughts about Zuccotti's Tahrir.

In the meantime, OWS and Tahrir activists connected through social media and discussed their campaigns, with topics ranging from how to deal with pepper spray in Oakland, to bullets in Cairo. Indeed, when Tahrir erupted later in 2011 against the SCAF, the Occupy movement issued a statement in solidarity with Egypt. "Our brothers and sisters in Egypt inspired us all with their courage over the ten months," the statement read. "Without them, would we have seen the Occupy Movement? How would our own struggle against austerity and cuts look without the model of the Egyptian revolution, and the knowledge that ordinary people can change the world?"[9] Such a feeling of solidarity was striking given that only a year before, a plan to build a Muslim community center and mosque in lower Manhattan near Ground Zero where the twin towers of the World Trade Center had fallen in 2001, had caused much controversy.

In their turn, Egyptian revolutionaries sent a message of solidarity to Zuccotti Park protestors. "We are now in many ways involved in the same struggle as yours," they proclaimed, maintaining that Tahrir and OWS were "one movement rooted in the systems of repression, disenfranchisement and the unchecked ravages of global capitalism."[10] In October 2011, Egyptian activists Asma Mahfouz and Ahmed Maher traveled to New York to join the Zuccotti Park protests, held a teach-in, participated in a march, presented an Egyptian flag with the message "From Tahrir to Wall Street." They exchanged ideas and experiences. Mahfouz urged the OWS to articulate a clear message and build coalitions to broaden the movement. In response an OWS coordinator affirmed "what effects Egypt, effects New York," adding that the "rights of persons worldwide and all semblance of free government has been highjacked by corporate interests.... We know we are together with only one choice—victory." In November 2011 the OWS planned to send a delegation of twenty activists to monitor the first parliamentary elections in Egypt, but the high cost prevented the plan. Earlier, the OWS activist Marisa Holmes had traveled to Cairo, where she visited Tahrir and discussed strategies with Egyptian activists; she reported how similar the scenes in Cairo and New York were.

Things were not so different in Spain, where the colossal protests had earlier energized those in Zuccotti Park. Stirred by the square dramas of the Arab Spring, the Spanish Indignados launched their own campaign on May 15, 2011, under the slogan "Real democracy now! We are not commodities in the hands of politicians and bankers."[11] Within a week, more than sixty central plazas across Spain were occupied, notably Madrid's Puerta del Sol that displayed "an uncanny resemblance to Tahrir Square in Cairo," where a sign read "From Tahrir to Puerto del Sol: Democracy for All." In what some called "Europe's very own Tahrir Square," tents were erected, assemblies formed, orderly discussions managed, alcohol discouraged, and multiple preparations were made to keep these unlawful occupations going. The passersby and tourists called in and engaged with the protestors, and activists raised a sign that said: "no house, no work, no future, but NO FEAR."

For them this was a "Tahrir generation" following a "Seattle generation and earlier a "Genoa generation." Some 650 messages of solidarity reached Los Indignados from around the world. Activists stated: "In the countries of Europe's periphery, emulating the popular uprisings in the Arab world, drawing warmth from Tunis's Qasbah and Cairo's Tahrir Square, people took back and took over the public space. The Arab Spring gave us confidence in ourselves and our collective ability to change the existing order." The Spanish activists established contacts and exchanged ideas with the counterparts in Egypt on their respective campaigns. They affirmed that the unemployed, pensioners, students, and disillusioned youth in Spain were rejecting the conventional party politics to emulate Arab revolutionaries to gain voice and live in dignity.[12]

Clearly the Arab Spring and the Tahrir moment altered, for a short time at least, the Western image of Arab societies as the bastion of religious intolerance and terrorism, presenting it instead as a symbol of peaceful, democratic, and imaginative uprisings for justice and freedom. But identification with Arabs and the Arab Spring had a greater meaning in Israel. For not only were Arabs and Muslims "represented as the ultimate Other of Israeli Jewish society usually through a securitized 'law and order' frame," but also because, as the sociologist Gershon Shafir has suggested, Israelis in general view themselves as part of the global "center" and the Arabs the "periphery." Moreover, the Israeli political elite disfavors attempts to democratize the Arab world, because a democratic Arab state is likely to oppose Israeli occupation policies, including the 1978 Camp David peace accord.[13]

Despite this, the tenets of the Tahrir repertoire circulated widely through posters, slogans, speeches, blogs, websites, videos, and tweets of members of Israel's most significant social justice movement. Emerged on July 14, 2011, the movement aimed to fight against income inequality, "piggish capitalism," increasing marginalization, and the declining status of middle classes. Beginning in Tel Aviv's "Rothschild Corner of Tahrir," the movement mobilized four hundred thousand protestors and occupied four hundred public squares. Youthful, tech-savvy, and indignant, the movement saw itself as part of a global struggle that originated from Tunisia and Egypt reaching the streets of Tel Aviv. "Netanyahu, if you will not be careful, you will feel the heat of Cairo," one sign read. Activists displayed a poem about an "Anxious [Tahrir] Square," highlighted the trinity "Mubarak, Assad, Netanyahu" in Rothschild Boulevard, and erected a large Arabic and Hebrew sign reading: "Erhal [leave]: Egypt is Here." A poster in Tel Aviv urged Israelis to "Walk Like Egyptians."

But identification with Egyptians and Arabs had limits. The Social Justice Movement in Israel held its own specificities thanks to the historical and demographic character of the Israeli state and society. Some 20 percent (1.4 millions) of Israel's population were Arab Palestinians who lived as "second class" citizens, notably in employment, education, and housing. Given the primarily Jewish composition of the movement, it was not certain if the term "people" in the demand "The People Want Social Justice" (in the manner of Arabic *al-sha'b yurid*) included the Arab citizens, let alone the 4.4 millions Palestinians who lived in the occupied territories. There was some limited cooperation at the local level with Palestinian citizens to organize joint demonstrations on such issues as social housing. But at the national level, the Justice movement did not include Palestinian activists, who then set up their own makeshift tents in Haifa and Jaffa. Thus, even though Israel's Justice Movement clearly invoked and identified with the tenets of the Arab Spring—its inventive liberated square, youthful energy, and its nonstop campaign against corrupt regimes—it was primarily a Jewish entity with limited involvement of Arabs; its notion of "justice" completely ignored the fact of occupation. No wonder Gershon Shafir wondered if the Justice Movement represented some kind of "Occupy Zionism."

CONCLUSION

Never before in its modern history did the Arab world enjoy such global identification as with the Arab Spring and its Tahrir moment. The Tahrir repertoire came to embody the new movements of the twenty-first century. The spirit of Tahrir connected social movements across the world to unite in their common claims against the consequences of neoliberal economy, rising inequality, precarity, and unresponsive party politics. The Arab uprisings and the global Occupy movements shared considerable common traits; they were youthful, consensus-based, and horizontal movements that derided hierarchy and institutional politics, and operated in liberated urban zones to experience an alternative social order. Their shared repertoires reflected the political trends after the Cold War, when the idea of public sphere a la Habermas had gained much popularity. Tahrir and its democratic moment represented the Habermasian public sphere par excellence.

But there were also fundamental differences. Whereas the Occupy movements in the West focused on the liberated squares as the models for true democracy, Arab activists meanwhile used those squares to change autocratic regimes. While Tahrir protestors wanted President Mubarak toppled, almost no one in the Zuccotti Park wanted the end of President Obama or any other political or business figure for that matter. Tahrir persisted until victory (even if that victory was short-lived), but Zuccotti surrendered. "We might have been evicted but that makes it a real spiritual and mental fight now," activists wrote in the Occupy website. "Let the story of Tahrir inspire us.... It was the fight that won the revolution." Even though the idea of Tahrir—both as a novel democratic community and a sustained campaign against a corrupt rule—went global, at times it took on specific meanings shaped by the local and national histories. For instance, in the capitalist West the occupation of space took a special value and meaning—it was a defiance of property rights. Zuccotti Park was a private property and its occupation illegal but was immune from police curfews that would apply to public parks. This was not an issue in the Arab world where the boundaries between the public and private is often blurred, and infringement on public space remains an aspect of cultural and political life. In Israel the Justice Movement did identify itself with the tenets of the Arab Spring, but its Rothchild Tahrir, its liberated square, included primarily Jewish citizens. Participation of the Arab citizens remained limited, and there was no room in the movement for the Palestinians in the occupied territories.

Yet our world has become such an integrated and interdependent place that makes circulation of knowledge an integral fact of transnational connection. Despite cultural differences, diverse societies on the globe—whether in the United States, the Middle East, Africa, or Latin America—do share certain underlying values and institutions. Cultures are in constant exchange; they lend, borrow, adopt, and indigenize. Good ideas can find their way out in the world despite massive disparities in global power relations and flows of knowledge.

NOTES

1. See Jeffery Alexander, *Performative Revolution in Egypt: An Essay in Cultural Power* (London: Bloomsbury Academic, 2011); Alain Badiou, "Tunisie, Egypte: Quand un vent d'est balaie l'arrogance de l'Occident," *Le Monde*, February 18, 2011; Slavio Zizek, "For Egypt, This Is the Miracle of Tahrir Square," *The Guardian* (February 10, 2011); and Helga Tawil-Souri, "Power of Place," *Middle East Journal of Culture and Communication* 5 (2012): 86–95.

2. Jeroen Gunning and Ilan Zvi Baron, *Why Occupy a Square?* (New York: Oxford, 2014), 259.

3. See *Time Magazine*, special issue "The Protestor," December 26, 2012.

4. Peter Beaumont, "Global Protest Grows as Citizens Lose Faith in Politics and State," *The Guardian*, June 22, 2013.

5. Schwartz, "Pre-Occupied."

6. Schwartz, "Pre-Occupied."

7. Anne Barnard, "Occupy Wall Street Meet Tahrir Square," *New York Times*, October 25, 2011.

8. "Occupy Wall Street: A US Version of the Arab Spring," *The Week*, October 3, 2011.

9. "OWS Report: Calling Occupy: Stand With Egypt," NYCLAW, November 11, 2011, https://nyclaw01.wordpress.com/2011/11/20/nyc-labor-against-the-war-11-20-ows-report-calling-occupy-stand-with-egypt/.

10. Jack Shenker and Adam Gabbalt, "Tahrir Square Protestors Send Message of Solidarity to Occupy Wall Street," *The Guardian*, October 25, 2011.

11. "Spain's Indignados and the Mediated Aesthetics of Nonviolence," *Media/Anthropology*, July 14, 2013, https://johnpostill.wordpress.com/2013/07/14/spains-indignados-and-the-mediated-aesthetics-of-nonviolence/.

12. Andy Price, "From Arab Spring to Spanish Summer," *New Compass*, May 24, 2011; and Pablo Ouziel, "Spain's Tahrir Square," *Common Dreams*, May 18, 2011, http://new-compass.net/articles/arab-spring-spanish-summer.

13. Dana Kaplan and Gal Levy, "The Arab Spring in Israeli Media and Emergent Conceptions of Citizenship," *Arab Media & Society* 24 (Summer/Fall 2017), https://www.arabmediasociety.com/the-arab-spring-in-israeli-media-and-emergent-conceptions-of-citizenship/; and Gershon Shafir, "Rothschild Corner in Tahrir Square?" paper delivered at a conference on the Arab Revolts: Causes, Dynamics, Effects, Columbia University, April 13, 2012. My account of Tahrir in Tel Aviv draws largely on Shafir's paper.

FURTHER READING

Bayat, Asef. *Revolution without Revolutionaries: Making Sense of the Arab Spring.* Stanford, CA: Stanford University Press, 2017.

Gitlin, Tod. *Occupy Nation: The Roots, the Spirit, and the Promise of Occupy Wall Street.* New York: IT Books, 2012.

Schwartz, Mattathias. "Pre-Occupied: The Origins and Future of the Occupy Wall Street." *New Yorker*, November 28, 2011.

Tufekci, Zeynap. *Twitter and Teargas: Power and Fragility of Networked Protests.* New Haven, CT: Yale University Press, 2017.

TWENTY-ONE

Islamizing Radicalism

Olivier Roy

THE TERM "RADICALIZATION," which is regularly used to describe a relatively recent (since the end of the 1970s) phenomenon in the Middle East and more generally among Muslim populations, refers in fact to two different trends, even if they often overlap. The first is the political violent radicalization in the name of Islam that makes jihad or "holy war" an individual religious duty. The second is the expansion of a fundamentalist and literalist form of devotion, usually referred to as "Salafism." Both trends represent a break with the more traditional forms of political mobilization (Arab nationalism or the Islamist ideology as promoted by the Muslim Brothers) and devotion (the local cultural Islams, Sufism, and the various legal schools of thought).

ISLAMIC FUNDAMENTALISM

If you compare pictures of street life in Cairo, Amman, or even Istanbul in the late 1960s with pictures taken in the late 1990s, the change is obvious: there are almost no women wearing headscarves in the first, while thirty years later there is an overwhelming presence of them. Everywhere new mosques are built, religious signs appear in the streets, and it is more difficult for the non-Muslim foreigners to eat in the open during the holy month of Ramadan. On a lesser scale, the same phenomenon appears among many second-generation Muslim migrants in the West: some young Western-educated people became "born-again" and suddenly adopted an ostensible way of practicing Islam, by scrupulously following religious dietary and dressing norms.

These attitudes have been explained as a "return to Islam," but in fact they do not correspond to a return to any national traditions: neither the scarf put on by young executive Muslim women in London or Paris, nor the impressive face veil (*niqab*) often worn with gloves and stockings by devout customers shopping in commercial malls were used by their mothers or grandmothers. New bookshops offer an accessible literature, made of up of simple booklets explaining, "What is Islam?" In the length of a few dozen pages, the text is usually comprised of a long list of *dos* and *don'ts*, warning about salvation, blaming the dominant culture as having turned pagan, and vituperating against Westernization.

Not all the actors of this Islamic revivalism could be called "fundamentalists" and even fewer "radicals." Many are just trying to recast religious norms and values in an environment that is more and more secularized and Westernized, including in very traditional Muslim-majority countries. But there is clearly a powerful movement that claims to reject modernity, with the exception of technology (the Internet is a great vector of fundamentalism). These "born-again" Muslims usually call themselves Salafis (the supporters of the righteous forefathers, who are the Prophet and his direct followers). Salafis tend to look to Saudi "Wahhabism" (the official sect in Saudi Arabia) for their models and mentors. Networks of Salafi madrasas (religious schools) have spread not only in the Middle East but also in South Asia, Europe, and Africa. Tens of thousands of young men, who very often did not find their way in the state educational system of their countries, received scholarships to join Salafi boarding schools in the Gulf region. Upon graduation, they return to their country of origin and open their own mosque or religious school.

The spread of Salafism has obvious social consequences: discrimination against women, calls for censorship, lobbying to impose laws inspired by sharia, pressure on other religious minorities, excommunication of Muslims who do not share their views, attacks against "blasphemous" activities, and denouncing of "apostates" (Muslims leaving Islam), and more. In the West the Salafis reject integration and are prone to either *hijrat* (returning to a Muslim country) or some sort of self-ghettoization that allows them the least amount of interaction possible with the dominant Christian or secular society. Salafism is obviously contributing to the radicalizing of social relations. But is Salafism a cradle of political radicalization and violence?

In fact, most Salafists are "quietist"—that is, they don't advocate an Islamic revolution, and they even reject political contestation of the existing rulers. During the Arab Spring uprisings in late 2010 and early 2011 the positions of the different Salafist groups were very contrasted. In Tunisia the small Salafi fringe of the Tunisian youth adamantly condemned the democratic movement and accused the Islamist Nahda Party of turning traitor because it accepted elections and, once in power, did nothing to impose sharia law. Their Egyptian Salafi counterpart which enjoyed a far larger constituency, created the Al-Nour Party and decided to support the military intervention of General Abdel Fattah al-Sisi against the government headed by the Muslim Brothers. In Libya the Salafi armed groups, who followed Imam Rabee al-Madkhali, a politically moderate but religiously orthodox Saudi preacher, sided with General Khalifa Haftar against the local branch of the so-called Islamic State (ISIS).

Nowhere did the Salafis try to take the political power. Salafism is the clear example of a radical religious trend that proposes to come back to the fundamentals of Islam as expressed by the Quran and the Tradition of the Prophet, that has a "neutral" or at least nonmilitant approach to politics. The recent crackdown on religious "extremism" by the Saudi Crown Prince Mohammed Ben Salman (2017–present) seems to indicate that Salafis will be urged by their Saudi sponsors to be more mainstream and less rigorous. But a recurrent question, in the Middle East and the West, is to what extent Salafism has fueled, directly or indirectly, the wave of violent radicalism that is expressed by the call for jihad and by the wave of terrorism.

JIHAD AND RADICALIZATION

Jihad is a term found in the Quran. It expresses, among other meanings, a call to fight "in the path to God" (*fi sebil-allah*). There is a debate about the general meaning of the root of the word *jhd*, which means to "make an effort," "to strive toward piety." The military meaning and interpretation of the word jihad is just one among others. However, in the context of the Prophet Mohammed's struggle to defend and impose Islam, the term clearly refers also to a war waged for God. Nevertheless, this notion of jihad, as developed in the legal Islamic tradition, has little to do with "radicalization." In the course of history both the Muslim rulers and the *ulama* (the religious scholarly class) endeavored to limit the conditions under which one could declare and participate in jihad, precisely in order not to let such a potent ideological weapon get in the hands of potential opponents or religious dissenters. Jihad was never included into the five religious "pillars" of Islam (that is, the five obligations one must follow to be defined as a Muslim—namely the testimony of faith, the five daily prayers, the fast, the religious tax, *zakat*, and pilgrimage). Jihad was traditionally defined as a collective duty to defend a part of the Muslim territory under attack. This duty was incumbent on the local population and rulers, was limited in time and space, and had to be officially declared by the competent religious authorities. In a word, no individual could call for jihad or bestow on himself the quality of being a "jihadi."

What is new in the contemporary Muslim world is that from the 1960s on, various circles, not necessarily in contact with each other, started to promote a more radical concept of jihad. One of the leading intellectual figures to promote the new definition has been Sayyid Qutb (1906–1966), a chief ideologue of the Egyptian Muslim Brotherhood. He stated that there was no longer a clearly defined Muslim territory due to the fact that contemporary Muslim societies were no longer "Islamic"; they had returned to a state of paganism (*jahaliyya*) because they ignored the basic tenets of the religion. An ever more radical actor, a graduate from Cairo University in electrical engineering and a self-taught religious leader, Muhammad Abd-al-Salam Faraj (1954–1982), defined "jihad" as the "neglected obligation," a personal and permanent obligation.

According to Faraj, "jihad" implies the right to kill Muslim political leaders who are not trying to implement the Islamic law (*sharia*) in their country. Faraj established a small radical group that was responsible for the assassination of President Anwar Sadat of Egypt (1981), accused of being a traitor after signing the Camp David Accords, or the Arab-Israeli Peace Treaty (1978). For the first time, jihad and terrorism were explicitly associated. Jihad was not to be fought on the frontiers but at the very core of the Muslim societies: this call is precisely what appears as "radical" in the eyes of the mainstream religious leaders. How to excommunicate (*takfir*) somebody who claims to be Muslim and practice the five pillars? *Takfirism* is a neologism that is often used among mainstream Muslim clerics and thinkers to refer to radicalism. For them a Muslim radical is somebody who, without any personal legitimacy, takes into his own hands the right to decide who is a good Muslim and who is not and, more dangerously, the right to punish him.

But the first organized international movement of jihad (Islamic jihad), which appeared just after the assassination of Sadat, was not initially associated with terrorism. On the contrary, it extolled the fight at the frontier of the Islamic world and rejected terrorism. The fusion between *takfirism*, terrorism, and jihad would come later, with Osama Bin Laden (1957–2011). In the meantime, the global jihad movement was launched in the early 1980s by Abdullah Yusuf Azzam, a Palestinian Muslim Brother with a Jordanian passport who was teaching in Saudi Arabia. He called for the recruitment of an Islamic international brigade of devoted and pious fighters who would go to Afghanistan to join the Afghan jihad—that is, the armed insurrection against the communist regime supported by a Soviet expeditionary corps since 1979.

Azzam defined jihad as a permanent, global, and individual duty, incumbent to any Muslim in the world physically able to join the fight. For him, as long as Islam is under threat, Muslims should live in a permanent state of war. He concluded from the perspective of world history that Islam has been under siege since the past two centuries due to both Western imperialism, followed by neocolonialism, and the Russian drive toward the south, not to speak of the stealth cultural colonization of the Muslim mind. But for him, the aim of jihad was not to establish an Islamic state into Afghanistan—that was the duty of the Afghans themselves. Beyond the short-term objective of expelling the Soviet troops from Afghanistan, the idea was to create a body of "global Muslims" whose commitment was solely to the world community of Muslims (the *ummah*) without any specific ties to a family, a tribe, a nation, or an ethnic group. War for the new jihadists was a sort of ritual of purification and trial; whatever their origin, they were bound by a strong esprit de corps. In the fight there are two options: death or victory. In the case of victory in Afghanistan, they were supposed to travel to other endangered Muslim territories and to proselytize among the Muslim youth through their personal commitment to the cause of God.[1]

In brief, action and commitment became the main mottos of this generation of jihadists, which differed from the Salafists. The foreign jihadi volunteers were under strict instruction not to try to impose sharia on the Afghans, although many Afghans complained that the jihadists endlessly criticized the Afghan way of practicing Islam, specifically with regard to burying their dead. They were also instructed not to indulge in endless debates on interpreting the acts and sayings of the Prophet (*sunna* and *hadith*) or in delivering fatwas (religious authoritative advice). Abdullah Azzam was himself a Muslim Brother, not a Salafist, and his concern was to justify jihad through religious arguments and quotations, not to rule on daily forms of devotion. More important, he did not advocate terrorism. During the time he headed the movement, there had neither been attacks outside Afghanistan nor targeting of Soviet diplomats or citizens elsewhere in the world.

This jihadi movement attracted thousands of foreign volunteers, mainly Arabs. They were called "the Arabs" by the Afghans, even if among them there were some Kurds, Turks, or Indians. When they eventually returned to their countries of origin, they were dubbed "Afghans" by the local population. Among them was Osama Bin Laden, whose organizational skills put him at the head of the logistical services. The movement was supported by the Pakistani Intelligence Services. Inside Afghanistan it allied mainly with the Afghan party Hezb-i-Islami of Gulbuddin Hekmatyar, an Islamist political movement without any Salafi background. To summarize, the concept of global jihad was not born among religious fundamentalists like the Salafis. It was first of all a movement of militants.

FROM JIHAD TO TERRORISM

After the Soviet withdrawal from Afghanistan in February 1989, thousands of global jihadists who survived the war returned to their countries of origin where they founded radical Islamic parties. In Algeria, for example, they founded the Islamic Salvation Front (FIS) in 1989 and a few years later, the Armed Islamic Group (GIA). When prevented to return to their countries of origin, they started to travel from place to place, avoiding arrest, and dreaming of turning the Afghan jihad into a global one. After the assassination of Abdullah Azzam in 1989, Osama Bin Laden took the leadership of the movement and turned it into the infamous al-Qaeda. It was a real transformation. Al-Qaeda gave up any endeavor to control a territory and chose global terrorism as the main course of action, starting with the first, and unsuccessful, attack on the World Trade Center in New York in 1993. It was followed by attacks against US embassies in Nairobi, Kenya, and Tanzania (1998) and against the Navy Destroyer the USS *Cole* in Yemen (2000). Most of the militants at that time were Arabs from countries of the Middle East.

To justify the shift from supporting a local jihad in a war of resistance against an invading foreign army, to a global terrorist campaign targeting also civilian activities, al-Qaeda developed the concept of a global resistance against a plot waged by the "crusaders" (that is, the West) to dominate or even destroy the Muslim community. Bin Laden's first appeal to global jihad was published in 1996. It did not catch the attention of Western governments but circulated underground in the fledging new world of the Internet.[2]

Once again, the movement's ideology contained little theology: it was enough for Bin Laden to quote some verses of the Quran to give a veneer of legitimacy to the struggle. Military and terrorist training were deemed more important than religious learning. There were no religious leaders at the head of al-Qaeda, even if Bin Laden's deputy, the Egyptian Ayman al-Zawahiri who was a physician by training, took the role of the religious brain of the movement.

Al-Qaeda never tried to establish an "Islamic state" anywhere. According to Bin Laden, Western military power was too strong to be directly confronted. The objective was to undermine Western societies from inside, through terrorism, in order to deter their governments to send troops into Muslim countries. Contrary to the Salafis, al-Qaeda never launched any kind of movement of predication and conversion to Islam. They preached radical violence, not religion, and the many youth who joined them, including converts, did not start their path toward radicalization in a religious school. From the early 1990s, the strategic priorities of the jihad movement shifted from local jihad to a global fight against the West. Initially, the movement targeted the United States but later extended to European countries by using terrorism against any kind of meaningful target. They attacked symbols as much as people. In fact, terrorism in Europe is more of psychological warfare than an endeavor to destroy the military or economic capacity of the enemy.

HOME-GROWN JIHADISTS

What changed in the mid-1990s was not the strategy of al-Qaeda but the recruitment of its followers. A new pool opened up in the West itself. In the summer of 1995 a spate of terrorist attacks against railway trains took place in France, in Paris and Lyon. The radical militants (led by the French/Algerian Khaled Kelkal) involved in the action were second-generation Muslim migrants with at least one convert (David Vallat). This was the first apparition of the "home-grown terrorist" that would plague the West during the following decades. While the attack of September 11, 2001, still involved a majority of terrorists coming directly from the Middle East (and specifically from Saudi Arabia), the operating cell was set up in Germany. Since that time, almost all terrorist actions in the West were made by young radicals who were born or at least educated in the West and became radicalized there.

This demonstrates a shift in the patterns of terrorism waged in the West in the name of Islam. Instead of being connected with specific Middle Eastern conflicts (the occupation of Palestine, for instance), they refer to a global jihad, which is waged on two distinctive kinds of fronts. First, local conflicts labeled as religious were seen as a way to participate in some sort of a global jihad. These local wars attracted international militants who traveled from jihad to jihad. From the 1990s the jihadist route consisted mainly of Afghanistan, Chechnya, Bosnia, and Yemen. Following the American military intervention in Iraq in 2003, global militants went to Iraq, where the town of Falluja embodied for a time the fierce opposition to the US invasion. After 2012 they massively flocked to Syria under the black banner of ISIS.

The second front was domestic terrorism in Europe. From Lyon in 1995 to Barcelona in 2017 and Trèbes in France in March 2018, the "home-grown terrorists" would strike around the very places they were living, without real strategic consideration. This "glocalism" (from local to global) is a general pattern of the new forms of Islamic radicalism. From 1997 to 2014 this global activism was managed by al-Qaeda, which organized the travels of Western volunteers to training camps (mainly in Afghanistan, Pakistan, and Yemen) and masterminded terrorist attacks in the West, usually by sending back some of the volunteers to let them recruit new young radicals who lived in Western countries. The deadliest attacks after 9/11 occurred in Madrid (2004) and London (2005), followed by a spate of less sophisticated individual attacks. The last attack directly connected to al-Qaeda was the murder of the journalists of *Charlie Hebdo* in Paris in January 2015. From 2015 on, ISIS took over al-Qaeda in the leadership and management of global jihad. ISIS attracted thousands of volunteers from all over the world who joined jihad in Iraq and Syria, while masterminding deadly assaults in Europe—the worst attack being the Bataclan in Paris in November 2015.

WHO ARE THE NEW RADICALS?

The new radicals do not come from traditional Muslim societies and milieus, they are Westernized. They do not care about the traditional conflicts that mobilize public opinion in the Middle East (such as the occupation of Palestine). They don't indulge in religious disputations and they even don't care to set up a sustainable "just" Islamic society. They do "propaganda by the deed" and are fascinated by death. Most of the terrorists who went into action in the West died either by blowing themselves up or by waiting for the police to kill them without trying to escape.

The same is true for the foreign jihadists who joined ISIS in Syria and Iraq: they were mainly used in suicide military operations and had such a high rate of fatality that few survived the fall of ISIS and returned to their countries. This fascination with death is visible in the aesthetics of violence—as in the staging of gruesome executions, a trademark of ISIS. The great strength of ISIS is to play on a Western youth culture. For instance, video games like "Call of Duty" and other games that use gore aesthetics resonate with a young audience with access to ISIS propaganda through the Internet. Facebook and YouTube have been full of videos and pictures of beheadings and executions, which were enthusiastically "liked" before social media companies cracked down on these kinds of posts. Academic research done on audiences of ISIS propaganda show that many young people, including converts, were frenetically looking and sharing their visual productions.[3] In other words, the radicalization process here is not a religious process; the fascination with death is equally important. ISIS did not need a large clandestine network of propaganda; it is enough to let the propaganda materials circulate on the Internet.

To summarize, even if there is not one well-established profile of radicals, different studies on the radicals show some common patterns. First, the great majority of radicals acting in the West since 1995 is made of two categories: second-generation Muslim migrants and converts. There are almost no third-generation radicals, even though some twenty-three years have passed since the terrorist attacks of the group of Lyon in 1995. Second, about half the radicals have a past experience of prison and petty delinquency. In fact, the jails, much more than the mosques, are the main places of radicalization. Third, very few radicals have a past of long-standing piety, and most of them are religiously illiterate.

Fourth, it is largely a generational phenomenon: the young radicals usually break with their parents who are not seen in their eyes as good Muslims. They rely on peers, brothers, and friends for their religious identity. Since 1997, there has been an astonishing proportion of siblings in the terrorist cells in Europe, as well as among volunteers going to Syria with ISIS. Fifth, they are radicalized on the margins of the local Muslim communities, in the framework of a close-knit cell made of (fellow Muslim) brothers and friends. They are not connected with larger organizations, social movements, or religious networks. The radicals do not appear as vanguard or harbingers of a larger mass movement of rebellion or protest. This is the case both in the West and in the Middle East.

The high percentage of converts (about 25 percent from the United States to Germany) shows that radicalization is chosen per se and is not the consequence of a long incubation in a Salafi milieu. What attracts these youth is not religion—most religious people are not radical—it is precisely the radicalism of al-Qaeda and ISIS that attracts them. The strength of al-Qaeda and particularly of ISIS is that they have created a narrative where absolute revolt (suicide bombing, total rejection of the society, destruction of symbols of the past) is cast into an Islamic narrative of jihad, caliphate, salvation, and avenging the suffering global Muslim community (*ummah*).

In the imaginary of the radicals, Global jihad has replaced the World Revolution of the leftists of the 1970s (as the Baader-Meinhof group). The virtual global *ummah* has replaced the virtual international proletariat. Propaganda by the deed (terrorism) serves as the main tool of action, and the "Islamic State" has replaced the "liberated areas." While the Western radical left is fighting globalization and defending the "local" (Occupy Wall Street), it has little appeal for those who feel uprooted, those without any local place to identify with, who wish to join a global movement. In the marketplace of violent global anti-imperialist movements, there is nowadays only al-Qaeda and Daesh—that is, there is only jihad.

CONCLUSION

Violent radicalization is not simply the consequence of a radicalization of the religious fundamentalist discourse. Nor is it merely related to Islam, as shown by the large spectrum of diverse forms of violent and nihilist attitudes, as expressed by the "Columbine" syndrome of young high school students killing their friends, teachers, and themselves. But the Islamist narrative of jihad provides an effective and ideologically coherent framework that could deliver some hope to a nihilist generation—namely, salvation and paradise. It is this deadly connection between nihilism and spirituality that should be addressed to fight the fascination with the global jihad.

NOTES

1. The writings of Abdullah Azzam, where these ideas are expressed, are easily accessible on Internet in different languages. The most influential of his writings is probably *Join the Caravan*—a call for the youth to join jihad.

2. See "Osama Bin Laden's Declaration of Jihad against Americans" (Salem Press, 1996).

3. Jeffrey Fleishman, "Islamic State and Its Increasingly Sophisticated Cinema of Terror," *Los Angeles Times*, February 26, 2015, www.latimes.com/entertainment/movies/la-et-mn-ca-isis-video-horror-20150301-story.html; and Steve Rose, "The Isis Propaganda War: A Hi-Tech Media jihad," *The Guardian*, October 7, 2014, www.theguardian.com/world/2014/oct/07/isis-media-machine-propaganda-war.

FURTHER READING

Hegghammer, Thomas, ed. *Jihadi Culture: The Art and Social Practices of Militant Islamists*. Cambridge, UK: Cambridge University Press, 2017.

Neumann, Peter. *Radicalized: New Jihadists and the Threat to the West*. London: IB Tauris, 2016.

Roy, Olivier. *Globalized Islam*. New York: Columbia University Press, 2004.

——. *Jihad and Death: The Global Appeal of Islamic State*. Translation from French by Cynthia Schoch. New York: Oxford University Press, 2017.

TWENTY-TWO

Global Movement for Palestine

Ilana Feldman

IT HAS BEEN MORE THAN SEVENTY YEARS since the Palestinian *nakba* (catastrophe) of 1948, when approximately 750,000 Palestinians were displaced and dispossessed. It has been over fifty years since the *naksa* (setback) of 1967, when Israel occupied the West Bank and the Gaza Strip, bringing all of historic Palestine under Israeli control. Over these decades Palestinians have struggled in various ways, and with only intermittent successes, to resist the ongoing colonization of their land, the continued dispersal of the population, and their persistent exposure to violence and assault. In this struggle they have looked, with varying degrees of hope, for support and solidarity from other people—near and far. Palestine's Arab neighbors have offered rhetorical support, but this rhetoric has often been at odds with the policies pursued by these states.

These policies have also often been at odds with the commitments of their populations. Palestine had a place, both rhetorical and operational, in Third-Worldist politics, although this alliance's moment has largely past. In the United States and, differently, in Europe the political forces arrayed against Palestinians and in support of the Israeli state long made it difficult for Palestine to be easily taken up by progressive movements that would seem natural allies. This situation has begun to change—indeed it has changed to a considerable degree. And along with that change a well-funded counter-movement has emerged that seeks to shut down speech and activity in support of Palestinians.

The Boycott, Divestment, and Sanctions (BDS) movement has been at the center of these trends. BDS is a genuinely global movement, but this chapter concentrates on what it looks like from the United States, where I am situated and what I know best. When thinking about the place and politics of BDS, it is crucial to remember that it is a movement that has its roots in Palestine. It emerges from a call by Palestinian civil society groups for international solidarity and asks specifically for people to take up BDS as the most effective form of such solidarity in the current moment. Debates about Palestinian politics that take place in Washington, DC, or in Tel Aviv, often presume to dictate to Palestinians the correct form of political activity. BDS reverses this fundamentally colonial position. It recognizes that Palestinian political strategy has to emerge from Palestinian society and also that international actors who want to support Palestinians need to take their cues from them. In thinking about their own political strategies, internationals are asking first, "What have Palestinians asked of us? What forms of horizontal support in a struggle for justice have they called for?" Asking these questions—and hearing the answers—is not the end of deliberations about political strategy. But a global solidarity movement that acknowledges Palestinians as genuine compatriots will give their voices and their calls the weight they deserve.

THE BIRTH

In 2005, 170 Palestinian civil society organizations launched a call for BDS. This call was followed two years later by the establishment of the BDS National Committee (BNC) to coordinate that campaign. The campaign makes three fundamental demands that: Israel (1) end the occupation of the West Bank and Gaza; (2) recognize the right of Palestinian citizens of Israel to full equality; and (3) respect the rights of Palestinian refugees to return to their home. The call asks universities, pension funds, and other institutions to divest of holdings in Israeli companies and from international companies involved in violating Palestinian rights. It asks individuals and institutions to boycott Israeli companies and institutions that are complicit in these violations. Academic and cultural boycott campaigns have been a central part of this effort. The third prong in the BDS strategy, and no doubt the hardest to implement, is to push states to impose sanctions on Israel as long as it continues these violations.

The occasion for the call (which one might argue was long overdue) was the one-year anniversary of the International Court of Justice (ICJ) ruling that the separation wall being built in the West Bank was in violation of international law.[1] With no Israeli action in response to this ruling, or to the subsequent General Assembly call for Israel to comply, the BDS call recognized that without significant external pressure, Israel would continue to flout international law. But the BDS call was not only a response to Israeli intransigence, it was also a recognition of the failures of Palestinian political leadership. The Palestinian Authority, established in the West Bank and Gaza as a result of the 1993 Oslo Accords, had proved itself incapable of advancing Palestinian interests or resisting the expansion of Israeli controls over Palestinian lives and seizure of Palestinian lands. The turn to BDS was part of an effort to relocate Palestinian politics to the grassroots.

The call was also a recognition of the importance of working against the fragmentation of Palestinian society that has been a hallmark of Israeli practice since 1948. Even with the massive displacement of Palestinian population in the process of establishing the state of Israel, around 150,000 Palestinians remained within the borders of the new state and became (distinctly second-class) citizens. Governed by military rule for the first twenty years of Israel's existence, Palestinian citizens were also treated by the state as multiple groups of "minorities" (Muslims, Druze, multiple Christian communities, Bedouin) rather than as a community of Palestinians. This effort at internal fragmentation—which Palestinians have increasingly resisted—goes along with other efforts to keep the parts of the dispersed Palestinian community separated. Since the implementation of the Oslo Accords, the West Bank and Gaza have been increasingly isolated from each other. Israeli policy made travel between the two territories ever more difficult. And Palestinian political leaders have further contributed to this separation through the territorial expression of the power struggle between Fatah and Hamas.[2] Another consequence of the Oslo Accords, reflected in the policy priorities of the Palestinian Authority, was that the interests of refugees living outside of Palestinian territory were largely left aside. The demands of the BDS campaign bring the three primary segments of the Palestinian population into the same political frame.

GLOBAL ANTECEDENTS

Perhaps the most frequently cited antecedent to the Palestinian BDS movement is the global resistance to apartheid in South Africa. Boycott, divestment, and sanctions were all central to the efforts to undermine this racist regime. But South Africa is by no means the only case where boycott tactics were used to support political justice agendas. One can think of the Salt

March in colonial India in 1930, the sugar boycott in British abolition politics in 1792, as well as the sixteen-year grape boycott in defense of farmworkers in California and the Montgomery Bus Boycott in support of civil rights in the United States. Boycott, divestment, and sanction, in one form or another, is a time-honored strategy for applying political pressure on recalcitrant regimes.

Even if it does not achieve immediate results, and it rarely does, boycott, divestment, and sanction takes an important step in both withdrawing support for unjust regimes and adding to the financial and political costs of maintaining such systems. BDS campaigns also help change the conversation about these conditions among outsiders. As writers Paul Di Stefano and Mostafa Henaway have noted: "One critical, yet often overlooked, way in which the international solidarity movement helped to support the South African struggle was through the creation of an alternative narrative to that disseminated by the apartheid regime."[3] There is no doubt that the variety of BDS campaigns launched in support of Palestinians have created openings for a broader conversation about Israel and Palestine, even when BDS is not adopted.

In South Africa the African National Congress (ANC) called for an international boycott campaign—one plank in a broader resistance strategy—as early as 1952. Apartheid did not end until four decades later. The length of the struggle and the breadth of tactics it required is a good reminder to those embarking on BDS activities in support of Palestinians that it will not be a short campaign. The South African experience is also a rejoinder to those who argue that the fact that a quick resolution does not seem likely is reason not to pursue these tactics. BDS opponents also sometimes suggest that the greater global consensus that apartheid must end, as compared to the divided opinions about Israel's racial distinctions, is another reason to avoid these tactics. But that argument forgets just how long the South African government received support from the United States. It was the CIA who alerted South African security forces to Nelson Mandela's whereabouts in 1962, leading to his twenty-seven years imprisonment. As late as the 1980s, Ronald Reagan pursued a policy of "constructive engagement" with the apartheid regime, seeking to encourage, but not insist on, reform. This policy is not dissimilar to recent US efforts to influence Israeli policies in the occupied territories (especially around settlement building). The Reagan administration continued to insist that the ANC was a dangerous radical movement. It was in no small part due to pressure from the anti-apartheid movement in the

United States that Congress eventually overrode its veto and imposed sanctions on South Africa.

Even as the South Africa campaign provides inspiration for Palestinian BDS, and even as there are many important lessons to take from this experience, there are also significant ways that the current effort is different from anti-apartheid BDS. Perhaps the most notable is the structure of the boycott. The guidelines of the Palestinian Campaign for the Academic and Cultural Boycott of Israel (PACBI) are very clear that the boycott it calls for is of institutions, not individuals. In the South African case the boycott was comprehensive. The institutional boycott promoted by PACBI is certainly intended to have an impact on individuals—the aim of BDS is to increase pressure for change across Israeli society and government—but it does not impede individual access to international conferences or academic institutions. Another distinction between the two movements is that the ANC (and the international solidarity movement that supported it) had a clear position about the state of the future polity in South Africa: one governed by the principle of one-person one-vote. The Palestinian BDS campaign does not take a position about future political form (one-state or two-state) but is rather focused on addressing the fundamental rights of the different segments of the Palestinian population: those inside Israel, those living under occupation, and refugees in the diaspora.

INTERSECTIONS

If one of the political benefits of BDS for Palestinian politics is its refusal of the fragmentation of Palestinian community, one of the benefits of BDS for global politics is the way it can contribute to efforts to work against the fragmentation of political consciousness and organizing in progressive politics more generally. BDS does not just insist on the relevance of the Palestinian political struggle to a broad array of intersecting concerns, it makes a concrete "ask" that gives people an opportunity to enact their progressive visions in a more comprehensive manner. Palestine has long been the exception in the landscape of progressive politics—as the appellation PEP (progressive except for Palestine) captures with great clarity. The consequences of this excision of Palestine from the terrain of some progressive politics is not just that Palestinians do not get the support they deserve, but that progressive analyses and political practices are hampered by an inadequate understanding of the landscape of global injustice. For instance, to comprehend a repressive policing apparatus in the United States, one needs to understand the global circulation of techniques and equipment that leads Israeli security firms and strategies to be deployed in cities in the United States. If we do not think about Palestine, we cannot fully understand Ferguson, Missouri.[4]

Israel and its supporters have long tried to claim the progressive political space, in an effort to undercut support for Palestine among progressives abroad. In a practice that has been termed "pinkwashing," Israel has tried to position itself as a haven for gay rights (and to a lesser extent for women's rights) within a "barbaric" Middle East. StandWithUs, a right-wing US-based Israel support group, developed a campaign it called "ipride" to tout Israel's gay-friendly credentials. As the Israeli daily *Haaretz* reported on the effort: "Tel Aviv's burgeoning gay scene may be the single most effective Israel-advocacy instrument in the Zionist toolbox, according to participants of a new program which uses Israel's vibrant gay culture to improve the country's image abroad."[5] The linking of gay rights with a country's "civilizational" status is not unique to Israel. The queer theorist Jasbir Puar has called this phenomenon "homonationalism" and describes its widespread deployment.[6] But increasingly these efforts to launder the occupation through a picture of a progressive society are backfiring. Many gay activists have rejected being enlisted as often unwilling participants in Israel's occupation politics.[7]

As feminist activists have grappled with the question of Palestine, they have had to confront a long-standing problem internal to Western feminism in which women from the North have imagined themselves as saviors of their sisters in the South. As part of a broader process of trying to "decolonize" feminism, scholars and activists have been working toward a more comprehensive view of what constitutes a gendered analysis. That is, feminist issues are not limited to matters of reproduction, family structure, or even the position of women in the workplace. Imperialism, colonialism, racism, and occupation are all crucial to feminist analysis and practice. And this is so not only because women suffer from these injustices but because each deploys gender politics in its efforts at control and suppression. In the Palestinian instance, activists have insisted: "It is our responsibility as transnational feminists to challenge simplistic and flawed explanations that would peg 'Muslim culture' as the key determinant of Palestinian women's experiences of oppression. We need to listen to Palestinian women's rights activists and feminist academics."[8] The endorsement of the boycott of Israeli academic institutions by the

National Women's Studies Association (NWSA) in December 2015 is evidence of the success of these efforts.

One of the most important political movements to arise in the United States in the past few years has been the Black Lives Matter movement. Originating in a hashtag coined in the wake of the murder of Trayvon Martin and making the simple and powerful statement that, despite appearances and too many government policies to the contrary, Black lives do indeed matter, the movement has developed since 2013 to provide a comprehensive vision for racial justice in America. And this vision includes Palestine. The Movement for Black Lives platform, issued in 2016, includes a call to cut US military expenditures and to redirect those funds toward domestic infrastructure and community well-being.

In explaining this position, the statement makes an explicit link to Palestine: "The US justifies and advances the global war on terror via its alliance with Israel and is complicit in the genocide taking place against the Palestinian people.... The results of this policy are twofold: it not only diverts much needed funding from domestic education and social programs, but it makes US citizens complicit in the abuses committed by the Israeli government."[9] This solidarity has not been unidirectional. When protesters were on the streets in Ferguson, Missouri, after the police killing of Michael Brown, supportive tweets came from Palestine. And what they offered was not just moral support but also practical advice for dealing with tear gas.[10] Along with this advice, they also called attention to the fact that the tear gas canisters used by the Israeli army against Palestinian protesters were, like those used by police in Ferguson, "made in the USA."[11]

Political attitudes toward Palestine are not only changing among populations that might be viewed as "outsiders" to the question of Israel-Palestine. They are also changing dramatically among American Jews, a group that Israel has long claimed as its own. Zionism has always been contested among Jews, but that contest has generally not been reflected in the positions of significant Jewish community organizations. This is beginning to change. Nowhere is the change more noticeable than on college campuses and among young people in general. Increasingly, young Jews in the United States either actively reject Zionism or simply do not see it as a matter close to their hearts. These trends are confirmed in a recent report by a pro-Israel marketing collective known as "Brand Israel Group" (BIG). According to its study, "the gap between Israel-supporters and detractors is widening. The current Israel advocacy programs are not working, and Jewish college students are the leading defectors from Israel support." According to the report, support for Israel among Jewish college students dropped 27 percentage points between 2010 and 2016. Notably, "the more the study participants knew about Israel, the less favorably they felt about the country."[12]

And organizations are arising to respond to this changing political landscape. Although still small in size relative to the behemoth that is the American-Israel Political Action Committee (AIPAC), groups like Jewish Voice for Peace (JVP) are staking a place for themselves in Jewish politics. JVP supports BDS. There are also organizations, such as Open Hillel, that do not themselves take a position on BDS, but which reject the attempt by so-called mainstream Jewish organizations to label BDS anti-Semitic and to deny this politics a place in Jewish conversation. Open Hillel describes its position: "Open Hillel promotes pluralism and open discourse on Israel-Palestine in Jewish communities on campus and beyond. We aim to eliminate Hillel International's Standards of Partnership for Israel Activities, which exclude individuals and groups from the Jewish community on campus on the basis of their views on Israel."[13] Continuing efforts to demonize BDS campaigners and Palestine solidarity organizations are likely to contribute to the trends that BIG documents and laments.

CHALLENGES

The profound shift in progressive politics, emanating from a multiplicity of spaces, is tremendously significant, but it would be incorrect to interpret these shifts as forecasting an easy road for BDS politics. Entirely excluding Palestine from progressive politics may be harder than it used to be, but there are still many barriers to real confrontation of the question and to the adoption of political positions and tactics that are supported by and likely to help Palestinians themselves. Even among people who are not likely to respond to arguments that Palestinians are simply terrorists whose threat to Israel must be eliminated, there are still difficulties in seeing Palestinians as compatriots. This challenge was evident in the debate in the American Anthropological Association (AAA) about whether to adopt a boycott of Israeli academic institutions. After an overwhelming vote in support of boycott on the floor of the AAA business meeting—a meeting whose attendance set AAA records—the proposal was ultimately defeated by a mere thirty-nine votes out of more than five thousand cast among the entire membership.

One frequently voiced concern about taking up the boycott was about the effects of a boycott on "our Israeli colleagues." This is a legitimate question, but notably it was never posed in a comparative framework. People who fretted about Israeli colleagues did not ask: "How do we weigh the effects of boycott for our Palestinian colleagues versus the effects on our Israeli colleagues? What are our differential obligations to both?" The absence of concern for Palestinian academics among those worried about the academic careers of Israeli anthropologists is telling. It suggests that for a significant segment of American anthropologists, Israelis are perceived as "near" and Palestinians as socially "distant"—that Israelis are often read as "our colleagues" while Palestinians are not. This attitude does not mean that these anthropologists have no concern for Palestinian lives, but this concern is often expressed in the language of "aiding" and "helping" people who are not viewed as compatriots. The hierarchies of value that are embedded in these positions make it possible for some to argue against boycott without serious engagement with the Palestinian call to pursue precisely this tactic. A global movement for solidarity with Palestinians will have to grapple with these continuing hierarchies that limit whose voices are heard in political debate.

BDS alone will not accomplish Palestinian political aims, and no one imagines that it will. It is one plank in a multifaceted political struggle. Like any solidarity politics, it is likely to have the largest effect when and if it is widely enacted alongside a vibrant political movement and strategy among Palestinians. One immediate impact of BDS activities is a change in political conversations about Israel and Palestine. BDS is not just about solidarity from afar; rather, it is a means of taking actions to work to change the policies "at home" (especially in the United States and Europe) that help sustain the status quo in Israel. The boycott call that emanates from Palestine does not only ask for international participation in a global struggle but for citizens in countries like the United States to recognize the complicity of their government, and therefore their own complicity, in supporting Israeli occupation and degradation of Palestinian lives. It asks Americans, and others around the world, to work to change these policies.

Growing grassroots support for BDS has been met with well-funded campaigns to demonize its supporters and even to legislate against boycott activity. In the United States right-wing billionaire Sheldon Adelson has provided significant financial support for anti-BDS campaigns on college campuses.[14] The Israeli government is also dedicating considerable resources to this effort. Boycott suppression even found its way into assistance for rebuilding in the aftermath of Hurricane Harvey, which devastated the Houston area in September 2017. The small suburb of Dickinson, Texas, population twenty thousand, conditioned its provision of grant money to residents on their verification that they do not boycott Israel.[15] This remarkable effort to tether disaster assistance to a particular political view was met with widespread outrage. The American Civil Liberties Union (ACLU) pointed out that boycotts are a constitutionally protected activity and promised to defend people's rights to protest. Under pressure, the town eventually removed the requirement.[16] But it seems certain that this incident will not be the last of its kind. The struggle around BDS is not only about whether to stand in solidarity with Palestinians but is also about fundamental political freedoms in the United States and around the world.

NOTES

1. Barkan and Abu-Laban, "Palestinian Resistance and International Solidarity."

2. In a particularly low moment, in the summer of 2017, the West Bank–based, Fatah-led Palestinian Authority asked the Israeli government to cut back the electricity supply to the Hamas–controlled Gaza Strip.

3. Paul Di Stefano and Mostafa Henaway, "Boycotting Apartheid from South Africa to Palestine," *Peace Review* 26, no. 1 (2014): 21.

4. Kristian Davis Bailey, "The Ferguson/Palestine Connection: As the Unrest Continues, the St. Louis Police Collaboration with Israel Underscores Connected Struggles," *Ebony*, August 19, 2014, www.ebony.com/news-views/the-fergusonpalestine-connection-403#axzz4keDhpQSN.

5. Cnaan Lipshiz, "Israel Advocates Play Gay Card," *Haaretz*, June 12, 2009, www.haaretz.com/israel-advocates-play-gay-card-1.277825.

6. Jasbir Puar, *"Terrorist Assemblages": Homonationalism in Queer Times* (Durham, NC: Duke University Press, 2007).

7. See Sarah Schulman, "Israel and Pinkwashing," *New York Times,* November 22, 2011, www.pinkwatchingisrael.com/.

8. Simona Sharoni et al., "Transnational Feminist Solidarity in Times of Crisis," 663.

9. Movement for Black Lives, https://policy.m4bl.org/invest-divest/ (accessed June 21, 2017).

10. Imani Jackson, "How Palestinian Protesters Helped Black Lives Matter," *USA Today*, July 1, 2016, www.usatoday.com/story/opinion/policing/spotlight/2016/07/01/how-palestinian-protesters-helped-black-lives-matter/85160266/.

11. Robert Mackey, "Advice for Ferguson's Protesters from the Middle East,"

New York Times, August 14, 2014, www.nytimes.com/2014/08/15/world/middle east/advice-for-fergusons-protesters-from-the-middle-east.html?_r=0.

12. Amanda Borschel-Dan, "'Devastating' Survey Shows Huge Loss of Israel Support among Jewish College Students," *Times of Israel,* June 21, 2017, www.time-sofisrael.com/devastating-survey-shows-huge-loss-of-israel-support-among-jewish-college-students/.

13. "Mission and Vision," Open Hillel, www.openhillel.org/about/.

14. Nathan Guttman, "Secret Sheldon Adelson Summit Raises up to $50M for Strident Anti-BDS Push," *The Forward,* June 9, 2015, http://forward.com/news/israel/309676/secret-sheldon-adelson-summit-raises-up-to-50m-for-strident-anti-bds-push/.

15. Jessica Schulberg, "Houston Suburb Conditions Hurricane Relief Money on Residents' Vow Not to Boycott Israel," *Huffington Post,* October 20, 2017, www.huffingtonpost.com/entry/dickinson-texas-hurricane-harvey-israel-bds_us_59ea2 eofe4b00f08619e9776.

16. Michael Wilner, "Under Pressure, Houston Town Untethers Hurricane Relief from BDS Test," *Jerusalem Post,* October 28, 2017.

FURTHER READING

Barkan, Abigail, and Yasmeen Abu-Laban. "Palestinian Resistance and International Solidarity: The BDS Campaign." *Race and Class* 51, no. 1 (2009): 29–54.

Darwich, Lynn, and Haneen Maikey. "The Road from Antipinkwashing Activism to the Decolonization of Palestine." *WSQ: Women's Studies Quarterly* 42, no. 3–4 (2014): 281–85.

Davis, Angela. *Freedom Is a Constant Struggle: Ferguson, Palestine, and the Foundations of a Movement.* New York: Haymarket Books, 2016

Rabkin, Yakov. *A Threat from Within: A Century of Jewish Opposition to Zionism.* New York: Zed Books, 2006.

Sharoni, Simona, et al. "Transnational Feminist Solidarity in Times of Crisis: The Boycott, Divestment and Sanctions (BDS) Movement and Justice In/For Palestine." *International Feminist Journal of Politics* 17, no. 4 (2015): 654–70.

Wiles, Rich. *Generation Palestine: Voices from the Boycott, Divestment and Sanctions Movement.* New York: Pluto Press, 2013.

TWENTY-THREE

Human Rights, Indigenous and Imperial

Lori Allen

FOR AT LEAST THE PAST CENTURY, people in the Middle East, North Africa, and West Asia (hereafter referred to as "Middle East") have been trying to obtain their human rights. Whether demanding national independence and self-determination from European colonial rule, or calling for freedom from police brutality and authoritarian governments, human rights have been a rallying cry for political action across the Middle East. People have not always pursued their struggles under the banner of "human rights" specifically, but the language of rights has been an important part of efforts to obtain freedom for nations, communities, and individuals in the region.

Although the struggle for rights has been important, there has also been a wariness of, and sometimes cynicism toward, the human rights *industry* for the ways it can smuggle in foreign intervention dressed as liberation. The industry consists of a large web of nongovernmental organizations (NGOs), professionals that staff them, donors, lobbyists, government agencies, and their funding organs. Many people are suspicious of the ways foreign funding for rights projects that feeds this industry in the Middle East can impose agendas that are not really for local benefit. So, on the one hand, the language of human rights is empowering for rights activists. But on the other hand, many in the Middle East recognize that the rights industry may actually undermine activists and obstruct local efforts toward creating conditions to ensure people's rights.

The malleability of the human rights system is part of what has made it such a rich forum for political struggles of many kinds, and a feature of broader debates over big issues like the rights of women in Islam, the rights of citizens to change their governments, and the rights or duties of states to intervene on behalf of vulnerable populations being deprived of their rights under other governments. The language and laws of rights remain a tool for those fighting for liberation across the Middle East. The human rights system is not just an external regime imposed artificially onto the peoples and societies of region. People from the region craft their own instruments and practices of human rights, often through processes of intense and sometimes acrimonious deliberation.

People from the Middle East have made important contributions to shaping many aspects of the global rights system and to building the institutions that exist to make human rights something real in the world. Jurists, politicians, and diplomats from the Middle East—men and women like Charles Malik, Bedia Afnan, Jamil Baroody, Fayez Sayegh, and Halima Embarek Warzazi who were themselves products of political and social change in the region—have shaped ideas about the importance of national self-determination, economic justice, women's rights, and other rights principles. They have contributed to the struggles over ending colonialism, they have offered critiques of the "responsibility to protect" doctrine, they have fought for workers' and children's rights as well as for the right to be free of military occupation. They have articulated the genuine concerns of people in the Middle East and struggled for them in terms of rights. They also have objected to the instrumentalization of human rights that furthers external political projects. The human rights system is itself a forum in which people seek to define the meaning and substance of rights in ways that make sense to them, and in which they try to defend them on their own terms. Contrary to some stereotypes that the region is inhospitable to ideas of liberty and individual and collective rights, it has actually been a place where people have struggled to define and defend human rights.

HUMAN RIGHTS BEGINNINGS

Charles Malik, an intellectual from Lebanon, was one of the drafters of the United Nations Declaration of Human Rights (UDHR) in 1948, and an influential member of the UN Human Rights Commission. His overriding belief was in the importance of developing international agreements that could address the "all-fundamental problem of personal liberty." Malik's Christian and Lebanese background shaped his approach to human rights. His Christian faith contributed to his focus on individual dignity and freedom, and to his view that human rights were inalienable and a fundamental part of God-given natural law. As historian Andrew Arsan has argued, Malik's belief that Lebanon was an exceptional refuge for people of multiple religious faiths informed his commitment to the protection of minorities and individuals. In Malik's view, the core problem of his era was "the struggle between the human person and his own personality and freedom on the one hand, and the endless pressure of groups on the other, including, of course, his own nation." Without the checks on power that human rights could provide, these pressure groups might "dictate to the person what he ought to think, what he ought to do, what even he ought to believe and hope for."[1]

Another Lebanese man, Jamil Baroody, was Saudi Arabia's representative at the UN, and a member of the UDHR drafting committee. In UN debates Baroody expressed what many in the recently decolonized states and still decolonizing nations believed, namely that the enjoyment of human rights "depended on the exercise of a fundamental right—the right of self-determination of peoples and nations."[2] As Malik observed, the principle of self-determination generated "'zest'... amongst people in 'non-Western lands.'"[3] The Iraqi delegate to the UN, Bedia Afnan, was another important figure who contributed to drafting early human rights documents, particularly as a member of the UN Third Committee. She ensured that the principle of equal rights for women was included in the later human rights covenants that make up the International Charter of Human Rights (the UDHR, the 1966 International Covenant on Civil and Political Rights, and the 1966 International Covenant on Economic, Social, and Cultural Rights).[4] Afnan had long been working for women's rights, initially as a member of the secular Iraqi Women's Awakening Club established in 1923. Afnan, who became a diplomat during a particularly liberal period of Iraqi history marked by state-sponsored feminism, fought hard to defend the principle of women's rights as human rights. In her debates at the UN, she insisted on the universalism of human rights that extended to women and small nations.

ANTICOLONIAL RIGHTS STRUGGLES

Struggles for self-determination began the moment Europeans took over Arab lands in the early nineteenth century. As Arab nationalism spread across the region in the late nineteenth century, demands for national sovereignty and freedom from European powers were grounded in historical, cultural, linguistic, and social ties to the region. Nationalists were encouraged by what seemed to be American support for their demands for national autonomy. In a speech to Congress in 1918, US President Woodrow Wilson said, "What we are striving for is a new international order based upon… universal principles of right and justice.… 'Self-determination' is not a mere phrase.… It is an imperative principle of action."

Despite Wilson's lofty liberal sentiments, European powers divided up the Ottoman Empire as the spoils of war among themselves. And despite promises that imperial greed would no longer be the motivating force of international relations, European states turned the Middle East into a patchwork of territories under their colonial control. This new form of colonialism was barely disguised by the new label of "mandates." European "tutelage" was supposedly needed for "peoples not yet able to stand by themselves under the strenuous conditions of the modern world," as Article 22 of the League of Nations Charter described non-Europeans. Wilson was among those "liberal internationalists" after World War I who had struggled to get the United States to sign on as a member of the League of Nations. But American isolationist tendencies in that period meant that the League would become the provenance of European powers that sought to facilitate peaceful international cooperation, while making imperial rule more humane. The League of Nations devised the mandate system, whereby European states would manage and administer other territories and peoples across the Middle East, Africa, and elsewhere.

Arab representatives flooded the League of Nations with petitions demanding their national rights. They sent delegations regularly to plead their case in Geneva, where the League of Nations was based. They argued with tenacity, and they protested in print and in the streets at home. Nevertheless, their actions had little effect. The Permanent Mandates Commission in charge of Iraq, Palestine, and Syria was indifferent to Arabic public opinion. It did not consult Arabic newspapers nor hire Arabic translators for its research. This neglect on the part of the commission led the Lebanese author George Antonius to decry this "amazing state of affairs" at the League. Antonius's book, *The Arab Awakening: The Story of the Arab National Movement*, was a call to arms for Arab nationalists. It describes the development of Arab nationalism and explains and justifies it. In fact, the British Foreign Office instructed British consuls in the Arab world to read his book, and Antonius himself appeared before a British Royal Commission on January 18, 1937, in an attempt to influence British policy on behalf of Arab national rights. He told the commissioners that such disregard for Arabs at the League of

Nations often gave "the Arabs the feeling that their case was going by default, that their petitions and their memoranda were dismissed rather summarily after a perfunctory examination."

Indeed, more often than not, their petitions—considered by at least one League official as "often naïve and badly worded"—were discarded without review, their pleas unheeded and arguments ignored.[5] One prolific petitioner, Syrian Druze leader Shakib Arslan (known at home as "the prince of eloquence"), who represented the Syrian-Palestinian anticolonial opposition, made regular claims for Arab freedom and independence to the powers that were represented in Switzerland. Grasping fully the Europeans' hypocritical justifications of their rule, Arslan described their colonizing history as one of "injustices, cruelties, spoliations, thievery, massacres, and absurdities of all kinds…a will to civilize and co-opt in view of a better future!'"[6] Arslan and others had identified contradictions within the human rights system. Westerners proclaimed the importance of universal rights and liberties but obstructed their attainment among people in the Middle East. The condemnations of Arslan and others, neither naive nor badly worded, did not yield self-determination in the Middle East, which was not achieved for most until the 1940s and 1950s. This dynamic around human rights and its critique would be repeated throughout every era, just as people would continue to demand their rights and struggle to create the political and economic conditions that would enable their realization.

From the early 1950s, the United Nations officially recognized self-determination as a right of all peoples, enshrining it in General Assembly resolutions on decolonization and in human rights conventions. Although self-determination is a generally accepted principle of international law, reasserted in almost every human rights instrument and document today, groups including the Palestinians (millions of whom live under Israeli military occupation) and Sahrawis (people living in the western part of the Sahara desert claiming independence from Morocco) have yet to enjoy this right to even a limited degree. Official declarations of liberty did not necessarily mean real freedom from foreign domination for all people, nor did self-determination guarantee the enjoyment of other human rights.

Among people throughout the Third World, the "right to development" was widely recognized as a key element of self-determination. A predominant argument among people in recently decolonized states was that international economic justice was a condition for the true fulfillment of human rights. The Declaration on the Establishment of a New International Economic Order

(NIEO) spelled out the principles and strategy for states to achieve economic autonomy. An Algerian jurist, Mohammed Bedjaoui, who had been a legal adviser to the National Liberation Front (the main nationalist movement during the Algerian War against the French colonial power), helped consolidate support for the NIEO. In the NIEO Declaration, adopted by the UN General Assembly in May 1974, members of the UN "solemnly proclaim[ed their] united determination to work urgently for the Establishment of a New International Economic Order based on equity, sovereign equality, interdependence, common interest and cooperation among all States, irrespective of their economic and social systems which shall correct inequalities and redress existing injustices, make it possible to eliminate the widening gap between the developed and the developing countries and ensure steadily accelerating economic and social development and peace and justice for present and future generations." Similar to earlier arguments about political self-determination as a prerequisite for human rights, Bedjaoui considered the right to development and economic self-determination to be "the precondition of liberty, progress, justice and creativity. It is the alpha and omega of human rights, the first and last human right, the beginning and the end, the means and the goal of human rights."[7]

Political and economic self-determination were important axes of discussion and strategizing among leaders across the Middle East for decades and remain so. But these were not the only frameworks within which people living through the colonial era and postcolonial transitions sought to construct their societies, build their polities, and determine the rules and norms that would allow people to thrive, or even just survive, within them. Other debates centered on questions of religion and how Muslims should relate to the human rights system and its claim to universality. How women's equality could be achieved, how workers' rights could be guaranteed, and how refugees could be protected were additional concerns.

ISLAM AND HUMAN RIGHTS

The extent to which Islam is "compatible" with human rights is an issue about which scholars, pundits, and religious and human rights practitioners have had much to say. Across the Middle East and throughout Muslim-majority societies, people take different approaches to how they incorporate Islam into local human rights institutions. Some draw on the juridical traditions of Islam to make claims to specific rights, while others point to Muslim intellectual history to justify the relevance of human rights in their particular contexts. There are several international agreements that articulate a set of shared rights standards in relation to Islam. Some explicitly draw on Islam as part of their justification to show they are in accord with religious tradition. Among them are the 1981 Universal Islamic Declaration of Human Rights, the Cairo Declaration on Human Rights in Islam (adopted in 1990 by forty-five of the Organization of the Islamic Conference member states), the 2005 Covenant on the Rights of the Child in Islam, the 2004 Arab Charter for Human Rights, and the 2014 Statute of the Arab Court of Human Rights. Each document spurred a debate about what aspects of Islam should be highlighted in a human rights framework.

One of the principal areas of focus in the debate about Islam and human rights has been the question of Muslim women's human rights and the role of religion. The relationship is often presented primarily as an ideological issue, a conflict between a local tradition, Islam, and the global demands for universal human rights. But this simple dichotomy does not capture the various approaches to this issue. Some make the case for the presence of human rights provisions within the Islamic tradition guaranteeing equity for women, if not equality. (Equality would imply that there is no distinction between men and women, an unsupportable position from this perspective.) Article 6 of the Cairo Declaration of Human Rights, for example, underscores both woman's equality to man "in human dignity," and points to distinctions in their "duties."

Others make the claim that Islam, through reinterpretation, can be seen to support, or be made to support, women's rights as articulated in international documents. Ebrahim Moosa is one scholar who calls for such an approach, and contends that Islam-based moral premises can contribute to a rights system that is compatible with secular human rights. Another important voice in these debates is Khaled Abou El-Fadl, who argues from a different angle that liberal conceptions of individual autonomy, human rights, and individual freedom should be incorporated into Islam. Azizah al-Hibri, legal scholar and founder of Karamah: Muslim Women Lawyers for Human Rights, has made the point that violations of women's rights (and of human rights in general) in Muslim societies are due to political problems, educational deficiencies, and ignorance of Islamic legal protections for women.

There are also scholars and thinkers, sometimes referred to as Islamic feminists, who engage in debates of Islamic jurisprudence to challenge gender inequality. Writers such as Amina Wadud, Asma Barlas, and Asma Lamrabet have developed emancipatory readings of the Quran and provide religiously based arguments for the protection of women's rights. An organization engaged in this kind of religiously based advocacy is the Voice of Libyan Women, a group that campaigns for greater political participation by women and against domestic violence. In Saudi Arabia, protests against the laws prohibiting a woman from traveling or marrying without the permission of a male guardian have also drawn on religious hermeneutics. The transnational Musawah (meaning "equality" in Arabic) movement has been part of a campaign for women's rights in Saudi Arabia and similar efforts elsewhere. Their actions are being carried out through online petitions, social media, and protests in the streets. Musawah provides women with educational tools and encourages them to learn about the support for women's rights within the Islamic tradition.

IMPERIALIZING HUMAN RIGHTS

Of course, not everyone who lives in the Middle East is Muslim, and Islam is not the focal point or framing discourse for all rights struggles. The struggle for women's rights took a distinct form during the colonial period, when women fought for national independence, while the imperial powers tried to justify their "civilizing mission" on the back of claims that women needed liberation from repressive Arab and Muslim men. Anthropologist Lila Abu-Lughod has demonstrated how "the moral crusade to save Muslim women" and "fantasies of rescue by 'the world community'" have also propelled many more contemporary conflicts, using restoration of the rights of Arab or Muslim women as an alibi.[8]

One rescue ideology was enshrined in 2005 when the UN member states endorsed the "Responsibility to Protect" (R2P) doctrine. The R2P doctrine justifies military action when a state fails to respect the rights and well-being of the people in its territory. It is based on a claim that the international community has a responsibility to intervene, including militarily, to protect populations from serious abuses like genocide, war crimes, ethnic cleansing, and crimes against humanity. Many scholars and rights activists view the R2P doctrine with suspicion, as it has served as justification for Western intervention in the Middle East. R2P action is clearly shaped by procedural ambiguities, political biases, colonial and Orientalist legacies, not to mention highly selective application. For instance, the United States has invoked R2P in Libya and Iraq (two oil-rich countries) but has turned a blind eye to Palestinian civilians who have been victims of war crimes, according to the UN Human Rights Council. As critical human rights analysts Fateh Azzam and Coralie Pison Hindawi have written: "From an Arab perspective, inaction on Palestine symbolizes at its worst the double standards that have plagued the international community for too long."[9]

To be sure, "the instrumentalization thesis of human rights" does not capture the full dynamic or motivations for how individuals, groups, or states act through the human rights system on behalf of or with others. But, as the human rights scholar Ayça Çubukçu has argued in her analysis of the World Tribunal on Iraq and the international military intervention in Libya led by the United States, "the particular vitality of the cosmopolitan ethos of human rights in justifying imperial occupations" remains a significant political dynamic worthy of continued critical interrogation.[10] Israeli "pinkwashing" is another example in which there are obvious political motivations behind the deployment of rights discourse. In this rather unsubtle PR strategy, Israel promotes itself as a state that can provide a safe-haven for LGBTQ Palestinians and others. The Israeli government uses gay rights to try to bolster its liberal credentials and shift attention away from its settler colonial occupation of Palestine. The promotion of religious freedom as a universal norm has likewise been mobilized in political ways. For example, the need to intervene militarily to protect Middle Eastern Christians has featured heavily in debates around US foreign policy. As political scientist Elizabeth Shakman Hurd's research has shown, American history has long been shaped by ambitions abroad that are justified through social projects and proclaimed religious and moral ideals.

The cynical use of human rights is not limited to actions at the state level. Citizen groups seeking to further their own political agendas and defend their repressive ideologies have appropriated human rights principles and legal mechanisms too. The plight of persecuted Christians in Syria, Iraq, and around the Middle East has become a rallying cry for conservative religious groups in the United States that have Islamophobic and pro-Zionist projects at their core. Coauthors Nicola Perugini and Neve Gordon recount another instance of human rights inversions in their book *The Human Right to Dominate*, in which they trace the emergence of Israeli settler NGOs such as Regavim (the National Land Protection Trust). Regavim and other groups tout their activism protecting Israelis' human rights, when its real goal and effect is furthering settler colonialism in Palestine. The brazen appropriation of rights is apparent in the work of these settler organizations when they literally cut and paste claims for Palestinian rights and transform the language, labeling Palestinian communities as settlements in their legal arguments for Palestinian dispossession. This tactic reveals the extent of the human rights system's political malleability and its manipulation.

For the most part, the majority of human rights work in Israel-Palestine remains focused on advocating for Palestinians living under military occupation, and for Palestinian citizens of Israel living under a discriminatory legal and political regime in that country. Organizations focused on the rights of, for example, refugees, children, women, and workers specialize in trying to activate distinct legal and advocacy networks that are dedicated to the protection of specific groups' rights. Defense for Children International–Palestine Section (DCI-PS) is one example of a human rights NGO that has successfully documented the Israeli mistreatment of Palestinian children. They have reported on the torture of children in Israeli jails and the persistent aggressions of Israeli settlers that often ends in the injury and death of Palestinian children. DCI-PS has also documented attempts by Israeli forces to recruit Palestinian children as informants and their use of children as human shields, actions that are in blatant violation of international legal prohibitions against recruiting or using children in armed conflict.

Despite the diligence of DCI-PS and many other Palestinian human rights NGOs working to inform the international community about the human rights violations that are an inherent feature of the Israeli occupation and its apartheid-based legal system that marginalizes Palestinian citizens, the abuses continue unabated. While the enormity of the gap between what is espoused in legal principles and international agreements and what is practiced on the ground may be particularly obvious in the case of Israel's treatment of Palestinians, it is a standard feature of the human rights system: principles and agreements often remain stuck at the level of pronounced ideals.

WOMEN'S RIGHTS, WORKERS' RIGHTS

Starting in the 1990s, as the number of human rights organizations mushroomed across the Middle East and elsewhere, the framing of specific groups' rights as human rights became more widespread. In pursuing women's rights as human rights, women's rights activists in the region have engaged with human rights standards in their efforts to reform their countries' Personal Status Codes that regulate marital and family relations. They are an important source of legal guarantees of fundamental rights as spelled out in the Convention on the Elimination of All Forms of Discrimination against Women (CEDAW). In 2004, Moroccan women were victorious in their struggle for changes to their state's Personal Status Code, which included the near eradication of polygamy, raising the legal age of marriage for girls from fifteen to eighteen, and making divorce a legal prerogative for women and not only men.

As late as 2017, in Lebanon and Jordan, women's rights activists achieved another victory in the repeal of laws that gave rapists the right to marry their victims and avoid punishment. In Lebanon migrant domestic workers are denied their basic rights, and the vast majority of them are deprived of their freedom of movement as employers confiscate employee passports as a matter of course. The visa "sponsorship" system in Lebanon, as in Jordan and Gulf Cooperation Council countries, ties migrant employment conditions to their sponsoring employer, a system that leaves workers vulnerable to a range of abuses. Women workers are vulnerable in particularly acute ways. Coalitions of women's NGOs have also pushed for employment rights, including the rights of domestic workers, in countries such as Tunisia.

The fight for workers' rights is another arena of struggle that is not always framed in terms of human rights, but economic and workers' rights are covered in many international human rights agreements. A basic precept of the human rights system is that human rights are indivisible—meaning that all rights are of equal value, and that they are interconnected and mutually constitutive and they cannot be separated. However, it has been especially important that rights pertaining to economic conditions and conditions of labor are underscored specifically in the UDHR and other international agreements. The UDHR includes the right to work, the right to just and fair conditions of employment, the right to form and join trade unions, and the right to a standard of living adequate for health and well-being. The International Covenant on Economic, Social and Cultural Rights (ICESCR), adopted in 1966, enshrines the economic, social, and cultural rights contained in the UDHR in more developed and legally binding form. The right to work, which requires governments to ensure protections for people working in informal sectors, includes the right to employment without discrimination and access to structures that address unfair dismissal as well as the right to safe conditions at work.

Another regional rights agreement, the Casablanca Protocol of 1965, called on members of the Arab League to grant to Palestinians the same worker rights as those of citizens. Other standards on rights relating to specific groups detail their economic rights (such as women, children, and migrant workers), as does the Arab Charter on Human Rights. As with rights agreements the world over, however, the words on paper remain high ideals far from the reality on the ground. Palestinian refugees in Lebanon are still prohibited from working in many professions. Millions of Syrian refugee children living in Jordan, Lebanon, Turkey, and across Europe are denied their right to education. The deprivation of this right often leads to their economic and sexual exploitation. Without governments' political and financial commitment to establishing mechanisms for the protection of these vulnerable groups, state signatures on international rights covenants are worthless.

When considering that in 2017 one of the world's largest humanitarian crises began in Yemen as the result of the assault by the Saudi-led Arab coalition (which the United States and the UK backed), one might ponder the efficacy and relevance of the human rights system in the world today. Regardless of how many human rights agreements and monitoring mechanisms are established, so long as economic systems that promote vast disparities of wealth between the rich and poor persist, human rights will be violated. As wars rage, killing, injuring, and sickening thousands, producing millions of refugees and internally displaced people, human rights cannot be guaranteed. Without structural change to existing economic and political arrangements, the human rights system can accomplish little. In the view of some, the human rights system may actually exacerbate these problems. By framing such structural inequalities and large-scale political hostilities besetting the Middle East as harms to individuals, or as problems that can be addressed by monitoring, "naming and shaming," and circulating reports, which are the standard activities of human rights NGOs, the human rights regime may draw attention and energy away from more effective action aimed at fixing the root causes of rights violations. These are systemic causes requiring systemic change.

GLOBAL ADVOCACY AND LOCAL VIOLATIONS

One indication that human rights advocacy still matters is the persistent persecution of rights advocates by governments throughout the region.

State repression of human rights activists continues in various countries, from Egypt to Saudi Arabia. Repression of rights advocates takes the form of incarceration, travel bans, freezing of bank assets, and harassment. Some rights advocates have been condemned on charges relating to human rights NGOs' acceptance of foreign funding, while others have been sentenced for "insulting the judiciary." In 2016, for instance, Israel passed a law that, in effect, targets NGOs and human rights groups that are critical of Israeli policy, especially those advocating for Palestinian rights, requiring such organizations to publicize the sources and extent of their foreign funding. Opponents of the law in Israel and abroad perceive it to be an authoritarian measure that exemplifies the trend toward fascism in Israeli society. While Israel and the Palestinian Authority have long sought to stifle human rights activism, the repression of people working on behalf of Palestinian rights has now extended to countries in Europe and North America, where organized campaigns of intimidation against advocates of the Boycott, Divestment, and Sanctions (BDS) movement have picked up pace, including through legislation aimed at criminalizing criticism of Israel. In Turkey, another country that has moved toward authoritarianism, human rights defenders, including Amnesty International's Turkey director, have been imprisoned.

Another sign that rights matter is the creativity with which people across the Middle East continue to struggle for them. The Arab Uprisings, a series of revolts that spread across the region in 2011, called for social and economic justice and an end to authoritarian governments. In countries such as Egypt and Tunisia, worker unions with many years of experience in political organizing were among the groups that supported these revolts. They sparked an outpouring of creative, often humorous, political expression in the form of poetry, graffiti, murals, music, and independent news media. The uprisings were political mobilizations calling for democracy that would enable full citizen rights and participation in self-governance (not just the democracy that would spread economic liberalization). Although the revolutionaries' aspirations for consequential citizenship, political inclusion, and social and distributive justice remain unfulfilled, people throughout the region continue to work toward these goals. They fight not just for individual rights or the rights of specific groups, but for broader change that would allow everyone to thrive, to live more freely, with autonomy, and in conditions in which they can define the meaning and substance of those values for themselves.

1948	United Nations Declaration of Human Rights (UDHR)
1960	United Nations General Assembly Declaration on the Granting of Independence to Colonial Countries and Peoples
1965	Casablanca Protocol
1966	International Covenant on Civil and Political Rights (ICCPR)
1966	International Covenant on Economic, Social, and Cultural Rights (ICESCR)
1974	Declaration on the Establishment of a New International Economic Order (NIEO)
1974	Charter on the Economic Rights and Duties of States (CERDS)
1979	Convention on the Elimination of All Forms of Discrimination against Women (CEDAW)
1981	Universal Islamic Declaration of Human Rights
1990	Cairo Declaration on Human Rights in Islam
2005	Covenant on the Rights of the Child in Islam
2008	Arab Charter for Human Rights
2014	Statute of the Arab Court of Human Rights

NOTES

1. Malik, "Proposing Ground Rules for Committee Debates on Human Rights."

2. Burke, *Decolonization and the Evolution of International Human Rights*, 44.

3. Andrew Arsan, "'A Unique Little Country': Lebanese Exceptionalism, Pro-Americanism and the Meanings of Independence in the Writings of Charles Malik, c. 1946–1962," in *Decolonization and the Cold War: Negotiating Independence*, edited by Leslie James and Elisabeth Leake (London: Bloomsbury, 2015), 116.

4. Waltz, "Universal Human Rights: The Contribution of Muslim State"; and Burke, *Decolonization and the Evolution of International Human Rights*, 11.

5. Michael Provence, "Protest, Counterinsurgency, and the League of Nations in Syria," unpublished paper.

6. Quoted in Raja Adal, "Shakib Arslan's Imagining of Europe: The Coloniser, the Inquisitor, the Islamic, the Virtuous, and the Friend," in *Islam in Inter-War Europe*, edited by Nathalie Clayer and Eric Germain, 156–82 (London: Hurst, 2008), 160.

7. Quoted in Isabella D. Bunn, "The Right to Development: Implications for

International Economic Law," *American University International Law Review* 15, no. 6 (2000): 1425–67, 1435.

8. Lila Abu-Lughod, *Do Muslim Women Need Saving?* (Boston: Harvard University Press, 2013), 26.

9. Fateh Azzam and Coralie Pison Hindawi, "The Arab Region," in *The Oxford Handbook of the Responsibility to Protect*, edited by Alex Bellamy and Tim Dunne (Oxford, UK: Oxford University Press, 2016), 454.

10. Ayça Çubukçu, "On Cosmopolitan Occupations: The Case of the World Tribunal on Iraq," *Interventions: International Journal of Postcolonial Studies* 13, no. 3 (2011): 425, 428; and Ayça Çubukçu, "The Responsibility to Protect: Libya and the Problem of Transnational Solidarity," *Journal of Human Rights* 12 (2013): 40–58.

FURTHER READING

Burke, Roland. *Decolonization and the Evolution of International Human Rights.* Philadelphia: University of Pennsylvania Press, 2010.

Douzinas, Costas. *Human Rights and Empire.* New York: Routledge Cavendish, 2007.

Malik, Charles. "Proposing Ground Rules for Committee Debates on Human Rights." United Nations Commission on Human Rights, February 4, 1947. www.gwu.edu/~erpapers/humanrights/casestudies/ERandHR%20case%20study%20PDF.pdf.

Sayegh, Fayez. "Papers, No. 27, Dr. Fayez Sayegh, Racism and Racial Discrimination. Published posthumously in 1982 from a taped speech delivered in 1976." International Organisation for the Elimination of All Forms of Racial Discrimination (EAFORD), 1982, pp. 1–9.

Waltz, Susan. "Universal Human Rights: The Contribution of Muslim State." *Human Rights Quarterly* 26 (2006): 799–844.

TWENTY-FOUR

Cosmopolitan Middle East?

AN INTERVIEW WITH SEYLA BENHABIB

Linda Herrera

> For me, cosmopolitanism involved the recognition that human
> beings are moral persons equally entitled to legal protection in
> virtue of rights that accrue to them not as nationals, or members
> of an ethnic group, but as human beings as such.[1]
>
> SEYLA BENHABIB

SEYLA BENHABIB, A LEADING PHILOSOPHER on cosmopolitanism
and the rights of others, shares an intellectual and philosophical lineage with
Immanuel Kant, Hannah Arendt, and Jürgen Habermas.[2] These towering
figures have advanced ideas around (global) citizenship, universal democracy, international cooperation, and human rights. Yet Benhabib stands
apart from her predecessors insofar as she did not herald from Europe and the
German intellectual tradition of the eighteenth through the twentieth centuries, although she would come to participate in and advance that tradition.
Benhabib was born in Istanbul in 1950, a "child of Ataturk's Republic," of a
Sephardic Jewish family that traced their lineage back centuries. But to call
her merely a Turk, an Istanbulite, a Jew, or even a woman, would blunt the linguistic, cultural, religious, historical, and political layers and experiences that
have informed—in subtle and explicit ways—her influential canon of work.[3]

I first glimpsed into Benhabib's family and intellectual biography in the
introduction to her 2011 book *Dignity in Adversity*. Commenting on how her
descendants left Spain and arrived in the Ottoman territories in the fifteenth
century, Benhabib noted: "When my ancestors tried but failed to persuade
Christian authorities to permit the Jews to stay in Spain, they, like thousands
in that period, left to seek refuge in the Ottoman Empire. Islam for them
was not a religion of war and jihad but a religion of tolerance that respected

the Jews and granted them the 'right of hospitality,' in Kant's sense."[14] In this short passage we witness how Benhabib takes her family history to address larger questions about persecution, migration, hospitality, Islam, tolerance, and respect—themes that remain utterly timely in the twenty-first century.

In an effort to further tease out connections between biography, cosmopolitanism, and the global Middle East, I contacted Professor Benhabib for an interview. I hoped we could explore ways that growing up in Turkey and experiencing the world with the political and cultural sensibilities of her place and time might have informed her work. She graciously accepted and made time in a busy period in the fall term of 2017. Initially she was reticent to talk about herself and seemed to consider the exercise somewhat self-indulgent. But as the conversation progressed, it unfolded how her family life, schooling, political awakenings, and lived experiences were indeed connected to her contributions and canon of work on cosmopolitanism, multiculturalism, sovereignty, feminism, rights, and migration, among other themes. Benhabib's life and canon of work embody the very idea of "global Middle East." We began with a discussion of her family genealogy and progressed to our own turbulent times.

LH: What is the history of the Benhabib family, and how did they arrive in Istanbul?

SB: We came to Turkey right after the [Spanish] Inquisition [which started in 1478]. The larger family may have gone from Spain to Rhodes, to Jerusalem certainly, to Gallipoli and Salonica [the Greek port city]. My father grew up in Gallipoli, which [is] not at all far from Salonica on the Greek side of what once was common Ottoman territory. We can trace back the family name to generations of rabbis in Salonica. In fact, the closest ancestor we were able to identify with my name, which is difficult when you're talking about the fifteenth century, was a rabbi with the Arabic name, Itzhak Ibn Habib. The very name Benhabib, which many people assume to be Arab and Muslim, in fact has a long history dating back to a centuries-old Sephardic Jewish community. At that time most Jews were either in the service of the Islamic court or they were protected by the Muslim kingdoms of that period. So it's not unusual to have the Arabic as well as the Hebrew versions of the name in the family.

LH: What has it meant for you to carry the Benhabib name?

SB: I mean, look, it's very simple. Nobody knows what kind of a name exactly it is. Most people who know anything about the Middle East think it's an Arabic name. When I go to France, it's assumed immediately that it is Algerian, and there's no question about it. When I go to Israel, they want to Hebraize my name and make it Ben Haviv. They ask me why I keep the Arabic "Habib?" They want to know why I'm attached to it. Haviv, Habib, it's the same word. Even as an established and prominent academic, in many countries of the world I deal with the question about identity. I mean, it's just in my name itself. They want to know: "Who are you?" "Oh, you're a Jew! Really?" "We thought that you were an Algerian." "We thought that you were a Moroccan." "We thought you were so-and-so."

LH: Is there a tradition in your family of scholars, a genealogy that led you into philosophy?

SB: There was, there was. The earliest identifiable ancestor was a rabbi from Zamora in northwestern Spain. My paternal grandfather was a rabbi in a smaller community in Gallipoli, but he also had his grocery business next to that. But I think the most influential thing for us, because we are three girls, was my mother's faith in education. My mother was a very brilliant student who went to a French [primary] school and after that, to the Italian Lycée. She was given a scholarship to go to Italy around 1938, but my grandmother said, "No child of mine is going to go off to Italy in this point in time." The following year she was married off to her [maternal] cousin, my father. It's very common throughout the Middle East for people to marry their cousins.

In our case, our mother was very influential in forming our educational ambitions, but among our cousins as well there are about six or seven university professors. So there must have been some kind of sociological law we were following. My closest relative here in New York is an economics professor at NYU, another one used to be a professor of aeronautics down in Virginia. We have cousins who are professors in Israel, et cetera. So there is clearly a kind of generational formula or something there. The older generation, the parents, were all basically businesspeople.

LH: Did your mother attend schools run by Christian missionaries?

SB: My mother (Paloma Ben Habib) went to a Catholic school directed by the *soeurs* (nuns). Some of the top educational schools for boys and girls in Istanbul were originally led by Catholic priests. But the agreement with Atatürk in order for them to remain in the country was that there would be no proselytizing. My mother never faced any conversion experience of any kind. But they were Catholic schools and Italian schools, run mainly by Catholic nuns.

LH: How would you describe your childhood in Istanbul?

SB: My childhood experience was very much that of a child of Atatürk's Republic. And that had its own contradictions because my family are Sephardic Jews. I grew up basically in a section in Istanbul that was quite modernized, one can even say Westernized. Istanbul itself was quite divided into different segments: the Asian part was always considered a little more, let's put it this way, "Oriental," although that also changed in my lifetime. I grew up in the western part of Istanbul, the European part that was closer to areas like Taksim Square, which your readers will know as Gezi Park, where the revolt and demonstrations against Erdogan took place in 2013. Taksim Square is exactly the area where Gezi Park was and that square is quite symbolic of the Turkish Republic because in the middle of Taksim Park stands a big statue of Atatürk during the time of the war of liberation.[5] It's surrounded by a lot of lights and flower stands.

LH: What language(s) did you speak at home?

SB: We were a multilingual family. I grew up with three, and eventually four languages: Turkish, French, Ladino—which is a special kind of Spanish that the Jews of Spain spoke, and then in school, English. For my mother's generation it was different. After Ladino, French was the language in which my mother was most comfortable.

LH: What schools did you attend?

SB: I went to a Turkish elementary school, which was obligatory for [primary school] for most children of my generation. The pattern for most of the middle class or upper middle classes in Istanbul, and not just for the minorities (that is to say, not just for the Jews, the Greeks, the Armenians), was that [after primary school] most children in this milieu applied to go to foreign-language schools. There were French, Italian, German, Austrian, British, and American schools. I went to a British middle school for girls for five years and then I transferred for my high school (years 9–12) to the American College for Girls (established in 1863).[6] But my sister, for example, went to an Italian school and finished up there. My youngest sister went to the American school from grades 6–12. Istanbul of the 1950s was an extremely cosmopolitan place, as I'm sure were Cairo and Beirut. It was the Levant, or the remains of the Levant, let's put it that way.

LH: You lived in Istanbul during a time of tremendous political change and upheaval. How did events from that time affect your family life?

SB: My childhood corresponded to the multiparty opening in Turkey when Atatürk's Republican Party now had a rival, the Democrat Party (DP). Basically, most of the Jewish community that I knew supported the

Democrats because they were less statist (*étatiste*), less disciplinarian, more Western, and free market–oriented. But then in the 1960s came the first military coup against the corruption of the Democrat Party and the execution of Prime Minister Adnan Menderes (on May 27, 1960). I remember my father listening to the trial process every night on the radio; there was no television then. It was a shock that in his lifetime he would have seen a prime minister executed. That was enormous. I was just ten in 1960.

It's interesting, I'm going to digress a little here, there were some moments in the early history of the AK Party, Adalet ve Kalkınma Partisi (the Justice and Development Party) when Menderes's memory was being revived against the Kemalists who actually were persecuting those who did not belong to the Kemalist bureaucracy. But Menderes himself was a completely, totally secular man. Nonetheless, he was heavily supported by the rural bourgeoisie in Turkey, if I may use that term. Turkey has a large peasantry, but nonetheless it is a country full of small towns. It's not like a latifundia territory in Latin America, a vast peasantry dominated by landlords. Some Kurdish areas have more of the latifundia structure, but most of central Turkey has towns with people who have land and have businesses. This rural group had already started flexing its muscle in support of the Democrat Party. And they have gone on to support the AK Party. But the funny thing is, the Democrat Party of my time was not an Islamist party at all, although it was being supported by the pious Muslim gentry.

LH: What effect did the Arab-Israeli conflict and the events leading up to the Turkish coup in 1972 have on you?

SB: The Israeli-Palestinian conflict, or Middle East conflict, was beginning to seep into Turkey. Turkey had very friendly relations with Israel. Zionism and Kemalism bear a lot of resemblance to each other because they are state-building ideologies. They [support] a secular elite that is modernizing and share a strong belief in a state leading civil society. Throughout the 1960s, most Turkish Social Democrats and Socialists used Israel as a model of what was possible for socioeconomic development. After the Six Day War in 1967, everything changed. Israel's victory gave rise to a big backlash.

I can tell you that the first time the Turkish-Jewish community began to feel insecure was after the events of September 6–7, 1955 [the Istanbul riots were mob attacks against the Greek minority, in which Armenians and Jew were also harmed]. It's funny, right? Israel's triumph all of a sudden made them feel more insecure because something snapped at that point. I think that the world was shocked that Israel triumphed over the Arab countries.

Particularly, nobody expected Egypt to have been defeated in the way in which it was. Something started changing at that point. There was the formation of a militant movement. Turkey had a lot of class struggle in those days. But militant movements were now established in relations with the PLO (Palestine Liberation Organization) camps. There were people who were getting training in Palestinian camps in Lebanon and bringing back the idea of an armed struggle to Turkey.

My family and our extended family started getting worried out of their mind. I had just graduated from the American College for Girls and had a scholarship to go to Brandeis University in Massachusetts. I left Istanbul in September 1970, just as things were entering a very politically tense period. The military coup took place in 1972. A month later my family left for Israel. I had no intention of going to Israel myself.

LH: What motivated your family to leave the place they called home for generations and move to Israel?

SB: That's an excellent question. I was a bit taken aback when they first did, and I'm not sure I quite understood what exactly this location would mean for the family. At the time, I already had developed my position around the Israel-Palestine issue. I was very much part of a movement for reconciliation, a two-state solution. It was clearly at odds with my mother's position at the time. In Israel she became a "dove" and my Father and she voted only for the Israeli Labor Party (Marah). We fought a lot. My father preferred not to listen to the fights. My sisters were too young, but I was quite progressive. My mother was convinced that I was going to end up in the hands of the Turkish police, and so she wanted me to get out of there as soon as possible. In retrospect, she was not wrong. At the minimum I would have been detained, maybe not imprisoned, but certainly interrogated and faced Turkish detention. It was quite an existential and volatile time, let's put it this way. These things are never, never easy.

I think that my mother was a Zionist in the sense that she really believed that we would never be an equal citizen in Turkey. She did not dislike Turkey, this was her home. But she did not believe that there was going to be equal citizenship and freedom for the Jews of Turkey. And so, she thought she wanted to go to Israel. My father was actually more neo-Ottoman, if I may put it that way. My father was softer about these questions. He really liked Turkish people, got along with them. And it was not a very happy move for him. In fact, he fell quite ill shortly after he went to Israel. And then one of my sisters left for California, so that [is why] my mother is buried in

California. My father passed away in Israel. I wouldn't say that for our family this was a successful move; it was not.

LH: Did you feel the same way as your mother, that the Jewish community could never have equal rights in the Turkish system?

SB: No, I didn't. I was always arguing, both with the family and Turkish friends, including boyfriends. I felt that one had to prove that one was equal. One had to prove that one was free. And particularly in the left progressive community that I was beginning to share with intellectuals, activists and so on, it was taken for granted that we would be, that we were equal. I think I wasn't as attentive to the fact that Turkish republicanism was not liberal, that this republicanism would go up to a certain point in integrating minorities but not farther. For example, I had cousins who served in the Turkish army. But non-Muslims would never be given the rank of officer. So they always remained at lower levels. There were hardly any Jewish university professors, which is an academic profession all over the world. There were very few, maybe one or two, journalists. We lived [in] what at times was referred to as a "golden ghetto." You know, the non-Muslims could practice their trade, could practice their profession, and they could make money, but they weren't really part of the public life of the country. So, in that sense, this cosmopolitanism wasn't like Salonica in the nineteenth century. It wasn't like that. And even Atatürk's Turkey was much more, in its public sphere, dominated by a Turkish Muslim majority.

One thing that has stayed till today in the Middle East is that it's very difficult to cross these ethnic or religious lines. Nobody in my family had married a Muslim person up until then. Imagine, about fifty generations. There was no intermarriage, there were no conversions. We only have one cousin who did marry a Muslim girl. It's not as if we were that observant or fanatical, nothing like that. I think we were what you call "high holiday Jews" in the United States. You know, one celebrated this, one celebrated that. We were very secular. But still, one did not go outside the group. And it was very threatening when one did it. My generation was beginning to feel the full force of what it meant to be so confined. And I was completely in revolt against this. And that led to a lot of conflict in the family.

LH: How did your family receive your first marriage to a German national?

SB: My first husband was German with repressed Jewish ancestry on his father's side. By then, I had graduated from Yale in 1977; taught there for two years and in 1979 left for Germany to study with Jürgen Habermas. I was faraway from my family. My father passed away in 1984 and I got married to my first husband in 1986, although we had been together before then. I think that people probably shook their heads, but my academic career had taken such an unusual and "successful" turn in conventional terms that they did not know what to make of me. My mother accepted my decision.

LH: After your family emigrated to Israel, did you return to Turkey?

SB: Yes, I went back to Turkey many times. I still had close friends whom I was working with. The first time I went back was for a visit in 1972. I realized that something was just completely different. How shall I put it—it's not that I didn't feel safe, I mean one always has to watch one's back as a woman in a country in the Middle East. But something else was happening. There was the emergence at the time of the Grey Wolves [Bozkurtlar], the militant ultra-nationalist Turkish party. They are very well-known in Germany.

The streets of Istanbul were beginning to feel more and more threatening. And when the 1972 military coup came against the resurgence of the left and sectors of armed struggle, quite a few of my friends were arrested and detained and interrogated. I was part of the student movement and a sympathizer of the general left opposition at the time. But the crackdown was pretty severe. Many of the intellectuals at the universities were arrested during the 1972 military coup. Very strong unions were forming, there were demands for more equity in the rural countryside, and that was also the beginning of the Kurdish liberation movement. From that point onwards—we are still thirty years away from the rise of Islamism—there was intense militarization. And in 1980, another coup came. I would describe this period in Turkey as the pacification of the class struggle.

LH: How did living through the political upheavals of Turkey of the late 1960s and 1970s influence your thinking about cosmopolitanism?

SB: Cosmopolitanism has so many different meanings. Philosophically, cosmopolitanism is an abstract position, it's not what most people understand by it. It means a commitment to the moral dignity of every human person. In that sense, it is very much a kind of a liberal modernist position. Legally, as a student of Hannah Arendt, I would say it is the right to have rights. There are certain rights that should accrue to individuals, not in virtue of their status of citizenship of belonging, but as human rights. And culturally, cosmopolitanism to me is a position that understands that cultures are promiscuous. Cultures are always constituted through the interaction of the "we" and the "they," both historically and psychologically. So I guess maybe what I am predisposed to, given my own background, et cetera, is I'm predisposed to be a skeptic towards any kind of identitarian movement. Certainly, I have my philosophical and political objections against nationalism, and what it has brought about, the miseries it has caused. But my history predisposes me towards accepting pluralism, and also that otherness is constitutive of one's identity.

LH: At what point did you move to Germany, and what was your reception there as a Turkish academic?

SB: From Brandeis I went to Yale, and in 1977 I completed my PhD. I was hired as an assistant professor. I taught at Yale and in 1978 I met Jürgen Habermas at a lecture. I had written my dissertation on Hegel. I said to him, "I want to come to Germany to study with you." The following year I got an Alexander von Humboldt fellowship, and I arrived in Germany in June 1979. Habermas was at the Max Planck Institute at the time, and I must say he was the best teacher I had. Not in the sense that he was a pedagogue or teacher in any conventional sense, but just watching and listening to him listen to other people's lectures and ask questions was an incredible experience. We had a weekly colloquium, where I learned a tremendous amount. My first book, *Critique, Norm and Utopia* (1986) is a product of those years and is quite philosophical. It dealt with basically the transformation of critical theory from Hegel to Habermas.

These years were an astonishing experience at first. But they were also familiar. I always said to myself that Frankfurt was halfway between home in Istanbul and the United States. It fell in this in-between space between Istanbul and Boston, or Istanbul and New York. It is true that the years that I went to Germany, I was an exception. I was treated very well, precisely because the whole idea of a Turkish woman who had studied Hegel, had written on him, and was interested in the Frankfurt school, for a lot of people it was like a categorical confusion. Compared to today, there were hardly any non-German academics. The few who were there were mainly American or British. There was hardly anybody of Middle Eastern origin, nothing like the kind of transformation that we have seen in the last twenty years in German public life. When I go to Germany now, it is indeed astonishing to see how much more diverse and multicultural the intellectual community is. Germans may deny multiculturalism from morning until night, but they have become a multicultural society. There are three generations of people now who are not of German origin but who have spent their lives in that country.

German academics and intellectuals are very solidaristic once the initial ice is broken. So I always felt extremely well treated in the academic community. I made an effort to learn German very rapidly. I think it is one of the most difficult languages I know, but I did the whole thing. I went to the Goethe Institutes and I learned four months of German grammar. That I started speaking the language quite early helped me to break the ice as well. But Germany was not an easy country in those years. There were still leftovers of the anxiety about the Red Army Faction (RAF, Rote Armee Fraktion in German). I remember shortly after I arrived, there was the request that university professors take an oath of loyalty to the constitution, the government, but to what exactly, it was not clear. And the whole Habermas community was quite conflicted. Habermas himself, to the best of my knowledge, did not take that oath.

LH: Did the condition of the Turkish guest workers in Germany influence your thinking on rights and citizenship?

SB: Absolutely. When I lived in Germany I could see what the Turkish guest worker community was going through. A lot of the experiential impulse behind my work on the rights of others comes from this experience of ten years or more in Germany of observing their situation and discussing and conversing about it. The Turkish guest workers were not very vocal in the 1970s, but as the years went by, in the mid-1980s, the first conflicts started showing up. There were strikes, big workers' strikes, in which Turkish and German workers participated. The IG Metall [IGM, the dominant metalworkers union in Germany] is one of the very famous trade unions in Germany. But things began to get quite conflictual when the splits between Turks and Kurds became visible. Segments of the guest worker community were beginning to identify as Kurdish, and I think there were Kurdish people coming in from Iraq at that time as well. If I'm not mistaken, this may have been the time of Saddam's first gas attack in Halabja.[7] The composition of the community was changing, and there was a growing presence of Kurdish people and languages in Frankfurt. The Kurdish and Turkish communities were moving apart, and things began to get very tense from then on. But for me at the time, the most important social movement was the woman's movement. Questions about multiculturalism and citizenship, the rights of others, would come a little later.

LH: How did you get involved in feminist thought?

SB: At the time, I was concerned about reconciling critical theory with some of the insights of feminism. Like other colleagues like Nancy Fraser and Jessica Benjamin, I was young and disturbed by the absence of any kind of explicit address of gender difference, of women's equality. I was beginning to make an attempt to bring in some themes from feminist ethics into Habermas's theory. At that point, the experience of the women's movement from the United States, the second generation of the women's movement, was influencing my perspective on the development of critical theory which was then followed close thereupon in 1992 with the book *Situating the Self: Gender, Community and Postmodernism in Contemporary Ethics*. This was my second book. [I later developed an interest in the work of] Hannah Arendt, which opened my eyes to this issue of the right to have rights, and why or how at the end of the twentieth century, we were still experiencing the condition of rightlessness.

LH: What is the state of cosmopolitanism is these times of polarization, populism, and reactionary nationalism?

SB: I prefer the expression "cosmopolitanism without illusions" these days because our times are hardly a period hospitable to cosmopolitan hopes and beliefs.[8] One has to see the nativist authoritarian and autocratic nationalisms of our times—Recep Tayyip Erdoğan (Turkey), Narendra Modi (India), Rodrigo Duterte (Philippines), Viktor Orbán (Hungary), Vladimir Putin (Russia), Donald Trump (United States), and now Jair Bolsonaro (Brazil)—as the opening salvo of a huge competition among capitalist states. The world is reconfiguring itself geopolitically and economically and giving rise to a lot of anxieties among citizens of established nation-states who want to keep their income levels and quality of life. As the world economy and the geopolitics of superpowers reconfigure themselves, people withdraw to what they know and want to defend it at all costs.

This is the only way we can explain the tremendous hostility to migrants and refugees even when the numbers do not warrant it. They symbolize the weakness of the imaginary boundaries of the nation. A cosmopolitan perspective gives one a sense of history and culture by highlighting the interdependence of, and exchanges among, cultures which have always characterized human societies. Cosmopolitanism emphasizes intelligent human cooperation in order to solve global problems. It resists the demonization of the "other"; his/her reduction to any enemy figure by emphasizing "the otherness within" each of us. Ironically, our times need more, not less, cosmopolitanism than ever.

1. *Epigraph*: Benhabib, *Dignity in Adversity*, 9.

2. See Benhabib, *Rights of Others*.

3. This nearly two-hour interview took place between the author and Seyla Benhabib at the latter's apartment in New York on October 28, 2017. This chapter is an abridged and edited transcript from that discussion.

4. See Benhabib, *Dignity in Adversity*, viii.

5. Mustafa Kemal Atatürk (1881–1938) was the first president of the Republic of Turkey after the fall of the Ottoman Empire. He held the office from 1923 until his death in 1938.

6. The American School for Girls eventually became Robert College, and the university is now Boğaziçi.

7. "The Halabja chemical attack (Kurdish: Kîmyabarana Helebce), also known as the Halabja Massacre or Bloody Friday, was a massacre against the Kurdish people that took place on March 16, 1988, during the closing days of the Iran–Iraq War in the Kurdish city of Halabja in Southern Kurdistan." "Halabja Chemical Attach," Wikipedia, http://bit.ly/2CEdry5 (accessed December 30, 2018).

8. The phrase "cosmopolitanism without illusions" is the title of the introductory chapter of Benhabib, *Dignity in Adversity*.

FURTHER READING

Benhabib, Seyla. *Critique, Norm and Utopia*. Chicago: University of Chicago Press, 1986.

———. *Dignity in Adversity: Human Rights in Troubled Times*. Malden, MA: Polity, 2011.

———. *Exile, Statelessness, and Migration: Playing Chess with History from Hannah Arendt to Isaiah Berlin*. Princeton, NJ: Princeton University Press, 2018.

———. *Feminism as Critique: On the Politics of Gender*. Exxon Lecture Series. Saint Paul: University of Minnesota Press, 1987.

———. *Situating the Self: Gender, Community and Postmodernism in Contemporary Ethics*. New York: Routledge, 1992.

———, with Jerry Waldron, Bonnie Honig, and Will Kymlicka. *Another Cosmopolitanism: Hospitality, Sovereignty and Democratic Iterations*. Edited by Robert Post. New York: Oxford University Press, 2006.

CONTRIBUTORS

AMRO ALI is a writer, public intellectual, and sociologist at the American University in Cairo, a member of the Arab-German Young Academy of Sciences and Humanities, and an associate of the Sydney Democracy Network. His research interests include Arab public spheres, Mediterranean studies, cities, citizenship, exile, technological modernity, and political philosophy. His work can be found at www.amroali.com.

LORI ALLEN is a reader in anthropology at SOAS University of London. Her book *The Rise and Fall of Human Rights: Cynicism and Politics in Occupied Palestine* won the book prize of the Association for Political and Legal Anthropology. Her articles on human rights, Palestinian politics, and affect have appeared in *Cultural Anthropology, MERIP, Comparative Studies in Society and History,* and elsewhere. Her second book, *A History of False Hope: Investigative Commissions in Palestine,* analyzes a century of Palestinian engagement with international law.

ASEF BAYAT is Catherine and Bruce Bastian Professor of Global and Transnational Studies, and professor of sociology and the Middle East at the University of Illinois at Urbana-Champaign. His research areas range from social movements and social change to religion and public life, urban space and politics, and the contemporary Middle East. His latest books include *Post-Islamism* (2013), *Life as Politics: How Ordinary People Change the Middle East* (2013), and *Revolution without Revolutionaries: Making Sense of the Arab Spring* (2017).

HAMID DABASHI is Hagop Kevorkian Professor of Iranian Studies and Comparative Literature at Columbia University, where he is a founding member of both the Institute for Comparative Literature and Society and the Center for Palestine Studies. His most recent books include *The Shahnameh: The Persian Epic as World Literature* (2019) and *Reversing the Colonial Gaze: Persian Travelers Abroad* (2020).

KHALED FAHMY is Sultan Qaboos bin Sa'id Professor of Modern Arabic Studies at the University of Cambridge. His research interests include the social and cultural history of the modern Middle East, with a specialization on nineteenth-century

Egypt. He is the author, most recently, of the award-winning *In Quest of Justice: Islamic Law and Forensic Medicine in Modern Egypt* (2018).

ILANA FELDMAN is professor of anthropology, history, and international affairs at George Washington University. She is the author of *Governing Gaza: Bureaucracy, Authority, and the Work of Rule, 1917–67* (2008), *Police Encounters: Security and Surveillance in Gaza under Egyptian Rule* (2015), and *Life Lived in Relief: Humanitarian Predicaments and Palestinian Refugee Politics* (2018). She is the coeditor (with Miriam Ticktin) of *In the Name of Humanity: The Government of Threat and Care* (2010).

MICHAEL FRISHKOPF is professor of music, director of the Canadian Centre for Ethnomusicology, adjunct professor of medicine, and adjunct professor of religious studies at the University of Alberta. His field and action research, centering on the Arab world and West Africa, includes music and Islam, music and development, global health, music as medicine, music and architecture, digital repositories, virtual and augmented reality, and machine learning. His work can be found at frishkopf. org and m4ghd.org.

WALEED HAZBUN is the Richard L. Chambers Professor of Middle Eastern Studies in the Department of Political Science at the University of Alabama. He teaches international relations, US foreign policy, and the politics of travel. He previously taught at the Johns Hopkins University and the American University of Beirut. He is the author of *Beaches, Ruins, Resorts: The Politics of Tourism in the Arab World* (2008) and serves on the editorial board of the *Journal of Tourism History*.

LINDA HERRERA is professor in the Department of Education, Policy, Organization, and Leadership at the University of Illinois at Urbana-Champaign with research areas in global studies in education, youth and digital transformation, and critical Middle East studies. Her books include *Cultures of Arab Schooling: Critical Ethnographies from Egypt* (edited with C. Torres, 2006); *Wired Citizenship: Youth Learning and Activism in the Middle East* (2014); *Revolution in the Age of Social Media* (2014); and *Educating Egypt* (2021).

AHMED KANNA is an associate professor of anthropology at University of the Pacific. Kanna is author of *Dubai, The City as Corporation* (2011) and, with Amelie Le Renard and Neha Vora, *Beyond Exception: New Interpretations of the Arabian Peninsula* (2020).

JOHN TOFIK KARAM is the director of the Lemann Center for Brazilian Studies and an associate professor in the Department of Spanish and Portuguese at the University of Illinois at Urbana-Champaign. His first book, *Another Arabesque: Syrian-Lebanese Ethnicity in Neoliberal Brazil* (2007), won awards from the Arab American National Museum and the Brazilian Studies Association and has been translated into Arabic and Portuguese. His forthcoming book is *Manifold Destiny: Arabs at an American Crossroads of Exceptional Rule* (2021).

FATEMEH KESHAVARZ directs the School of Languages, Literatures, and Cultures at the University of Maryland–College Park and holds the Roshan Chair in Persian

Studies. She has lived, studied, and taught in Iran, Europe, and the United States. Her work is focused on Persian lyric poetry and the literary process of encountering the sacred. Keshavarz has appeared on *On Being, On Point*, and other NPR programs to discuss the relevance of the writings of Rumi to current issues and concerns. She hosts the podcast *Radio Rumi*.

LALEH KHALILI is a professor of international politics at Queen Mary University of London and the author of *Heroes and Martyrs of Palestine* (2007); *Time in the Shadows: Confinement in Counterinsurgencies* (2013); and *Sinews of War and Trade: Shipping and Capitalism in the Arabian Peninsula* (2020).

TIMOTHY MITCHELL is a political theorist and historian specializing in the modern Arab world, the history of energy, and the political economy. Educated at Cambridge University and Princeton University, he is the William B. Ransford Professor of Middle Eastern Studies at Columbia University, where he also holds an appointment in the School of International and Public Affairs. His books include *Colonising Egypt* (1988); *Questions of Modernity* (2000); *Rule of Experts: Egypt, Technopolitics, Modernity* (2002); and *Carbon Democracy: Political Power in the Age of Oil* (2011).

EBRAHIM MOOSA is the Mirza Family Chair of Islamic Thought and Muslim Societies in the Keough School of Global Affairs with appointments in the department of history and a concurrent faculty in the Law School at the University of Notre Dame. He codirects the Contending Modernities project at Notre Dame and leads the Madrasa Discourses project. Moosa's interests range from studies in al-Ghazali to modern debates in Islamic law and ethics as well as traditional educational systems, especially the madrasas of South Asia. He is the author of *Ghazali and the Poetics of Imagination* (2005) and *What Is a Madrasa?* (2015), with multiple publications on ethics, bioethics, Islamic history, and Islamic thought.

ROBERT MORRISON is George Lincoln Skolfield Jr. Professor of Religion at Bowdoin College. A specialist in the history of science in Islamic societies and Jewish cultures, he works at the intersection of the history of science with religious studies. His current book project addresses the broader question of intellectual exchange between Islamic societies and the West in the 1400s and early 1500s.

KAMRAN RASTEGAR is professor of comparative literature at Tufts University, where he directs the Center for the Humanities. He is the author of the books *Surviving Images: Cinema, War and Cultural Memory in the Middle East* (2015) and *Literary Modernity between the Middle East and Europe* (2007) and edited the special issue *Authoring the Nahda: Writing the Arabic Nineteenth Century* for the journal *Middle Eastern Literatures* (2013).

OLIVIER ROY is a professor at the European University Institute (Florence). He is the scientific adviser of the Middle East Directions program at the Robert Schuman Centre for Advanced Studies. He has been a senior researcher at the French National Center for Scientific Research since 1985. Roy received an Agrégation de Philosophie and a PhD in political sciences. He is the author of *The Failure of Political Islam*

(1994), *Globalized Islam* (2004), *Holy Ignorance* (2010), and more recently *Jihad and Death* (2017), *In Search of the Lost Orient* (2017), and *Is Europe Christian?* (2019).

EDWARD SAID was born in Jerusalem in 1935 and died in New York in 2003. He was University Professor of English and Comparative Literature at Columbia University and the author of more than twenty books, including *Orientalism* (1978), *The Question of Palestine* (1979), and *Culture and Imperialism* (1993). A leading literary critic, humanist, and public intellectual, Said was a lifelong advocate of the Palestinian cause.

AHMAD SHOKR is an assistant professor of history at Swarthmore. His writings on historical and contemporary political issues have appeared in *Arab Studies Journal, Middle East Report, Jadaliyya, Critical Historical Studies,* and *Economic and Political Weekly.* He is also a contributor to several edited volumes, including *The Journey to Tahrir: Revolution, Protest, and Social Change in Egypt* (2012) and *Dispatches from the Arab Spring: Understanding the New Middle East* (2013).

JEANNIE SOWERS is an associate professor of political science at the University of New Hampshire. Her main areas of research explore political and environmental change in the Middle East and North Africa and the impacts of war on civilians and ecosystems. Her publications include *Environmental Politics in Egypt: Experts, Activists, and the State* (2013), the coauthored *Modern Egypt: What Everyone Needs to Know* (2019), the coedited *Journey to Tahrir: Revolution, Protest, and Social Change in Egypt* (2012), and a number of articles and book chapters. She holds a PhD from Princeton University and a BA from Harvard University.

TED SWEDENBURG is a professor of anthropology at the University of Arkansas. He is the author of *Memories of Revolt: The 1936–39 Rebellion and the Palestinian National Past* (1995, 2003) and coeditor of *Displacement, Diaspora and Geographies of Identity* (1996) and *Palestine, Israel and the Politics of Popular Culture* (2005). His recent work focuses on the politics of popular music in the Arab and Islamic world and their diasporas.

SAMI ZUBAIDA is Emeritus Professor of Politics and Sociology at Birkbeck, University of London, and a professorial research associate of the Food Studies Centre at SOAS. He has written and lectured widely on religion, culture, law, and politics in the Middle East as well on the history and sociology of food, including *A Taste of Thyme: Culinary Cultures of the Middle East* (edited with R. Tapper, 2000) and *Food, Politics and Society: Social Theory and the Modern Food System* (with Alex Colas, Jason Edwards, and Jane Levi, 2018).

INDEX

Arab Charter on Human Rights, 310, 315
"Arab Gulf," 241, 243t; defined, 240; problems with the term, 240–41; terminology, 240, 250n2
Arab–Israeli War of 1967. *See* Six-Day War
Arab League, 315
Arab revolt in Palestine (1936–1939), 165
Arab Spring (Arab Uprisings), 4, 17, 216, 269–71, 283–84, 316; aftermath, 236–37; goals, 8; impact on Western image of Arab societies, 278; Indignados Movement and, 274–75, 277, 278; Israel and identification with tenets of, 278–80; kuyifas and, 172; Occupy movements and, 274–77, 279–80; Salafist groups and, 283–84; Tahrir Square and, 172, 270–74, 279
Arab Winter, 4
Arabian-American Oil Company (ARAMCO), 243, 246–47
"Arabic science," 11–12, 35
Arafat, Yasser, 166
arak, 127–28
ARAMCO (Arabian-American Oil Company), 243, 246–47
Arendt, Hannah, 326, 329
Argentina, 260
Arslan, Shakib, 308
art and power, 11
astrology, 37
astronomy, 36–42, 38f; Indian, 37–38, 41–42, 47
Athens, protests in, 275
Audarson, Jon, 167
Auerbach, Erich, 88
Azzam, Abdullah Yusuf, 286
Azzam, Fateh, 312

Baghdad Pact, 109
Bahaullah, 32
Bahrain. *See* "Arab Gulf"
Baroody, Jamil, 306
Bedjaoui, Mohammed, 309
beer, 126–27
Beirut, 16, 79, 141, 213, 215, 229, 233, 234
belly dance *(raks el-sharq)*, 148–51, 151f, 154–56, 263

Ben Habib, Paloma (Seyla's mother), 321, 322, 324–26
Ben-Gurion, David, 111
Benhabib, Seyla, 14–15; on cosmopolitanism, 319; father, 320, 321, 323–26
Benjamin, Walter, 219
Berman, Jennifer, 166
beverages, 126–30. *See also* water
Bialik, 79
biblical Israel, 26
"biblical right" to Palestine, Israel's, 5, 6
bin Laden, Osama, 5, 285, 287
Bīrūnī, Abu Rayhan al-, 38, 45–46
Black Lives Matter, 299
Black Panther (film), 157
Bonet, Nai, 150–51, 151f
Bonhoeffer, Dietrich, 31
Bouazizi, Mohammed, 269
Bourdieu, Pierre, 80–81
Boycott, Divestment and Sanction (BDS) movement, 64, 293–94, 302; aim, 297; birth, 294–95; campaigns against, 300, 301, 316; challenges, 300–302; demands, 294; global antecedents, 295–97; impact, 296, 297, 301; intersections, 297–300; support for, 300, 301
boycotts, 295–97, 301–2
Brand Israel Group (BIG), 299
Braschi, Giannina, 65–66
Braudel, Fernand, 210
Brazil, 253–55, 259–62, 264
Britain, 214, 217, 226, 307; Aden and, 113, 210, 213, 214, 216, 217; alcoholic beverages and, 127–28; Arab revolt in Palestine (1936–1939), 165; balance-of-payments crisis, 190; cinema and, 135; Egypt and, 4, 7, 17, 104, 109, 206, 217 (*see also under* British occupation and imperialism); financial crisis, 190; Iran and, 189, 190, 193; Iraqi oil and, 187; kufiyas and, 164, 165; Lavon Affair and, 109; ports and, 113, 214, 216; Six-Day War and, 190
British Conquest of Egypt (1882), 104, 199
British Empire, 212
British occupation and imperialism, 242–44; occupation of Egypt (1882–1956), 198, 199, 226; withdrawal from Gulf, 190; withdrawal from Suez, 109. *See*

dance, 149–52; belly, 148–51, 151f, 154–56, 263

Dante Alighieri, 85–86

Darwish, Mahmoud, 82–83

Day of Rage, 270–71

Dayan, Moshe, 114, 115

De Sica, Vittorio, 67

Declaration on the Establishment of a New International Economic Order (NIEO Declaration), 307–8

Defense for Children International–Palestine Section (DCI-PS), 313

desalination, 177, 178, 182

development, right to, 308, 309

Di Stefano, Paul, 296

Diab, Amr, 147

Dibb, Humberto Domínguez, 258

"Didi" (song), 154

Dignity in Adversity (Benhabib), 319

Dīn Bukhari, Jamāl al-, 39, 39

Diouf, Sylviane, 158

drink, 126–30. *See also* water

Dubai, 15–16, 235, 241; as "cosmopolitan," 15–16; development, 235, 236; labor market, 16, 245, 247, 249; ports, 216–20 (*see also* Jabal Ali); privatizing labor relations, 249; tourism, 225, 235, 236

Dubai Creek, 214

Dubai Ports World (DP World), 215, 218, 220

Dunkin' Donuts advertisement, 164–65

East India Company, 127, 212, 214

economic liberalization/economic "reform," 136, 201, 203, 225, 231, 232, 256, 257. *See also* free-market policies; neoliberalism

economic self-determination. *See* self-determination

Ecuador, 259

effendiya, 165

Egypt: 2013 Egyptian, 93; Britain and, 4, 7, 17, 104, 109, 206, 217 (*see also under* British occupation and imperialism); post-revolution land reform, 107, 110, 113. *See also* Nasser, Kamal Abdel; Salah, Mohammed "Mo"

Egypt–Israel relations, 108–10, 231

Egyptian revolution of 1952, 106–7, 201; aftermath, 136–37

Egyptian revolution of 2011, 93. *See also* Tahrir Square

Egyptian–Czechoslovak arms deal, 109–11

El Salvador, 168, 260

El-Fadl, Khaled Abou, 310

Ellmann, Richard, 86

émigrés, 84–85

energy: nuclear, 183–84; water and, 182–84. *See also* oil

energy conservation, 182–83

Evangelical Christians and Israel, 5–6

exceptionalism, 3, 6

exile, 13, 77–89; fictional writings about, 83–86; loss and, 77–79, 82–83, 85, 87, 88; nationalism and, 80–82, 87; refugees and, 78, 80, 81, 84

exiled poets, 79, 80, 82

exiles, 13; resentment toward non-exiles, 84

expatriates, 84

exploitation of workers. *See* labor exploitation

fabric. *See under* cotton

Facussé, Miguel, 260

Faiz, Faiz Ahmed, 79

Fanon, Frantz, 63

Faraj, Abd-al-Salam, 285

Faraj, Muhammad Abd-al-Salam, 285

female labor force, 248–49

feminism, 298, 306; critical theory and, 328–29; Palestine and, 298

feminists, Islamic, 310–11

film. *See* cinema

financial crisis of 2007–2008, 236

folkwaysAlive!, 146

food, 9, 10, 130–31; language and lineage, 121–24; "Mediterranean cuisine," 129–30; movement to the east, 124–26. *See also* culinary culture

France, 108; arms sales to Israel, 108; Egypt and, 108. *See also* Suez Crisis

Free Officers Movement (Egypt), 106–7, 201

"free ports," 214, 217

freelancing, 249

free-market policies, 137, 203, 204, 232, 256.

tourism, 225; development of, 225–26, 228–31; "Dubai model" for, 236 (*see also* Dubai: tourism); Israeli, 230–33; and new "global" cities in the Gulf, 234–35; and the "New Middle East," 231–33

transcendence, poetics of, 66–72

transcultural exchange, 36, 47

transnationalism, 241

"transregional," 35

transregional (scholarly) exchange, 36, 39, 41–43, 45, 47

transregional scientific culture, 11, 35, 36

Trump, Donald J., 8

Tunisia, tourism in, 228–33

Tunisian Revolution, 236, 269, 284

Turbay Ayala, Júlio César, 259

"turcos" ("Turks") in Latin America, 253–62

Turkey, 184, 316, 322–26; citizenship and citizenship rights in, 324, 326, 328; Democrat Party (DP), 322–23

Turkish military coups: 1960 Turkish coup, 323; 1971 Turkish military memorandum, 323, 324, 326; 1980 Turkish coup, 326

Ṭūsī, Naṣīr al-Dīn al-, 39

Ulugh Beg, 41–42

Unilateral Declaration of Egyptian Independence, 104

unions. *See* labor strikes

United Arab Emirates (UAE), 95, 220; cinema in, 138; emergence as business center, 235; energy resources, 183–84; female workforce, 248; tourism, 236; water supplies, 184. *See also* "Arab Gulf"

United Arab Republic, 112–13

United Nations (UN), 306

United States: Iran and, 189–94; Israel and, 115, 193; military–industrial complex, 188. *See also specific topics*

United States Department of State (State Department), 190, 192, 193

Universal Declaration of Human Rights (UDHR), 8–9, 305, 306, 314

Urban Outfitters, 162–64, 169

"virtual water," 182

Wahhabism, 283

Warda, Amr, 91–92

water, 177–79; energy and, 182–84; safe drinking, 180, 181; "virtual," 182

water conservation, 182–83

water pollution, 180, 181

water scarcity, 177, 178, 182, 183

water stress, measuring, 179–81

Water Stress Index, 179

water uses and misuses, 181–83

Weil, Simone, 86

Welspun India, 205

Welspun India scandal, 195, 205

"West, the," 61

West Bank, 230, 232, 294, 295

White, Micah, 275–76

White Rose, The (film), 135

Wilson, Woodrow, 307

wine, 126–28, 130

women in labor force, 248–49

women's rights, 314, 329; Islam and, 310

women's rights activists, 313–14

workforce. *See* labor force and labor market

World Tribunal on Iraq, 312

World War I, 254; aftermath, 201, 307

World War II, 146–47; aftermath, 106, 225, 240

worldliness, 66–68, 72; Abbas Kiarostami and, 69, 70, 72, 140, 141, 143; idea of, 3

Xenophon, 62

Yahweh, 26–27, 27f

Yarur, Juan, 255–57

Yemen: 1962 Yemeni coup, 113; water scarcity, 180, 181. *See also* Aden

Yemeni Civil War (2014–present), 8, 12, 315

Yemeni port workers, 216, 217

Yushij, Nima, 70

Za'im, Husni al-, 106

Zarathustra, 65

Zidane, Zinedine (Zizou), 97

Zionism, 82, 259, 279, 299, 324; Kemalism compared with, 323

Zoroaster, 62, 65–66. *See* Zarathustra

Zuccotti Park (New York City), Occupy Wall Street (OWS) protests in, 275–77, 280

Founded in 1893,
UNIVERSITY OF CALIFORNIA PRESS
publishes bold, progressive books and journals
on topics in the arts, humanities, social sciences,
and natural sciences—with a focus on social
justice issues—that inspire thought and action
among readers worldwide.

The UC PRESS FOUNDATION
raises funds to uphold the press's vital role
as an independent, nonprofit publisher, and
receives philanthropic support from a wide
range of individuals and institutions—and from
committed readers like you. To learn more, visit
ucpress.edu/supportus.